Fame at Last

Fame at Last

Who *Was* Who According to
the *New York Times* Obituaries

John C. Ball, Ph.D.,
and
Jill Jonnes, Ph.D.

**Andrews McMeel
Publishing**

Kansas City

00 01 02 03 04 RDH 10 9 8 7 6 5 4 3 2 1

Library of Congress Cataloging-in-Publication Data

Ball, John C.
    Fame at last: who was who according to the New York times obituaries / John C. Ball
    and Jill Jonnes.
        p. cm.
    Includes bibliographical references.
    ISBN 0-7407-0940-2
        1. Obituaries—United States. 2. Biography—20th century. 3. Celebrities—Obituaries. 4.
    United States—Biography. 5. United States—Social life and customs—20th century. I.
    Jonnes, Jill, 1952- II. Title.

CT220 .B25 2000
920'.009'04—dc21
                                                                        00-031484

Design by Peter Lippincott

ATTENTION: SCHOOLS AND BUSINESSES

Andrews McMeel books are available at quantity discounts with bulk purchase for educational, business, or sales promotional use. For information, please write to: Special Sales Department, Andrews McMeel Publishing, 4520 Main Street, Kansas City, Missouri 64111.

Contents

List of Tables and Figures   vi

Acknowledgments   ix

1. *Fame at Last* and the Database That Made It Possible   1

2. The Millionaires Who Do Not Live Next Door   19

3. Pioneering Women   43

4. Outstanding Blacks   69

5. Eminent Physicians   89

6. Prominent Academics   115

7. Successful Publishers and Authors   141

8. Corporate and Financial Titans   167

9. Creative Philanthropy   201

10. Leading Judges, Politicians, and Lawyers   227

11. Criminals   265

12. Hollywood and TV People   281

13. Inventors Who Changed Our World   323

14. Revolutionaries of Fine Food and Drink   347

15. People with Utterly Unusual Lives   367

16. Some Final Thoughts on Success and Fame   385

Appendices   392

Index   400

List of Tables and Figures

1-1.	Rank of Forty-two Occupations by Amount of Obituary Coverage	7
1-2.	The Nine Dominant Occupational Groups in the Obituary Database	10
1-3.	Education of Those in the Obituary Database, by Sex	11
Figure 1-1.	Highest Education or Highest Degree Attained by Those in the Obituary Database	12
1-4.	The Overall Apex of Fame: The Longest Obituaries	13
1-5.	Leading Causes of Death: The U.S. Population and the Obituary Database	16
1-6.	Age at Death of Those in the Obituary Database, by Sex	17
2-1.	Corporate Ownership and Occupations of Millionaires in the Obituary Database	21
2-2.	Occupations of the Millionaires in the Obituary Database, by Sex	27
2-3.	Education of the Millionaires in the Obituary Database, by Sex	30
2-4.	The Apex of Fame: Millionaires in the Obituary Database	36
3-1.	Careers of the Women in the Obituary Database	44
3-2.	The Apex of Fame: Women in the Obituary Database	58
4-1.	Occupations of Blacks in the Obituary Database, by Sex	71
4-2.	Education Attained by Blacks in the Obituary Database	72
4-3.	U.S. Population: Education Attained, by Race	72
4-4.	U.S. Population 25 Years of Age or Older with Advanced Degrees, by Sex and Race	73
4-5.	The Apex of Fame: Blacks in the Obituary Database	76
5-1.	Undergraduate Colleges Attended by Medical School Professors and Physicians in the Obituary Database	92
5-2.	The Apex of Fame: Medical School Professors and Physicians in the Obituary Database	94
5-3.	Physicians in the United States by Type of Practice	96
6-1.	Undergraduate Colleges Attended by the College Professors in the Obituary Database	117
6-2.	The Apex of Fame: College Professors in the Obituary Database	118
6-3.	U.S. Population: Education Attained, by Sex	122
6-4.	The Apex of Fame: College Presidents in the Obituary Database	136

7-1.	Education of the Authors in the Obituary Database	143
7-2.	Books Sold in the United States, 1987 and 1996	145
7-3.	The Apex of Fame: Best-Selling Authors in the Obituary Database	150
7-4.	The Apex of Fame: Critically Acclaimed Authors in the Obituary Database	162
8-1.	The Apex of Fame: Corporate Executives in the Obituary Database	172
8-2.	Undergraduate Colleges Attended by the Executives in the Obituary Database and by *Forbes'* Top 800 CEOs	174
8-3.	Degrees Obtained by the Executives in the Obituary Database and by *Forbes'* Top 800 CEOs	175
8-4.	The Apex of Fame: Financial Executives in the Obituary Database	190
9-1.	Education of the Philanthropists in the Obituary Database, by Sex	203
9-2.	The Apex of Fame: Philanthropists in the Obituary Database	204
10-1.	The Apex of Fame: Judges in in the Obituary Database	230
10-2.	Career Characteristics of the Judges, Members of Congress, and Lawyers in the Obituary Database	234
10-3.	The Apex of Fame: Members of Congress in the Obituary Database	244
10-4.	The Apex of Fame: Lawyers in the Obituary Database	256
11-1.	Forty-one Criminals in the Obituary Database and Their Type of Offense	270
12-1.	The Apex of Fame: Actors in the Obituary Database	284
12-2.	The Apex of Fame: Actresses in the Obituary Database	288
12-3.	The Apex of Fame: Hollywood and Other Producers in the Obituary Database	298
12-4.	The Apex of Fame: Directors, Managers, and Designers in the Obituary Database	302
13-1.	The Apex of Fame: Inventors in the Obituary Database	326
Appendix A-1.	Occupational Groups in the U.S. Workforce and the Obituary Database	392
Appendix A-2.	The 176 Millionaires in the Obituary Database	394

Acknowledgments

The manuscript profited greatly from a cogent review by Dr. Roger H. Shannon. Rabbi Robert Rothman carefully perused the text and provided exemplary advice. Paul L. O'Brian and Henrietta Johnson also read the manuscript and offered valuable suggestions. My son, Dr. Charles J. Ball, was most helpful in revising the tables and chart.

This project would not have been feasible without the dedicated assistance of Wilson Chu. Students from Johns Hopkins and Loyola Universities who assisted in compiling the database were Christy Fusco, Everett L. Hamner, A. Jeannette Hamner, Jennifer L. Pummell, and Mary Helen Berk.

Many thanks to all those who gave their time to read portions of the manuscript, including Peggy Sarlin, Christopher Ross, Victor Romita, and Heidi Syropoulos. Robin Murphy, longtime follower of the *New York Times* obituaries, kindly read the whole manuscript. Anne McCracken was always an enthusiastic supporter, ultimately giving the manuscript a helpful once-over. Our agent, Gareth Esersky, quickly sold the book proposal to Andrews McMeel, where Christine Schillig has been an attentive editor.

—John C. Ball and Jill Jonnes

1

Fame at Last and the Database That Made It Possible

Every day more than a million Americans read the *New York Times*. A great many are avid followers of one section in particular: the obituaries. Here are the life stories of everyone from the mighty chairman of IBM to the guy who introduced single-wrap cheese slices. Part of the pure pleasure of the *Times* obits is their incredible variety. On a typical day we meet a retired Yale professor who was an expert on the ancient Syrian city of Ugarit, a Michigan crooner who sang with the Four Tops for more than forty years, a California doctor who developed better ways to remove lung clots, and a senior manager at NASA responsible for explorations to Jupiter and Mars. Here in the obits, Americans successfully pursue all manner of goals: money, knowledge, justice, art, the perfect crime, or a wonderful meal.

No American obits carry more cachet or gravitas than those appearing in the *New York Times*, the self-anointed paper of record. For many Americans, a prominent obit in the *Times* is the final seal of earthly success. Posterity can learn of your life and accomplishments, how you became well regarded or reviled, and who you left behind. Obits go back to Greek and Roman times. The word itself comes from the Latin *obiit,* meaning simply "he [or she] died." It is not surprising, then, to learn that obits are one of the best-read parts of the newspaper. (In two major surveys of daily news consumption in 1982 and 1987, the obits proved more popular than news about the president or the Congress and TV listings.)[1]

What is most striking about contemporary *New York Times* obits is how completely they focus on professional accomplishment and success. The ever-astute editor Michael Kinsley noticed this in a 1992 essay on obits headlines.[2] He was fascinated by an obit on "Dr. John

1

Hotson, 95, Unraveler of Elizabethan Literary Puzzles." He wondered what else this man had done in his ninety-five years on earth. Perhaps, wrote Kinsley, "he may have bred a wonderful family or done thousands of kindnesses to others, but the *Times* does not concern itself with that sort of thing."

Exactly. The *Times* concerns itself almost exclusively with professional and public accomplishment. And its obits range from ones on the predictably eminent statesmen to the completely quirky—as in "Authority on Sounds of Whales Was 88." Virtually all those found worthy of a *Times* obit were successful in their chosen fields, and many were also famous. The accumulated obits document, above all, an extraordinary record of success and fame in late-twentieth-century America.

There are apparently no set rules or standards about who will or will not get an obit, but it certainly improves the odds considerably to be a New Yorker, to be connected in some way to the *Times*, to be very famous, very creative, and/or very rich, or to have performed conspicuous public service—say, many distinguished years in Congress. We can pretty much guess that if "Bernard Baruch, Jr., Stock Exchange Member, 90" had not been the son of the famous Bernard Baruch, Sr., he might not have made the *Times* at all. There may be 1.5 million waitresses in America and 2 million janitors and cleaners, but few if any have received obits in the *Times*. While the occasional beloved street entertainer might get an affectionate obit farewell, by and large *New York Times* obits are the hard-to-enter preserve of the nation's elite.

It is very instructive to hear what the *New York Times* itself says is important when doing an obituary. Longtime *Times* editor A. M. Rosenthal once explained that when the paper chooses who rates precious space and attention, it puts the highest value on creativity—"a talent never matched, like Fred Astaire's, or one that opened new fields, like Walt Disney's. . . . In addition to creativity of performance, there was creativity of intellect: Felix Frankfurter . . . and a kind of creativity of character, a sense that there is a life whose very living will always have meaning: Helen Keller, Martin Luther King, Jr."[3] In short, the *Times* concentrates on those it feels have made a constructive contribution to society, with special attention to those who have been path breakers and innovators. Inevitably, this *does* skew the obits toward those in the arts and media, people who are dedicated to being creative and anxious to obtain publicity or make people aware of their work and activities.

The *Times* has about two thousand obits prepared and ready.[4] Some of the more renowned among our citizenry, not receiving the awaited phone call for an obit interview, take it upon themselves to write letters to the *Times* obit editor, giving a premortality spin to their time on earth. Once someone is dead, the *Times* gets the word through a multitude of channels—everything from the wire services (AP and Reuters obits make up 15 percent of those run) and foreign newspapers to family and friends. Hundreds flow in daily, but only a handful make the paper.

Several decades ago, the *New York Times* made a conscious decision to devote more space and systematic reportorial energy to obits. From 1964 to 1976, *Times*man Alden Whitman, a short, amiable man who affected capes, attained a modest fame as the man with the ghoulish assignment of roving the world interviewing great men and women before they died. Whitman's colleagues called him "The Mortician" and often inquired, "Who'd you pack away on ice today?" In recent years, most would agree, the obit writer supreme has been Robert McG. Thomas, Jr. Nominated in 1995 for a Pulitzer Prize for "spot news," he displayed an extraordinary talent for rich, deft details, the telling quote, the meaningful story. Just as we were finishing *Fame at Last*, a long and admiring obit appeared of Thomas himself. Dead from cancer at age sixty, he was warmly described as a Yale dropout whose own "career turbulence" had made him especially sympathetic and friendly to "underachievers and late bloomers."

And while an obit in the *Times* is a great coup for many, it is not always received uncritically. *Times*man Richard Shepard, obits editor for a year in the 1980s, recalled in a history of the *New York Times* how he had "approached my telephone with some trepidation each morning."[5] Some complaints were easily rectified—a misspelled name, say. But after that things got more difficult. Who was a man's real wife? Had the person been a founder of the company, as a daughter claimed, or the cofounder, as the company claimed?

For those who hope to get an obit, *New York Times* editor Rosenthal offers this advice: "It is best to die before noon, 2 p.m. at the latest, so that there will be decent time for justice to be done before the early-evening deadline of the first edition—and less inconvenience to the staff. All those interested in having the *Times* sum up their lives, even briefly, should avoid dying on Saturday, when the deadline is very early."[6] One should also avoid dying during primary and election seasons, when the obits section is accorded far less space than usual. The column inches you should have had may end up allotted to the Republican primary in New Hampshire.

For the less exalted, whether you make it in may well depend on who else has died and who's on hand to write obits. After all, this is a daily newspaper with all its chaos. If, say, the dance writer is on vacation when a certain ballerina dies, that hardworking artist will probably get short shrift. One obits editor lamented the inadequate coverage of a longtime society figure: "We just did not have a really good Old Money person to write the piece. I do now. I still don't have a good military person. In other words, a certain amount is just luck and happenstance."

The *Times* has little to say about most people's personal lives or their success as wives, fathers, friends, or all-around human beings. But there are tantalizing clues in the standard paragraph listing survivors. Here we usually learn the person's marital status and if there were children or grandchildren. Thus one wonders, did the expert on mother-child bonding deliberately have no children? Or was that a great heartbreak? Do all the children of this famous person live on the opposite coast because they needed to put distance between them? Or was there some other factor at work? Why didn't the great love psychologist have any wife, any children? Five wives? Five husbands? What were the stories behind those marital multiplicities? Sometimes, if people are very famous and their marriages are a large part of their reputation, we may learn the answer, but usually those dry listings are all that we know from the *Times*.

In this century, the practitioners par excellence of the art of the obit have been the British.[7] Part of the charm of the British obits is that they *do* judge people as people and tell us something of their personal lives, classifying someone as a grump or a delightful friend, a devoted husband or an indifferent mother. Never in the *New York Times* would we see poet Laura Riding, companion and muse to Robert Graves, described as being "of cleverness unsanctified by humility, of power unredeemed by benevolence, and above all of human presumption swallowed up by the vast indifference of eternity." And what of the wonderful British obit describing Christopher Robin Milne (famous because he was the son of *Winnie-the-Pooh* author A. A. Milne) "as gloomy as the moth-eaten old donkey Eeyore"?

In more genteel days of British newspapering, writes Lord Noel Annan, "Connoisseurs of obituaries learnt to read between the lines. [There was] certain coded language. 'He died suddenly' was a euphemism for suicide. 'He died unmarried,' well, one could make of that what one wished. 'He died in Northhampton' could mean [a person] had lost his marbles before the end and had died in the hospital there for the insane."

But in these tell-all times, euphemism is out on both sides of the Atlantic. One no longer expects the kindliness of *de mortuis nil nisi bonum*—of the dead speak only good—from the modern obit. Nowadays, if you sold your soul to get reelected—like Governor Orval Faubus of Arkansas—be prepared to have that harsh truth mentioned in your obit.

For both the daily readers of the obits and the journalists who write them, the obits are an ad hoc daily enterprise: interesting people die and get written up. One of the authors of this book, Dr. John C. Ball, has had a long career as a sociologist studying large groups. He looked at the obits and saw not just random lives but richly detailed information about America's greatest achievers in fields as diverse as computers and cooking. By gathering the *New York Times* obits in a systematic way into a computerized database, he surmised, one could learn a great deal about America's elite, who they are, what fields they're in, what schools they attended. Once this database was up and running, Dr. Ball began collaborating with Jill Jonnes, author and historian, on this book.

Fame at Last uses 9,325 *New York Times* obits of Americans to consider in a systematized way what constitutes success and fame in the

United States as we enter the new millennium. (The 1,600 foreigners in the database were excluded from this book.) The combined stories and data create a portrait of where America has been and where it's going. Each year about 2.5 million Americans die; about 1,800 of them, or about one in 1,400, get *New York Times* obits. The individual obits are minidramas about achievement, renown, wealth (sometimes), and even failure that provide a gold mine of information. The *New York Times* goes far beyond the pro forma approach of a *Who's Who* in its obits. While it provides such standard information as age, occupation, education, and advancement, it also often describes a person's specific role in business or history, adversities overcome, hardscrabble youth, and odd turns of fate.

Exactly what information is included in the database? Starting in the fall of 1993 and continuing for the next six years, every obit was collected every day, for a total of just over 11,000. First, each obit was categorized into one of four classes based primarily on length: Type 1 had forty inches or more of coverage, and it included one or more photographs (this was 3.5 percent of the total). Type 2 had one photo and less than forty inches of coverage (33.8 percent). Type 3 had no photo but a bylined story (22.2 percent). Type 4 had neither a photo nor a byline (40.5 percent).

Probably *the* most telling fact is the *length* of each person's obituary. The number of column inches allotted to each soul conveys just how famous or important the *New York Times* thinks that someone is. Some merit two inches, some two pages. In turn, those accumulated inches in the database form the basis for ranking whole groups. For instance, authors are eighth in the average length of their obits, as indicated in Table 1-1.

Each obit was cut out and filed; then relevant information was abstracted, coded, and entered in the computerized database. That basic information included name, age, headline, sex, race, cause of death, nationality, place of residence, level of education and colleges attended, occupation, political party, and religion. Much of this detailed work of creating and analyzing the database during the past six years has been done by a dedicated staff supervised by the authors.

TABLE 1-1. *Rank of Forty-two Occupations* by Amount of Obituary Coverage*

Rank	Occupation	Number of Obituaries	Average Obituary Length
1.	Members of Congress	86	25.0"
2.	Singers	142	18.0"
3.	Judges	174	17.6"
4.	Military personnel	152	16.9"
5.	U.S. government: State, Defense	147	16.8"
6.	Actors/actresses	428	16.4"
7.	Athletes	241	16.4"
8.	Authors, writers, poets	457	16.2"
9.	University presidents	108	15.8"
10.	State government (not New York)	92	15.7"
11.	Real estate executives	90	15.7"
12.	Engineers, inventors	123	15.7"
13.	Fashion and interior designers	76	15.7"
14.	Hollywood and TV directors	137	15.0"
15.	Artists	205	14.9"
16.	Dancers	134	14.8"
17.	Radio and TV broadcasters	90	14.7"
18.	U.S. government: Domestic departments	81	14.5"
19.	Clergy	164	14.3"
20.	Reporters, journalists	174	14.3"
21.	Architects, landscape designers	79	14.0"
22.	University professors	816	13.6"
23.	Composers	89	13.6"
24.	Musicians	266	13.6"
25.	Small-business owners	177	13.4"
26.	Major business executives	470	12.6"
27.	Philanthropists, art patrons	102	12.5"

(continues)

TABLE 1-1. *Rank of Forty-two Occupations* by Amount of Obituary Coverage*

Rank	Occupation	Number of Obituaries	Average Obituary Length
28.	Playwrights	79	12.4"
29.	Publishers	118	12.4"
30.	Sports coaches	108	12.3"
31.	Hollywood, stage, TV producers	168	12.3"
32.	Medical school professors	286	12.3"
33.	Museum directors, curators	89	12.3"
34.	Civic leaders	110	11.5"
35.	Practicing doctors	178	11.3"
36.	Media executives	139	11.2"
37.	Financial executives	276	11.2"
38.	Editors	179	11.2"
39.	Lawyers	349	11.1"
40.	Public relations, advertising people	132	10.4"
41.	School administrators	153	10.4"
42.	Small-business executives	234	10.3"
	Total obituaries in forty-two occupations:	**7,938**	
	Average length of obituaries		**13.9"**

*Occupations with at least seventy obituaries in the obituary database.

Note: The total of 7,938 obituaries represents 85.1% of the 9,325 obituaries in database.

The unique aspect of the database is that it focuses almost entirely on prominent and accomplished Americans in a wide range of endeavors. We are as likely to meet a *Fortune* 500 CEO as an outstanding entomologist "who was one of the world's foremost experts on mosquitoes." And while one could certainly argue about some of the choices made by the editors of the *New York Times*, it is our preeminent newspaper and brings great institutional authority and credibility to its coverage. And it is the one national newspaper that daily runs obits about such a broad range of people, offering real insight about who and what we as a society view as important.

The database yields a national profile of our most important and influential occupations. How was this determined? Simply by the sheer numbers of men and women representing any given field. Two thirds of the men and women in the database had careers in one of nine high-status fields: business, academia, government, law, medicine, acting, books, sports, and journalism, as is shown in Table 1-2. What really underscores the elite nature of the obits is comparing the database's top eighty-five occupations with those of the overall U.S. labor force.[8] The *New York Times* people are almost completely (99 percent) concentrated in arts and media careers, higher education, business executive positions and professional sports, which are classified as "Management and Professional Specialty." In the American workforce overall, not even 30 percent of people fall into those categories. In the database, such medium-status jobs as sales, production, and service were barely represented or absent. Even within high-status work, an author, professional athlete, or actress has a ten times greater chance of getting a *New York Times* obit than a doctor or a lawyer.

One of the most striking findings is educational level, as indicated in Table 1-3. If you want to appreciate just how important education has become to success, look no further than this database. Dr. Mary Howell, a onetime dean at Harvard Medical School, had a Ph.D. in developmental psychology, a medical degree, and a law degree from Harvard. While she was an overachiever even among our group, the fact is that those with *New York Times* obits were *five times* as likely to have a college education than the general American population who were their peers. Sixty percent held college degrees. (Even today, not quite a quarter of Americans have completed college.) The database also enables us to make educational comparisons among the different occupational groups—and to note that almost a fifth of those with college degrees in the database attended just four schools: Harvard, Princeton, Yale, and

TABLE 1-2. *The Nine Dominant Occupational Groups in the Obituary Database*

Rank	Occupational Group	Number of Obituaries	Percentage of Database	U.S. Labor Force*	Chance per 1,000 of an Obituary in the *New York Times* †
1.	Business executives	1,657	17.8	2 million companies	0.8
2.	University professors	856	9.2	709,000	1.2
3.	Government officials	690	7.4	811,000	0.9
4.	Lawyers and judges	523	5.6	774,000	0.7
5.	Doctors and medical school professors	464	5.0	750,000	0.6
6.	Authors	457	4.9	93,000	4.9
7.	Sports figures	445	4.8	82,000	5.4
8.	Actors, Actresses	428	4.6	74,000	5.8
9.	Journalists	411	4.4	365,000	1.1
	Total	**5,931**	**63.6**	**5,658,000**	**1.0**

* There were 125 million men and women in the U.S. labor force in 1995; 5.7 million (4.5 percent) of these were in one of the above nine occupations. But 63.6 percent of the 9,325 obituaries in our database were of men or women in these nine occupations. *Source: Statistical Abstract of the United States; 1996*, Table 637.

† This is the approximate chance per 1,000 that a person in each occupation will obtain an obituary in the *New York Times*. Thus, actors and actresses are ten times more likely to have an obit than doctors.

Columbia. Thirty percent of our database people held higher degrees, as shown in Figure 1-1, in contrast to 4.5 percent of the U.S. population of comparable age or 8.5 percent of the current population.[9]

TABLE 1-3. *Education of Those in the Obituary Database, by Sex*

Education	Men (N = 7,705) (%)	Women (N = 1,620) (%)	Total (N = 9,325) (%)
1. High school or less	2.7	4.9	3.1
2. Some college	9.5	11.7	9.9
3. College graduate (no higher degree)	20.2	21.5	20.4
4. Master's or equivalent degree	7.7	8.8	7.9
5. Ph.D. degree	13.4	10.0	12.8
6. Law degree	12.8	3.4	11.2
7. M.D. degree	5.8	1.9	5.1
8. Two or more of nos. 5–7	0.9	0.4	0.8
9. Religious and other	2.5	0.9	2.2
10. Not stated	24.5	36.6	26.6
Total	**100.0**	**100.0**	**100.0**

Still, the database has an obvious limitation. It covers only six years of time. Many important people are alive and kicking, still making their mark. And many influential people, of course, died before 1993. Although the *New York Times* is a national newspaper (and even international in its coverage, as 15 percent of the obits are of foreign nationals), it does emphasize local news and events. This local emphasis is reflected in its obituaries, with some one third of the Americans (35.5 percent) being residents of New York State. Nonetheless, most of the obituaries refer to persons throughout the nation, and every state is represented in the database. (While this book deals only with *New York Times* obituaries, the database is ongoing and now incorporates obits from the *Times* of London and the *Globe and Mail* of Toronto.)

Crowning this massive database is the Overall Apex of Fame, the twenty-eight longest obits appearing since 1993. This Apex of Fame, as shown in Table 1-4, is topped (as one might expect) by the only

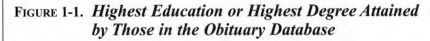

FIGURE 1-1. *Highest Education or Highest Degree Attained by Those in the Obituary Database*

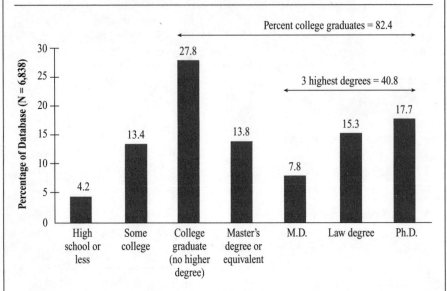

1. The highest level of education attained was stated for 6,838 persons in the obituary database (73.4%). Those for whom incomplete education data were indicated (26.6%) tended to have less education and fewer degrees.

2. The educational level and degrees of those included in Figure 1-1 are an underestimate of their formal education as only the highest degrees are shown; graduate study not culminating in a degree is omitted from the chart.

American president in the database, Richard M. Nixon, who was given twice as much coverage as the number two person, singer Frank Sinatra. While certain listings in this overall Apex of Fame—such as Supreme Court Justices—are not surprising, others are. Yet the very diversity of those who merited more than a hundred column inches and often front-page coverage when they died underscores the uniqueness and value of these obits as a way of looking at American society. We feature a specific occupational Apex of Fame in almost every chapter, and sometimes more than one. These Apexes provide a fascinating look at who is most famous in each group: the most famous women, the most famous lawyers, the most famous philanthropists, and so on.

TABLE 1-4. *The Overall Apex of Fame: The Longest Obituaries*

Rank	Name (Age at Death)	Obit Date	Occupation	Obit Length	Number of Photos
1.	Richard Nixon (81)	04/24/94	U.S. president	510"	13
2.	Frank Sinatra (82)	05/16/98	Singer/actor	236"	12
3.	Jacqueline Kennedy Onassis (64)	05/21/94	Wife of John F. Kennedy	210"	10
4.	Joe DiMaggio (84)	03/09/99	Baseball player	209"	10
5.	Warren Burger (87)	06/26/95	Supreme Court chief justice	158"	4
6.	William Brennan, Jr. (91)	07/25/97	Supreme Court justice	152"	2
7.	George Wallace (79)	09/15/98	Alabama governor	151"	7
8.	Harry A. Blackmun (90)	03/05/99	Supreme Court justice	150"	3
9.	Saul Steinberg (84)	05/13/99	Cartoonist	147"	14
10.	Jerome Robbins (79)	07/30/98	Dancer	128"	4
11.	Mickey Mantle (63)	08/14/95	Baseball player	127"	7
12.	Willem de Kooning (92)	03/20/97	Artist	127"	6
13.	Dr. Benjamin Spock (94)	03/17/98	Pediatrician; author	125"	3
14.	Alger Hiss (92)	11/16/96	Diplomat; spy	121"	7
15.	James Stewart (89)	07/03/97	Actor	120"	9
16.	James Reston (86)	12/08/95	Journalist	119"	5
17.	Barry Goldwater (89)	05/30/98	Presidential candidate; U.S. senator	119"	5
18.	Lewis Powell, Jr. (90)	08/26/98	Supreme Court justice	119"	4

(continues)

TABLE 1-4. *The Overall Apex of Fame: The Longest Obituaries*

Rank	Name (Age at Death)	Obit Date	Occupation	Obit Length	Number of Photos
19.	Allen Ginsberg (70)	04/06/97	Poet	117"	4
20.	Clark Clifford (91)	10/11/98	U.S. secretary of defense	116"	3
21.	Paul Mellon (91)	02/03/99	Philanthropist	115"	5
22.	Jessica Tandy (85)	09/12/94	Actress	112"	6
23.	J. William Fulbright (89)	02/10/95	U.S. senator	109"	3
24.	Dean Rusk (85)	12/22/94	U.S. secretary of state	107"	4
25.	Gene Kelly (83)	02/03/96	Dancer	106"	5
26.	Yehudi Menuhin (82)	03/13/99	Violinist; conductor	106"	4
27.	Ella Fitzgerald (79)	06/16/96	Singer	102"	3
28.	Roy Lichtenstein (73)	09/30/97	Artist	102"	5
	Total			**4,075"**	**167**
	Average			**145.5"**	**6.0**

Note: These twenty-eight are the longest obituaries to appear in the *New York Times* during the six-year period of the database; the total number of obituaries included in the database was 9,325.

Naturally, when it came time to figure out how we would write about this vast sea of impressive humanity, we were very much guided by the patterns that had emerged from the database. Many of our chapters look at the high-status career areas that stood out as the most important: business, medicine, government, media and entertainment, academia, publishing. We also decided to do chapters that we thought would be interesting or just plain fun, chapters on specific groups that are not defined by standard occupations but certainly tell us something about where we have been going as a society: women, inventors, blacks, millionaires, food folk, criminals, and philanthropists. For our final chapter, we wrote about the free spirits, those so unusual they fit no niche.

How then did we choose the 350-some achievers profiled in the following fifteen chapters? While the Apex of Fame in each chapter may seem like the obvious source, it was not necessarily so. What we looked for were not just the most famous people but the most innovative, the most pioneering, those with a fresh take, a different vision. These were the Americans whose ideas and work really changed our nation—generally for the better, but not always. We looked at people who played major roles in the great technological revolution that has swept our world and at those who were highly influential in the tremendous generation of wealth, the great expansion of opportunity. We looked always for people whose influence had been felt widely. Thus among the doctors we included the physician who pioneered the mammogram as a tool against breast cancer. Few know his name, but all over America women now get mammograms. One of the great charms of the *New York Times'* obituary section is the folks whose *names* we wouldn't recognize but whose accomplishments we do.

And while the obits are about people's lives, one remains curious about why someone died. As Table 1-5 shows, just under a third of the time no explanation is given. But for the remaining two thirds, our database can say what kills off America's elite, and it is not much different from what kills off the population as a whole. The biggest cause is cancer, followed by heart disease, and, as the distant third and fourth, strokes and pneumonia. For men, AIDS has been a significant factor. Almost one in a hundred people died in automobile accidents.

And of course, as people age, many read the obits to keep score and weigh the odds. As writer Joseph Epstein explained, "Now that I have hit sixty, I find it much more comforting to begin a day in which the obituary page lists three people who died in their nineties and one who made it to 105."[10] Assuming Mr. Epstein is looking mainly at other men, we can say, as indicated in Table 1-6, that there are not many such days. Only 1,060 of the 7,705 men in the database died between the ages of

TABLE 1-5. *Leading Causes of Death: The U.S. Population and the Obituary Database*

Leading Causes of Death	U.S. Population , 1995*		Obituary Database†	
Cause of Death	Number	Percent	Number	Percent
1. Heart diseases	737,563	31.9	1,819	29.2
2. Cancer	538,455	23.3	2,337	37.5
3. Cerebrovascular diseases	157,991	6.8	500	8.0
4. Pulmonary diseases	102,899	4.5	192	3.1
5. Accidents	93,320	4.0	247	4.0
6. Pneumonia, influenza	82,923	3.6	272	4.4
7. Diabetes mellitus	59,254	2.6	55	0.9
8. AIDS	43,115	1.9	242	3.9
9. Suicide	31,284	1.4	53	0.9
10. Liver diseases, cirrhosis	25,222	1.1	42	0.7
11. Kidney diseases	23,676	1.0	79	1.3
12. Homicide, legal intervention	22,895	1.0	17	0.3
13. Septicemia	20,965	0.9	—	—
14. Alzheimer's disease	20,606	0.9	104	1.7
15. Atherosclerosis	16,723	0.7	50	0.8
16. Others: Infections, hepatitis, Parkinson's disease, ALS, drug overdose, others	335,241	14.5	225	3.6
Total	**2,312,132**	**100.0**	**6,234**	**100.0**

*The New York Times Almanac, 1998, p. 394.
†3,091 obituaries did not give the cause of death.

ninety and ninety-nine, or about 14 percent. As for those who made it beyond one hundred, there were only 61, less than 1 percent.

While the database provides a great deal of original career information, to best convey the reality of these careers in the greater universe of work we have also drawn on a wide range of other sources, including the mother lode of the U.S. Census, the *Economist, Time*, the *New York*

TABLE 1-6. *Age at Death of Those in the Obituary Database, by Sex*

Age at Death (years)	Men Number	Men Percent	Women Number*	Women Percent	Total Number	Total Percent
7–29	21	0.3	8	0.5	29	0.3
30–39	111	1.4	25	1.5	136	1.5
40–49	330	4.3	69	4.3	399	4.3
50–59	574	7.4	137	8.5	711	7.6
60–69	1,118	14.5	174	10.7	1,292	13.9
70–79	1,905	24.7	336	20.8	2,241	24.0
80–89	2,525	32.8	453	28.0	2,988	32.0
90–99	1,060	13.8	373	23.0	1,423	15.3
100–123	61	0.8	44	2.7	105	1.1
Total	**7,705**	**100.0**	**1,619**	**100.0**	**9,324**	**100.0**
Average Age	**75.8**		**77.6**		**76.1**	

* The age at death for one woman was not stated.

Note: In 1996, the life expectancy for the U.S. population was: Males = 73.0 years; females = 79.0 years; total = 76.1 years (*Statistical Abstract of the United States, 1998*, Table 128).

Review of Books, the *New Yorker*, *Forbes, Fortune*, the American Medical Association, the American Bar Association, the Screen Actors Guild, the Author's Guild, and *Publishers Weekly*, along with a range of specialized books on law, TV, publishing, and food.

Notes

1. Charles Winick, "AIDS Obituaries in the New York Times," *AIDS & Public Policy Journal*, Fall 1996, p. 148.
2. Michael Kinsley, "Death Warmed Over," *New Republic*, December 21, 1992.
3. Arthur Gelb, A.M. Rosenthal, and Marion Siegel, *New York Times Great Lives of the 20th Century* (New York: Times Books, 1988).

4. Richard F. Shepard, *The Paper's Papers* (New York: Times Books, 1996), p. 284.
5. Ibid., p. 285.
6. Gelb, Rosenthal, and Siegel, *New York Times Great Lives of the 20th Century.*
7. "The Obituarist's Art," *Economist*, December 24, 1994–January 6, 1995, pp. 64, 65, 68.
8. For a comparison with the U.S. labor force, see Appendix A-1.
9. *Statistical Abstract of the United States, 1998*, Tables 260, 262. See also Jeremy Kahn, "Is Harvard Worth It?" *Fortune,* May 1, 2000, pp. 200–204.
10. Joseph Epstein, "Speaking of the Dead," *Weekly Standard*, February 2, 1998, p. 33.

2

The Millionaires Who Do Not Live Next Door

Florida Citrus Baron

A Pioneer of Silicon Valley

A Hunch Led Him to Create Kitty Litter

Right after World War II, Navy veteran Edward Lowe, twenty-seven, was helping out in his father's sawdust business in Cassopolis, Michigan, when a neighbor came by wanting to make a purchase. Her poor cat was having trouble coping with the freezing sand in the outdoor litter box. Lowe suggested that rather than sawdust, the woman try a bag of kiln-dried granulated clay. His father, "who sold sawdust to factories to sop up grease spills, had begun offering [the clay] as a fireproof alternative." When the neighbor returned within the week seeking more clay for her feline, young Lowe thought he might be onto something. He bagged the clay up, wrote "Kitty Litter" on the side, and began making the rounds of pet stores and cat shows with his product. The rest, as they say, is history.

Cats, long relegated to the outdoors because their "highly concentrated urine is one of the most noxious effluences of the animal kingdom," were now welcomed into the nation's hearths and homes. By 1985, according to the *New York Times* obit of Edward Lowe, the notoriously independent feline had taken over from the loyal dog, surpassing it as the nation's preferred pampered pet. By the mid-1990s, more than 60 million American cats were consuming $650 million worth of litter, a third of that being the original Kitty Litter brand.

19

As the millions rolled in, Lowe, who had grown up dirt poor, indulged in lavish living, buying a three-thousand-acre estate in southwestern Michigan and twenty-one other homes. And then there were "a 72-foot yacht, a stable of quarter horses, a private railroad and an entire Michigan town."

The millionaires in the *New York Times* obituaries are not the frugal businessmen and plumbers who populate the best-selling how-to book *The Millionaire Next Door*[1], the 3.5 million Americans who have accumulated a million dollars in assets. (In the sequel, *The Millionaire Mind*,[2] that figure had risen to 4.9 million American millionaires.) The *Times* people are mostly multimillionaires or even billionaires, mainly businessmen and bankers, but also some showbiz sorts and professionals. Many would certainly satisfy the higher millionaire standard Andrew Hacker sets in his book *Money* of a million a year in *income*.[3] In the mid-1990s, 68,000 American households filing tax returns had at least a million dollars in income, a fourfold increase from 1979, even adjusted for inflation! Just as eye-popping, by 1999 you needed at least $625 million to make *Forbes'* list of the four hundred richest Americans.[4] In recent decades the United States, with its sturdy economy and robust stock market, has been generating unprecedented wealth. By 1997, the number of Americans earning $1 million or more per year had risen to 142,500.[5] As more and more people get rich, many Americans are obviously wondering how they, too, can become millionaires.

In the *New York Times* obits, we get a chance to learn about people who got rich doing everything from telling jokes to making widgets. Of the 9,325 Americans in our database, 176 were identified as working millionaires, and these are listed in the appendix. These are men and women who made a fortune or actively expanded an enterprise. Like Edward Lowe of Kitty Litter fame, three quarters of these millionaires are in business or finance. Also like Edward Lowe, almost half started their own companies. And as shown in Table 2-1, two thirds became owners of their companies.

In this chapter we learn who the *New York Times* millionaires are through answering such basic questions as: What were their businesses

TABLE 2-1. *Corporate Ownership and Occupations of the Millionaires in the Obituary Database*

Occupation	Number	Percent
Founder and owner of a company	84	47.7
Later owner of a company	36	20.5
Executive of a company	20	11.4
Arts and entertainment careers	24	13.6
Professions	12	6.8
Total	**176**	**100.0**

Note: More than two thirds of the millionaires (68.2 percent) were owners of their companies.

or occupations? How important is business ownership? How do they compare with the "Millionaires Next Door"? To what extent did they make it from the bottom up? How many of them inherited wealth? What was their family background? What was their education, and how many attended elite colleges? What work ethic influenced their success? Does becoming a successful multimillionaire differ notably from other kinds of career success?

Sometimes the prologue to millionairehood is a string of failures. For much of his adult life, Benjamin Eisenstadt certainly seemed dogged by bad luck. He emerged from St. John's University law school in New York just as the Depression struck in 1929. Though first in his class, he was unable to get launched in law. Stymied, he ran cafeterias, ending up during World War II with a thriving place across from the Brooklyn Naval Yard. After the war was won, his clientele disappeared. He converted the space into a not-very-successful tea factory. Then, writes the *Times*, came "the brainstorm that changed the way Americans dispense sugar. The same equipment that injected tea into tea bags, he realized, could be used to put sugar into little paper packets." The big "Eureka!," however, still did not translate into savvy success. For when Eisenstadt proudly escorted big sugar executives through his factory as it churned out the revolutionary sugar packets, they just copied his brainstorm. And so his firm, Cumberland Sugar, limped along for another decade.

Then, in 1957, after almost thirty years of false starts and marginal success, Eisenstadt and his son Marvin concocted a "granulated low-calorie sugar substitute." This time he wised up and obtained a patent for what he named Sweet'N Low. The product was snapped up by weight-obsessed Americans, who by the 1990s were ripping open 50 million pink packets a year. The company also developed butter and salt substitutes, racking up sales of $200 million annually and employing 400 people in the same building that had once housed the ill-fated cafeteria. While Eisenstadt's late-life success is a testament to perseverance, it was not the norm among our millionaires. Most had become rich and successful by their late thirties.

Here were two men—Edward Lowe of Kitty Litter and Benjamin Eisenstadt of Sweet'N Low—living out the American Dream in all its glory, becoming millionaires by creating new companies that made domestic products, items useful to daily life. They are typical of *New York Times* millionaires because they have made their own fortunes. Fully four fifths of these millionaires were founders, owners, or executives of both new and established companies. Most of these people became very rich—multimillionaires—and most were entrepreneurs who made it on their own. Moreover, what really drives home the accomplishment of these *New York Times* millionaires is how many came up on their own. In our millionaire group, one quarter are from poor families, and another half are from working-class or middle-class backgrounds. All told, a full three quarters entered the world without a silver spoon in their mouths. This encouraging fact is similar to up-from-below data from *The Millionaire Next Door*.[6]

While Kitty Litter and Sweet'N Low are familiar brand names to every American, in the mammoth multitrillion-dollar American economy they are minor players. The big players are people such as Zalman C. Bernstein, a Wall Street legend who pooh-poohed the conventional wisdom by opening a firm in 1967 that accepted nothing but discretionary accounts. At the time these sorts of accounts—where brokers make investment decisions for their clients—were very much in bad odor, banned at most old-line brokerages as prone to exploitation and scandal. Yet what Bernstein had in mind was something so visionary—giving "comparatively small investors the benefits of professional money managers"—that it attracted student researchers from the Harvard Business School, who were dubious about the firm's prospects. In fact, it became "one of the world's largest independent investment companies, managing more than $80 billion in securities for 25,000 private and institutional clients . . . one of the most respected names on Wall Street."

Bernstein was an interesting character. After serving in the Navy in World War II, he studied economics and accounting at New York University, got a master's from Harvard Business School, and then spent three years with the Marshall Plan helping rebuild Europe. He returned to the United States and, when turned down for a job with Value Line Investment Survey, offered his services without pay, thereby landing the position. He also worked at several other securities firms before launching his own business. Rough, gruff, and a great smoker of cigars, Bernstein developed a reputation as an unusual interviewer. Not only were prospective employees subjected to various personality tests, they often had to play chess or backgammon with the boss so he could check out their competitive qualities and tolerance for cigar smoke. Wall Street has always been a popular destination for aspiring millionaires, what with its concentration of wealth and potential. In the long bull market, it's really been booming. In 1996, at least 1,500 people on Wall Street made a *minimum* of $1 million each.[7]

And today, certainly, the tens of millions of middle-class American investors who have prospered thanks to several good decades on Wall Street are partially indebted to men such as Bernstein. For he was one of the pioneers who made it possible for average people to have access to experienced money managers. He was not an easy man, one gathers, what with his three wives. But late in life he became a devout Orthodox Jew, lived modestly in Jerusalem, and gave hundreds of millions of dollars to Israeli and other causes.

While Bernstein was a legend in the canyons of Wall Street, David Packard was famous the world over as one of the founders of Silicon

Valley, by the 1990s a new magnet for millionaire wanna-bes. (In 1996, there were reported to be 186,511 millionaires in Silicon Valley[8], with hundreds more created each month as companies went public.) In classic Horatio Alger fashion, Packard and his partner, William Hewlett, engineering graduates of Stanford University, began their innovative company from a Palo Alto garage (now a state landmark) with all of $538 in cash. Together they created what the *Times* called "the prototype of the modern technological company and one of the most widely admired corporations in the world." A multinational company, Hewlett-Packard had $31 billion in revenues in 1995 and employed 100,000 people. While best known today for such products as the first handheld calculator and ink-jet printer and a host of scientific items, the company began as a maker of instruments for electronic testing and measuring.

Andrew Hacker, in *Money,* shows that the eight hundred largest U.S. firms in manufacturing, retail, transportation, utilities, and finance together employ 20 million citizens, or 169 per 1,000 working Americans. To create a company of that size and stature—as David Packard helped do—is truly a monumental achievement. Yet David Packard endeared himself to the public and his employees by his disdain for pomposity of all kinds. Given a chance to blow his own horn—he was once asked what his proudest moment had been—he refused, advising instead, "Do something useful, then forget about it and go on to the next thing. Don't gloat about it." At times, Packard's down-to-earth philosophy could have comical consequences. In 1961, the company's senior managers flew to Manhattan to celebrate the company's listing on the New York Stock Exchange. Rather than take taxis downtown from their hotel off Central Park, Packard insisted they all take the subway, whereupon they all got lost.

Packard advocated what came to be known as "The H-P Way"—a work environment that encouraged "individual motivation, initiative and creativity." To him, this meant sharing company profits with employees, allowing employees to work flexible schedules, and affording easy access to managers. He liked to amble around the shop floor, encouraging employees to open up with their ideas and problems. Another maxim was "management by objective," which boiled down to executives actually articulating what they wanted done and then giving employees free rein to do it. The very existence of the H-P Way highlights the problem of corporate hugeness, whether at Hewlett-Packard or any other business that needs to stay nimble to maintain and replicate its initial success.

These millionaires—Lowe of Kitty Litter, Eisenstadt of Sweet'N Low, Bernstein of Wall Street, and Packard of Silicon Valley—typify the *New York Times* millionaires. Three quarters of those in our database are concentrated in business or finance, with two thirds of the 176 men and women being owners or executives of American corporations; more than 20 percent of them were in finance and real estate.

Where are the *New York Times* millionaires geographically? They could be found scattered over thirty states and in one foreign country. But half were living in New York, California, or Florida by the end of their career. From this one could rightly conclude that if you want to make money, it certainly makes sense to head where the money is. Two New Hampshire brothers, Richard and Maurice McDonald, hoping to make a million, headed to Hollywood and the glitter of the movie industry. When that didn't pan out, they opened a hot-dog stand by the Santa Anita racetrack before moving on in 1940 to a small drive-in barbecue joint near San Bernardino. After eight years, their hearts still set on being millionaires, they closed the place, which was popular but no gold mine. Then they completely revamped their whole operation, working to deliver "reasonably priced food at a rapid pace." Their kitchen was redesigned to mechanize all possible tasks, and whatever food could be prepared ahead of time was. Dick felt they needed a visible symbol and suggested golden arches: "I thought the arches would sort of lift the building up." Their architect was appalled. Nonetheless, recalled Dick, "They worked. It was luck, I guess."

The new place, McDonald's, was such a success with its fifteen-cent burgers, ten-cent fries, and twenty-cent milk shakes that by 1955 the brothers had sold twenty-one franchises and opened another nine outlets on their own. Our whole concept was based on speed, lower prices and volume," Dick said. A veteran milk shake machine salesman named Ray Kroc made a special trip to see what his best customers were up to.

Watching through the clear glass walls, Kroc saw white-clad restaurant staff swiftly serving a long line of customers in a spick-and-span space. Wowed by the concept, he asked for the right to sell franchises. In 1955, Kroc opened his first McDonald's in Des Plaines, Illinois. A year later he bought the business outright from the McDonaldses for $2.7 million.

At age fifty-one, Dick McDonald had attained his goal of becoming a millionaire. He headed home to Bedford, New Hampshire. By the time Dick died in mid-1998, Ray Kroc had developed Dick's fast-food concept almost into a science and the McDonald's Corporation spanned the globe, with twenty-three thousand outlets in 111 countries and annual sales in excess of $33 billion. Dick McDonald, who had dreamed up not just the golden arches, but also the ever-changing outdoor sign of how many burgers had been sold, must have been amazed as that figure soared into the billions.

While the McDonaldses set out on a determined quest to become millionaires, a certain number of fortunate Americans exercise a unique talent and get rich along the way. These tend to be the quarter of our millionaires (including most of the women) who are not businesspeople. As seen in Table 2-2, they are found in a wide range of careers, including entertainment and traditional professions. Hollywood people account for about 11 percent of the millionaires, while the rest—a handful each—are sports figures, professors, lawyers, authors, and one doctor. One of the authors was Erma Bombeck, the beloved humor columnist who made a fortune poking fun at the tiresome humdrum of housewifery and child raising. A typical Bombeck line about dirty ovens: "If it won't catch fire today, clean it tomorrow."

Bombeck was a housewife living in a Dayton, Ohio, suburb, a middle-class mom of three school-age children in the early 1960s. "That's when I used to sit at the kitchen window year after year . . . I decided it wasn't fulfilling to clean chrome faucets with a toothbrush. At 37 I decided it was my time to strike out." Way back in junior high, she had written a humor column. In high school she had worked at the *Dayton Journal-Herald* as a copy girl and then after college as a reporter before leaving to marry. But now her kids were in school all day and she was bored. Bombeck convinced the local suburban weekly to carry her early

TABLE 2-2. *Occupations of the Millionaires in the Obituary Database, by Sex*

Occupation	Men (N = 160) (%)	Women (N = 16) (%)	Total (N = 176) (%)
Major corporation	48.1	6.3	44.3
Smaller business	6.3	12.5	6.8
Finance, real estate	20.6	18.8	20.5
Publisher, media business	3.1	—	2.8
Inventor, architect	3.1	6.3	3.4
Hollywood, TV	7.5	43.8	10.8
Sports	3.1	—	2.8
Author	1.3	12.5	2.3
University professor	1.9	—	1.7
Lawyer	3.8	—	3.4
Doctor	0.6	—	0.6
Union leader	0.6	—	0.6
Total	**100.0**	**100.0**	**100.0**

Note: There were no millionaires in the following occupations: dancer, musician or composer, artist, editor or photographer (there was one female TV journalist), medical or law school professor, college president or official, teacher or museum curator, judge or law enforcement official, farmer, government official.

columns, and within the year her old employer, the *Journal-Herald*, had not only signed her on for three columns a week but gotten her syndicated. And so, by 1969, "At Wit's End" was running in two hundred newspapers. Readers chuckled at her off-the-wall send-ups of suburban life and felt that her very jibes ratified the value of their choices.

It can safely be said that very few print journalists will ever be millionaires. They are generally wage slaves of the middling sort. But Bombeck advanced her prospects in three ways: she appealed to a huge underserved audience—suburban moms—became a TV star (albeit a minor one), and wrote best-selling books. From 1975 to 1986,

Bombeck appeared twice a week on ABC's *Good Morning America,* thereby enlarging her audience (and earning potential) by many millions. Not surprisingly, her years as a TV personality coincided with the peak years of her column. By the mid-1980s, more than nine hundred newspapers carried her column. The five books she published during her TV years—with titles such as *The Grass Is Always Greener over the Septic Tank* (1976) and *Motherhood: The Second Oldest Profession* (1983)—sold more than 15 million copies. The next three-book contract she signed was said to be worth $12 million. Not bad for a housewife who was always burning or breaking things!

Even while she was raking in the millions, Mrs. Bombeck knew better than to abandon her material. She still cleaned and shopped and complained about the hubby and kids like every suburban homebody. "If I didn't do my own housework, then I have no business writing about it. I spend 90 percent of my time living scripts and 10 percent writing them."

Entering showbiz has always been one of the great long shots. But in the postwar years it was one way for black Americans to become millionaires. Flip Wilson was the "first black entertainer to be the host of a successful weekly variety show on network television." Born during the Depression, one of eighteen kids abandoned by their mother, he spent his childhood in foster homes and then in reform school. He reunited with his father for a few years before joining the Air Force. There, "his knack for creating outlandish stories and acting them out in various dialects" earned him the nickname "Flip." By the time he left the service in 1954, he had decided to be a comedian.

While working as a bellhop in a San Francisco hotel, he convinced the manager to let him perform a comedy skit in the hotel nightclub. He became a regular, eventually setting out to tour and hone his material. By 1965, he had made it to the Big Apple as an MC at the Apollo Theatre. The proverbial big break came when Johnny Carson asked comedian Redd Foxx who the funniest comedian was. When he heard the unfamiliar name Flip Wilson, Carson booked him on his late-night TV talk show. At a time of great racial strife, Wilson came across as funny, black, and lovable in a wacky way. He was a great hit on the Carson show, and soon a regular on a whole host of variety shows. From

1970 to 1975, he had his own top-rated network show featuring him as "such outrageous, over-the-top characters as the Reverend Leroy of the Church of What's Happening Now and Geraldine, the sassy but proud black woman." By the time Wilson left—his show still top-rated—his income had soared to more than a million dollars a year. In 1979, he explained, "I accomplished what I set out to do. I wanted the whole cookie and I got it. Now I want to spend more time with my [five] children—make sure they don't go through what I did."

Wilson's strength was apolitical humor. He loved whimsical, historical riffs on topics such as Christopher Columbus looking for America and Ray Charles: "His humor is universal. He has the talent to make blacks laugh without anger and whites laugh without guilt." Just as Erma Bombeck enabled housewives to laugh at their lives, Flip Wilson allowed Americans of all races to enjoy his "distinctively black voice." Both comics had the ability to connect with whole new audiences. And so we see that people who make large fortunes are often tapping into unnoticed needs, sometimes of the psychic sort.

Three of our featured millionaires had advanced degrees, one a B.A. and several others nothing beyond high school. One of the outstanding and surprising facts about these millionaires is that as a group they were far better educated than their peers, as shown in Table 2-3. They were five times as likely to have a college degree than the U.S. population of comparable age. Of those who attended U.S. colleges, 67 percent went to the top fifty colleges, while 37 percent went to the eight Ivy League schools. The male millionaires were six times as likely to have advanced degrees as their peers. A quarter of the male millionaires had higher degrees, with eighteen men having law degrees, as well as five Ph.D.s and two M.D.s.

When it came to education, there was a big gap between the men and the women, which reflects the larger number of female millionaires in entertainment. In contrast to the 60 percent of men with a college degree, only a fifth of the women had one. And not a single woman had an advanced degree.

While most of our millionaires own businesses, some have become wealthy through a special talent. Take Ben Feldman, "whom industry

TABLE 2-3. *Education of the Millionaires in the Obituary Database, by Sex*

Education	Men (N = 160) (%)	Women (N = 16) (%)	Total (N = 176) (%)
Did not complete high school	13.1	18.8	13.6
High school graduate (but no college)	6.9	12.5	7.4
Some college	8.1	18.8	9.1
College graduate (no higher degree)	32.5	25.0	31.8
M.A., M.S., M.B.A., etc.	8.8	—	8.0
Ph.D.	3.1	—	2.8
M.D.	1.3	—	1.1
Law degree	11.3	—	10.2
Pharmacy degree	0.6	—	0.6
Not stated	14.4	25.0	15.3
Total	**100.0**	**100.0**	**100.0**
Attended college (%)	65.6	43.8	63.6
Graduated from college (%)	57.5	25.0	54.5
Achieved a higher degree (%)	25.0	—	22.7

experts called the greatest life insurance salesman of all time."
Everyone knows that responsible people—especially family men and
women raising children—should have life insurance. And according to
the U.S. Census Bureau, several hundred thousands earn a living selling just that.[9] But Feldman inhabited some other superplanet of salesmanship. By the end of the 1970s, wrote the *Times*, "Combining a
soft-sell approach with a hard drive to succeed, Mr. Feldman . . . was
selling more insurance annually as a single agent than 1,500 of the
1,800 insurance agencies in the country." Four years into his career in
1946, he broke the $1 million mark. Thirty years later, when others
might have begun to slow down, Feldman became the first person to
sell $100 million in life insurance in one year. This was a salesman of

such phenomenal dimensions that he was the subject of several books. All told, in five decades Feldman sold more than $1 billion in coverage as a New York Life Insurance agent working in eastern Ohio. His clientele were "owners of small factories, mills, and businesses."

Feldman seemed born to sell life insurance. A native of New York City, he dropped out of school at sixteen and briefly worked for his father in the poultry business. But he joined New York Life in 1942 and never looked back. His secret? Truly, no one could probably ever meaningfully deconstruct the unique quality of such salesmanship. Those hungering to know Feldman's secret can only read that he employed "a more positive approach that would harness a buyer's best instincts."

But the reality is that most millionaires are entrepreneurial business-people, men and women whose driving ambition and slightly different view of the world give them an advantage. Jack M. Berry was born on a farm northeast of Memphis, Tennessee, and, though he finished high school, there was no money for him to go to college, as there had been for his older brother. However, that married brother lived in New York, where he sold citrus from his in-laws' Florida groves to mom-and-pop grocers. Wrote the *Times*, "According to family legend, Charles [the brother] was a playboy who needed somebody to do the work and found his little brother well suited for the task . . . while [he] concentrated on New York night life." When the carousing brother died of a heart attack in 1942, Jack had saved enough to buy the business. But Jack soon realized that the very business that he had acquired—essentially brokering Florida oranges to small New York groceries—was doomed. Chain supermarkets, which were coming on strong, contracted directly with the Florida growers for their supplies.

But something else was also happening: All over the nation, health-conscious Americans were starting to swig down o.j. with breakfast every day. The demand for oranges—not to peel and eat for a snack but to make into frozen concentrate—was soaring. Jack Berry scouted central Florida, prime citrus-growing territory with its dry soil, and began buying groves. By 1950, he had moved down to Winter Haven. Along with many others, he rode America's obsession with vitamin C to prosperity. Then came the killer freeze of 1962, which wiped out half the state's citrus crop. In the wake of this, Mr. Berry decided to buy six thousand acres in southern Florida, soggy terrain viewed as utterly inferior for growing good citrus. The other citrus barons rolled their eyeballs at this foolish move, but eventually had to concede that yes, Berry's drainage canals worked and yes, his groves were doing okay. "It was not until 1982, when another freeze devastated crops in central Florida but left the Berry harvest untouched, that his pioneering created a stampede. Since then more than 100,000 acres of southwestern Florida have been converted to citrus crops." Meanwhile, Berry's gamble was paying off big-time because citrus prices had soared and he had the goods. He used some of that income to pay $25 million in cash for another sixteen thousand southwestern Florida acres, thereby expanding his total citrus holdings to forty-five square miles. By 1993 he had made *Forbes'* list of the four hundred richest Americans, with $280 million in assets—and all because Americans love orange juice.

Thomas H. Davis was a Winston-Salem boy who just kept on figuring out new ways to stay near what he loved best: airplanes. Growing up in North Carolina, he was among the millions enthralled by Charles Lindbergh's 1927 transatlantic flight. During high school, he took up flying and while he was away at college, he made money teaching others to fly. But after coming home for the summer and selling airplanes, he quit school, soon bought out his employer, and named his company Piedmont Aviation. Just before World War II hit, Piedmont's ten employees were selling one hundred planes a year. During the war, Davis discovered a lucrative niche training military pilots and soon had a hundred employees. Then, "Just because the war was over, I didn't want to turn them out in the cold."

Once again, Piedmont Aviation changed its game plan, this time entering the commercial aviation business. Piedmont Airlines was a regional carrier whose average route was less than one hundred miles long. All those takeoffs and landings shot up the costs of running the company. "To save money, the company made lightning-fast turnaround times at the terminal its specialty." Once on the ground, the "pilot would kill one engine but keep the other running as passengers exited and others came on board." Piedmont became one of the nation's most profitable airlines, and by the time US Airways bought it in 1987, Piedmont had 21,500 employees and annual revenues of $2.5 billion.

Until the last year of his life, Davis continued to be an avid flier, sometimes taking out the restored Taylor E-2 from his student-pilot days. "I still enjoy flying around and looking at the countryside," he said in 1995. "It's a lot of fun." And thus does a life passion segue into a life accomplishment.

Davis made his fortune pretty much up in the clouds. Sarah Korein, a Manhattan real estate mogul, made hers firmly on the ground. She was a *rara avis* of her generation, a female millionaire who made her money herself. She and her husband were immigrants who landed in New York City in 1923. In 1931, they bought a six-story apartment building in East Flatbush in Brooklyn for $6,000 so all the family members could live rent free. It would be another ten years before the Koreins bought more real estate, this time a large apartment building in the Bay Ridge section of Brooklyn. Thinking she would need to replace the refrigerators to entice tenants, Mrs. Korein bought dozens and stashed them in the building's empty swimming pool. Then came World War II, and both refrigerators and apartments were in short supply. She rented her building with no problem *and* sold the refrigerators at a tidy profit.

Thus was launched a businesswoman who by the time she died owned such famous (and, need we add, wildly valuable) Manhattan properties as Lever House on Park Avenue, the giant Equitable Building downtown, and Penn Plaza, the city's fifth largest office building—not to mention the Delmonico Hotel on Park Avenue, the Swiss Center on Fifth Avenue, and two apartment towers on Central Park South. And those were just the name properties.

Her secret? Always looking for solid value. According to the *Times*, "Mrs. Korein made use of the nonamortizing mortgage, under which she would pay slightly higher interest rates but nothing toward principal, thus freeing cash for further investments. By the time the loan itself came due, her properties typically had appreciated so much in value that Mrs. Korein could easily pay off the amount." Said one business colleague, "All her properties, without exception, did nothing but increase in value"—a hard record to beat.

What can we say overall about the sixteen female millionaires in our database? They were found in three fields: Hollywood and entertainment, book authors, and business. In the first group we find people such as actress Ginger Rogers, singer Tammy Wynette, and producer Dawn Steel. Among the authors were Bombeck and astrologer Linda Goodman. And there were the six businesswomen who did everything from running banks to starting a chain of stores.

Risk taking is a common theme in the life histories of millionaires. Berry took a flier on untested citrus terrain and emerged triumphant. Bernstein opened a whole new kind of Wall Street brokerage. And then there was Mel Fisher, the biggest gambler among all our *New York Times* millionaires. This was a guy engaged in the ultimate risky enterprise: hunting for undersea treasure. Fisher was the poster boy of optimism, able to press on "despite skeptical investors, mixed luck in the law courts, a leaky houseboat home, debts" and the drowning deaths of a son and daughter-in-law. His mantra as he headed off for another day's search: "Today is the day." Another favorite maxim: "Finders keepers." Asked why he had chosen such an uncertain life, he often said, "For the fun, the romance and the adventure."

Like most of the *New York Times* millionaires, Fisher entered the work world with a college degree. Fittingly, his was in hydraulic engineering, which he studied at both Purdue and Alabama University. Then he headed west and opened a chicken farm in California, certainly the antithesis of fun, romance, and adventure. But that didn't last long. Soon Fisher had opened a diving shop in Redondo Beach and fallen under the spell of treasure hunting. Reported the *Times*, "He is said to have been heartened by his finding of a doubloon under water at the Florida coast in the 1960's." Shortly thereafter, he moved his family to Florida.

Fully focused on his quest for treasure, over the years he found "hundreds of thousands of gold and silver coins, jewelry and bars from old-time Spanish shipwrecks in the waters off Florida." His great quest, the Holy Grail, was for the "cargo of a single treasure-packed galleon, the Nuestra Senora de Atocha, which sank in 1622 near the Florida Keys." In 1985, his son Kane finally located the ship, whose treasure turned out to be worth $400 million.

Like Eisenstadt of Sweet'N Low, Mel Fisher's family was involved in his business. When he died, he had been married to his wife for forty-eight years. And while we tend to think of the rich as having serial marriages and families, less than 38 percent of the male millionaires married more than once. Almost two thirds of the women, however, married more than once. The number of offspring of those married (four did not marry) varied from none to nine, averaging out to 2.7 children per millionaire.

Mel Fisher was an endearing romantic, a genuine old salt who loved the sea and its secrets. We cherish such impractical sorts and cheer their triumphs. But most millionaires are far more pragmatic. A good example is J. Reese Phifer, a southern lawyer who made his money through aluminum screens. Born in Tuscaloosa, Alabama, Phifer and his brother grew up helping around their father's grocery store. Reese earned a B.A. in commerce and a law degree from the University of Alabama. Around the time he set up a law practice, he also learned to fly, a skill he put to use during World War II. Not only did he train Allied pilots, he helped ferry planes to Europe, thereby seeing some of the world beyond the South. When he returned, like many a veteran, he was restless. Said his brother, "He told me that he wanted to get into manufacturing. He said that's where the money was. He looked all over for something that wasn't manufactured in the South. He came up with screen because we use more screen in the South than anywhere else."

So in 1952, Phifer started the Phifer Aluminum Screen Company. Again, his brother: "He was doing the selling himself. He'd get in the plane and sell the wire and then come home and help make it. He had a little bitty office with one secretary and the guy who helped him set up the looms." Renamed Phifer Wire Products in 1956, it expanded continuously. By 1998, it employed a thousand people who produced "more than half the world's aluminum insect screening and more than 60 percent of the world's fiberglass insect screening." Phifer saw early on that a lawyer could sell only so many billable hours, whereas a businessman could sell ever-expanding numbers of his product—in his case, screens.

Most businesspeople like Phifer deliberately pursue wealth and are often very generous with what they make. But occasionally a very different impetus is at work. Such was the case with Dr. David H. Smith, chairman of pediatrics at the University of Rochester Medical School. As a medical professor, Dr. Smith worked on the problem of meningitis caused by the bacterium *Haemophilus influenza* type B, or Hib. This was a very dreadful disease, and by the early 1980s, said the *Times*, "20,000 cases of Hib invasive disease in preschool children were reported to the Federal Centers for Disease Control. In about 12,000 of those cases, the children had meningitis, an inflammation of the brain and spinal cord membranes that can be fatal or cause permanent brain damage."

TABLE 2-4. *The Apex of Fame: Millionaires in the Obituary Database*

Name (Age at Death)	Obit Date	Occupation
1. Frank Sinatra (82)	05/16/98	Singer/actor
2. Benjamin Spock (94)	03/17/98	Pediatrician/author
3. James Stewart (89)	07/03/97	Actor
4. Harry Helmsley (87)	01/06/97	Real estate developer
5. Roy Rogers (86)	07/07/98	Singer/actor
6. George Abbott (107)	02/02/95	Producer
7. Ginger Rogers (83)	04/26/95	Actress/dancer
8. George Burns (100)	03/10/96	Actor/comedian
9. James Michener (90)	10/17/97	Author
10. Joseph Baum (78)	10/06/98	Restaurant executive
11. Red Skelton (84)	09/18/97	Actor/clown
12. Gene Autry (91)	10/03/98	Actor; businessman
13. Carl Sagan (62)	12/21/96	Astronomer; author
14. Roberto Goizueta (65)	10/19/97	Business executive
15. Fred Trump (93)	06/26/99	Real estate developer
16. Sarah Korein (93)	11/04/98	Real estate investor

Dr. Smith believed that a Hib vaccine could be developed, but he could not interest a pharmaceutical company in it. "He was so determined to do this," said his wife, "that he quit his job and mortgaged the house and founded" Praxis Biologics in 1983. Two years later, the first vaccine for older children had been developed. Seeing the possibilities, American Cyanamid bought Praxis in 1989 and Dr. Smith served as chairman and chief scientific officer of the combined company. In 1990, a vaccine won approval to be used in infants as young as two months old. By 1997, the number of reported cases of Hib-caused meningitis had plummeted to 258, from 12,000 cases more than a decade earlier. In 1996,

Accomplishments and Fame	Amount of Wealth*	Obit Length
Singer and film actor	$$$	236"
Infant/child care books	$	125"
Made more than eighty movies; national icon; won Oscar	$$	120"
Helmsley-Spear	$$$$	90"
Movies, records	$$	90"
Broadway giant involved in more than 120 plays	$	90"
Made seventy movies; won Oscar; humble upbringing	$	87"
Movies, shows; won Oscar	$$	86"
Novels	$$$	78"
Restaurant Associates; Four Seasons	$	69"
TV, movies; began in vaudeville shows	$	66"
Movies; owner of radio and TV stations and baseball team	$$$	66"
Professor; TV series host	$	60"
Coca-Cola president; turned company around	$$$	60"
Postwar master builder	$$$	60"
Dealing style; owned famed properties in New York City	$$	59"

(continues)

TABLE 2-4. *The Apex of Fame: Millionaires in the Obituary Database*

Name (Age at Death)	Obit Date	Occupation
17. Samuel Fuller (85)	11/01/97	Director
18. Phil Hartman (49)	05/29/98	Actor/comedian
19. Charles Luckman (89)	01/28/99	Real estate developer
20. Howard Cosell (77)	04/24/95	Broadcaster
21. James Rouse (81)	04/10/96	Real estate developer
22. Thomas Watson, Jr. (79)	01/01/94	Business executive
23. Tammy Wynette (55)	04/08/98	Singer
24. Dawn Steel (51)	12/22/97	Producer
25. William Levitt (86)	01/29/94	Real estate developer
26. Flip Wilson (64)	11/27/98	Comedian
27. Melvin Belli (88)	07/11/96	Personal injury lawyer
28. David Packard (83)	03/27/96	Business executive
29. Seymour Durst (81)	05/20/95	Real estate investor
30. Avery Fisher (87)	02/27/94	Business executive
31. Jack Kent Cooke (84)	04/07/97	Businessman
32. Bebe Rebozo (85)	05/10/98	Real estate; banker
33. John Goldwater (83)	03/02/99	Cartoonist
34. Ann Corio (85)	03/09/99	Actress
35. Zachary Fisher (88)	06/05/99	Real estate developer
36. Harold Geneen (87)	11/23/97	Business executive

* $ = Millionaire: $1 million to $19 million; $$ = Multimillionaire: $20 million to $99 million; $$$ = Supermillionaire: $100 million to $999 million; $$$$ = Billionaire, stated as such.

Note: Most of the millionaires with the longest obituaries were business leaders or those involved in Hollywood, TV, or other media. Of the thirty-six in the Apex of Fame for millionaires, sixteen were in business and fifteen in entertainment. The five other Apex millionaires included three authors, a doctor-author and a lawyer. Of the Apex millionaires, five were women. All thirty-six millionaires with the longest obituaries received extensive coverage: each had forty or more column inches of coverage and a photograph.

Accomplishments and Fame	Amount of Wealth*	Obit Length
Films	$	56"
TV shows *Saturday Night Live, Newsradio*; movies	$	56"
Luckman partnership	$	56"
Sports on TV	$	55"
James W. Rouse & Co.	$	54"
I. B. M. president; computer manufacturing pioneer	$$$	53"
Country music	$	53"
Columbia; Paramount Studio chief	$	52"
Levitt & Sons	$$	51"
TV show host	$	50"
Flamboyant style and huge settlements	$$	48"
Cofounded Hewlett-Packard; Silicon Valley pioneer	$$$	46"
Durst Organization	$$	44"
Founded Fisher Radio, Philharmonic Radio; philanthropy	$$	44"
Owned broadcasting stations and sports teams	$$$	42"
Private investor; friend of Richard Nixon	$	42"
Archie Comic Publications	$	41"
Burlesque queen on Broadway	$	41"
Helped alter New York City skyline	$$$	41"
Made ITT a global conglomerate	$$	40"

Dr. Smith shared the Albert Lasker Award for Clinical Medical Research, one of his profession's most prestigious prizes. His noble and very successful ambition to help the sick just happened to make him a multimillionaire.

Then there's luck. You may remember Dick McDonald attributing his choice of the golden arches to good luck. Most people feel that some aspects of their good fortune are just that: luck! And in some cases, it's absolutely true. Thus we have one multimillionaire, Sheila Ryan, who won the $55 million Florida lottery jackpot in 1988.

This made her the largest individual lottery winner in U.S. history. A New York widow who had moved to Florida, Mrs. Ryan worked part-time selling real estate. After her extraordinary windfall, she said, "I think it was by the grace of God I won. I realized there must have been a reason He gave me the money, so I decided to give some of it to senior citizens and the homeless." To that end she set up a charitable foundation that underwrote everything from low-cost housing to paying overdue rent to spare single mothers and their children from eviction. When Mrs. Ryan died, only $16.6 million of the jackpot had been paid out, and so, like many an American millionaire, her philanthropy will live on.

What, then, can we conclude about the millionaires we encounter in the *New York Times* obits? From the database, we know that most of them started new companies, generating new wealth not just for themselves but for their employees and business associates. Most rose through their own initiative. Only one quarter came from affluent families. The men were far better educated than their peers. Owning a company was the principal route to success for two thirds of these people. The women were more likely to succeed in nonbusiness venues. Most on our list were multimillionaires, and some were billionaires. As seen in Table 2-4, their fame was often associated with great wealth; most in the apex of fame were multimillionaires or billionaires.

From the stories of their lives, we know that certain character qualities are important: being entrepreneurial, persevering, and innovative; going against the conventional wisdom at times; taking risks; and working hard.

Notes

1. Thomas J. Stanley and W. D. Danko, *The Millionaire Next Door* (Atlanta: Long Street Press, 1997).
2. Thomas J. Stanley, *The Millionaire Mind* (Kansas City, Mo.: Andrews McMeel, 2000), p. 4.
3. Andrew Hacker, *Money* (New York: Touchstone, 1997), p. 69.
4. Peter Newcomb, editor, "The Forbes 400," *Forbes* Oct. 11, 1989, p. 169.
5. David Cay Johnson, "Reducing Audits of the Wealthy, I.R.S. Turns Eye on Working Poor," *New York Times*, December 15, 1999, p. A1, C31.
6. In *The Millionaire Next Door* it is reported that 80 percent of U.S. millionaires are "first-generation rich" p. 3.
7. Hacker, *Money,* p. 75.
8. Bettina Flores and Jennifer Basye Sander, *The Millionaire$$ Across the Street* (Chicago: Dearborn Financial Publishing, 1999), p. 135.
9. In 1997, there were 724,000 insurance agents, brokers, and service workers; see *Statistical Abstract of the United States, 1998*, Table 687.

3

Pioneering Women

Ardent in Politics and Romance

Hawaiian Surfing Champion

First Woman to Be a Reporter at CBS

In life as in death, Jacqueline Kennedy Onassis was "one of the world's most famous women, an object of fascination to generations of Americans." The *New York Times* lavished two full pages on her obituary, including ten mesmerizing photos. There she is as a young society child in an old-fashioned riding habit, as an enchantingly beautiful bride with Senator John F. Kennedy, and in glowing First Lady mode.[1] Then there is the terrifying blur of the assassination followed by the grief-stricken but dignified widow with her two small children. The final two photos show her brief jet-set period with her second husband, Greek shipping magnate Aristotle Onassis, and then the Doubleday senior editor, still glamorous and youthful at sixty-three, attending a gala opera evening with her longtime but little-known companion, businessman Maurice Templesman.

Of the two thousand or so obituaries that run each year in the *New York Times*, only 17 percent are of women. In our *New York Times* database, of the 9,325 Americans, 1,620 are women. The average length of a woman's obit was almost sixteen inches. Of course, this group generally reflects a generation born long before the women's movement, and one would expect that percentage to rise dramatically in coming decades as women rack up more accomplishments in the public arena. After all, in 1955, just over a third of American women worked, while today that figure is 60 percent.[2]

TABLE 3-1. *Careers of the Women in the Obituary Database*

Area of Fame	Percent
Entertainment: Performers and others (N = 465)	(33.0)
Actresses	11.1
Singers, dancers	7.9
Designers, directors, producers	5.8
Musician, composer, artists	5.4
Sports	2.8
Education careers (N = 222)	(15.7)
Professors: college, university, seminary	7.8
Education administrators	3.3
Museum or library director	2.3
Teachers, tutors	2.3
Authors, journalists, editors (N = 213)	(15.1)
Authors	9.7
Editors, reporters, photographers	5.4
Government and civic leaders (N = 155)	(11.0)
Federal government leaders	3.6
Civic leaders	3.3
Advocates, party leaders	2.3
State and local government leaders	1.7

When we look at the obits, 87 percent of the women were famous for their career accomplishments, while the remainder were notable for their family connections (e.g., as a wife or daughter of a famous man) or were famous heiresses and/or socialites. Almost half the successful working women were clustered in the arts, as Table 3-1 shows. A full third were performers, with actresses accounting for more than a tenth of all those featured. Professors and others in education accounted for 16 percent. Writers and editors accounted for another 15 percent. After that, the women had careers in government (11 percent), business (10 percent), medicine (6 percent), law, fashion, and others (8 percent).

Area of Fame	Percent
Business executives (N = 146)	(10.4)
Corporate executives	5.7
Media executives	2.5
Other business and labor executives	2.2
Medical people (N = 91)	(6.5)
Professors of medicine, doctors	2.6
Nurses, social workers, therapists	2.6
Hospital administrators, others	1.2
Lawyers, others (N = 118)	(8.4)
Lawyers	1.7
Judges	1.0
Fashion and interior designers	2.1
Religious leaders and others	3.6
Total (N = 1,410)	**100.0**

In this chapter we look at a cross section of America's most successful women, many of them pioneers in their fields. Some triumphed by playing by the old rules, some prevailed by acting as if those rules did not apply to them, while others challenged the old strictures and became the first woman this or the first woman that. Many of them changed the way we think about a woman's place in the world; others changed our world—whether by helping us take charge of money, designing truly comfortable (but stylish) clothes, or opening up the fields of health, media, or sports. Of the 125 million Americans now in the workforce, 46 percent are women.[3] And the percentage of women with college degrees rose from 5.2 percent in 1950 to 15.4 percent in 1997.[4]

Jackie Kennedy Onassis straddled the pre- and postfeminist eras, having served as the perfect postwar wife and mother before seeking a career as a book editor in the more liberated 1970s. Ironically, her extraordinary fame did not really come from either of her roles as wife or editor. This most famous American woman—whose obit was twice as long as that of any other female in the database—had long since transcended her actual occupations to become an international icon of style and glamour. Jackie Kennedy was, one suspects, a one-of-a-kind historical figure. Certainly no Helen Keller, she nonetheless embodied a kind of elegance, dignity, and determined privacy that was enormously appealing to people. Her true accomplishment in life was creating herself and her whole way of living and being. As President Kennedy commented in amusement after a state visit to France, "I am the man who accompanied Jacqueline Kennedy to Paris—and I have enjoyed it." When we look at the qualities that differentiate a certain number of the successful and famous women from their male peers, Jackie Kennedy epitomizes them. As unpalatable as this may be, for some women, great beauty, marriage, and an elegant image remain very real paths to success and fame in a way that simply is not true for men.

Moreover, Jackie Kennedy was that rare creature who remained in that exalted state of fame through the sheer power of her elegant persona. And it seems that once Jackie understood that for her, visual image was crucial, she ceased having anything public to say. The molding of her image extended to even small details. Jackie Kennedy was a chainsmoker, but she was careful never to be seen or photographed in the act. Over the decades, her reticence made her only the more alluring.

If marrying well was the road to success in the old days, probably no woman so completely embraced that route as Pamela Harriman, at her death U.S. ambassador to France but best known for "her history of captivating some of the world's richest and most attractive men on two continents, and marrying three of them." Harriman herself explained, "I was born in a world where a woman was totally controlled by men. I mean, you got married and there was kind of no alternative. The boys were allowed to go off to school. The girls were kept home, educated by governesses." Thus, by the terms of the old rules, she triumphed. But what makes Harriman so fascinating and a true transitional figure is that she also triumphed under the new rules, a striking example of feminine power unleashed.

Born into a declining British aristocratic family, young Pamela was seen as an unfashionable country girl when she "came out" in London society in 1938. But Prime Minister Winston Churchill's ne'er-do-well son proposed on the first date, they married, and Harriman's rise began. With her husband away at war, the young Mrs. Churchill became the center of Winston Churchill's social set, having affairs with such powerful men as John Hay Whitney, the U.S. ambassador, and CBS broadcaster Edward R. Murrow. After the war, she divorced Churchill, for whom she had produced the desired heir, and then lived on the Continent, the mistress of such rich and prominent men as Aly Khan and Baron Elie de Rothschild. In 1960, she went to New York, met producer Leland Hayward, and married him. When he died eleven years later, she married Averell Harriman, a lover from the London war years and heir to the $100 million Union Pacific railroad fortune. She became a U.S. citizen and an exuberant supporter of the beleaguered Democratic Party, boning up on policy matters, constantly raising money, and producing opinion pieces for the press.

But what made that all possible was an extraordinary talent for cultivating powerful men—whether as friends or lovers—and a series of marriages that gave her access to huge wealth and power. She was not—like Jacqueline Kennedy—a great beauty, but she had a tremendous sense of style and gave absolute rapt attention—"geisha-like" devotion—to the men in her life. Her biggest accomplishment in the last phase of a life where she was always "one of the most vivacious women on the international scene" was raising millions of dollars, rebuilding the Democratic Party, and helping elect Bill Clinton president.

In her final decades, she reinvented herself as a major political patron and power broker. When Averell Harriman died in 1986, Pamela Harriman really came into her own, eventually receiving a plum reward: ambassadorship to France. Here, finally, she could operate in her own

right as the person with the power. The *New York Times* described her as
a signal success who loved the "16-hour days dealing with questions of
international trade, NATO expansion and the war in Bosnia, and working the telephone to Washington late into the night." She rejected the
general view of herself as a highly focused gold digger: "Those were
the people I met. Everything in life, I believe, is luck and timing."

In that era when "men controlled everything," Harriman was just one
of the best known of the femmes fatales. Another was Kay Halle, and
some of her beaus may sound familiar. This "glamorous Cleveland
department store heiress . . . once showed a friend a list of sixty-four
men who proposed to her, among them a youthful Randolph Churchill
and an aging Averell Harriman." A slender blond society beauty who
settled in Washington, D.C., after World War II, Halle never did marry,
becoming "famous for surprising wealthy suitors by showing up for
dinner dates with several less well-heeled admirers in tow." Another
glamour girl out of the prefeminist era was Dorothy H. Hirshon,
described as "one of the most beautiful girls in Southern California."
Among her high-profile husbands were John Randolph Hearst and CBS
founder William S. Paley. Not only was she sketched by Matisse and
photographed by Cecil Beaton and Horst, but her Long Island estate,
Kiluna Farm, had twenty-two servants!

These were women who played by the old rules and did pretty well.
One does not feel so sanguine about Wanda Toscanini Horowitz, dutiful
daughter of conductor Arturo Toscanini and handmaiden wife of pianist
Vladimir Horowitz. The *New York Times* described her as a woman who
"wore a permanent scowl and was famous for her fiery temper." When
asked about her life, which had been given over to the endless needs of
these two geniuses, she exploded, "Don't talk to me about them. My
father made me neurotic and my husband made me crazy. . . . I have my
own personality. But now, at this point in life, I wish I would have done
something for me."

Considered the most musically talented of Toscanini's four children,
Wanda aspired to be an operetta singer. But the severe judgment of her
brilliant father dissuaded her. She feared even practicing piano when he
was present. "A mistake was like a stab in his stomach," she once said.

Instead, she married Horowitz and followed in her mother's footsteps, acting as all-around factotum despite a stormy and troubled marriage that produced one unhappy daughter. It became Wanda's job to pack her husband's "bags and see to it that he had every comfort of home on the road, from the proper curtains and bedding in his hotel room to the filet of sole and asparagus he favored in his later years. She screened his telephone calls, fought with managers and saw that record jackets—and the recordings inside them—were just so."

When Vladimir Horowitz died in 1989, Leonard Bernstein recognized her sacrifice: "You cared for him and guarded him through a series of neurotic crises the world may never know nor understand; and you returned him to us time and again, refreshed, renewed and ever greater." In short, she had fulfilled the traditional role as helpmate to the men in her life.

There were, of course, working women before the feminist revolution of the 1970s.[5] But they tended to be found in traditional fields, such as acting. One of those in the Women's Apex of Fame was Ginger Rogers, who danced her way to success with Fred Astaire in a series of frothy musicals, such as the classic *Swing Time*. At age fifteen young Ginger was already the champion Charleston dancer of Texas, whereupon she hit the vaudeville circuit. She traveled with her mother, Lela, a woman completely devoted to nurturing her daughter's talent and career, and times were not easy. "There was never enough money," Rogers would recall. "I always had to roll down my silk stockings and carry a doll when we bought train tickets so I could go half-fare. If we had $3, we always figured out how to tip for the trunks and still eat."

All that early touring prepared her for Broadway, and at twenty-two this lithe blond beauty and Astaire were whirling together toward movie stardom. By 1941, Ginger Rogers was America's highest-paid woman with a $355,000-a-year studio contract. When her movie career petered out, she returned to Broadway and the stage. Along the way, in good Hollywood style, she married and divorced five times but had no children. Always, she had a creed that guided her career and kept her working, "The most important thing in anyone's life is to be giving something. The quality I can give is fun and joy and happiness. This is my gift."

Martha Gellhorn was one of those who proceeded as if the existing rules for females could be ignored, becoming in the course of things the "premier war correspondent of the 20th century," according to writer Ward Just. "She began during the civil war in Spain in 1937 and ended several wars and more than 50 years later in Panama." Gellhorn was acclaimed not just as a journalist but also as a short-story writer. Educated at Bryn Mawr College, she had been a reporter for ten years, becoming friendly with such powerful people as Eleanor Roosevelt, when she "went to Spain with nothing but a knapsack and $50" to cover the conflict for *Collier's Weekly*. During World War II, she started off in London, reporting on the Blitz. Come D-Day, "she stowed away on a hospital ship and snuck ashore as a stretcher bearer. . . . When the Allies liberated Dachau, she was there to write about it."

The *New York Times* described Gellhorn as "a cocky, raspy-voiced maverick who saw herself as a champion of ordinary people trapped in conflicts created by the rich and powerful." In her war reporting, she always focused on civilians and foot soldiers. From Dachau, she wrote, "Behind the barbed wire and the electric fence, the skeletons sat in the sun and searched themselves for lice. They have no age and no faces; they all look alike and like nothing you will ever see if you are lucky."

She was married briefly to a Frenchman, for five years to Ernest Hemingway—whom she left because he was "jealous and bullying"— and then to a *Time* editor. After that she gave up, declaring "married life too boring." After World War II, she adopted a son, raising him in the many countries she lived in as an expatriate. Looking back, she would say to friends, "I was physically lucky and was paid to spend my time with magnificent people."

While Gellhorn triumphantly crashed a man's field—war reporting— through her own chutzpah, Mary Roebling blazed the money trail as "the first woman to head a major American bank, the Trenton Trust Company" at the behest of the men in her family. In 1958, she also became the first female governor of the American Stock Exchange and "a tireless advocate of a greater role for women in the country's economic affairs." In a 1965 speech, she said that "the American woman has almost unbelievable economic power, but American women, like women of all civilized nations, do not use the influence their economic power gives them." Roebling worked to change that.

She was born in suburban New Jersey, where her father was a telephone company executive and her mother a music teacher. While still a teenager, she married a musician, and when she was widowed three years later, she went to work at a Philadelphia investment house to support her daughter. At night she took courses in business administration at the University of Pennsylvania. She then married Siegfried Roebling, a wealthy businessman and engineer whose family was famous for designing and building the Brooklyn Bridge. During this time, she stayed home raising her child.

Siegfried Roebling died when his wife was just thirty, leaving her once again a widow but with the consolation of a large block of stock in Trenton Trust. Her father and father-in-law urged that she "try her hand at running the bank," citing her previous experience and, perhaps most important, "her common sense." And so, in 1937, she became the bank's president. Reported the *Times*, Trenton Trust "grew substantially and she was its president or chairman until 1972." By that time, "300 other American women had become presidents or chairwomen of banks." In 1978, Roebling helped establish the Women's Bank of Denver, the first nationally chartered bank founded by women. She felt that such banks could "be better listeners for women and give them more time, advice and direction. . . . It's a psychological thing, really." Women like Roebling played an important role in helping American women appreciate the power and importance of money.

Some of our women pioneers would probably agree with Pamela Harriman that to some degree their destinies were shaped not by any career planning but by "luck and timing." A woman such as the aristocratic Sister Dorothy Parish, for instance, would never have been allowed to develop a high-powered decorating and design firm had the Depression not brought hard times on both her blue-blooded stockbroker husband and her father. But once Parish started her own business (taking on as her partner Albert Hadley much later, in 1962), she never looked back. Nor did she have to, for as more and more Americans became wealthy in the postwar years, nesting and decorating became national pastimes.

Born in New Jersey hunt country, Parish had a silver-spoon upbringing that included finishing school (but no high school diploma or college) and frequent trips to Europe. After her marriage, she had a home in Manhattan and a farmhouse in Far Hills, New Jersey. Her artful interiors in the country revealed an enormous talent. When her family needed more income, she opened a firm that would make her the "grande dame of American interior decorating" over six decades and reshape the American home. Most memorably, in the 1960s, she created what came to be known as American country style, marked by simple furniture, painted floors, patchwork quilts, and throw rugs. One admirer wrote, "No one else in America does a room with such patrician aplomb, such life-enhancing charm, such a lack of gimmickry or trendiness."

Clearly, Parish's family status and connections were crucial in opening doors and securing clients. For instance, Mrs. Parish lent her famous eye and advice to redoing the dowdy Kennedy White House, until one day an annoyed First Lady "fired Sister for telling little Caroline to keep her feet off the upholstery." Ultimately, however, it was a combination of Parish's unique eye, hard work, and deeply held ideas that caused *Vogue* to deem her "the most famous of all living women interior designers." Parish was very clear about where she stood: "What seems important to me is permanence, comfort and a look of continuity in the design and decoration of a house. The happiest times of my life are associated with beautiful, familiar things and family."

While Sister Parish sought to liberate American homes from stiff, highly formal and uncomfortable furnishings, clothes designer Vera Maxwell pursued the same goal with women's wardrobes. She was "one of the pioneers of women's sportswear. . . [designing] clothes that were casual, comfortable and classic." So influential were her easy-to-wear creations that she was honored with two retrospectives, one at the Smithsonian Institution in Washington, D.C., and one at the Museum of the City of New York. Matching separates in comfortable styles was considered revolutionary, as was the forerunner of the jumpsuit that she designed.

Vera Maxwell spent part of her childhood in Europe and then graduated from high school in New Jersey. At that time she saw dance, not designing, as her destiny and danced for five years with the Metropolitan Opera Ballet. When she married Mr. Maxwell, she left the ballet and took up modeling on Seventh Avenue, where she began her love affair with fashion. She went to London to study tailoring and put in stints at various fledgling American sportswear houses. Until then, the great fashion designers had been largely French and male: Charles Worth, Paul Poiret. But then came Coco Chanel, who was Maxwell's idol, and Maxwell, too, aspired to make "timeless clothes that women could move around in."

It is hard to imagine, in our present day of rampant hype and fashion superstars, that Vera Maxwell blazed that path first. According to the *New York Times*, "Mrs. Maxwell became known as a designer in the 1930s when American fashion was struggling to be born and most designers toiled anonymously. She achieved fame with such designs as a weekend wardrobe of a collarless jacket with four patch pockets that she made in tweed and in gray flannel to be mixed and matched with a short pleated flannel tennis skirt, a longer tweed skirt with pressed-down pleats and a pair of flannel cuffed trousers—all designs so classic they could still be worn today." The star designer with a signature style had come to America, helping to launch a genuine home-grown fashion industry.

In 1947, not long after divorcing her second (and last) husband, she formed her own company, Vera Maxwell Originals. The 1950s were her heyday, and by 1960, seven hundred stores around the country were carrying her designs. But with fab Brits such as Mary Quant in the ascendant, Maxwell faltered. Her 1964 line "bombed," and so "I decided to lay fallow for a while." In 1970, she returned to designing, offering her loyal followers "tasteful classic suits, coats and dresses" that they could wear for years. Today American sportswear, with its emphasis on stylish comfort, dominates not just the fashion world but the real world, all thanks to Vera Maxwell and others in that long-gone vanguard.

Postwar America, with its roaring prosperity, became an enthusiastic society of consumers, buying houses, cars, clothes, and a slew of household gizmos and gadgets. How best to sell things—market research—became an important and lucrative field unto itself. This new field proved friendly to women such as Florence Skelly Altman, who developed "many techniques that are now standard in market research, including the use of simulated test markets to estimate the potential of new products." When Procter & Gamble test-marketed Pampers in Peoria, Illinois, in 1961, it was using one of Florence Skelly's ideas that landed her in the Market Research Hall of Fame.

Her longtime partner Daniel Yankelovich explained, "She had a great flair for the numbers side of the business, but saw the human implications of the numbers like no one I have ever known." When Skelly did a study of younger Americans in the late 1960s with Yankelovich and another longtime partner, Arthur H. White, she helped coin the term "baby boomers." But more important, said White, "The study revealed gender and race problems, that we had a society in which large segments of the population were not treated as well as other segments and that attitudes about institutions were changing. . . . We saw that most people did not want to accept everything an employer or the Government said." The coming turbulence of the sixties and seventies was foreshadowed in that study.

Discrimination against women was straightforward in the fifties.[6] When Florence Skelly went with White and another colleague to attend a meeting of the board of the New York Stock Exchange, she was not allowed in, only the two men. But she kept her good humor, which apparently was one of her great strengths. "She was a wonderful, witty person," said Yankelovich, who was her partner with White in two different firms, "very funny but serious at the same time, which is a great combination. Our clients loved her, and she loved the business."

Women were tolerated and even welcomed in new kinds of businesses—whether interior decorating, fashion, or market research. But they found the early going very tough when breaking into the most prestigious, male-dominated professions: medicine and law. Dr. Mary Howell, "who championed medical careers and better health care for women," was one of a handful of female physicians to merit a major obit in the *New York Times* in recent years. Howell became a doctor in the early 1960s, when many believed that an expensive medical school education was squandered on women. After all, they were just going to get married, quit, and have children. When she was well established as a medical leader, Dr. Howell described "the slights, condescension, jokes and outright hostility she endured as a medical student and intern from school administrators, faculty members and male students. Even female patients often feared that a female doctor was inherently inferior."

In 1969, she joined the staff of the Harvard Medical School as an instructor in pediatrics, and by 1972 she found herself associate dean for student affairs, a job she viewed as a token gesture to satisfy demands for female administrators. But she exploited this highly visible position and Harvard's great prestige for all they were worth. While there, she "sent out questionnaires to female medical students throughout the country, asking them about their status and attitudes towards them." This led to a book about discrimination against women in medicine titled *Why Would a Girl Go into Medicine? Medical Education in the United States: A Guide for Women.* Not wishing to ruffle feathers at Harvard, Dr. Howell published under a pseudonym, but the information was highly useful to those pressing for a better deal for women doctors in training.

In this same era, Dr. Howell was a busy activist in the new field of women's health, organizing the first national women's health conference at Harvard, helping to found the National Women's Health Network, a lobbying group that represented the fast-forming grassroots groups dedicated to women's health issues, and turning out articles for magazines and for the groundbreaking *Our Bodies, Ourselves: A Book by and for Women.*

When we look at the huge number of women now practicing as doctors—160,000—and the much greater emphasis and attention on women's medical issues, there is no question that Dr. Mary Howell was a true pioneer.[7] Her organizational skills and writings had a profound effect on women's health.[8]

The number of women with college degrees rose from 5.2 percent in 1950 to 15.4 percent in 1997. Our *New York Times* women were far more educated than that, with just under half holding a college degree and almost 20 percent having higher degrees. (There was no educational information for a full third of the women in their obits, so that figure might be higher.) Almost a hundred of these women attended Ivy League schools, and another 166 attended top fifty schools. The thirty American women who made it into our Apex of Fame, shown in Table 3-2, fall into three groups. First, there are the 30 percent of the women famous because of their families or their socialite status. Second are famous actresses, singers, or athletes, who make up about a quarter of the total. The remaining thirteen women span a wide range of careers: Congress, writing, medicine, Hollywood production, interior design, and real estate.

Marie Lambert was one of the first to storm the barricades of law. Graduating at the top of her class from New York University Law School not long after World War II, she worked for a number of Wall Street law firms "but left because she was told to specialize in trust and estate law, which she considered 'women's work.'" Fed up with that, Lambert decided to pursue personal injury law, a real man's world. Even here she found herself initially getting the dregs, "negligence cases that no one else would touch." Her style—shambling into the courtroom with shopping bags stuffed with her legal papers—made her opponents underrate her and the jury embrace her as an ordinary person. As her loser cases turned into winners, she began to earn the respect of her male peers. In 1974, the New York State Trial Lawyers Association elected her president.

Three years later, in 1977, she ran and won election as a judge in Manhattan's Surrogate Court. There was a certain irony, for this was the very field she had spurned as a young female attorney. But in fact, this was quite a powerful position, and for twelve years she presided over "disputes pertaining to wills and estates, and formalized adoptions. She directed the flow of millions of dollars a year by appointing guardians for those too young or too feeble to handle their accounts, designating lawyers to manage wills that had no assigned executors, and awarding legal fees." This "gregarious, street-smart lawyer" turned out to be as every bit given to cronyism, bad temper, and strong will as any man, which made her less than popular. "As Surrogate, she ruled over the dying wishes of the very rich and the very famous, a role she relished." Her most famous case was "settling the war over the half-billion-dollar estate of J. Seward Johnson, an heir to the pharmaceutical fortune." Apparently she gave the former maid turned wife turned widow such a hard time that the woman decided to settle.

Whatever Marie Lambert's flaws, she was a tough woman who took on a male preserve and showed that women too could litigate and judge. Today almost half of law school students are women (compared to 4 to 5 percent in Lambert's day), and almost a quarter of practicing lawyers, or 240,000, are women.[9]

If Madelon Talley, "one of Wall Street's first female executives," had a hard time making her way in the male world of big money and big finance, there is little sign of it in her obit. A book about Wall Street in the 1960s by John Brooks described her as "a New York housewife who had tired of full-time housewifery" when she went to the Dreyfus Corporation in 1969 as an assistant analyst. A year later, in 1970, when she was approaching forty, she was promoted to comanager of the Dreyfus Leverage Fund, becoming "the first female fund manager on Wall Street." She spent most of the next decade at Dreyfus, rising to manage several funds and become a member of the firm's executive committee. During this time, she also earned her B.A. from Sarah Lawrence. Talley was certainly one of the few "female pioneers" whose obit included no tale of unfair treatment.[10]

Having become known "as one of the sharper financial minds around," Talley was then appointed in 1979 as New York State's director of the Division of Investments and Cash Management. She would be responsible for managing the state's $16 billion common retirement fund. The New York State controller who hired her said, "Madelon Talley set the procedures and processes for the retirement funds, so that when the markets started to rise in 1982, when the Dow Jones industrial average was at 800, we were set. It was a very, very major contribution." She seems to have been something of a restless sort, or maybe just versatile, but after her short but important stint for New York State, she was active in various financial groups, had her own hedge fund, and did a fair amount of writing and speaking on the importance of investing.

Today we take for granted the inevitable television news pairing of male and female coanchors. But in the late 1950s, on-air television was

TABLE 3-2. *The Apex of Fame: Women in the Obituary Database*

Name (Age at Death)	Obit Date	Accomplishments and Fame	Obit Length
1. Jacqueline Kennedy Onassis (64)	05/21/94	Wife of John F. Kennedy; became Icon of Fame	210"
2. Jessica Tandy (85)	09/12/94	Actress	112"
3. Ella Fitzgerald (79)	06/16/96	Singer	102"
4. Pamela Harriman (76)	02/06/97	Socialite; politics; wealthy husbands	95"
5. Bella Abzug (77)	04/01/98	U.S. congresswoman	92"
6. Rose Kennedy (104)	01/23/95	Mother of President Kennedy	88"
7. Ginger Rogers (83)	04/26/95	Actress	87"
8. Nicole Simpson (35)	06/23/94	Wife of O. J. Simpson	80"
9. Doris Duke (80)	10/29/93	One of the richest women in America	79"
10. Claudette Colbert (92)	07/31/96	Actress	77"
11. Lucille Lortel (98)	04/06/99	Off-Broadway producer, patron	76"
12. Barbara Jordan (59)	01/18/96	U.S. congresswoman	74"
13. Betty Shabazz (61)	06/24/97	Wife of Malcolm X	72"
14. Diana Trilling (91)	10/25/96	Literary critic; writer	67"
15. Oveta Culp Hobby (90)	08/17/95	U.S. secretary of health, education, and welfare; WAC founder	66"
16. Betsy Whitney (89)	03/26/98	Socialite; philanthropist	65"
17. Sadie Delany (109)	01/26/99	Schoolteacher; author, *Having Our Say*	62"

a male preserve. Nancy Hanschman was an ambitious young woman who grew up in a suburb of Milwaukee, earned a degree in English, Spanish, and Portuguese from the University of Wisconsin in 1948, and

Name (Age at Death)	Obit Date	Accomplishments and Fame	Obit Length
18. Marjory Douglas (108)	05/15/98	Conservationist; writer	60"
19. Martha Gellhorn (89)	02/17/98	Journalist; wife of Ernest Hemingway	59"
20. Irene Zambelli (82)	07/11/98	Socialite	59"
21. Florence Griffith Joyner (38)	09/22/98	Track star; Olympic gold medalist	59"
22. Sarah Korein (93)	11/04/98	Real estate fortune	59"
23. Helen Wills Moody (92)	01/03/98	Tennis champion	58"
24. Jean Dalrymple (96)	11/17/98	Producer of musicals and plays	58"
25. May Sarton (83)	07/18/95	Poet; novelist	56"
26. Sister Parish (84)	09/10/94	Interior designer	55"
27. Margaret Chase Smith (97)	05/30/95	U.S. senator	55"
28. Greer Garson (92)	04/07/96	Actress	55"
29. Mary C. Rockefeller (91)	04/22/99	First wife of Governor Nelson Rockefeller	54"
30. Alice Tully (91)	12/11/93	Philanthropist	53"
31. Tammy Wynette (55)	04/08/98	Singer	53"
32. Dawn Steel (51)	12/22/97	Hollywood producer	52"
33. Mary S. Calderone (94)	10/25/98	Doctor and advocate of sex education	52"

Note: Jessica Dubroff (80"), age 7, is not included.

headed to Manhattan in search of an "interesting job." Stymied, she then tried Washington, D.C., where she eventually landed a spot as a researcher for the Senate Committee on Foreign Relations. If ever there was a woman who understood deep in her soul the power of connections and contacts in a place like Washington, it was Nancy Hanschman. This bright, attractive woman was soon dating various senators. And when she heard that CBS was looking for somebody to produce a radio show about the political scene in Washington . . . she talked her way into it. She did well as a producer and by the mid-1950s moved up to become associate producer of *Face the Nation*. At her urging, the Speaker of the House made his national television debut on the show.

In February 1960, CBS television news made her its first female correspondent. She covered the presidential elections, beginning with Senator Hubert Humphrey and then following Lyndon Johnson all the way to the national convention. In 1962, she married a wealthy real estate investor and became Nancy Dickerson. "It was an indication of her place in the social firmament that when she married Mr. Dickerson," wrote the *New York Times*, "a party was given in her honor, hosted by President Lyndon B. Johnson, Justice Arthur Goldberg of the Supreme Court and Senator Abraham Ribicoff of Connecticut." In 1965, the Dickersons moved, bought the historic estate Merrywood in McLean, Virginia, and began throwing fabulous parties that only added to Nancy's luster as a major Washington insider whose contacts could produce scoops. "My social life always seems to revolve around business," she said.

After several years at CBS, Dickerson moved over to the NBC bureau in Washington and worked there until 1970, delivering such exclusives as LBJ's decision to have Senator Humphrey as vice president and a rare interview with House Speaker Sam Rayburn. She then realized the advantages of ownership and began her own production company. Some of her outstanding shows were a documentary, "784 Days That Changed America—From Watergate to Resignation," "Being with John Kennedy," and her 1980 interviews for PBS with Egyptian President Anwar el-Sadat, Israeli Prime Minister Menachem Begin, and Saudi Foreign Minister Saud el-Faisal.

Television, being a new medium, was relatively friendly to women. Hollywood was not, especially as, after the advent of TV, the studios found themselves producing fewer and fewer movies. Dawn Steel was a pioneer, the "first woman to head a major movie studio and who played a prominent role advancing other women to top jobs in Hollywood." However, like TV, contacts and relationships were extremely important. How Dawn Steel ended up in Hollywood is itself an instructive tale.

From a troubled family living "on the wrong side of the tracks" in Great Neck, New York, Dawn Steel completed a year at Boston University; then she ran out of money and returned to New York to attend New York University's School of Commerce, where she studied marketing. One of her first jobs was at *Penthouse*, coming up with X-rated mail-order products. One of her great hits was an amaryllis plant, whose phallic appearance before it bloomed was the selling point. While in Europe looking for gift ideas, she decided that Gucci toilet paper was an amusing and potentially profitable notion. She formed her own company, Oh, Dawn!, and soon had the Gucci toilet paper and was facing a lawsuit by the company. She persuaded a big-time lawyer named Sid Davidoff to represent her, and the whole silly story was soon spread through the tabloids. After the case was settled out of court, she asked Davidoff if he would use his contacts in Hollywood to get her a marketing job. Jeffrey Katzenberg at Paramount hired her. "She was highly opinionated, extremely self-confident, had a fantastic sense of humor and was someone of enormous taste and style," he said. "Maybe under the facade she was scared and intimidated by it all, but I didn't see a scintilla of that."

She herself thought her humor was an important factor: "I was funny. I wasn't heavy furniture. I made them laugh and entertained them. And the other thing was that I could identify a good idea. Not a lot of people can do that. That was my gift."

And when she had a good idea, she pushed for it—hard. Producer Dan Melnick compared her to a tank: "She would just lower her head and charge through all the red tape and bureaucracy. She's the most determined woman in the business." She did not appreciate being branded abrasive and hard-nosed and expressed her hurt in her 1993 autobiography, *They Can Kill You, but They Can't Eat You: Lessons from the Front*.

At Paramount, she became head of production and oversaw a string of major hits: *Flashdance, Footloose, Top Gun, The Untouchables, Fatal*

Attraction, and *The Accused.* In late 1987, she became president of
Columbia Studios and oversaw *Awakenings, Flatliners, Ghostbusters 2,*
and *Casualties of War.* As an independent producer after 1991, she made
Cool Runnings, Fallen, and *City of Angels.* The films she loved best had
stories not unlike her own, of "outsiders with outlandish ambitions who
overcome numerous obstacles." A female colleague explained, "She had
a formula for many of her movies that carried a simple truth: You want
something, you work incredibly hard, you get it."

Writer/director Nora Ephron explained the larger importance of
Dawn Steel: she "certainly wasn't the first woman to become powerful
in Hollywood, but she was the first woman to understand that part of her
responsibility was to make sure that eventually there were lots of other
powerful women. She hired women as executives, women as producers
and directors, women as marketing people. The situation we have today,
with a huge number of women in powerful positions, is largely because
of Dawn Steel."

In an entirely different field, Rell Sunn, an international surfing
champion, was one of a generation of women who opened sports to
women at all levels. A native of Mekaha on Oahu, Sunn grew up just
"three blocks from one of the world's most storied surfing beaches, a
reef-ringed stretch of water where big waves abound." She began surfing at age four, as Hawaiian women had long done before missionaries
discouraged it. As there were no women's competitions, she entered the
men's competitions, almost always making the finals. She encouraged
other women to start surfing, and eventually enough were doing so for
her to found the Women's Professional Surfing Association with its own
tour and prizes for women.

She competed around the world, in Australia, California, South
Africa, and such unlikely venues as France. In 1982, she was the top-
ranked woman on the longboard. At this time, she was engaged in what
would become a fourteen-year battle with breast cancer. Her bravery
endeared her to her fellow Hawaiians. Whenever she got out of the hospital, she headed straight for the ocean: "Surfing was the best therapy."
She arranged her own memorial service. Reported the *Times,* "After her
ashes were scattered over the water, several hundred surfers made a

final ride with Ms. Sunn, whose middle name, Kapolioka'enukai, means 'heart of the sea.'" She had also, through her example and organization building, enabled thousands of women to experience the joys of physical prowess and athleticism.

Many of the women we have met were pioneers, opening new fields and opportunities for those coming along. Rose Blumkin is just one of those amazing business dynamos who is an inspiration. She "founded the Nebraska Furniture Mart in 1937 [and] helped her son and grandchildren build it into the nation's largest home furnishings store." In 1984, Warren Buffett's legendary group, Berkshire Hathaway, bought majority control of her company. At the time Buffett, one of the nation's investment and business gurus, said of Rose Blumkin, "Put her up against the top graduates of the top business schools or chief executives of the *Fortune* 500 and, assuming an even start with the same resources, she'd run rings around them."

So who was Rose Blumkin to get such kudos? She was the classic poor immigrant from Russia, who began working in the struggling family grocery at age six. By the time she was sixteen, she was the manager with six people under her. At twenty she married and three years later, in 1916, headed to the United States to join her husband, who had fled the Russian draft. The newlyweds moved to Omaha, Nebraska, had four children, and operated a secondhand clothing store. Then Mrs. Blumkin borrowed five hundred dollars and started a furniture business. Her philosophy: "Sell cheap, tell the truth, don't cheat nobody."

The road to business greatness was not smooth at first: "When furniture manufacturers stopped selling directly to her after bigger customers in Omaha complained about her low retail prices, she traveled to Kansas City, Missouri, Chicago, and New York, bought from department stores and still undersold her rivals." When her son returned from World War II, he too began to put in seven-day, seventy-hour weeks. She had a falling-out with her grandsons over the business, retired at age ninety-five, and then returned and set up a rival store across the street. Within two years it was profitable and had become Omaha's third largest carpet outlet. Not bad for a woman about to turn one hundred!

And so we see, again and again, that successful women are those who take control of their own destinies. They start their own companies. They begin professional organizations. They write books that promote them and their points of view, their causes. Most of the women in this chapter are quite famous, if not to the world at large, then within their own professions and fields. One who is not but played an important role is a little-known government researcher in the U.S. Labor Department named Catherine East. From this position, having ready access to reams of factual information about discrimination against women, she was able to arm those pushing for equal rights for women. For instance, when a journalist named Vera Glaser appeared interested in the issue, Catherine East contacted her, offering whatever facts and figures she might need. The ensuing five-part series on discrimination against women gained wide attention. "A lot of the facts came from Catherine," said Glaser.

Then, in 1963, East helped produce a government report, *American Women,* that described the still lowly status of women and proposed the establishment of federal and state commissions on women. From these, she knew, would come pressure on government to lead the way. And in fact, she headed numerous such task forces, many of which steadily advanced rights and protections for working women. East also pushed the early feminists to start an organization comparable to the NAACP and is thus viewed as a major influence in the founding of the National Organization of Women.

Many decades into the women's revolution, Felice Schwartz suggested that all was not as rosy and simple as just banishing discrimination at work. After all, many women who worked had husbands and children, and for some it was all proving too much. By recognizing this and daring to discuss it and offer solutions, she stirred up an unfriendly storm: "What I said then and still say is that women face many, many obstacles in the workplace that men do not face. I was saying to the group of men at the top, 'Rather than let women's talents go to waste, do something about it.'"

Her solution was a "parent track," which was swiftly denounced as the "mommy track." She herself had spent a decade at home raising three children and then in 1962 founded Catalyst, which "focused in its early years on lobbying employers to allow women to combine family and part-time work. The organization pioneered several job-sharing pilot projects in which two women shared a full-time job. It also undertook studies on family issues in the workplace."

Schwartz spread her ideas through two books, *How to Go to Work When Your Husband Is Against It, Your Children Aren't Old Enough and There's Nothing You Can Do Anyhow,* published in 1968, and *Breaking with Tradition: Women and Work, the New Facts of Life*, published in 1992.

The final woman in our chapter is not really a pioneer but someone who, like so many of us, did not really know what her calling was in life—until she stumbled on buttons. Lives in which serendipity plays a role are in their own way reassuring to those who are not marching toward some definite calling. Diane Epstein was a native of New York who was adopted by an aunt in Chicago. After graduating from the University of Chicago and studying at the Art Institute of Chicago, she went to New York and held a series of editing jobs. But by her late twenties, she harbored the uneasy feeling that books were not her destiny.

One day, after buying a nice jacket for work, Epstein decided to replace the rather cheesy buttons. When she arrived at her favorite little button shop, it was shuttered; the owner had died. Then, reported the *New York Times*, "acting on what she recalled only as an inspired whim, Ms. Epstein tracked down the owner's heirs, paid them $5,000 for the entire stock of several hundred thousand buttons dating to the 1930's, and then, with no place to keep them, rented the store." She had no game plan but thought it would be a fun venue in which to throw a party. On that occasion, one of the guests, Millicent Safro, an antiques restorer, looked at the "jumble of crushed and torn cartons of buttons" and offered to help Epstein at least get them organized. As the two women sorted through the boxes and boxes of buttons, a customer wandered in and purchased "six red buttons for a penny apiece in what may or may not have been a bargain." The business and a lifetime partnership were thus launched.

Epstein and Safro began a crash course in buttonry, determined to figure out the worth of their inventory. Within several years, both had become experts in the field and had moved their shop, Tender Buttons, to 143 East Sixty-second Street, a long, narrow ground-floor space crammed floor to ceiling with more than a "million ancient, antique and modern buttons in a profusion of materials, shapes and sizes." The store became a mecca of beautiful and unusual buttons for those who cared about such stylish details. This being Manhattan, the shop served many a celeb, from designers such as Bill Blass to beauties such as Isabella Rossellini to the dandyish writer Tom Wolfe. Apparently, the advice Epstein always gave was that buttons "should never speak louder than the dress or jacket they adorn."

Inspired by the diminutive and whimsical nature of her stumbled-upon passion, Epstein became enamored of all things small. Most charming of all were her "'little' dinners, generally served on small plates on children's furniture." She also, fittingly, lived in a tiny town house on Manhattan's Upper East Side.

To truly appreciate how differently women's lives and prospects are handled today in the obituaries, one has only to peruse Janice Hume's *Obituaries in American Culture,* a historical study. She looked at eight thousand obituaries that appeared in three distinct periods. What was striking were the women's obituaries of the nineteenth century, when women were portrayed almost exclusively in terms of their relations to men—mother, wife, daughter, sister. The women were much praised for being modest, helpful, and virtuous. Today, women can generally expect to be judged—as are the men—on their accomplishments.

Notes

1. For brief biographies of all First Ladies, see: Carl Sferrazza Anthony, *First Ladies*, vols. 1 and 2 (New York: William Morrow, 1990 and 1991).
2. *The Wall Street Journal Almanac, 1999,* p. 239.
3. *Statistical Abstract of the United States, 1998,* Table 647.
4. *Statistical Abstract of the United States, 1998,* Table 262.

5. Lydia Bronte, *The Longevity Factor* (New York: HarperCollins, 1993), chap. 12.
6. Margaret W. Rossiter, *Woman Scientists in America* (Baltimore: Johns Hopkins University Press, 1995), chap. 5.
7. *The Wall Street Journal Almanac, 1999*, p. 558; in 1996, there were 157,387 female doctors.
8. Jennifer Steinhauer, "For Women in Medicine, a Road to Compromise, Not Perks," *New York Times* February 29, 1999, p. Al.
9. Richard L. Abel, ed., *Lawyers: A Critical Reader* (New York: New Press, 1997), pp. 24–25.
10. Doug Henwood reports that only 5 to 10 percent of the top jobs in investment banking are held by women; see his *Wall Street* (New York: Verso, 1998), p. 78.
11. Janice Hume, *Obituaries in American Culture* (Jackson, Miss.: The University Press of Mississippi, 2000).

4

Outstanding Blacks

Broke Color Barrier to Get Ph.D.

First Black Cabinet Member

Lawmaker of Resonant Voice

In America, education is generally *the* key to advancement, opportunity, and success. For that reason, black civil rights strategists initially targeted schools, determined to widen access to the coveted and all-important degrees. In 1946, the NAACP recruited Ada Louise Sipuel Fisher, an honors graduate of Langston College, to apply to the University of Oklahoma Law School. The state, with its strict segregation laws, fended off admitting Fisher to its all-white law school for two years, saying it would open a black law school. Her lawyer, Thurgood Marshall of the NAACP, pressed the U.S. Supreme Court, which (still hewing to its "separate-but-equal" doctrine) ordered the state to make good. With no black law school in sight, Fisher was admitted to the regular law school in 1949, but with cruel caveats: "She was forced to sit in a raised chair apart from other students behind a sign reading 'Colored.' And she had to use a side door to the cafeteria and sit at a table separated by a chain from the rest of the room; a uniformed guard was posted to prevent interracial mingling." Fisher's heart was not in law but in history, and she ended up as a history professor at her original alma mater. But her disgraceful treatment did much to convince people in her state of the immorality of segregation, and eventually Oklahoma was forced to open its graduate schools to the many black students clamoring for admission. It must have been a sweet day in April 1992 when Mrs. Fisher became one of seven regents governing the University of Oklahoma.

In the *New York Times* obituaries we meet a wide spectrum of accomplished black Americans, many with stirring personal histories. While this chapter features a number of luminaries, most are lesser-known black pioneers who opened doors that had long been shut, allowing their race access to the kinds of education, opportunities, jobs, and wealth that whites have often taken for granted. Five percent (462) of the overall obits database feature blacks. Of these, 104, or almost a fourth (22.5 percent), are women. Like the women in our *New York Times* obits database, black Americans are clustered in certain careers that were more open to them, as shown in Table 4-1. Notably, 32 percent of the men and women excelled in the performing arts, while almost 12 percent of the black male obits are for sports figures. The large number of black actresses, singers, and dancers with obits explains why the ratio of black women to black men is somewhat higher than in the overall database, where women make up only 17 percent of the total. After the performing arts and sports, the two leading fields were education and government. The average obit length of all 462 blacks was just over seventeen inches. If being black were an occupation, this group would be in third place after members of Congress and singers in their average obit coverage.

Not surprisingly, considering barriers like those encountered by Mrs. Fisher, our *New York Times* database blacks had lower levels of college education than our whites, as is shown in Tables 4-2, 4-3, and 4-4. Of the 462, just over 42 percent had a B.A. This level of college education is almost triple that of even the current general black population. Also, forty-five people, or 30 percent, had graduated from the top fifty schools, with seventeen holding Ivy League degrees. There were 176 people whose education was not known. However, what is unusual is how many of these blacks went on to get higher degrees—enough that the percentage of blacks holding an advanced degree equals that of the overall database, or 31 percent. But this level of higher education is eight times greater than that of the overall U.S. black population (31.2 percent versus 3.8 percent).

Among the lesser-known pioneers was Walter Ridley of Virginia, who became "the first black person ever to obtain a doctorate from a

TABLE 4-1. *Occupation of Blacks in the Obituary Database, by Sex*

Occupation	Men (N = 358) (%)	Women (N = 104) (%)	Total (N = 462) (%)
Performing arts	29.3	37.5	31.2
Media arts	8.7	8.7	8.7
Sports	11.2	4.8	9.7
Government and civic	9.8	14.4	10.8
Education	10.6	13.5	11.3
Law	6.7	2.9	5.8
Medicine	4.7	2.9	4.3
Business	8.1	2.9	6.9
Other occupations	8.1	1.9	6.7
Not in labor force	2.8	10.6	4.5
Total	**100.0**	**100.0**	**100.0**

state-supported university in the South." Ridley grew up in Newport News, Virginia. His mother was a music teacher, and his father, the son of a slave, had risen from shipyard hand to founder of a bank. Ridley graduated from Howard University and also got a master's there. When he applied to the University of Virginia for a graduate degree in education in the 1940s, it solved its dilemma by paying for him to attend graduate school in the North. By 1950, federal courts had forced Virginia's higher education system to open to blacks. Dr. Ridley, then the forty-one-year-old chairman of psychology at all-black Virginia State College, began a Ph.D. program at the University of Virginia's School of Education in Charlottesville. "Why shouldn't I go?" he asked. "My father has been paying taxes in this state since before I was born, and I am entitled to study here." He retained his position at Virginia State and made the long commute.

In 1958, Dr. Ridley began "what he regarded as his most significant academic work, as president of the small black Elizabeth City College."

TABLE 4-2. *Education Attained by Blacks in the Obituary Database*

Highest Education	Men (N = 358) (%)	Women (N = 104) (%)	Total (N = 462) (%)
High school or less	5.0	11.5	6.5
Some college	14.5	8.7	13.2
College graduate* (no higher degree)	9.8	15.4	11.0
Higher degree†	33.2	24.0	31.2
Not stated	37.4	40.4	38.1
Total	**100.0**	**100.0**	**100.0**

Note: Of the 144 higher degrees attained, 44 were in law, 39 were Ph.D.s, and 14 were in medicine.

* Percentage of college graduates: 42 percent of 462 men and women.

† Percentage who attained a higher degree: 31 percent of 462, or 74 percent of those who completed college.

TABLE 4-3. *U.S. Population: Education Attained, by Race*

Year	4 Years of High School or More		4 Years of College or More	
	Whites	Blacks	Whites	Blacks
1960	43.2	20.1	8.1	3.1
1970	54.5	31.4	11.3	4.4
1980	68.8	51.2	17.1	8.4
1990	79.1	66.2	22.0	11.3
1997	83.0	74.9	24.6	13.3

Source: Statistical Abstract of the United States, 1998, Table 260.

He oversaw the raising of academic standards and the expansion of the student body and campus, "laying the groundwork for its elevation to university status in 1969." He also made a point of opening the school

TABLE 4-4. *U.S. Population 25 Years of Age or Older with Advanced Degrees, by Sex and Race*

	U.S. Population	Percent with Advanced Degree
Total	170,581,000	7.8
Male	81,620,000	9.4
Female	88,961,000	6.3
Race		
White	144,058,000	8.1
Black	19,072,000	3.8
Other: Asian, etc.	7,401,000	12.9

Source: Statistical Abstract of the United States, 1998, Table 262.

to white applicants and was president when the first white student entered the college.

Stephen J. Wright was president of top-rated Fisk University for almost a decade. But what distinguished him were his creative efforts in "broadening educational opportunities for black America." The son of a doctor in Dillon, South Carolina, Wright was a paragon of education: he had a bachelor's degree in chemistry from Virginia's Hampton Institute, a master's in education from Howard University, and a doctorate from New York University. A talented musician, he taught music in high schools for a while before beginning his academic climb through various black colleges. As president of Fisk from 1957 to 1966, he began to exercise his influence in a broader way, convincing the other black colleges to start requiring their students to take the Scholastic Aptitude Tests. While this meant finding testing sites that would allow black students in, it also made black students and colleges think about college admissions on the same terms as white students. When Wright retired from Fisk in 1966, he became president of the United Negro College Fund, helping to raise money for some thirty historically black schools. He also joined the College Board. The goal was to make attending college as much an option for ambitious black students as it was for others. Through all these many demanding jobs, reported the *New York Times,* Wright had such a voracious appetite for knowledge that he read a thousand pages a day. Over the years, this much-in-demand man served on two dozen boards and commissions and received more than a dozen honorary degrees.

These early pioneers in expanding higher education for blacks paved the way for those challenging the most die-hard southern states in the 1960s. One of the most famous of the segregation challengers was Hamilton E. Holmes, "who braved the hostility of racists to integrate the University of Georgia with Charlayne Hunter in 1961 and went on to a distinguished career in medicine." Beginning in 1959, lawyers for the NAACP went before the courts to argue that these two fine students deserved admission to their state university. Holmes had been valedictorian, class president, and cocaptain of his high school football team. The U.S. Supreme Court agreed and ordered state officials to comply. On January 9, 1961, these two bookish young people joined the seven thousand white students enrolled at the Athens, Georgia, campus. "Within a short time a group of youths, swelled by some 1,500 spectators, were jeering Ms. Hunter and shouting, 'Go home, nigger, and don't come back.'" Two days later, "a howling, cursing mob of about 600 students and a few outsiders laid siege to Ms. Hunter's dormitory. The disturbance raged out of control for nearly an hour before it was ended by the police, using tear gas and fire hoses." Hamilton Holmes, who had given up the friendly pleasures of all-black Morehouse College in Atlanta to press this crusade, spent two largely isolated years proving that blacks were as entitled to a state education as whites. "He was amazing," said Charlayne Hunter-Gault, now a well-known reporter, "He had quiet dignity, scholarship. He wouldn't let anything stand in the way of his desire to become a doctor."

Having braved the racist heart of the university system, Hamilton Holmes further steeled himself and "became the first black student admitted to the Emory University Medical School in Atlanta." He received his medical degree in 1967 and went on to become an orthopedic surgeon. When he died, he was an associate dean at Emory as well as a faculty member at his medical school alma mater and chairman of the orthopedic unit at Grady Memorial Hospital in Atlanta.

In light of what he was subjected to, one can understand Dr. Holmes's reluctance to have anything to do with the University of Georgia. But in 1983, he overcame his lingering bitterness and became its first black trustee. When presented the university's bicentennial medal a year after that anniversary, Dr. Holmes said, "I have come to really love this university. People look at me and say, 'You're crazy, man. How can you love that place?' But I will never forget this, and I will cherish it forever."

The trailblazing of a Dr. Holmes certainly matters, for physicians are our best-paid professionals, with orthopedists and other specialty surgeons earning an *average* of $300,000 a year.[1] The number of black *male* doctors has risen since 1970 from 18 of every thousand doctors to 23 of every thousand.[2]—not a huge jump. At the same time, the numbers of black female doctors rose from 4 of every thousand doctors, to 12 of every thousand, a threefold increase.

The Apex of Fame for blacks, as is shown in Table 4-5, is a pretty good reflection of who's in the database. There is a big group of performers and artists, followed by government and political types such as Los Angeles Mayor Tom Bradley and Stokely Carmichael and a sprinkling of athletes and writers, and one educator, a president of Howard University.

Singer Ella Fitzgerald, who has the longest obit of any black American, was never viewed as a civil rights activist. However, she represented a generation of enormously talented and personable black entertainers who won the hearts of millions of white fans and almost certainly played a role in advancing equal rights for their race. When Fitzgerald died at age seventy-nine, she was the most celebrated jazz singer of her generation. In a career that spanned six decades and involved constant touring, "her perfect intonation, vocal acrobatics, clear diction and endless store of melodic improvisation—all driven by powerful rhythmic undercurrents—brought her nearly universal acclaim."

Though Fitzgerald became famous as a singer, her early ambition was to be a dancer. As a young teen, when she lived in Yonkers, New York, she was half of a couple that performed in clubs around New York City. Then in 1932, her mother died suddenly, and Ella moved from the suburbs to Harlem to live with her aunt. At seventeen, she entered an

TABLE 4-5. *The Apex of Fame: Blacks in the Obituary Database*

Name (Age at Death)	Obit Date	Accomplishments and Fame	Obit Length
1. Ella Fitzgerald (79)	06/16/96	Jazz singer	102"
2. Ronald Brown (54)	04/04/96	U.S. Commerce secretary	85"
3. Eldridge Cleaver (62)	05/02/98	Black Panther leader	84"
4. Barbara Jordan (59)	01/18/96	U.S. congresswoman	74"
5. Stokely Carmichael (57)	11/16/98	Civil rights revolutionary	73"
6. Betty Shabazz (61)	06/24/97	Wife of Malcolm X	72"
7. Tom Bradley (80)	09/30/98	Mayor of Los Angeles	70"
8. Sadie Delany (109)	01/26/99	Schoolteacher; author, *Having Our Say*	62"
9. Coleman Young (79)	11/30/97	Mayor of Detroit	60"
10. Florence Joyner (38)	09/22/98	Track star; Olympic gold medalist	59"
11. Adolphus Cheatham (91)	06/03/97	Jazz trumpet player	55"
12. Henry Lewis (63)	01/29/96	Conductor	54"
13. Joe Williams (80)	03/31/99	Jazz singer	54"
14. Dorothy West (91)	08/19/98	Harlem Renaissance writer	50"
15. Flip Wilson (64)	11/27/98	Comedian; host of TV shows	50"
16. Ralph Ellison (80)	04/17/94	Novelist, *The Invisible Man*	48"
17. Archie Moore (84)	12/10/98	Boxer	48"

amateur contest at the Apollo Theater, singing two songs that won her first place. Band leader Chick Webb liked her talent but was put off "because she was gawky and unkempt." When she did join his band, her career took off. She recorded her first hit, "A-Tisket, A-Tasket" with Webb. Wrote the *New York Times*, "The record became a popular sensation and made her a star."

Name (Age at Death)	Obit Date	Accomplishments and Fame	Obit Length
18. A. Leon Higginbotham, Jr. (70)	12/15/98	Federal judge	48"
19. Cab Calloway (86)	11/20/94	Jazz bandleader; singer	47"
20. Wardell R. Lazard (44)	05/13/94	Investment banker	45"
21. Wilma Rudolph (54)	11/13/94	1960 Olympic track star	45"
22. Buck Leonard (90)	11/29/97	Negro League Baseball player	44"
23. Betty Carter (69)	09/28/98	Jazz singer	42"
24. James Nabrit, Jr. (97)	12/30/97	Howard University president	39"
25. Marion Motley (79)	06/28/99	Hall of Fame football player	39"
26. Helene Johnson (89)	07/11/95	Poet of Harlem; librarian	38"
27. Bessie Delany (104)	09/26/95	Dentist; author, *Having Our Say*	38"
28. Richard Berry (61)	01/25/97	Songwriter of *Louie, Louie*	38"
29. Spottswood W. Robinson III (82)	10/13/98	Civil rights lawyer; judge	38"
30. Austin Hansen (85)	01/25/96	Photographer	37"
31. Moneta Sleet, Jr. (70)	10/02/96	Photographer	37"
32. Juanita K. Stout (79)	08/24/98	Pennsylvania state judge	37"

During the 1940s, Ella Fitzgerald became "as great a master of bop as she had been of swing." She had been constantly recording, turning out huge hits as well as junk novelties. But by the late 1940s, she had backed into an artistic corner: "I had gotten to the point where I was only singing be-bop [and] I had no place to sing." She then had the good fortune to hook up with Norman Granz in what would become "one of the most productive artist-manager partnerships in the history of jazz." Granz persuaded Fitzgerald to undertake a series of landmark "Songbook" albums that introduced her to a vast nonjazz audience. Recalled Ella, "He produced 'The Cole Porter Songbook' with me. It was a turning point in my life." She went on to record albums of the songs of Irving Berlin, Harold Arlen, the Gershwins, and many other outstanding composers, concentrating on material that was "almost consistently commensurate with her artistry, and her career soared."

When rock 'n' roll eclipsed jazz in the sixties and seventies, Ella Fitzgerald recorded a series of albums that "found her groping insecurely for a new pop identity." She had split from Granz but now returned to his label and jazz. Through it all, she continued to tour until deteriorating health kept her off the stage except for occasional concerts. When awarded an honorary doctorate of music at Yale, she commented wryly, "Not bad for someone who only studied music to get that half-credit in high school." But the quip belies a lifetime of steady hard work devoted to nurturing a gigantic talent.

The extreme segregation that was the norm through World War II presented real economic opportunities to ambitious black businessmen who catered to their race. Their success and wealth in turn made them powerful and pivotal people in a community struggling for full access to the American Dream. A. G. Gaston was "a black multimillionaire businessman in Alabama who used his money and influence in the cause of civil rights." Gaston was an inspiring bootstraps story if ever there was one. Born in Demopolis, a hundred miles southwest of Birmingham, he was the grandson of a slave. He lost his father when still a boy, whereupon his mother went to the city to work as a maid and he was raised by his grandmother.

After serving in the Army during World War I, Gaston moved to Birmingham and held a lowly job at a coal company. But he saved and hustled, making small loans to fellow workers, while also selling peanuts, digging holes, and painting boxcars. "Start somewhere" was his lifelong business maxim. By 1923, he had launched an insurance company aimed at blacks and then a funeral home. Reported the *Times*,

"Both prospered, and as the years went by his holdings included a chain of insurance companies, radio stations, a savings and loan institution and other businesses." To remind himself and others of how far he'd come, "he kept a tinted photograph" showing a lanky seven-year-old "standing by an ox cart in front of an unpainted cabin."

When the civil rights movement really got going, Gaston played an important but quiet role, both as a liaison between wary whites and blacks and as a financial bulwark. He easily posted $5,000 bail for Martin Luther King and Ralph Abernathy when they were jailed in Birmingham. His motel provided a meeting spot for King and other organizers (and was subsequently firebombed). And when civil rights marchers were en route from Selma to Montgomery, they found a welcoming place to stay at one of Gaston's farms.

When militant blacks derided him as an Uncle Tom, Gaston responded that what black people needed was "a Martin Luther King of economics who will fire the people up like they're being fired up for civil rights. It doesn't do any good to arrive at first-class citizenship if you arrive broke."

Generations of discrimination have indeed been a serious hindrance to black Americans' accumulating and generating major wealth. Consider that since *Forbes* began tracking the wealthiest Americans in 1982, a thousand have been identified and only five have been black.[3] As rich as Gaston was—estimated at having $30 million to $40 million—he was small potatoes on a national scale, not even close to the minimum cutoff of $640 million needed to make the *Forbes* list in 1999.[4] Only a handful of black business and media moguls such as Oprah Winfrey or Bill Cosby have that kind of money.

As we have seen, the real money in America is made in business, and one of the ironies of the end of segregation is that corporate America, which once largely ignored blacks, is happy to target them as consumers, meaning they are no longer a natural and easy niche for black businessmen. Because the post–civil rights black middle class was largely concentrated in secure government jobs, one suspects that it will be their children or grandchildren who will make real inroads in business and wealth accumulation.

Another southern businessman who provided a friendly haven to both blacks and whites was Robert H. Paschal, "the Atlanta restaurateur and entrepreneur whose perfectly seasoned fried chicken sustained the civil rights movement." He and his brother, James, were partners for fifty years, from the time they moved to Atlanta in 1947 from the unpromising Thomson, Georgia, and opened a lunch counter near the city's black colleges. Their excellent chicken sandwiches eventually enabled them to open a hotel that featured a soon-to-be-famous lounge called La Carousel. "As the city's first black-owned hotel, Paschal's was a source of immense pride in the black community. La Carousel drew integrated crowds to see headliners like Aretha Franklin and Ramsey Lewis."

When the civil rights movement took off, the Paschals supported it by offering meeting space and free food. The Atlanta sit-ins, the March on Washington, and Mississippi Freedom Summer were all partly planned there. Congressman John Lewis recalled that "he ate his first meal in Atlanta at Paschal's after arriving from Alabama to work for the Student Nonviolent Coordinating Committee. He also remembered that the last time he ever saw Dr. King was at Paschal's." Congressman Lewis observed, "Some of the decisions that affected the direction of the country were made in that restaurant."

When black politicians became a force in Atlanta, the Paschals benefited by having a crack at such local plums as concessions at the new airport. Though the brothers eventually retired, their chicken remained a local legend: "It was crispy, tender, spicy and always delivered to the table steaming hot by one of a coterie of friendly and gracious waitresses."

Pleasant social venues are important for first building bridges and then building networks. That was certainly the conclusion of William Burwell Fitzgerald, "a Washington community leader and an entrepreneur who over 30 years built a small thrift institution into one of the country's largest black-owned businesses." For while he was building up Independence Federal Savings Bank into "the first fully integrated but minority-controlled savings bank in the nation," he was also assiduously networking through his Thursday lunches at the bank. He saw the lunches, which were famous for the Bloody Marys, as a way of bringing together people who otherwise would not be dining together. He hoped that mingling the traditional Washington power elite with neighborhood activists and other community-minded citizens would create new alliances and attitudes: "That's why I spend a lot of time and energy on these luncheons."

Fitzgerald, who had lived in Washington, D.C., since childhood, took some real estate courses at American University and worked numerous jobs as a young man, including stints as a taxi driver and a construction worker. Then he discovered real estate and founded Burwell Realty Company. After the 1968 riots scorched whole neighborhoods and traditional lenders turned their backs, Fitzgerald and eight associates formed Independence S&L to provide loans to residents and businesses. While the institution's assets were never huge—$269 million—it and Fitzgerald were always activist. He belonged to dozens of organizations that ran the gamut from the Cerebral Palsy Foundation to the Urban League.

The second biggest occupational group for black men in our obits group is sports. And the black male athlete with the longest obit is boxer Archie Moore, born in Georgia and raised by an aunt and uncle in Saint Louis. His "legendary career spanned almost three decades . . . [and included winning] the light-heavyweight championship when he was well into his 30s." Moore was a genuine character who created a persona that set the stage for the boxer-as-star-and-personality. Moore began boxing in the mid-1930s and was doing okay, but by the early 1950s, he needed a major fight to boost his career. When the current light-heavyweight champ, Joey Maxim, refused to enter the ring against him, Moore began a letter-writing campaign to big sports writers to pressure Maxim. Finally Maxim agreed, but on the condition that he be guaranteed $100,000 of the purse. Moore arranged it, won the title in a fifteen-round unanimous decision, and didn't worry that he had come away with only $800. The ensuing fame and publicity introduced the public to an amusing, almost whimsical fellow who never gave a straight answer on where and when he had been born, for a start.

Moore also became famous for his mysterious eating habits, long kept secret by his insistence on dining behind a screen when journalists were around. Apparently in 1940, while in Australia, Moore had met an aborigine who had taught him to chew meat to extract the juices, then spit the rest out. And there was his morning sauerkraut drink flavored with lemon juice. But all these were closely guarded training secrets until he published his late-life autobiography. Along the way, he married five wives and had three daughters and four sons.

Once Moore had triumphed over Maxim, he began to pursue a fight with reigning heavyweight champ Rocky Marciano. Better known now and richer, Moore this time launched a $50,000 advertising campaign that included a "wanted" poster of Marciano that finally embarrassed the champ into meeting Moore, a decade his senior, in the ring. When they fought on September 21, 1955, Moore managed to knock Marciano down once but otherwise fared badly. When the referees asked Moore to cede the fight after the eighth round, he refused. "The only way to go out in a championship fight is on your back," he declared. In the next round Marciano obliged him.

Despite that setback, Moore remained light-heavyweight champ until 1962, when he lost his title for refusing to fight up-and-coming challengers. He continued to be a force in boxing, acting as a trainer and adviser, and coaching the Nigerian boxing team at the 1976 Olympics. In the early 1990s, when former heavyweight champion Floyd Patterson tried a comeback, Moore coached him, teaching him "his secrets of escapology and breathology."

Perhaps it took a black athlete, one who was sensitive to being "owned" by a team, to serve as "the pioneering figure in the legal attack on baseball's reserve clause that foreshadowed the era of free agents." The athlete was Curt Flood, who was an All-Star center fielder for the Saint Louis Cardinals for twelve seasons and played in three World Series. But then, as the team was faltering in 1969, the owner decided to trade Flood and two other players. Flood refused and demanded his freedom to play for whichever team "makes me the best offer."

What made Flood a pioneer in liberating the whole field of athletics was "his stiff resolve regarding the unfairness of baseball's virtual enslavement of players and his courage in challenging a system that perpetuated this condition." He sued for his freedom, and his lawyer was former Supreme Court Judge Arthur J. Goldberg. A ten-week trial and two-thousand-page transcript did not in the end demolish baseball "slavery," but it created a crack and emboldened other players to bring suits that eventually demolished the reserve clause. Wrote the *Times*, "As a result, before another generation had passed, salaries in all sports soared." In short, Curt Flood set the stage for the revolution, helping athletes of all kinds attain the sort of wealth that had long been the preserve of the owners.

The civil rights movement focused heavily on two critical areas: education and politics, both of which are important sources of power and wealth. Government is a major occupational category for blacks in our database: 10 percent of the men and 16 percent of the women. The *New York Times* obits remind us of just how recently blacks ascended to meaningful electoral and political clout. Robert C. Weaver was certainly one of the pioneers, the first secretary of housing and urban development and the first black person appointed to the Cabinet. Weaver, a Washington, D.C., native, had not one but three degrees from Harvard University, including a doctorate in economics. He then further cemented his cerebral reputation by writing four books on urban affairs. In 1933, he became an aide to Interior Secretary Harold L. Ickes, the first of numerous managerial positions he held in federal agencies in the ensuing decades. During this period he was an active "behind-the-scenes strategist in the civil rights movement." "Fight hard and legally," he said, "and don't blow your top."

Weaver was part of President Franklin Delano Roosevelt's "Black Cabinet." Just before the 1940 election, FDR's press secretary managed to outrage the black community by his abusive treatment of a black police officer. Roosevelt, concerned that this would cost him an important voting bloc, called Weaver late one night wondering whether a placating speech would put things right. Weaver seized the moment, telling the president, "I don't think a mere speech will do it. What we need right now is something so dramatic that it will make the Negro voters forget all about [the press secretary] and the Negro cop, too." This brought about a series of appointments that were firsts: the first black Army general, the first black civilian aide to the secretary of war, and first high-ranking aide to the head of the military draft.

Weaver was very much the man that Democratic administrations consulted when it came to the black vote. Eventually John F. Kennedy appointed him head of the House and Home Finance Agency and then tried to raise that to a Cabinet rank. Southern members of Congress rose in fury. Interestingly, when Lyndon B. Johnson successfully did the same thing five years later, making Weaver head of Housing and Urban Development, the congressmen who had been so much against Weaver now voted for him. It was a real tribute to Weaver's political skills.

Moreover, Weaver's push to increase the numbers of high-visibility blacks in government showed a shrewd appreciation of his race's best prospects for the immediate future. In his book *Money*, Andrew Hacker writes, "Over forty percent of blacks who earn more than $40,000 are employed by government, and the proportion grows to more than half if we add quasi-public positions in health and education and social agencies." Without government jobs, says Hacker, "there would not be much of a black middle class."[5]

Men like Weaver, working tirelessly behind the scenes, made possible real electoral gains for up-and-coming politicians such as Cleveland's Carl B. Stokes, "whose election as the first black mayor of a major city in 1967 became a symbol of a changing America." This great-grandson of a slave defeated not just any politician but the grandson of President William Taft! Stokes's brother, Congressman Lewis Stokes, credited his brother's mayoral win with inspiring "black Americans to aspire to higher political office all over the country." Stokes was also the "first black Democrat elected to the [Ohio] Legislature in 1962." And he was also "the first black anchorman of a television news show in New York."

Stokes's story is another of those extraordinary stories about people who succeed against great odds. His father died when he was two, and his mother, a maid, raised her two sons in a public housing project. Stokes dropped out of high school and was working in a foundry when World War II came along. He served overseas and then returned to earn first his high school diploma and then his B.A. at Cleveland College of Western Reserve University. One suspects that his was a life very much changed by World War II. Like many others of his generation, the war opened whole new horizons and possibilities, while the G.I. Bill of Rights almost certainly made his college education possible. Stokes eventually became a lawyer, working as a probation officer while attending Cleveland-Marshall Law School.

Stokes won the mayoralty in a white-majority city: "I went into every white home that would let me in there and every hall that would have me. I don't sit back. Carl Stokes doesn't sit back." His lifelong regret was the way the 1968 Glenville riots destroyed all real hope of uniting Cleveland. And so, after two terms as mayor, he moved to New York in 1972 to become a popular TV anchorman. By 1983, he had returned to Cleveland, where he served as a municipal judge for a decade. When he died, he was serving as U.S. ambassador to the Seychelles.

Like Weaver and Stokes, Barbara Jordan was a political pioneer: "In 1966, she was elected as the first black state Senator in Texas history, and went on to be the first woman and first black elected to Congress from Texas." But she was also a politician's politician, a protégé of that master of maneuvering, Lyndon B. Johnson, who made it her business to assimilate the process and its details completely. That prowess made it possible for her to "ascend to the post of Speaker pro tem in the Texas Senate six years after having arrived there as a political oddity and an outcast." But it was her extraordinary eloquence that made her famous. She was a magisterial, riveting speaker "who stirred the nation with Churchillian denunciations of the Watergate abuses of President Richard M. Nixon."

Born in Houston, Jordan did not notice that her family was poor, because "so was everyone around us." From a young age, she knew she "never wanted to be run of the mill," and she applied her considerable intelligence and energy to making sure she wasn't. At age eleven she quit her piano lessons, thereby eliminating teaching music as a fallback job. She attended Houston's segregated public schools, then graduated magna cum laude with debating honors from all-black Texas Southern University. (Her father worked a second job in a warehouse to pay her way.) She got her law degree from Boston University in 1959, returned home, and plunged into local politics, directing voter drives in the 1960 JFK-LBJ presidential race. Then she ran for the state legislature herself, losing "her first two bids for elective office in rough-and-tumble, racism-tinged bouts. But she succeeded when state legislative districts were finally redrawn."

What motivated her political career? Here was her advice to college students: "Reaffirm what ought to be. Get back to the truth; that's old, but get back to it. Get back to what's honest; tell government to do that. Affirm the civil liberties of the people of this country. Do that." Afflicted with multiple sclerosis, she retired after three terms in the House to teach at the University of Texas at Austin. There her students knew her as "never being without a copy of the Constitution in her purse."

In the last hundred years, the routes to success and fame for black Americans have been largely entertainment and athletics, careers that are based on pure, raw talent and require very little in the way of formal qualifications. You don't need a college education, much less an advanced degree. Nor do you need to pass a bar exam or leap any other hurdle. You perform, people are enthralled, and you begin to rise to stardom. Nonetheless, even in entertainment, there have been stereotypes. Henry Lewis, an exception, "broke racial barriers in the music world as the first black conductor and music director of a major American orchestra, the New Jersey Symphony."

A musical prodigy, his talent at the double bass got him a scholarship to the University of Southern California. Though he did not graduate, already at age sixteen he had joined the Los Angeles Philharmonic Orchestra, becoming the "first black instrumentalist in a major American orchestra," not to mention the youngest. When he went in for military duty in 1954, he found himself conducting the Seventh Army Symphony in Stuttgart, which gave him the experience needed to work under Zubin Mehta at the Los Angeles Philharmonic as assistant conductor when he returned home. Lewis created something of a sensation in 1960, when he married the famous opera star Marilyn Horne, a white woman. Despite many warnings by friends and family of the troubles they would face, they had a fruitful partnership, and she would describe her husband as "my prophet and my teacher and my right hand."

In 1968, Lewis, thirty-six, was appointed conductor and musical director of the New Jersey Symphony Orchestra, prevailing over 160 other candidates. This was a landmark event for blacks in classical music, and Lewis built the orchestra into a first-class operation, one that featured world-famous soloists such as Misha Dichter and Itzhak Perlman. The orchestra played Newark's ghettoes as well as Carnegie Hall. As Lewis became a famous, high-profile conductor jetting to guest appearances around the world, he began to attract criticism. Some said he was too easygoing in concerts, encouraging uneducated audiences to applaud at the wrong time. Some blacks denounced him for even conducting and presenting white music. Meanwhile, his own orchestra rebelled and went on strike, complaining about the grueling schedule and what they termed Lewis's "tyrannical" ways. To settle the strike, one demand was that he "refrain from frowning at rehearsals and performances"! And so, in 1976, Lewis left, but continued to be a much-in-demand maestro on the podium and for recording sessions. His marriage ended about the same time, but he and Horne always remained friends and colleagues.

The traditional domains of accomplishment for blacks have been entertainment and athletics, but those in the database also have many other kinds of talents. The Apex of Fame reflects that heavy emphasis on sports and the arts, as well as the focus in recent decades on politics and civil rights. As with the women, the list of blacks emphasizes pioneers, determined people whose education enabled them to raise their status and open up new opportunities, new fields, and new occupations.

Notes

1. Andrew Hacker, *Money* (New York: Touchstone, 1997), p. 126.
2. Ibid. p. 156.
3. Ibid. p. 94.
4. "The Forbes 400,"edited by Peter Newcomb, *Forbes*, October 11, 1999, p. 169.
5. Hacker, *Money*, p. 157. Also see Ellis Cose, "The Good News About Black America," *Newsweek*, June 7, 1999, pp. 29–40.

5

Eminent Physicians

Led Fight To Vanquish Childhood Diseases

Nobelist Who Helped Invent CAT Scan

Founder of Project HOPE

Each summer after World War II, American parents waited with quiet terror, wondering where and when polio, a viral infection of the nerves that can cause paralysis, would strike and which communities and families would be afflicted. In the PBS documentary "A Paralyzing Fear," one young Minneapolis doctor would recall the summer it came to his state: "Maybe two or three hours after a lot of these kids would come in with a stiff neck or fever, they'd be dead. It was unbelievable. . . . At the height of the epidemic, the people in Minneapolis were so frightened there was nobody in the restaurants. There was practically no traffic, the stores were empty. . . . A lot of people just took up and moved away, went to another city. It was really a disaster."[1] Postwar America had become so clean and sanitary that very young children no longer developed a natural immunity to the polio virus, paving the way for the terrifying epidemics that struck every summer. Frightened parents forbade their children to swim in public pools, and otherwise tried to keep them isolated and safe from this invisible crippler and killer. In 1952, polio swept through the country with unprecedented ferocity, with 58,000 cases and 3,000 deaths.

Consequently, few physicians are more famous than Dr. Jonas Salk, the man "who developed the first successful vaccine against poliomyelitis." When Dr. Thomas Francis of the University of Michigan was able to announce, on April 12, 1955, that Dr. Salk's vaccine had proven safe in a field trial of 440,000 people, the news, reported the

New York Times, "caused a public sensation probably unequaled by any health development in modern times." After several years of mass vaccinations, the number of polio victims plummeted to a dozen annually. No longer were the children's wards filled with suffering, crippled patients. President Eisenhower understandably praised Dr. Salk as a "benefactor of mankind." Summer again became a carefree season.

The fascination of the *New York Times* obits is that not only do we learn the details of the life of a famous doctor like Salk, we also learn of polio victims such as Mark O'Brien, forty-nine, "journalist and poet in iron lung." Stricken by polio as a boy in Sacramento, California, O'Brien was paralyzed from the neck down and at his death in July 1999 was one of about a hundred American polio victims still dependent on iron lungs to keep breathing. Determined to make a life for himself, O'Brien used an inflatable vest called a turtle shell to breathe when he forayed forth on his electric gurney, navigating the streets of Berkeley. One can only imagine what a huge act of will it was for him to earn degrees in English and journalism at the University of California in the 1980s. Then he began working for the Pacific News Service, composing his reports by using a stick to type. He also published poetry, including a volume called *Breathing.*

In truth, the great majority of children survived, but the aftermath was heart-wrenching. Some of polio's 600,000 victims were hospitalized for years, confined within huge machines called iron lungs that kept them alive. Others struggled valiantly through years of rehabilitation to walk again on crutches. The Salk vaccine, which used killed viruses, was too late for Mark O'Brien, but it saved many others. The Salk vaccine was soon largely replaced by Dr. Alfred Sabin's live oral polio vaccine, setting off a lifelong debate and rivalry between these two medical giants. Salk's fame enabled him to launch the Salk Institute in La Jolla, California, to which brilliant thinkers in many fields were invited to work on important problems. Dr. Salk continued his biomedical research, focusing heavily on AIDS. He also became something of a scientist-philosopher.

In this chapter, we look at people who have advanced medical science and our collective health during what has been called the Golden

Age of Medicine, the era when huge strides were made in understanding the body and eradicating age-old diseases. Infant mortality and child death rates plummeted, while the average life expectancy rose to seventy-six years.[2] It is a great truism that "if you have your health, you have everything," but the banality of the saying fails to convey the extraordinary distress of being ill or having a sick family member or friend. And so those who can explain, palliate, cure, or prevent sickness are giving a wonderful gift.

Our *New York Times* database has 464 doctors and medical professors, thirty-seven of them women. The average length of the medical obits is twelve inches. Of those in our group working in medicine, 407 hold M.D.s, 61 hold Ph.D.s, and 27 hold more than one advanced degree. The remaining 3 have a master's degree. Thirty-nine percent attended one of the top fifty schools, as Table 5-1 shows; of these 112, or 24 percent, went to Ivy League schools.

In the Apex of Fame for Medical Professors and Doctors, shown in Table 5-2, we see the incredible range of endeavors that are possible in the field of medicine. On top with a far longer obit than any other physician is pediatrician Benjamin Spock, a familiar and trusted name to millions of American parents who consulted his perennial best-seller on the proper care of babies and young children. Others in the Apex include Nobel Prize winners working in the most fundamental aspects of human biology, a family doctor who made house calls up to the end of his seven-decade career, pioneers in understanding different aspects of cancer, those who pushed exercise, founders of eminent institutions and leaders and lobbyists of various stripes.

When a colleague can say of a doctor that "Saul Krugman has done more to eliminate pediatric infectious diseases than any other person ever," we are looking at someone who has truly changed the world for the better. While chairman of pediatrics from 1960 to 1975 at the New York University School of Medicine, Dr. Krugman and his coworkers helped develop vaccines against once common childhood scourges such as polio, measles, and rubella. But "his crowning achievement" was figuring out that there were different hepatitis viruses, each transmitted in different ways. He won the Albert and Mary Lasker award for

TABLE 5-1. *Undergraduate Colleges Attended by Medical School Professors and Physicians in the Obituary Database*

College	Medical School Professors ($N = 286$) (%)	Doctors in Practice ($N = 178$) (%)	Total Professors and Doctors ($N = 464$) (%)
Ivy League	25.5	21.9	24.1
Rest of the top fifty	18.5	10.1	15.3
Other private colleges	16.8	12.9	15.3
Other public colleges	18.2	23.0	20.0
Foreign colleges	9.8	7.9	9.1
Not named	11.2	24.2	16.2
Total	**100.0**	**100.0**	**100.0**

Top fifty colleges (According to *Barron's,* 1995): Amherst College, Bates College, Boston College, Bowdoin College, *Brown University,* Bryn Mawr College, California Institute of Technology, Carleton College, Carnegie Mellon University, Claremont McKenna College, College of William and Mary, *Columbia University, Cornell University, Dartmouth College,* Davidson College, Duke University, Emory University, Georgetown University, Georgia Institute of Technology, *Harvard University,* Harvey Mudd College, Haverford College, Johns Hopkins University, Massachusetts Institute of Technology, Middlebury College, Northwestern University, Pomona College, *Princeton University,* Reed College, Rice University, Stanford University, Swarthmore College, Tufts University, University of California at Berkeley, University of California at Los Angeles, University of Chicago, University of Illinois at Urbana-Champaign, University of Michigan at Ann Arbor, University of North Carolina at Chapel Hill, University of Notre Dame, *University of Pennsylvania,* University of Texas at Austin, University of Virginia, Vassar College, Wake Forest University, Washington and Lee University, Wellesley College, Wesleyan University, Williams College, *Yale University.* The eight schools in italics belong to the Ivy League.

his "pivotal role in creating a vaccine against the hepatitis B virus," a disease that has afflicted not just children but about 300 million people worldwide.

Dr. Robert Guthrie was another physician working on behalf of children. The father of five, Dr. Guthrie had a mentally retarded son, John, born in 1948. Thus he knew firsthand the sadness of that affliction. Then, ten years later, in 1958, a niece was born with phenylketonuria

(PKU). Without early diagnosis and a special diet, this inherited disease affecting one in 10,000 newborns causes permanent brain damage and mental retardation. This was the calamity that befell his niece. Spurred on by this tragedy, within a few years Dr. Robert Guthrie had developed a three-cent PKU test for newborns. Such was the political climate that he had to overcome the opposition of doctors who saw mandatory screening as some form of socialized medicine. Today PKU screening is routine throughout the United States and twenty-five other countries. In the past three decades, it has been estimated, Dr. Guthrie saved some 30,000 children from becoming mentally retarded.

In 1996 there were about 664,000 practicing physicians in the United States, up from 311,200 in 1970.[3] At its best, medicine draws on the intellect and the emotions and creates an intimate bond between doctor and patient. At its worst, medicine leaves patients feeling as if they are just nuisances, as doctors seem more concerned with collecting fees or getting them out of the office. In the course of their duties, physicians regularly confront many of life's greatest dramas: birth, death, and the haunting sadness of prolonged debility and illness. Some doctors handle these better than others. The universality of human illness and suffering means that medicine, far more than most occupations, often operates at an international level.

Few other jobs pose such high hurdles for entry or such continuous lifetime monitoring and regulation. Doctors commonly must complete four years of medical school. The vast majority then go on to serve a grueling year of internship at a hospital, typified by long hours with little or no sleep. After internship, two thirds of American doctors specialize, spending several years (and sometimes more) in a residency that gives further training in a certain field, such as internal medicine, pediatrics, psychiatry, or surgery, as shown in Table 5-3. Doctors must have a medical license issued by the state in which they work. And so, not until they are in their late twenties or early thirties do most doctors begin the actual practice of medicine. Because incompetent physicians can inflict great harm, their prescribing habits are monitored, while state licensing boards require their attendance at continuing medical education courses.

TABLE 5-2. *The Apex of Fame: Medical School Professors and Physicians in the Obituary Database*

Name (Age at Death)	Obit Date	College Attended
1. Benjamin Spock (94)	03/17/98	Yale
2. Jonas Salk (80)	06/24/95	CCNY
3. Mary Calderone (94)	10/25/98	Vassar
4. Howard M. Temin (59)	02/11/94	Swarthmore
5. Philip Strax (90)	03/11/99	Not named
6. Hamilton Holmes (54)	10/28/95	U. Georgia
7. George Sheehan (74)	11/02/93	Manhattan C.
8. Charles Huggins (95)	01/15/97	Acadia U.
9. Hector Garcia (82)	07/29/96	U. Texas
10. William Walsh (76)	12/28/96	St. John's
11. Paul Zoll (87)	01/08/99	Harvard
12. Alexander Langmuir (83)	11/24/93	Harvard
13. Bernard Fields (56)	02/01/95	Brandeis
14. Oscar Auerbach (92)	01/16/97	NYU
15. Michael Pollock (61)	06/12/98	U. Arizona
16. L. Butterfield (72)	06/06/99	U. New Mexico
17. Louis West (74)	01/09/99	Not named
18. Helen Kaplan (66)	08/19/95	Syracuse
19. Harald Johnson (89)	09/07/96	U. Nebraska
20. Matthew Warpick (95)	01/10/97	Not named
21. Vernal Cave (78)	05/12/97	CCNY
22. Joseph Wolpe (82)	12/08/97	U. Witwatersrand (South Africa)
23. Harold Neu (63)	01/29/98	Creighton U.
24. Edwin Weinstein (89)	09/21/98	Dartmouth

Note: There were 286 medical school professors and 178 doctors in practice in the obituary database. The 26 with the longest obituaries represented less than 6 percent of these 464 professors and doctors.

Higher Degree (School)	Fame/Accomplishments	Obit Length
M.D. (Columbia)	Pediatrician; author of books on child care	125"
M.D. (NYU)	Developer of polio vaccine	91"
M.D. (U. Rochester)	Advocate of sex education	52"
Ph.D. (Caltech)	Discovered reverse transcriptase; Nobel	41"
M.D. (NYU)	Advocate of mammograms	38"
M.D. (Emory)	Surgeon who integrated University of Georgia	36"
M.D. (SUNY Downstate)	Cardiologist; running figure	33"
M.D. (Harvard)	Drug therapy for cancer; Nobel	32"
M.D. (U. Texas)	Led Hispanic rights group, American GI Forum	31"
M.D. (Georgetown)	Founder of Project HOPE	31"
M.D. (Harvard)	Development of pacemaker	31"
M.D. (Cornell)	Started Epidemic Intelligence Service	30"
M.D. (NYU)	Influenced direction of viral research	30"
M.D. (NYMC)	Linked smoking to cancer	29"
Ph.D. (U. Illinois)	Research on exercise	29"
M.D. (U. Colorado)	Pioneer in modern neonatology	28"
M.D. (U. Minnesota)	Psychiatrist who studied extremes	27"
Ph.D. (Columbia) M.D. (NYMC)	Pioneer in sex therapy	27"
M.D. (U. Nebraska)	Expert on rabies and arthropod-borne viral diseases	27"
M.D. (Not named)	Old-fashioned family doctor for 7 decades	26"
M.D. (Howard)	Brooklyn leader of medical, political, and social causes	26"
M.D. (U. Witwatersrand)	Pioneer in behavior therapy	26"
M.D. (Johns Hopkins)	Warned about bacterial resistance to antibiotics	26"
M.D. (Northwestern)	Reevaluation of President Wilson's death	26"

TABLE 5-3. *Physicians in United States by Type of Practice*

Field of Practice	Number of Physicians
Office-based private practice:	
Internal medicine	67,900
General and family practice	58,200
Pediatrics	31,500
Obstetrics and gynecology	28,200
General surgery	24,200
Psychiatry	22,600
Anesthesiology	22,000
Orthopedic surgery	16,600
Ophthalmology	14,300
Cardiovascular diseases	12,900
Diagnostic radiology	12,100
Emergency medicine	10,600
Other specialty	86,000
Total in private office-based practice	407,000
Hospital-based practice	
Full-time hospital staff	44,600
Residents, interns	86,800
Clinical fellows	4,700
Total in hospital-based practice	136,100
Federal-patient care, administration, research	22,500
Inactive or unknown	54,200
Total Physicians, Professionally Active (1994)	**619,800**

Source: *Statistical Abstract of the United States, 1996,* Table 179.

In his book *Money,* Andrew Hacker notes that medicine has been America's best-paid job for most of this century: "What has been unique about medicine is that virtually anyone who has a medical degree and who has completed a residency could count on finding a position that promised $100,000. . . no other profession starts people at that level."[4] Doctors would, of course, argue that this is just compensation for the grueling years spent in training, their specialized knowledge, and the long (and often erratic) hours most put in—not to mention the need to pay off sizable medical school debts. The high status and pay have attracted so many foreign doctors to practice here that they make up a fifth of the profession. The high status and pay can also be an irritant to those who feel the medical profession sometimes seems more concerned about preserving those privileges than practicing medicine.

Many of the physicians and scientists who have contributed most to the advancement of medical knowledge rarely, if ever, actually see patients anymore. Instead, they are primarily medical scientists whose discoveries have had profound implications for the understanding of the human body and often, but not always, have advanced the treatment of disease. They generally hold academic appointments at medical schools and publish their work in peer-reviewed scientific and medical journals. Some are authors of highly regarded medical textbooks that are standard works in their fields. They are frequently on the road attending meetings and conferences to deliver talks and hear about the work of their colleagues and rivals.

Dr. John J. Bonica, an anesthesiologist, dedicated his entire career to the problem of pain and pain relief. He was very much a hands-on physician who had a crash immersion in the wrenching realities of pain when treating wounded soldiers during World War II. As if that were not enough, his wife almost died while under ether anesthesia during the birth of their first child. That prompted him to develop far safer pain relief for childbirth based on epidural analgesia, which numbs only a woman's lower body. And Dr. Bonica himself suffered occasional bouts of debilitating pain from old wrestling injuries.

Dr. Bonica came to the United States as an Italian immigrant of ten. Still young when his father died, he helped support his family during the Depression by "shining shoes, hawking newspapers, and selling fruits and vegetables." He used his talent as a high school wrestler to enter the pro circuit, which paid his way through Long Island University and Marquette University School of Medicine. He trained in anesthesiology at St. Vincent's Hospital, was drafted into the Army, and then found himself chief of anesthesiology at Madigan Army Hospital. There the groaning wards of war wounded shaped his whole future.

During his career, Dr. Bonica founded and then directed the Multidisciplinary Pain Center at the University of Washington Medical Center in Seattle. Educating colleagues was his mission, for in their hands lay the true prospect of less pain for patients, whether acute or chronic. He wrote hundreds of articles and edited dozens of books. In 1953, he published a two-volume work, *The Management of Pain,* which was translated into six languages and used by doctors around the world. Dr. Bonica thought globally, for pain knows no borders. He promoted new and better treatments of pain worldwide, founding the International Association for the Study of Pain, which at his death had six thousand members in eighty countries. One has to look at Dr. Bonica as something of a medical missionary, a man who had a simple message—that pain can be conquered. Dr. Bonica then devoted his life to developing and disseminating the medical information and founding a movement—through articles, textbooks, organizations, and teaching—that could make that a reality.

Dr. Philip Strax was also a doctor with a mission, a "radiologist whose early and passionate advocacy of the mammogram helped revolutionize breast-cancer detection." Dr. Strax did not enter the medical field as a likely candidate for greatness. When he completed New York University Medical School in 1931, he headed right into private general practice in Manhattan. All was going along nicely until 1947, when his wife, Bertha, was diagnosed with breast cancer and died at age thirty-nine. "He was very much in love with her," said one colleague. "When they discovered it, he was shocked. It was a major blow to him. And he decided at that time that he was going to spend his lifework preventing that kind of shock from happening to anyone else, especially the patient."

Dr. Strax pioneered the use of X-rays to detect breast cancer in its earliest stages in an era when X-rays were used primarily to look at bones, not tissue. Though he had as yet no hard and fast proof of the value of X-rays, Dr. Strax opened two clinics in New York to provide cheap or free mammograms. Said another doctor, "He had that vision. He thought it was the right thing to do." To prove that X-rays were an important and powerful tool, Dr. Strax helped conduct a pathbreaking study with the Health Insurance Plan of Greater New York. Between 1963 and 1966, HIP provided mammograms and manual breast exams to tens of thousands of women forty to sixty-four years of age. A similar number in a comparison group received no such service. The study proved that these preventive measures had reduced breast cancer deaths by a third. When Dr. Strax and a colleague were honored some years later by the General Motors Cancer Research Foundation, the prize noted that they had "almost unilaterally changed medical thinking about early detection."

Today, every woman who learns she has breast cancer early enough to get life-saving treatment owes a big debt to this passionate crusading doctor. He authored several books about breast cancer, as well as three books of poetry. His patients from the breast clinics still spoke ardently of Dr. Strax years after he had retired. Said his daughter, "His most important theme is, always do more for others than is done for you."

Innovations in health care come in many forms. Some are preventive, such as Dr. Strax's mammography. Others involve technical advances. Dr. Harry H. LeVeen was chief of surgery at the Veteran Affairs Medical Center in New York when he invented a clever device that prevented "the often fatal buildup of fluid from severe liver diseases." The LeVeen shunt, available since the 1970s, became widely used by surgeons operating on the liver and prevents blood from flowing fatally in the wrong direction. Dr. LeVeen also invented a Dacron suture coated with Teflon known as Tevdek that is generally used to sew tissue together. These sorts of small improvements, little known outside their immediate arenas of application, are part of what constantly advances medicine.

Some technological improvements have a vast impact. Millions of people around the world today owe their lives to the presence of implanted pacemakers and defibrillators that keep their hearts functioning. Dr. Paul M. Zoll was the Harvard cardiologist who in the face of complete skepticism developed these lifesavers. When Dr. Zoll came back from World War II, every heart doctor carried a large jackknife at all times. Why? Because back then the "standard treatment for cardiac arrest was crude: a doctor would cut into the chest and squeeze the heart with his hand to pump blood through the body."

In that frontier era of rip-'em-open-to-save-'em, Dr. Zoll's novel idea was to electrically stimulate the heart externally to get it beating properly. In 1952, Dr. Zoll resuscitated two patients whose hearts had stopped by zapping them with electricity on the outside of their chests. Rather than excitement about his findings, there was thorough disbelief. Reported the *New York Times* in his obit, "After Dr. Zoll reported his findings at a scientific meeting, a close friend and leading cardiologist in Boston turned to Dr. Zoll's wife and said the device was a toy that would have little medical use." Fortunately for the world, Dr. Zoll pressed on. Later he would write, "Many people, including my own cardiac fellow, thought that it might be blasphemous, improper or unethical to keep a patient alive by such artificial means."

Dr. Zoll was a child of Boston who attended that city's most prestigious institutions: First Boston Latin School, then Harvard College, then Harvard Medical School. He interned at Beth Israel Hospital in Boston, trained further at Bellevue in Manhattan, and then worked as a doctor in England during the war. It was there, while watching a surgeon remove shrapnel from beating hearts, that he began contemplating electricity as a cardiac tool. When Dr. Zoll returned to Boston, he educated himself about electricity in order to design his machines. He developed external cardiac pacemakers. While these kept patients alive, it was no joy to be tethered to a large machine that, when used, sometimes caused burns and terrible pain. But they were a first step toward the tiny implanted pacemakers that are so commonplace today. In 1973, Dr. Zoll was duly recognized with an Albert and Mary Lasker Award.

As heart disease is one of our biggest killers, anything that can diminish its deadly toll is welcome. One of the simplest and most effective interventions is CPR, or cardiopulmonary resuscitation, today commonly taught and practiced around the world. It saves not only heart attack victims but also people who are choking or drowning. Dr. Archer

Gordon was a heart specialist who was hailed as the "father of CPR," though he properly pointed out that many had contributed to this enterprise. Yet he was a leading crusader who kept it all moving forward.

In the 1950s, while Dr. Gordon was at the University of Illinois, he did important studies showing the value of mouth-to-mouth resuscitation for choking children, rather than banging on the back. Reviving those in acute distress, a fairly common crisis, became his focus, and he worked with others to found a CPR Committee of the American Heart Association. They developed CPR, which combines mouth-to-mouth with chest compression techniques as a highly effective means of reviving the stricken. Dr. Gordon was then instrumental in developing mannequins that could be used to teach CPR and also wrote "Standards for CPR" for such major promoters of the technique as the American Medical Association, the American Red Cross, and the American Heart Association. Who knows how many men, women, and children all over the world have been saved by CPR? One suspects it has easily been millions in the last two decades.

For many, the aftermath of illness is a determined quest to recover and then stay healthy. The question then becomes how best to do that. Michael L. Pollock was among those who continually exhorted our sedentary society to exercise. He was "perhaps the nation's most respected expert on how much and how hard adults should exercise." He was not a medical doctor but a Ph.D. in exercise physiology who studied and quantified what kinds and amounts of physical activity most help keep one healthy. The author of three books and more than three hundred articles, he was a major force in convincing doctors that cardiac patients—including those coming off transplants—could significantly improve their recoveries through focused kinds of exercise, especially tailored weight training. Those who followed these regimens, he showed, "could prevent anti-rejection medication from reducing bone density. That, in turn, reduced the chance of brittle bones and stress fractures." The beauty of the exercise programs, said one colleague, was that "He helped patients help themselves."

Nor did Dr. Pollock limit his concern to just the ill. He was very much in the vanguard of the health and fitness movement that swept certain segments of America, giving us, among other things, health clubs and spandex. You may recall newspaper stories in the early 1990s recommending that adults engage in active aerobic activities such as running, bicycling, and swimming three to five times a week for at least twenty minutes. That was the highly respected advice of Dr. Pollock. Later he added weight training, especially for the elderly, to fend off excessive frailty. Of course, since these exhortations did not seem to bestir the nation's couch potatoes, the exercise establishment subsequently lowered the bar considerably, urging people just to get out for a walk around the block or garden a bit—anything to get them moving. But the numbers who exercise have not budged in a decade, still amounting to just one American adult in four. Pollock himself was a devoted exerciser despite serious arthritis. And no doubt antiexercise types might observe that regular exercise didn't keep Pollock from dying from a stroke at age sixty-one. Nonetheless, many Americans have taken his advice to heart and improved the quality of their lives through running, bike riding, weight lifting, and all the rest.

While cigarettes had long been tagged "coffin nails," for decades there was no hard proof that smoking actually caused disease. Dr. Morton L. Levin was the epidemiologist who first sounded the alarm in 1950. That year, he published one of two papers in the prestigious and authoritative *Journal of the American Medical Association* showing that "people who smoked had a greater chance of developing lung cancer." This is old hat today, a medical fact that many well-informed young people choose to believe will not apply to them. Yet, said the author of the other paper, "The idea that smoking causes lung cancer was revolutionary back then. The fact that we both submitted papers made others say there may be something to it."

Dr. Levin was an epidemiologist, someone who studies large groups in the population to divine health trends. He had degrees in pharmacy and medicine from the University of Maryland, as well as a doctorate in public health from Johns Hopkins. In 1936, he became the New York State Health Department's assistant director of cancer control. From 1938 to 1950, he followed the health of a large group of patients in Buffalo, New York. It was here that he found that "lung cancer occurred more than twice as frequently among smokers as among nonsmokers." From that time on, he was one of the earliest anti-tobacco campaigners.

For many, Dr. Levin's links were suggestive but not totally convincing. Some thought that maybe the problem lurked in Buffalo's water or air. But then, in the early 1960s, Dr. Oscar Auerbach produced what many acknowledged was the smoking gun: "the first evidence in human lung tissue of a link between cancer and smoking." Dr. Auerbach was a pathologist, a physician who specializes in studying human tissues as part of diagnosing and understanding disease. A real workhorse, Dr. Auerbach began examining two thousand slides of lung tissue a day, coding each for precancerous or cancerous symptoms. Then he found out which patients smoked. In one paper based on twenty-two thousand slides, he was able to show that cigarette smoking was indeed linked to cancerous cells. Dr. Auerbach then took the further trouble to determine the smoking levels of each patient whose tissue he was studying. He found that the more cigarettes, the greater the tissue damage.

Dr. Levin had not seemed headed for medicine as a teenager because he never even finished high school. But he later took exams, entered New York University, and, before graduating, entered New York Medical College and earned his M.D. in 1929. He spent most of his career at the Veterans Administration Hospital in East Orange, New Jersey. He taught at both his alma mater and the New Jersey Medical School.

Dr. Auerbach's work became famous with the groundbreaking surgeon general's 1964 report on the dangers of smoking. Dr. Auerbach then went beyond his vast pathological studies to teach eighty-six beagles to smoke. By the end of the experiment, twelve of the poor dogs had lung cancer. This was "the first instance of tumors produced in large animals exposed to cigarette smoke." The American Cancer Society, which underwrote much of Dr. Auerbach's research, trumpeted these striking results, but the Tobacco Institute, the industry apologists, held fast, citing "stressful laboratory conditions" as a possible cause. Dr. Auerbach also provided hope and impetus for smokers to quit by showing that human lung tissue gradually recovers when smokers stop smoking.

The number of Americans who smoke cigarettes has decreased dramatically since the 1960s, when people like Drs. Levin and Auerbach began to lay out the medical-scientific evidence about tobacco and cancer. One estimate was that 750,000 lives had been saved as the number of Americans who smoked dropped from close to one in two to one in four.

Many of the American physicians we have looked at thus far have won numerous honors, very often the highly coveted Lasker Award. But the most prestigious honor of all is international, the Nobel Prize in Physiology or Medicine. The prize has been awarded since 1901, and since World War II the prize list has been dominated by American scientists and physicians.[5] The prize honors "the most important discoveries or inventions" and immediately vaults its recipients to worldwide acclaim and recognition.[6] Dr. Charles B. Huggins of the University of Chicago, for instance, was a general surgeon who won the Nobel Prize in 1966 for helping "open the era of drug therapy for cancer and provide underpinnings of the modern treatment of prostate and breast cancer." Huggins grew up in Nova Scotia, the son of a pharmacist, graduated from Acadia University, got his M.D. from Harvard Medical School, and then trained as a general surgeon at the University of Michigan. He was one of the founding faculty members of the University of Chicago Medical School. Once there, he was a pioneer in understanding the physiology and biochemistry of the urogenital tract. He became interested in cancer because surgery and radiation were the usual treatment when he first began to practice.

In his research, done mainly on dogs, Dr. Huggins was able to show how male and female hormones, selectively used, could retard prostate and breast cancers. Dr. Huggins's great breakthrough was to show that cancer cells were not always "autonomous and self-perpetuating, as previously believed, but could be dependent on hormones or other chemical signals to grow and survive." These very original findings not only helped many cancer patients, they inspired whole new avenues of cancer research. Thus, the female hormone estrogen could be given to prostate cancer patients to retard their cancer. Dr. Huggins then went on to do further research on breast cancer, eventually showing that in a third of advanced cases, removing the ovaries and adrenal glands (the source of cancer-stimulating hormones) brought significant regression.

Why, one might ask, did twenty-five years elapse between Dr. Huggins's work and his receiving the Nobel Prize? Apparently because the first time the Nobel Committee awarded a prize for medical work related to cancer in 1926, it turned out that the medical advance did not stand the test of time. Once burned, twice shy. However, the Swedish prize committee did not want to wait too long, for there is no posthumous prize giving.

Unlike many successful medical scientists, Dr. Huggins was not an empire builder. Rather, he was single-mindedly focused on his lab research. He kept his lab small, doing his own experiments and shunning administrative responsibilities. His career advice to his colleagues was "Don't write books. Don't teach hundreds of students. Discovery is our business. Make damn good discoveries."

In 1981, Roger Sperry won the Nobel Prize in Physiology or Medicine for his studies of patients with split brains, whose importance was to "define the function of the corpus callosum, a thick bundle of some 200 million nerve fibers . . . [showing that] it served as a channel to pass information between the two hemispheres." Until Dr. Sperry's work, the received wisdom was that the left brain was dominant. The Nobel Prize press release noted that the left brain "can speak, write and make mathematical calculations . . . it is also the more aggressive, executive, leading hemisphere." But Sperry also showed that the right brain had important duties, including "the capacity for concrete thinking, spatial consciousness and comprehension of complex relationships." Sperry was able to demonstrate these differences first through monkey experiments, and then with a unique group of human subjects: epilepsy patients whose interbrain connecting tissues had been severed to bring relief from severe seizures. His brilliantly designed test procedures showed that with these people the two sides of the brain could no longer communicate! And because the two sides could not share or transfer information, he could truly discover the capacities of each hemisphere, yielding such specific facts as the right brain's minimal mathematics ability. It can perform only simple addition up to twenty; it cannot subtract, multiply, or divide at all!

Through elegant experiments with newts and other amphibians, Sperry showed that certain nerves are destined to hook up with others:

"The brain's wiring, in other words, is very specific, and particular pathways serve particular functions." Sperry was a doctor not of medicine but of zoology, with a Ph.D. from University of Chicago. He was a Caltech faculty member for three decades.

Dr. George Davis Snell won the Nobel Prize in 1980 for "milestone research that helped make human organ transplants possible." Dr. Snell had a Ph.D. from Harvard in science and then settled into a life of studying genetics at the Jackson Laboratory at Bar Harbor, Maine. His special province was histocompatibility, a term he coined, that examined how mice respond to transplanted tissue at the most basic level. Why did some mice's bodies accept these foreign organisms and others did not? His work helped show how and why, at the genetic level, some mice's immune systems were less likely to distinguish between their own cells and an invader's. This is science at its purest, but its medical applications are widespread, as the many who are alive today because of organ transplants know.

The man and woman who won the Nobel Prize in Physiology or Medicine in 1988 were highly unusual recipients because they were not on the faculty at a prestigious medical school or similar academic setting. George H. Hitchings and Gertrude Elion were industry scientists, he for thirty-three years the chief researcher and biochemist and she his colleague at the Burroughs Wellcome Company in Research Triangle Park in North Carolina. Founders of the field of chemotherapeutics, Dr. Hitchings and Ms. Elion won the prize for pharmaceutical research that "led to the creation of drugs to treat leukemia, gout, malaria, and disorders of the human immune system that eventually made organ transplants possible." They provided the underpinnings for the development of the AIDS medicine AZT.

A native of Washington State, Dr. Hitchings earned a B.S. and M.S. in chemistry at the state university and then his Ph.D. in biochemistry at Harvard. Ms. Elion was a native New Yorker who held a B.S. in chemistry from Hunter College and an M.S. from New York University. She could not initially find a job in a medical research laboratory because she was a woman. Instead, she taught high school science for a while, worked as a food analyst, and then, helped by personnel shortages caused by the war, finally got a job in 1944 at the Wellcome Research Laboratories as Dr. Hitchings's assistant. They would work together for the next four decades. "He had two arms of research," said Ms. Elion, "and I was one of them."

Their brilliant breakthrough was to introduce compounds into human cells just "slightly different than those that occur naturally. Those false building blocks would inhibit growth of unwanted cells, like cancerous ones, by fooling them into thinking that they were replacing themselves." Looking back on a long and productive career, Dr. Hitchings would say, "That was the key discovery from which everything else stems." Colleagues calculated that their drugs had saved more than a million lives. His son would say, "His greatest joy was meeting people whose lives were saved by his medicine."

Gertrude Elion, who won the Nobel Prize with Dr. Hitchings, is the only woman in this chapter. She is a perfect illustration of the great difficulties women have had getting into the highest echelons of science and medicine, a field with high formal hurdles. She sorely felt her lack of a Ph.D. and so entered a doctoral program at Brooklyn Polytechnic Institute. She commuted an hour and a half each way to take courses at night. But ultimately she had to give up because she could not finish without attending school full-time and she could not afford to give up her job.

Though Elion had been engaged at one time, her fiancé had died and she never married. Reported the *New York Times*, "Ms. Elion said she would not have advanced in her career if she had chosen to marry and have children because women were not encouraged then to work while their children were young." And so she chose to dedicate her life to science and medicine, bringing great surcease from pain and disease to millions through her medical breakthroughs. Fortunately, women no longer feel obliged to make such stark choices. Today young women make up more than one fifth of the profession (21.3 percent in 1996). This is a marked increase from 9.1 percent in 1975.[7]

One of the qualities of science and medicine is the varied routes that can lead to huge breakthroughs. Allan MacLeod Cormack won the Nobel Prize in 1979 for making possible the CAT scan, "the greatest advance in radiology since the first Nobel Laureate, Wilhelm Conrad Rontgen, discovered X-rays in 1895." It all began with Cormack's great love of stargazing as a boy in South Africa. Thinking he wanted to be an astronomer, Cormack took physics in college but soon encountered something more fascinating, subatomic particles. He put in two years of postgraduate nuclear physics at Cambridge University in England and then, wanting to marry and needing an income, he returned to the University of Cape Town. In 1955, a local hospital radiology department hired him on a part-time basis to fulfill a law requiring a nuclear physicist to monitor its X-ray operations.

Like many in the field, the chairman of radiology was concerned about not exposing patients to any more radiation than necessary. So he asked his new part-time physicist to "find a way to measure how much X-ray energy was absorbed by various parts of the body." Cormack knew almost nothing about X-rays and was quite amazed at the undifferentiated pictures they delivered. Bones, organs, and soft tissue all showed up on top of one another, making for a very difficult analysis of what one was seeing. As for the immediate problem of absorption, he figured the solution was to create an interior map of the human body: "The map would show which tissues and other materials were where by shooting X-rays through the body from many different angles, then using triangulation to derive a high-definition image of any cross section." Cormack, by now on the faculty at Tufts University in Boston, was deeply involved in other work, but he gradually developed the mathematical formula necessary to do this, demonstrated that it worked with some crude models, published his results, and correctly assumed that an engineer would take it from there. And so Sir Godfrey Newbold Hounsfield did. These two men, who had never met, shared the Nobel in 1979. Like the X-ray machine from which it sprang, the CAT scan was a huge leap forward for medicine, providing, for the first time ever, clear images of the inside of the human body. Thus Cormack received his Nobel relatively quickly.

One of the most striking aspects of modern medicine is the vital importance of institutions. While the majority of American doctors are still solo practitioners, the most powerful physicians operate out of the complex, sophisticated precincts of major medical institutions. Usually, these are medical schools with huge hospitals and major research labs, but some are government agencies. The 126 U.S. medical schools provide the infrastructure for much of this research advancement.[8] The top people at these institutions can be most influential in their fields. Witness Dr. A. McGehee Harvey, who "developed the first research-based school of medicine in the United States at the Johns Hopkins Hospital [in Baltimore] and trained an army of medical school leaders there." Not only was Dr. Harvey a much-honored and favored teacher who influenced the medical education of 2,151 medical students and nearly a thousand residents, he was also the author of *Differential Diagnosis,* which has gone through several editions, and the editor in chief of the important textbook *The Principles and Practice of Medicine.* Moreover, a number of Dr. Harvey's residents have gone on to their own glorious careers, sixteen as heads of departments and eight as deans in other medical schools.

Dr. Harvey's great contribution was his insistence on the relevance of medical research to the actual treatment of patients. He required his students and residents to always carry pads and pencils so they could write down as much information as possible about each patient. That process was intended to encourage new insights that could be put to work in the research lab. The results achieved in the lab were, in turn, to be applied to subsequent patients. "Dr. Harvey had a ripple effect," said one former student and Harvard medical dean. "The things I saw in him, the environment, the attitude toward patients, it all got burnished into me. . . . He would stop at a bed and really demonstrate how to gather information from a patient." In this way, said another alumnus, "He trained a whole generation of leaders in American medicine." The most effective institutions make possible the Dr. Harveys—highly dedicated, talented professionals who can use the strengths of the institutions to set a standard that becomes the norm. Dr. Harvey was himself a product of that same institution: he had gotten his M.D. at Johns Hopkins and received further training in England and then at Vanderbilt before serving during World War II in the South Pacific with the Hopkins 118th General Hospital.

Dr. Thomas C. Chalmers used the might of Mount Sinai Medical Center and its school of medicine in New York to impose greater rigor on the practice of medicine. When doctors treated patients, he felt, they should be getting the best care science—not anecdote—dictated. Thus he was "a pioneer in popularizing the use of randomized clinical trials to determine the best course of medical treatment." He first proved the power of such comparisons when studying patients recovering from hepatitis A. Should patients be obliged to undergo long periods of bed rest, as customary care demanded? Or might they resume their normal lives? Dr. Chalmers's randomized trials showed that what had long been believed was wrong: patients *could* return to active life.

As president of Mount Sinai, he established a department of biostatistics that would dedicate itself to considering the best choices in medicine based on research. He also promoted and practiced meta-analysis, in which one takes many studies of a particular disease or problem—say, what the best course of treatment for an arthritic hip might be—combines them, and arrives at a meaningful conclusion. Scientific analysis was a core medical belief of his. When Dr. Chalmers's own aching arthritic hip had him limping around with a cane, a friend recounted asking him, "Why not get the hip replaced [with an artificial one]?" and he would wince and say, 'Because the trials haven't yet concluded that such treatment is best.' He lived by his example."

One suspects that Dr. Chalmers's passion for scientifically based medicine may have come from growing up in a family of doctors in New York City. He must have observed numerous treatments administered by his grandfather and father that would later be viewed as questionable or even harmful. Certainly many had never been scientifically proven. Dr. Chalmers also had the vision, in 1983, to open the nation's first department of geriatrics in a medical school and give it equal stature with other long-standing specialties. After all, the nation's demography made it clear that in coming decades there would be a great need to understand and treat the problems of the old.

Dr. Alexander Langmuir was an institution builder of another sort. In 1949, armed with a Cornell degree in medicine and a Johns Hopkins degree in public health, he went to Atlanta to create the Epidemic

Intelligence Center for the U.S. Public Health Service. Out of the center, initially launched to deal with malaria outbreaks in the U.S. South, Dr. Langmuir built a far more ambitious empire known today as the U.S. Centers for Disease Control and Prevention. He personally trained the first 500 of the 2,200 doctors, statisticians, nurses, and others who worked there, and by the time they moved on to other state health departments and schools of public health, he had created a network inculcated in the Langmuir way.

As the center's chief epidemiologist from 1949 to 1970, Dr. Langmuir had his agency pioneering the active surveillance of infectious diseases. Systems were set up to "track dozens of diseases and to analyze patterns to take steps to prevent clusters and outbreaks from becoming epidemics." Dr. Langmuir was a physically big man who loved a good bureaucratic tussle. He had no qualms about standing up to recalcitrant local officials if they stood in the way of better public health. He prided himself that he and his corps practiced "shoe leather epidemiology": investigators were sent to the scene of a disease outbreak to assess everything, including food, air, and water, as possible disease vectors. His people sported lapel pins of a shoe with a hole in the sole. Back at the office, detailed reports were completed quickly and dispatched to any and all possibly relevant persons. This approach nipped many an outbreak in the bud. For instance, it helped solve the initial mystery of Legionnaires' disease, explained toxic shock syndrome, and identified the kind of hantavirus that was killing Native Americans in New Mexico. Dr. Langmuir spent his final career decades first at Harvard's and then at Johns Hopkins's school of public health, teaching incoming generations of epidemiologists and inculcating them in the power of surveillance.

Just as Dr. Bonica found his future work while tending the war wounded, so Dr. William B. Walsh found his calling while a Navy doctor in the South Pacific. When his ship anchored at certain islands, he was appalled by the unnecessary illnesses and deaths, especially among the children. He would later say, "Some of them had never had any real medical care in their life. I promised myself that if I ever got the chance, I wanted to do something about that sort of thing."

Dr. Walsh returned from the war and continued his medical training at Georgetown University Hospital. He became a cardiologist and joined the Georgetown staff as a professor of internal medicine. In 1958, his big break came: he was called in as a consultant after President Dwight D. Eisenhower had a heart attack. The two men hit it off, and Dr. Walsh became active in one of the president's pet postwar projects, the People-to-People program, aimed at providing professional expertise to developing nations. Dr. Walsh proposed a floating hospital ship that could visit overseas as requested. The Navy pulled out an old mothballed 15,000-ton hospital ship, and Dr. Walsh raised the money to refit it and paint huge letters on its side: HOPE. Arriving in the fall of 1960 at the remote Indonesian island of Sumbawa, HOPE found thousands of people lined up to see a doctor for the first time in their lives. In one of several books he wrote about this humanitarian project, Dr. Walsh reported that an Indonesian farmer who had a painful tumor removed said through an interpreter, "This is the first time in my memory, or the memory of the oldest man in my village, that foreigners have come and not taken rice from us. You are here to help us. We will not forget." For the next fourteen years, during the height of the Cold War, the ship HOPE traveled 250,000 miles to visit dozens of poor nations.

Dr. Walsh made Project HOPE his life's work. When the ship became too aged, it was retired, and HOPE expanded into a global organization active in dozens of nations. In the late 1990s, its major project was creating a new children's medical center in Shanghai aimed at treating 250,000 children a year. Dr. Walsh and Project HOPE exemplify the best of American medicine: the desire to improve the lot of ordinary people with all their ills and aches and pains; the creativity of smart people dedicated to that ideal of service against suffering; and the creation of institutions that can carry those high ideals into the future. There is nothing more heart-wrenching than the sight of a sick child, and that repeated experience had been enough to inspire a career that must have helped millions of people in some of the most backward spots on earth.

Notes

1. Jane E. Smith and Paul Wagner, *A Paralyzing Fear: The Triumph over Polio in America* (New York: TV Books., 1998), p. 3.
2. See Table 1-6 for life expectancy rates.
3. *Statistical Abstract of the United States, 1998*, Table 190; and for 1996, Table 179.
4. Andrew Hacker, *Money* (New York: Touchstone, 1997), p. 123.
5. Harriet Zuckerman, *Scientific Elite* (New York: Free Press, 1977); Elizabeth Crawford, "Nobel: Always the Winners, Never the Losers," *Science*, November 13, 1998, pp. 1256–1257; Also, for the role of U.S. funding, see "NIH Funds Support Nobel Laureates," *Newsletter of the NIH Alumni Association*, Spring 1999, p. 24.
6. The Nobel Prize Committee has an outstanding Web site at www.nobel.se/laureates/medicine that gives individual autobiographies of each of the Nobelists.
7. *The Wall Street Journal Almanac, 1999*, p. 558.
8. Abraham Flexner, *Medical Education in the United States and Canada* (New York: Arno Press and *New York Times*, 1972); Erwin H. Ackerknecht, *A Short History of Medicine* (Baltimore: Johns Hopkins University Press, 1982).

6

Prominent Academics

Expert on Ancient Greece

Optimistic Economist

Inspired Hubble Telescope

He was the classic academic, described in his obit as "the ultimate absent-minded professor, a brilliant eccentric using abstract economic theory to find solutions to everyday problems." After years of trying to interest the "real" world in his ideas, Columbia University economist William Vickery won the Nobel Prize in 1996 for "seminal work in many areas of public economics," and suddenly everyone was at his door. The media descended upon a garretlike office crammed with "file cabinets topped with cardboard boxes . . . prehistoric coffee cups, articles of clothing, broken eyeglasses . . . and walls of sloping books." There Dr. Vickery explained his long-proposed solutions to traffic jams and mass transit rush-hour crowds: If people had to pay higher fares for everything from bridge tolls to subway tickets during peak times, congestion would ease up. Basking in the opportunity to promote his ideas, he declared, "It feels swell. Ahhhh, at last." Three days later, the poor man was dead of a heart attack.

In this chapter we look at some of our most successful and accomplished professors and university presidents, the people who generate much of the nation's intellectual capital, the promoters of knowledge and inquiry. The professors make up the second largest group in the *New York Times* obits, after businesspeople, with well over 800 academics, 746 of them men and 110 women, or 10 percent of all the men's obits and 8 percent of all the women's. The average professor's obit is thirteen and a half inches long. The academics are an especially fascinating group, for their expertise covers the whole range of possible human knowledge, from the most abstruse physics to the study of Greek coins to Japanese history. There are about a half-million full-time faculty working at 3,600 public and private colleges and universities in the United States.[1] As might be expected, the vast majority of the professors in our database had advanced degrees, with three quarters holding Ph.D.s. With regard to colleges attended as undergraduates, almost half were from one of the top fifty colleges, as shown in Table 6-1. The second group in the chapter (who are described in detail later) are college and university presidents—another hundred-plus people—who have presided over the extraordinary expansion of higher education since World War II.

College Professors

With knowledge and education viewed as integral to success and advancement in many fields, professors have traditionally been respected, sometimes even revered figures, members of an intellectual high priesthood. Most have spent their careers isolated in ivory-tower campuses, quietly teaching for their departments, serving on committees, advising students, and turning out an occasional book or article. These institutional bastions, many of which are affiliated with religious institutions or serve targeted populations—say, women or blacks—are located in every state and serve as the source of most knowledge that is transferred from generation to generation. Success within academia is defined as becoming a tenured full professor in a top department in a prestigious school. But the professors in the *New York Times* obits have generally gained fame beyond the academy, often leading high-profile lives and promoting their particular ideas in far more public arenas. Almost all were ardent in trying to convey the importance of those ideas, and some changed our society dramatically.

Thirty-three professors made our Apex of Fame as shown in Table 6-2. Two thirds were working at the top fifty schools, with fourteen at Ivy League schools. Regarding their own education, almost half (46 percent) held degrees from one of the top fifty colleges. Almost another fifth (18 percent) were graduates of foreign universities, reflecting the

TABLE 6-1. *Undergraduate Colleges Attended by the College Professors in the Obituary Database*

College	Number of Professors	Colleges Attended* (%)
Ivy League	169	26.4
Rest of the top fifty	135	21.1
Others in the United States	337	52.6
Foreign	86	—
Not named	129	—
Total	**856**	**100.0**

*For the 641 professors whose attendance at specific colleges was stated.

brain drain from abroad to the United States that has been so important in certain fields, especially science.

Kenneth Bainbridge, "the physicist who directed the first test of an atomic bomb," was among the scientific mandarins who helped develop numerous key technologies during World War II, in his case radar. A Harvard professor when war broke out, he had established a major reputation for designing a mass spectrometer that could determine the masses of atomic elements. Then, in 1943, he went to the top secret Manhattan Project, taking with him his Harvard cyclotron. His task, code-named Project Trinity, was to test the atomic bomb in the desert south of Los Alamos, New Mexico. He had no qualms about this quantum leap into new levels of potential destruction: "It was obvious that in the space of a few years the war was getting dirtier and Hitler's threats and deeds gave me a somewhat bloodthirsty viewpoint on the war."

As the great day of the first test loomed on July 16, 1945, Bainbridge's "personal nightmare was knowing that if the bomb didn't go off or hangfired, I, as head of the test, would have to go to the tower first and seek to find out what had gone wrong." All went fine, and in that remote spot the Atomic Age was launched. After the United States

TABLE 6-2. *The Apex of Fame: College Professors in the Obituary Database*

Name (Age at Death)	Obit Date	College Attended as Undergraduate	School of Fame	Obit Length
1. Linus Pauling (93)	08/21/94	Oregon Agr. College	Caltech	99"
2. Meyer Schapiro (91)	03/04/96	Columbia	Columbia	87"
3. William Vickery (82)	10/12/96	Yale	Columbia	62"
4. Carl Sagan (62)	12/21/96	U. Chicago	Cornell	60"
5. Eugene Wigner (92)	01/04/95	School in Budapest	Princeton	59"
6. Henry Steele Commager (95)	03/03/98	U. Chicago	Amherst College	53"
7. Wassily Leontief (93)	02/07/99	U. Leningrad	Harvard, NYU	50"
8. Lyman Spitzer, Jr. (82)	04/02/97	Yale	Princeton	44"
9. Leon Edel (89)	09/08/97	McGill U.	NYU	41"
10. Subrahmanyan Chandrasekhar (84)	08/22/95	Presidency College (India)	U. Chicago	40"
11. Paul Erdos (83)	09/24/96	Not named	U. Chicago	40"
12. Robert Serber (88)	06/02/97	Lehigh U.	Columbia	39"
13. Robert Dicke (80)	03/05/97	Princeton	Princeton	38"
14. Daniel Crowley (76)	03/05/98	Northwestern	UC Davis	38"
15. Mirra Komarovsky (93)	02/01/99	Barnard	Barnard	37"
16. J. John Sepkoski, Jr. (50)	05/06/99	U. Notre Dame	U. Chicago	37"
17. Eqbal Ahmad (67)	05/13/99	Occidental College	Cornell	37"

Name (Age at Death)	Obit Date	College Attended as Undergraduate	School of Fame	Obit Length
18. Thomas Kuhn (73)	06/19/96	Harvard	MIT	36"
19. Kenneth Bainbridge (91)	07/18/96	Not named	Harvard	36"
20. John Clarke (83)	07/20/98	Columbia	Hunter	36"
21. Derek Barton (79)	03/19/98	U. London	Texas A&M	35"
22. Ellis Kerley (74)	09/12/98	U. Kentucky	U. Maryland	35"
23. Thomas McMahon (55)	02/19/99	Cornell	Harvard	35"
24. Americo Paredes (83)	05/07/99	U. Texas	U. Texas	35"
25. John Rewald (81)	02/03/94	U. Hamburg	CUNY	33"
26. Arthur Link (77)	03/29/98	Princeton	Princeton	33"
27. Robert Eisner (76)	11/28/98	CCNY	Northwestern	33"
28. John H. Yoder (70)	01/07/98	Goshen College	U. Notre Dame	32"
29. Frank Spencer (58)	06/03/99	Not named	Brooklyn College	32"
30. Robert Sobel (68)	06/04/99	CCNY	Hofstra	32"
31. Mario Savio (53)	11/08/96	San Francisco St.	Sonoma St.	31"
32. John W. Hall (81)	10/24/97	Amherst	Yale	31"
33. Abraham Katsh (92)	07/26/98	Not named	NYU	31"

Note: There were 856 professors in the database; the 33 in this apex represent 4 percent of them.

dropped atomic bombs on Hiroshima and Nagasaki, the Japanese surrendered. Dr. Bainbridge never regretted his role in developing the atomic bomb. But with the war won, he put his considerable clout as a Harvard scientist into actively opposing further nuclear testing, expanding the nuclear arsenal, and using atomic bombs in a first strike. But the genie of the Atomic Age could not be pushed back into the bottle, and the Cold War, with its nuclear threat, was soon being played out across the globe.

World War II demonstrated the tremendous creativity and progress possible when teams of smart scientists collaborated under military auspices to solve complex technical problems. The federal government became convinced that advanced knowledge of all kinds was extremely important. In 1958, 8,773 Americans earned Ph.D.'s from American universities. By the mid-1990s, after decades of U.S. largesse aimed at keeping up with the Russians, that figure had soared to more than 45,000 new Ph.D.'s a year. Today, higher education has ceased being a genteel cloister and has become a major industry employing 2.5 million people. Consider, for instance, that Harvard University's endowment tops $8 billion, more than the gross national product of certain poor countries. Half a million of those in academia are full-time faculty. For full professors, the average salary ranges from $60,000 in state schools to more than $100,000 in the Ivy Leagues. Superstars in certain fields can top $200,000. Add book contracts, lecture fees, and consulting work, and famous academics can make serious money. Andrew Hacker, himself a professor, notes in his book *Money* that "the basic work year for college faculties adds up to 90 days, not counting sabbaticals, which allow them every seventh year off. Most other Americans are expected to spend 250 days at their place of employment." And of course, professors with tenure have that rarity in our present marketplace: a lifetime employment guarantee.

However, the glory days of the academy seem past, at least from the point of view of all those freshly minted Ph.D.'s. Their prospects of getting a tenure-track job are slightly better than surviving the sinking of the *Titanic*—about 40 percent. The use of part-time faculty has doubled since 1970, and almost half of all teaching positions are part-time. This has left many unhappy people singing the overeducated, underpaid blues as they cobble together the lives of gypsy scholars, earning $2,000 a course (with no benefits) teaching here and there.

Meanwhile, college students pour in because higher education equals greater opportunities and earning power. America outstrips all other Western societies in its level of college graduates: one quarter of all adults, as shown in Table 6-3, or twice that of most European nations with the exception of the Netherlands.[2]

There are compelling economic (not to mention intellectual) reasons to pursue a college degree. In 1995, the typical twenty-five- to thirty-four-year-old male college graduate earned 52 percent more than those with only a high school diploma. In 1946, there were 2.4 million college students. Today, there are 9 million students attending 2,125 four-year schools (595 public, 1,530 private). Most college students attend larger public institutions, which are often metropolitan or statewide in scope; only 22 percent attend private colleges.[3] Many millions more attend two-year community colleges, and a million more attend college part-time.

Professors with powerful intellectual ideas or insights can have enormous influence. Dr. James Coleman, a University of Chicago sociologist, was such a man, for his "controversial studies laid much of the groundwork for and against the use of busing to desegregate schools in the 1960s and 1970s." His 1966 report to Congress concluded that disadvantaged black children performed better in integrated classes. This became the basis of massive busing to achieve racial balance, followed by massive white flight from the cities, leaving urban school districts—not to mention cities—even worse off. This mass flight also set an American pattern of avoiding social problems by moving farther and farther away from them, fueling the ever-widening suburban sprawl. When Dr. Coleman concluded eleven years later that busing had been a disaster, he was attacked for changing his mind. But what he had found in later studies was that poor black children did better only when the *majority* of their white classmates were middle-class. And as that mix rapidly disappeared, Dr. Coleman no longer saw any advantage to busing. This was a highly unpopular piece of news among civil rights

TABLE 6-3. *U.S. Population: Education Attained, by Sex (Persons 25 Years of Age and Older)*

Education	Male (%)	Female (%)	Total (%)
Did not complete high school	18.0	17.8	17.9
High school graduate (but no college)	32.1	35.5	33.8
Associate's degree	6.5	8.0	7.3
Some college	17.2	17.2	17.2
College graduate (no higher degree)	16.8	12.0	16.0
Advanced degree	9.4	6.3	7.8
Total (N = 170,581,000)	100.0	100.0	100.0

Source: Statistical Abstract of the United States, 1998, Table 262.

activists. "It was not a fashionable or pleasant scientific finding," recalled Gary Becker, a fellow sociologist at Chicago. And there arose a move to oust Coleman from the American Sociological Association. Said Becker, "Fortunately for the integrity of the association, that move failed."

One of the more fascinating aspects of the academy is how fiercely it resists change. This is in notable contrast to many other arenas in American life, where innovation is actively encouraged. But professors operate under a different dynamic. They normally become prominent through championing a particular idea or school of thought. This idea has usually won them tenure, appointment at a prestigious school, and respectful attention from colleagues and sometimes even the wider public. When, inevitably, someone comes along to challenge this respected idea with a new career-making viewpoint or interpretation, the old leaders defend their academic turf to the bitter end. What made Coleman unusual was his willingness to repudiate his own most lauded work. This was so unusual that his obit noted his "courage" in doing this.

An even more controversial academic was Harvard psychologist Richard Herrnstein, whose belief that intelligence was largely hereditary "drew intense hostility from liberal academics and support from con-servative theorists." Herrnstein was a good example of another impor-tant aspect of academia, having a powerful mentor, in his case Harvard behaviorist B. F. Skinner. Herrnstein was Skinner's star pupil while doing his Ph.D. and then joined Skinner at Harvard. His doctoral work consisted of classic behavioral studies showing that animals responded in direct proportion to the level of the reward, usually food, they were offered for doing something specific. But when he moved on to intelli-gence, Herrnstein stirred up the proverbial hornet's nest. Unlike Dr. Coleman, whose work had profound and ultimately disastrous real-life consequences for millions of Americans, Dr. Herrnstein mainly made a lot of people angry. His very ideas were distressing, especially to black Americans, who were hearing that slavery and Jim Crow were irrelevant to their poor standing in the American social sphere. Moreover, his views were contrary to a great many American beliefs. Biology was destiny? Not hard work? Not good education? Not loving parents?

With each succeeding book (concluding with *The Bell Curve*) advancing his basic thesis that "an inborn lack of ability would bar those of low IQ from career success, creating a 'biological stratifica-tion' into castes created on 'hereditary meritocracy,'" Herrnstein churned up more hostility. One suspects that but for Herrnstein's tenure, Harvard might have been glad to see such a hot potato move elsewhere. But the *Times* reported that Herrnstein had been "regarded with respect because . . . he understood and honored data," according to fellow psy-chologist Jerome Kagan.

Probably the most famous of our *New York Times* obits professors is Carl Sagan, a Cornell astronomer who "became one of the nation's best-known scientists by enthusiastically conveying the wonders of the uni-verse to millions of people on television and books." Unlike Vickery, the Nobel Prize economist, who had had a terrible time interesting any-one in his ideas about traffic, Sagan developed a vast following who yearned to hear his every thought about the universe. First of all, Sagan was absolutely passionate about his subject. By the time Sagan was twelve, he had already told his New York working-class family that he planned to be an astronomer. As he made his way up the academic food chain, earning his Ph.D. in astronomy and astrophysics from the University of Chicago, working at Berkeley, Harvard, and finally Cornell, Sagan wrote constantly, churning out more than six hundred scientific papers as well as popular articles. He was a wonderful writer, winning rave reviews and huge popular audiences for *Cosmos* and his Pulitzer Prize–winning *The Dragons of Eden: Speculations on the Evolution of Human Intelligence*. But above all, Sagan was handsome and telegenic. He understood that if you want to communicate in a big way today, you must do it on television. While other academics looked on with mixed disgust and envy, Sagan became a regular (twenty-six appearances) on *The Tonight Show* in the Johnny Carson era. "The show has an audience of 10 million people," said Sagan. "That's an awful lot of people, and those aren't people who subscribe to *Scientific American*." Moreover, the viewers were also the taxpayers whose dollars funded space science. When his book *Cosmos* was made into a thirteen-part PBS series, Sagan was able to discuss "everything from the world of the atom to the vastness of the universe" before an amazing 400 million people in sixty countries, the most widely viewed short-term television show until Ken Burns's *The Civil War* came along.

However, Sagan's great trump card was that he believed, along with many Americans, that "E.T." was really out there somewhere. Reported the *Times*, "Civilized life must be common in the universe, he said, because stars are so abundant and the Sun is a fairly typical star." Here was a brilliant scientist with terrific professional credentials agreeing with regular folks that aliens were almost certainly out there. Who could not be charmed by an astronomer who oversaw the space version of a message in a bottle thrown into the sea? As a part of NASA's *Voyager* team, Sagan had attached to the outside of that spacecraft "a 12-inch copper phonograph record inserted in an aluminum protective jacket. . . . It included greetings in many languages and from whales, a 12-minute sound essay, 90 minutes of music and a series of blips to be decoded into black-and-white and color photographs." Of course, it doesn't take a rocket scientist to understand why millions flocked to hear Sagan rhapsodize about the mysteries and wonders of space, while economist Vickery could interest no one in solving traffic jams and rush-hour snarls. Sagan's ideas offered romance, the vast unknown, all distant and wonderful, whereas Vickery just wanted people to relive their horrid, hopeless commute. Some ideas are intrinsically more enthralling than others.

While Carl Sagan became personally famous for making the universe more accessible, Lyman Spitzer, Jr., created a machine that is famous for doing the same. He was the "visionary theoretician of astrophysics and plasma physics who inspired the Hubble Space Telescope." Because the space telescope has generated a whole series of astonishing images and with them new knowledge, it is rather satisfying to learn of its origins. Spitzer was a very bright boy from Toledo, Ohio, whose father owned a paper box–manufacturing company. Spitzer had an elite education at Phillips Andover Academy and Yale and earned his Ph.D. in astrophysics at Princeton. He was one of the wartime science mandarins, in his case helping develop sonar. After the war, Spitzer went to Princeton to run its astronomy department and immediately began proposing some kind of space telescope. It took a few years, but an experimental model called Project Stratoscope was launched in 1954. Carried by balloons, it took cameras twenty miles high.

From that time on, Dr. Spitzer lobbied relentlessly for a space-based telescope. The truly successful scientist-professor is one who has not only powerful ideas but also the political clout to push them through. It took Spitzer decades, but NASA finally sent the Hubble into orbit in 1990. This $2.1 billion project was, wrote the *Times*, "the most complex and costliest undertaking in unmanned space study. It represented big science, conducted by battalions of scientists, engineers and technicians amid fierce competition and bureaucratic encumbrances."

But the Hubble was by no means Spitzer's only passion. He spent much of his career leading Princeton's Plasma Physics Laboratory, a pioneer in the as-yet-unsuccessful effort to create clean nuclear fusion by "replicating the process that makes the sun shine." The goal was clean, unlimited energy. Professor Spitzer once said of himself, "I have a weakness of character—a fascination with the spectacular. But then I have a sort of theory about our weaknesses being our strengths."

The essence of the academy is developing new knowledge and from that knowledge developing new ideas, new theories, new interpretations. For a businessperson, success is measured by the bottom line: how big did a company grow, how much money did it earn? For inventors, success is measured in numbers of patents, products developed, and the importance of those products. For academics, success is based on the power and influence of their intellect and their ideas, which are often—but not always—rewarded by tenured appointments at the nation's most elite schools. Successful academics advance and solidify their standing by writing important journal articles, editing leading journals in their fields, publishing books or textbooks, and energizing their professional organizations or organizing new ones. Many never seek any wider renown, perfectly happy to be stars in their own specialized world, be it electrical engineering or English literature. But those who seek to influence or educate the general public generally look to relevant governmental or cultural organizations to help reach much wider audiences.

Linda Schele, a University of Texas professor of art who "helped revolutionize Mayan scholarship" exemplifies the successful academic. She is also that much-admired American creature, the late bloomer. A studio art teacher at the University of Southern Alabama, she first visited Mayan ruins in 1970 with her architect husband, who, long fascinated by all things pre-Columbian, had proposed a trip to Mexico. Always a doer, Schele recruited three students to help photograph the sites to flesh out her art department's research slides. Their first stop was the city of Palenque. Reported the *Times*, "Dr. Schele was so taken with the breathtaking beauty of the site and so enthralled by the scholars she encountered there that the two-hour visit stretched to twelve days. By the time she got back to Mobile she had a new life's work."

And so, at the age of almost thirty, Dr. Schele began working on her doctorate in Latin American studies (still at the University of Alabama), including studying at Palenque or other sites. The conventional scholarly wisdom on the Mayans, whose heyday was the first thousand years after Christ, portrayed them as peaceable, highly advanced stargazers whose splendid monuments were covered with religious carvings and glyphs recording complex astronomical observations. Established scholars scoffed at those who suggested the glyphs might be anything obvious such as words, much less syllables of words.

But Dr. Schele and other younger scholars quickly showed that the glyphs were indeed syllables that formed words and that the fabulous Palenque monument carvings "provided an incredibly detailed history of the Palenque dynasty." For more than a dozen years, Dr. Schele was working with others to compile new translations from numerous sites that provided greater and greater details about this previously mysterious civilization. But the public did not quite appreciate these extraordinary advances until Schele helped organize a major exhibit at the Kimball Art Museum in Fort Worth in 1986. The Mayans turned out to be "a warring nation who tortured and sometimes sacrificed their captives, whose nobles engaged in blood-letting rituals to placate their gods and whose king was required to stick a rod through the shaft of his own penis on ceremonial occasions." Schele set out this fascinating new history in several books written with others, including *The Blood of Kings, A Forest of Kings,* and *The Code of Kings.* Always admired as an energetic dynamo, she was also known for being generous and helpful to others. She had even begun holding "workshops to teach the Mayan descendants how to read the language of their ancestors."

The story of a Linda Schele is wonderfully inspiring and romantic, because it suggests that our life's work does not always reveal itself right away. (Not many of us can declare at age twelve that astronomy is our destiny!) Another inspiring life story is that of Albert W. Tucker, a Princeton mathematician whose "ideas and teaching influenced economics and business in the postwar era." First off, Tucker came from a poor family in Ontario, Canada. And while his father had taught math before becoming a minister, Tucker was not obviously destined for scholarly greatness. He had to repeat his senior year of high school in the hope of upping his score on a state scholarship exam. He attended the University of Toronto and then moved on to Princeton for his doctorate. From the start, Tucker displayed no inclination to truckle to the senior faculty. In his first year as a graduate student, he so annoyed a professor that he was almost kicked out. His transgression? Protesting that the professor he was helping to teach calculus was moving too fast, failing to allow the students to grasp the material. A dean who mediated the dispute promoted Tucker.

Not surprisingly, Professor Tucker became a beloved mentor to a whole generation of great mathematicians. One described the math department of Tucker's era as "electric with ideas and the sheer joy of the hunt. . . . If a stray 10-year-old with bare feet, no tie, torn blue jeans and an interesting theorem walked into Fine Hall at teatime, someone would have listened." John Forbes Nash, Jr., one of the first generation of game theorists and a Nobel Prize winner in economics, recalled how Tucker championed his thesis work in the face of the formidable disapproval of Professor John Von Neumann, one of mathematics' great stars.

Not only was Tucker a great teacher and mentor, he made significant contributions to his field. And he did it after age forty-five, very rare among mathematicians. Tucker's subject was linear programming, a method of allocating scarce resources that was developed to address the military's logistical problems. Said the *Times*, "It is now used by the AT&T Corporation to design communications networks, by oil companies to run refineries and by the Navy to route its supply ships." With most of our academics, we can point very directly to their influence on our world. But Tucker's intellectual and mentoring accomplishments have filtered into daily life through the work of many other people.

Physics, math, history, and astronomy are familiar academic fields. But weather? Yes, the glory of higher education is that all spheres of knowledge are potentially fair game. Verner E. Suomi was a meteorologist at the University of Wisconsin at Madison "who developed weather-forecasting technology that makes it easier to plan space missions, agricultural irrigation and family picnics." Suomi was yet another one whose whole life direction was changed by World War II. At the start of that conflict, Suomi, a junior high school science teacher, enrolled in a civil air patrol course that included basic weather instruction. Captivated by heat, rain, and wind, he enrolled at the University of Chicago to study weather while teaching the subject to wartime flyers. His doctorate was the sort of work that makes nonacademics scoff: a study of sunshine falling on a field of corn. But Suomi realized from this close observation that "the entire planet Earth is simply one big cornfield, getting and losing heat and moisture—making weather—in ways that might be measured and predicted, if scientists were observant and their instruments precise."

His great gift to the world was the spin-scan camera that, when attached to a satellite circling twenty-five thousand miles above the globe, could send back photos that "revolutionized weather forecasting and studies of the earth's atmosphere." When a weatherperson on TV analyzes the images swirling over a continent, that is Suomi's legacy. He served briefly as chief scientist for the U.S. Weather Bureau and then went to Madison and cofounded the Space Science and Engineering Center. Suomi became the 103d recipient of the Franklin Medal, thereby joining such august company as Thomas Edison, Albert Einstein, and Orville Wright.

Of course, people who value knowledge and ideas above all else inevitably clash with those who passionately see the field a bit—or a lot—differently. According to the *Times*, Dr. Suomi "carried on a celebrated 30-year feud" with another meteorologist who had been such a close friend that they had helped each other build their houses. "Their rift appeared to grow from different approaches, with [the other] more interested in theory and Dr. Suomi in data-gathering, and from the storms generated by two towering egos."

Academics who successfully challenge much-cherished common-sense understandings of human experience provide a necessary reminder that life is not as simple as it might appear. Julian Simon, an economist who taught business at the University of Maryland, delighted in "taking on scientists, demographers and other academics who argued that mankind was stretching the resources of the earth to the breaking point." Professor Simon, who had both an M.B.A. and a doctorate in business economics from the University of Chicago, initially focused on mail-order marketing. But then he became interested in the issue of finite resources and challenged those who were predicted doom and gloom. His position was this: "First, humanity's condition will improve in just about every material way. Second, humans will continue to sit around complaining about everything getting worse."

Professor Simon was a professional optimist and contrarian. In 1980, he made what was to become a very famous wager about the consequences of the fast-rising world population. On one side was Stanford ecologist Paul R. Ehrlich, whose 1968 book *The Population Bomb* had predicted that "one-fifth of humanity would starve to death by 1985." Ehrlich bet that certain raw materials would become much more expensive as world demand rose. The *Times* described the wager thus: "The Ehrlich group bet $1,000 on five metals—chrome, copper, nickel, tin, and tungsten—in quantities that each cost $200 in October 1980, when the bet was made." If the prices rose, as the Malthusians expected, Mr. Simon would pay the difference. If the prices dropped, Ehrlich would. During the 1980s, the world population soared by 800 million, even as the store of these metals stayed the same. But their prices dropped, obligating Erhlich to eat humble pie and mail Simon a check for $576.07. He then declined Professor Simon's offer of another bet, this for $20,000.

Amos Tversky was a Stanford University cognitive psychologist who "changed the way experts in many fields think about how people make decisions about risks, benefits and probabilities." He and his wife and colleague, Barbara Tversky, showed that people were prone to finding "patterns and connections that were not really there" and proceeded to base their decisions on those. One famous 1988 study after the NBA play-offs showed that, contrary to the widespread belief, there was no "hot hand" in basketball, meaning that once a player had made a basket, he was no more likely to get another one. Yet fans liked to believe that, and so they did.

The Tverskys showed again and again that human decision making is far less rational than one might expect. One example they used was a person who had bought a ten-dollar theater ticket, gets to the theater, and realizes she has lost the ticket and will have to purchase another. At the same time, another person arrives at the box office to buy a ten-dollar ticket and realizes he has lost ten dollars in cash. The Tverskys showed that the person who had lost the ticket was unlikely to buy another, while the person who had lost the ten dollars was likely to go ahead and buy a ticket. Both would have been out the same amount—ten dollars—but they viewed the loss differently, and certainly not rationally.

Tversky grew up in Israel before emigrating to the United States to get a doctorate at the University of Michigan in 1965. He certainly had much firsthand experience with risk, fighting in the Israeli Army in three wars (in 1956, 1967, and 1973), and winning the highest honors for his bravery in rescuing a fellow soldier who had frozen in place after going out to set off an explosive.

All of our *New York Times* academics have been important for their ideas, but they followed a variety of paths in disseminating that knowledge and encouraging further work in their field. John W. Hall was a "missionaries' child who became a pioneer in the field of Japanese studies . . . an academic entrepreneur building up the fledgling field." Born in Kyoto, Japan, in 1916, Hall lived in Japan until he went off to prep school at Phillips Andover. Before then, a visit to the United States had driven home how foreign, remote, and unknown Japan was to Americans. Hall would make it his life's work to help the two countries get to know each other better, work made far more urgent by World War II and its aftermath. Hall graduated from Amherst College with a degree in American Studies, spent two years at Doshisha University in Japan, and then returned to be one of Japan scholar Edwin O. Reischauer's first graduate students at Harvard.

After World War II, Professor Hall became director of the Center for Japanese Studies at the University of Michigan. He also arranged to go to Japan to begin studying the actual records of one of the dynasties that had ruled feudal Japan from 1600 to 1868. Hall and other scholars showed that this had been not just a feudal era of masters and serfs but the beginning of modern industrialized Japan. Hall would set much of the postwar agenda of Japanese studies by organizing a massive six-volume work on the evolution of modern Japan authored by numerous historians. In 1961, he went to Yale and published his magnum opus, *Government and Local Power in Japan, 500 to 1700*. It was hailed as opening up more than a thousand years of Japanese history to the West. "Scholarly books rarely have a shelf life of more than a generation," said one colleague, "but this is a book that has always been on my syllabus and probably always will be."

Once at Yale, Professor Hall became a busy activist, trying to enlist foundations, other universities, and the Japanese government in support of Japanese studies. He was founder and chairman of the Japan–United States Friendship Committee and worked closely with the Japan Foundation, a Japanese government–supported entity in New York City. Eventually, the foundation gave $1 million to ten universities to support the field. The Japanese government honored him for his bridge building between the two nations with the Order of the Sacred Treasure, described as a scholarly knighthood. In this country, he was awarded the American Historical Association's award for scholarly distinction. And he certainly could look around and see the fruits of his life's work: new organizations, many up-and-coming scholars, and two major books.

A man like John Hall seems destined to be a Japan scholar. But James E. B. Breslin was a very different story. A Brooklyn native, he attended college there, then obtained a doctorate in English literature at the University of Minnesota. Breslin made quite a name for himself in the field of modern American poetry, writing essays and books, including a well-thought-of biography of William Carlos Williams. But then, in 1979, he had an epiphany. In New York and feeling desolate over the end of his first marriage, he wandered into a show of the paintings of Mark Rothko. He was captivated by Rothko's work. The paintings, he would later write, "create an empathetic space in which to confront emptiness and loss; they create environments for mourning."

Breslin finished a book on poetry that had long been in the works and then threw himself into a completely new endeavor, something that had nothing to do with poetry: a biography of Mark Rothko. For eight years, he immersed himself in art history and Rothko's work, even traveling to remotest Latvia to see where the great painter had grown up. When *Mark Rothko: A Biography* was published in 1993, longtime *New York Times* art critic Hilton Kramer proclaimed it "the best life of an American painter that has yet been written." Long respected, Breslin now vaulted to a new level of prestige, particularly because he was that rare academic creature—someone who had changed his field in mid-career. He became a beacon for others, explained a younger Berkeley colleague, because he had reinvented himself.

Bluma L. Trell also reinvented herself, becoming a classicist in her thirties after deciding that being a lawyer was dull. Professor Trell was hailed not only for her studies of ancient Greek architecture based on coins, but for her extraordinary teaching skills. The *New York Times* described a small woman with gray hair elegantly roped around her head. "Once Dr. Trell opened her mouth [and] got her arms moving . . . [she] began expounding on the intricacies of Greek culture, literature and the language with a passion few encountered in a teacher before or since." Her introductory Greek classes became legendary, as well they might, for they culminated with the students performing an ancient Greek play in "flawlessly enunciated Greek" garbed in homemade costumes and with homemade sets. Nor were her college students her only students. For fifty years, she led a group of friends in a once-a-week Greek reading group that worked its way through Homer, Hesiod, and other great writers of the ancient world.

Her academic specialty was the study of Greek coins to determine what certain famous buildings, now long lost, might have looked like. In 1945, she published a book that showed the likely appearance of the Temple of Artemis in Ephesus. Her reconstruction is on display at the British Museum. Almost three decades after that work, she coauthored with British Museum expert Martin Price *Coins and Their Cities: Architecture on the Ancient Coins of Greece, Rome and Palestine*. But ultimately, Professor Trell was that great find for students, a scholar who preferred teaching to research and publishing.

College Presidents

While success for college professors is measured by where they work and the power and influence of their ideas, success for college and university presidents is all about empire building. University presidents wield enormous power, presiding as they do over the educational enterprises that determine the life chances of millions of young people. Any college or university president who leaves behind a bigger, richer, better-thought-of school has achieved recognized success. While there are half a million full-time faculty, there are only some two thousand college presidents.[4] Our *New York Times* database features 101, with 6 being women. Their average obit is almost sixteen inches long. Their prominence as academic leaders in turn makes them sought after to serve on national and international advisory and planning bodies. Three quarters of the presidents held Ph.D.'s, or law or medical degrees. A full third graduated from one of the top fifty schools. The twenty-nine presidents who made our Apex of Fame, shown in Table 6-4, included twelve presidents from the top fifty schools, four of them being Ivy League schools, ten private universities, and seven state or city universities. In this group, 40 percent attended one of the top fifty schools.

Harlan H. Hatcher guided the University of Michigan through "a time of growth that lifted it into the ranks of the nation's elite research universities." While Hatcher presided from 1951 to 1967, enrollment more than doubled from 17,000 to 37,000, while the budget quadrupled, from $44.5 million to $186 million. Empire building means not just bringing in more bodies and money but creating visible legacies: new schools, new buildings. In Hatcher's case, this included new satellite campuses in Dearborn and Flint. But he saw his greatest legacy as a new and ambitious undergraduate library that pioneered long hours and open stacks: "Book circulation figures soared, and more faculty members began to require wider reading by their students."

Eric Walker of Pennsylvania State University came on the scene a bit later, from 1956 to 1970. During his era, enrollment tripled to 40,000, the number of faculty doubled, and more than one hundred new buildings went up, including the Milton S. Hershey Medical Center. Walker was very much a Harvard man, receiving his B.S. in engineering there, an M.B.A., and then a Ph.D. in general science and engineering. He taught at both Tufts and the University of Connecticut before returning to Harvard, where World War II found him "devising new types of torpedoes." The laboratory, the Underwater Sound Laboratory, was split in two, with Walker's group going off to the lush but isolated State College campus of Penn State. He was a productive scholar who wrote more than three hundred publications. One is charmed to read that in 1972 an Antarctic glacial ridge was named for him. Once established in State College, Walker never left the bucolic small-town setting, but he helped dramatically improve higher education for students throughout Pennsylvania.

Harvie Branscomb, chancellor of Vanderbilt University from 1946 to 1963, ambitiously shaped the school into one of the nation's elite institutions. He not only doubled the number of professors but also made the place more attractive by tripling their salaries and vastly expanding the number of buildings. The university budget quadrupled and the endowment more than doubled, reaching $88 million. The schools of engineering, divinity, and law all got their own buildings.

Branscomb was a personal example of the transforming qualities of a top-flight education. A native of Huntsville, Alabama, he received a degree from Birmingham College and then won a Rhodes scholarship to Oxford in the late 1930s. Oxford, where he began his career as a New Testament scholar, opened the doors to Columbia University and a Ph.D. in philosophy. Branscomb was an energetic scholar, publishing four books on the cultural and religious roots of Christianity. When he became chancellor of Vanderbilt, that energy went into building and expanding, creating a southern university that could rival some of the old-line Ivy League schools.

But running a university is inevitably a contentious undertaking, presiding as one does over so many people with ideas and strong beliefs. Branscomb got into headline-making trouble in 1960, when a black divinity student was expelled for leading civil rights sit-ins in Nashville. The president tried to negotiate a compromise of some sort but infuriated the black faculty when he stated, "The law has been the basis for much of the Negro's progress in the past and is the guarantee of their continued progress." The divinity dean and a dozen faculty resigned in outrage, and the student finished up at Boston University. Years later, Branscomb said that "the best course might have been to bury the issue in administrative procedures." (In another part of the country, Hatcher, at the University of Michigan, was condemned as an overly heavy-handed anti-Communist. But a trip to the USSR helped ease those criticisms. University leaders must be nimble walkers through the academic minefields.)

TABLE 6-4. *The Apex of Fame: College Presidents in the Obituary Database*

Name (Age at Death)	Obit Date	College Attended as Undergraduate	College/ Institution of Fame	Obit Length
1. Grayson Kirk (94)	11/22/97	Miami U. (Ohio)	Columbia	71"
2. Mary Bunting-Smith (87)	01/23/98	Vassar	Radcliffe	46"
3. Bob Jones, Jr. (86)	11/13/97	Not named	Bob Jones U.	42"
4. James Nabrit Jr. (97)	12/30/97	Morehouse College	Howard	39"
5. Terry Sanford (80)	04/20/98	U. North Carolina	Duke	38"
6. Jerome Wiesner (79)	10/23/94	Not named	MIT	37"
7. Hugh McKean (86)	05/08/95	Rollins	Rollins	35"
8. Laurence Gould (98)	06/22/95	U. Michigan	Carleton/ Explorer	32"
9. Alan Simpson (85)	05/08/98	Oxford U. (UK)	Vassar	29"
10. Harvie Branscomb (103)	08/01/98	Birmingham-S. Col.	Vanderbilt U.	28"
11. Douglass Cater (72)	09/16/95	Harvard	Washington	27"
12. William McGill (75)	10/21/97	Fordham	Columbia	25"
13. James Perkins (86)	08/22/98	Swarthmore College	Cornell	25"
14. Walter Ridley (86)	11/03/96	Howard U.	Elizabeth City College	24"
15. Richard Ruopp (65)	11/30/97	Iowa Wesleyan U.	Bank Street College	24"

Name (Age at Death)	Obit Date	College Attended as Undergraduate	College/ Institution of Fame	Obit Length
16. Dean McHenry (87)	03/30/98	UCLA	UC Santa Cruz	24"
17. Leon Goldstein (66)	01/10/99	CCNY	Kingsborough City College (NYC)	24"
18. Joseph Murphy (64)	01/19/98	Olivet (Michigan)	CUNY	23"
19. William McElroy (82)	02/21/99	Stanford	UCSD/NSF	23"
20. Julius Stratton (93)	06/24/94	MIT	MIT	22"
21. Albert Bush-Brown (68)	07/25/94	Princeton U.	Long Island U.	22"
22. Samuel Gould (86)	07/16/97	Bates	SUNY	22"
23. Edgar Shannon, Jr. (79)	08/26/97	Washington and Lee U.	U. Virginia	22"
24. Harlan Hatcher (99)	03/04/98	Ohio State U.	U. Michigan	22"
25. W. Wallis (85)	10/14/98	U. Minnesota	U. Rochester	22"
26. Robert Marston (76)	03/16/99	VMI	U. Florida/NIH	22"
27. Leo McLaughlin (84)	08/18/96	Georgetown U.	Fordham U.	21"
28. Rodney Felder (69)	01/26/97	SUNY—Albany	Finch College, (NYC)*	21"
29. Richard Cyert (77)	10/10/98	U. Minnesota	Carnegie Mellon U.	20"

* Finch College, a women's college, closed in the 1970s.

Note: There were 110 college presidents in the database. Of these, 103 were men and 7 were women.

Leaders in higher education are much in demand beyond their own campuses. And one suspects that in the interest of future fund-raising it is well worth the trouble to serve, as did Branscomb, as chairman of the U. S. Commission for UNESCO, as an educational consultant to the World Bank, and on numerous international bodies aimed at countering illiteracy and promoting education.

Lee Alvin DuBridge was a great empire builder at the California Institute of Technology, or Caltech. While he served as president from 1946 to 1969, the size of the campus tripled to ninety acres, the endowment quintupled to $100 million, the faculty doubled to 550, the number of buildings tripled to sixty-four, and the budget went up almost fourfold, to $30 million. The two-hundred-inch Hale Telescope on Mount Palomar opened during his tenure, as did the Jet Propulsion Laboratory. As if that were not enough for one man, DuBridge was also the founder of the local public television station and helped launch the California Museum of Science and Industry. Here was a man who understood that education should flourish beyond the campus.

DuBridge was born in Terre Haute, Indiana, and graduated from a small Iowa college before going on to take a graduate degree in physics at the University of Wisconsin. He taught at the University of Rochester and supervised construction of its cyclotron. During the war, he went to MIT to work on radar. The project was a great success and established DuBridge as an impressive administrator. With the war over, he headed west to Caltech, which was being overwhelmed with masses of new students who were too much for its facilities. Within four years of his arrival, President Harry S. Truman named him to the President's Science Advisory Committee, which he then chaired until 1958, when it became a full-time job. It was a job he would hold again for eighteen months under Richard M. Nixon after he retired from Caltech.

For those in tenured positions, being a professor is a high-status, low-risk occupation with great security and longevity. Fame (and the potential for wealth) comes through publishing outstanding papers or books and moving up the career ladder to prestigious universities. The academics in our Apex of Fame were mostly at major institutions, especially the Ivy League. However, overall, the professors in our chapter were those who were active and influential beyond the academy. The successful college presidents were generally empire builders at important schools.

Notes

1. Andrew Hacker, *Money* (New York: Touchstone Books, 1997), p. 137.
2. Ibid.
3. *Statistical Abstract of the United States, 1998*, Table 250.
4. In 1995, there were 2,244 four-year colleges in the United States: *Statistical Abstract of the United States, 1998*, Table 306.

7

Successful Publishers and Authors

Seminal Conservative Author

Helped Millions Take SATs

Saw Talent Others Didn't

The paperback revolution in publishing was truly that: a dramatic break with the past that forever changed the world of books. Traditionally, Americans who wanted to read a book had two options: to purchase an expensive hardcover book in a bookstore or borrow it from a public library. Thanks to publishing pioneers such as Ian Ballantine, Americans in the years after World War II enjoyed a cornucopia of paperback books sold at a fraction of the hardcover price and readily available in department stores, in drugstores, on newsstands, and in train and bus stations. Moreover, the rise of paperbacks stimulated whole new kinds of books—everything from enthralling mystery series such as Perry Mason to easy-to-carry nature guides. This, said one longtime publisher, was where Ian and Betty Ballantine made "their most distinctive contributions. They really helped make the genres of science fiction, western and mystery true mass market best sellers by nurturing a whole generation of novelists." When the couple ran Ballantine Books, they published the works of science fiction masters Ray Bradbury and Arthur C. Clarke and introduced beloved fantasist J. R. R. Tolkien, author of *The Hobbit* and *Lord of the Rings*.

In this chapter we look at the most influential and successful publishers, editors, and, above all, authors featured in the *New York Times* obituaries. These are the men and women who changed the face of books and reading in the United States over the last few decades. While the 457 authors do not make up a big percentage of the overall database, not even 5 percent, their average length of coverage—sixteen inches—puts them fifth in importance, after members of Congress, singers, judges, and actors and actresses. A striking 30 percent were women (almost double the rate of the overall database), reflecting the fact that writing is utterly democratic and grassroots, requiring no special training or degrees. Considering that these are America's top writers, it is interesting to see that while most attended college, only just over half earned a degree, as shown in Table 7-1. Just under a quarter of the group held some sort of advanced degree. Half of the men and a third of the women went to one of the top fifty colleges; almost 60 percent of those attended Ivy League schools. There was no education information in the obits for almost a quarter of the database group.

Despite the great rise in new kinds of media—everything from television to the Internet—books remain the enduring form of transmitting knowledge. Books are simple to use, last a long time, and can be read repeatedly. We still depend on books to introduce us to new information, entertain us in our idle hours, and connect our thinkers, dreamers, and storytellers to the wider populace. While many people author books, successful writers such as we find in the *New York Times* obits constitute a very small, elite group. The Authors Guild is the nation's biggest and most prestigious organization promoting and protecting the interests of writers. It has only 7,400 members. Unlike becoming a doctor, lawyer, or engineer, writing books requires nothing more than ambition, talent, and perseverance. Succeeding at it is another matter.

For writers, success can take two forms. They can be critically successful, their books highly praised and viewed as important—either from a literary standpoint or because they contribute new and important information and ideas. Or they can be popular successes, their books gaining little critical approbation while selling well or better than well. Sometimes important books are also popular successes. Most in our group were best-selling authors who also made millions of dollars from their work. To put this into perspective, only 5 percent of the titles that appear in bookstores sell more than five thousand copies.

TABLE 7-1. *Education of the Authors in the Obituary Database*

Education	Number*	Percent
High school or less	13	3.8
Some college	77	22.4
College graduate (no higher degree)	145	42.2
Master's or equivalent degree	62	18.0
Ph.D.	29	8.4
Law degree or M.D.	18	5.2
Total	**344**	**100.0**

* There were 457 authors in the database. Adequate information about their highest education was available in the obituaries of 344 (75 percent). Of those with adequate information, 74 percent were college graduates and 32 percent earned a graduate degree.

Ian Ballantine was not the first to introduce paperbacks to the United States. That was the work of Robert de Graff, who launched Pocket Books in 1939. But right on his heels came the Ballantines, who began selling Penguin paperbacks. When America entered World War II, the Ballantines worked closely with the U.S. military to make twenty-five-cent paperbacks easily available to soldiers. Wrote Betty Ballantine, "As the war wound down, the returning service men and women, habituated to the easy access and casual use of books, expected to find them just as readily available in civilian life. Moreover, in post-war America, thousands upon thousands of men and women went to college or school under the GI Bill of Rights. . . . Books became a familiar part of the 'baby-boom generation.'"[1]

Initially, these pioneering paperback enterprises simply printed cheaper editions of successful hardcover books that sold, for example, for twenty-five cents rather than two dollars. Early Penguin releases included such classics as H. G. Wells's *The Invisible Man* and P. G. Wodehouse's *My Man Jeeves*. Ian Ballantine was a New Yorker who graduated from Columbia University, where he wrote a paper explaining the great promise of paperbacks. He then attended the London School of Economics before heading home with his wife, Betty, his lifelong partner in publishing. But it was not until the Ballantines launched Ballantine Books in 1952 that Ian was able to act on his belief that paperbacks could have their own authors and subjects, thus vastly expanding the range of titles and topics. The economics of paperbacks made possible the first megasellers, paperbacks that sold an unheard-of million copies—books such as Dale Carnegie's *How to Win Friends and Influence People* and Dr. Spock's *The Commonsense Book of Baby and Child Care.* Early on, Ian Ballantine also saw the extraordinary power of movie tie-ins and began whenever possible to issue paperbacks, such as John Steinbeck's *The Pearl* and Borden Chase's *Red River,* to coincide with Hollywood openings. All these developments would gradually reshape what had once been a genteel profession—publishing—into a major industry.

The number of books published has exploded in the postwar years from sixteen thousand new titles a year to almost seventy thousand![2] The great bulk of these are paperbacks. Meanwhile, backlists of already published books mean that Americans today can choose from 1.5 million titles listed in R. R. Bowker's *Books in Print.* As we head into the new millennium, Americans are spending $26 billion a year to buy 2.4 billion books, two thirds of them paperbacks.[3] But however big a business publishing has become, as shown in Table 7-2, to a great extent it remains a craft industry dependent on a highly idiosyncratic product. After all, each book represents an enormous amount of time, effort, and commitment by an individual writer, almost always working on his or her own. While word processors have greatly speeded up and eased manuscript (and thus book) production, writing itself remains slow, solitary work.

At the same time that Ian Ballantine was helping create the paperback revolution, Paul Steiner was reshaping the publishing industry with his Chanticleer Press. Unlike Ballantine, whose enthusiasm for the possibilities of paperbacks even in college seemed to destine him for a life in books, Steiner had a more circuitous entry to publishing. A native of Vienna, he had studied law and then worked for a newspaper

TABLE 7-2. *Books Sold in the United States, 1987 and 1996*

Type of Publication	1987	1996
Trade	600,200,000	847,300,000
Adult trade	373,500,000	858,800,000
Juvenile trade	226,700,000	388,500,000
Religious	135,500,000	164,400,000
Professional	135,900,000	163,600,000
Book clubs	123,600,000	135,500,000
Mail-order publications	132,600,000	96,400,000
Mass-market paperbacks	441,400,000	516,300,000
University press	14,700,000	17,400,000
Elementary and high school	216,200,000	255,400,000
College	129,600,000	162,600,000
Subscription reference	1,100,000	1,200,000
Total	**1,930,800,000**	**2,360,100,000***

Source: The New York Times Almanac, 1998, p. 406.

* Of the 2.36 million books sold, 63 percent were paperbound and 27 percent were hardbound. (This does not include mail-order or subscription reference publications.)

publisher there until the Nazis came. He fled in 1939 and once in the United States survived by selling vacuum cleaners and working as a roofer before a Viennese friend who had started a publishing house in London asked him to start an American branch. By 1952, Chanticleer was independent and Steiner had developed a new publishing concept: book packaging. Traditionally, publishers had come up with their own books, which they developed from initial idea to final completed volume. Steiner's press—and the many other packagers who later joined the ranks—would come up with the idea or concept for a book, commission writers, illustrators, and photographers, and then deliver the completed text to a publisher, which took over from there.

One of Steiner's specialties was the illustrated coffee-table book, now a staple of the publishing industry and a much-relied-upon gift-giving solution. Some of his other great successes were illustrated nature guides, including *The National Audubon Society's Field Guide* and the *Pocket Guide* series, both published by Knopf. Both broke new ground by using photographs rather than drawings. Wrote the *New York Times*, "And, in a reflection of Mr. Steiner's acute sense of color and design, they also broke with tradition by grouping birds by size, shape and color rather than by type. It proved a winning formula. More than 10 million of the Audubon guides have been sold."

Books have many different kinds of power; they can charm, inform, solace, enrage, or inspire. Most powerfully, they can reframe how people see society, making new and different what was familiar. Almost anyone who is serious about ideas and changing the world in some fashion will gather his or her information and ideas into a book. But although many authors aspire to become catalysts for change, few succeed. Rachel Carson's *Silent Spring* scored a major triumph as an idea book, becoming the call to arms for the budding environmental movement. Idea books were what interested publisher Henry Regnery, "a one-time New Deal Democrat who became the godfather of modern conservatism as the publisher of the movement's leading theorists." The son of a Chicago "textile magnate," Regnery graduated from MIT, then studied under free market economist Joseph Schumpeter at Harvard. Regnery, who was very much an idea man, dedicated his life and his press to promoting the conservative viewpoint, publishing such well-respected authors as Albert J. Nock and James J. Kirkpatrick, while bringing out paperback versions of novelists and poets such as Wyndham Lewis and T. S. Eliot.

Regnery first came to wide notice when he published William F. Buckley's *God and Man at Yale* in 1951, which so outraged the liberal academy that the University of Chicago huffily canceled its Great Books contract with Regnery. But what truly put Regnery on the map was publishing Russell Kirk's *The Conservative Mind: From Burke to Santayana* in 1953. This was a seminal idea book that the *New York Times* described as being "greeted by conservatives as the second coming of Edmund Burke and providing the underpinning for the later development of conservative thought." Indeed, by 1981 Kirk had indeed seen his ideas triumph. No less than President Ronald Reagan hailed Kirk at a testimonial dinner in Washington, D.C., for helping "renew a generation's interest and knowledge" in the conservative viewpoint.

Russell Kirk is also in our *New York Times* database, having died in 1994. Here was a man, described as "a founder of the modern conservative movement in the United States," who understood the lasting power of the word, especially if printed in a book. He himself wrote more than thirty. *The Conservative Mind* "established his reputation and lent intellectual weight to the budding conservative movement" by arguing that it was not liberal ideas that defined America but conservative thought, as expressed by everyone from John Adams to Nathaniel Hawthorne. Kirk also founded a journal, *Modern Age* and wrote a column for *National Review* for twenty-five years and a syndicated newspaper column for the *Los Angeles Times* for another thirteen years.

From our present vantage point, the rise of the Right may seem predestined, but when Russell Kirk began promoting his ideas, they were anything but common or popular. A native of Michigan, he graduated from Michigan State University and earned a master's degree at Duke University and a doctorate of letters from St. Andrews University in Scotland in 1952. While writing his many books, columns, and essays, he was also "one of the most sought-after speakers on the college lecture circuit." He estimated that he had spoken at more than five hundred schools. What is charming to know about Russell Kirk is that even as he was turning out serious books about fundamental beliefs, he was also writing "works of mystery, suspense and fantasy in such publications as *London Mystery Magazine* and *Fantasy and Science Fiction.*"

As books became ever-bigger business, authors increasingly felt that they needed some heavy artillery in their corner. It came in the form of hard-driving literary agents. Paul Gitlin was a Harvard-trained lawyer and literary agent who "brokered multimillion-dollar deals for authors" and helped reshape "the economics of the book industry . . . when he designed the first combined hardcover-paperback deal by selling Pocket Books' *The Carpetbaggers* by Harold Robbins." Under so-called hard-soft deals, authors end up with bigger royalties from their paperback sales. Gitlin pioneered and promoted the literary auction, which forced publishing houses to pay authors top dollar for their manuscripts. Described as "gruff and charming, Mr. Gitlin was credited by one client, the novelist Irving Wallace, with winning the author a $2.3 million, four-book contract in 1972." Among Gitlin's many big-name clients were Sidney Sheldon, Barbara Taylor Bradford, and Cornelius Ryan. The assumption was that such juicy advances were not only fair compensation to big-time authors but would ensure that publishers gave full efforts to promotion in order to make the books best-sellers.

The best-selling writer is truly a *rara avis*. (For our Apex of Fame of best-selling authors, see Table 7-3.) For the reality is that few writers can even make a living writing books, and for that reason there are very few full-time writers. Most authors teach, are supported by spouses, or have other kinds of jobs. In the mid-1990s, the Authors League Fund, which helps needy writers, commissioned a survey of writers' income. The survey found that a quarter of those contacted had earned nothing from writing the previous year, and 16 percent had made less than $1,000. Only 9 percent had made more than $50,000. The conclusion: "Most established fiction and nonfiction writers and playwrights are not close to being able to support themselves from their writing." In contrast to all other occupations we look at in this book, the great majority of those who produce the "product" for the publishing industry—authors—cannot earn a living from that work.

Big sales and incomes make the successful authors standouts. When we produced the Apex of Fame for authors, we quickly saw that our most famous writers fell into two camps: those who had sold a great many books and those who had garnered much critical praise. So we created two Apexes of Fame, the first for best-selling authors, the second for critically acclaimed ones. Sometimes the best-selling writers also reaped praise, but we still assigned them to our first Apex. What came as something of a surprise was the fancy schools—Harvard, Princeton, Swarthmore, the University of Chicago—many of these popular writers had attended. It is also interesting to see the great variety of what sells, from bird guides to humor to cookbooks to history to novels.

Making the best-seller list became a highly visible sign of success when the *New York Times* began running its best-seller list after World War II.[4] Rare indeed is the writer who has made that list multiple times over the decades. When novelist James Michener died in 1997, his *Times* obit described him as having won the "Pulitzer Prize with his very first book, published when he was about 40," then becoming "one of America's favorite storytellers with grand-scale novels like *Hawaii, The Source* and *Texas*." He was also identified as "one of only eight authors who had written six or more No. 1 best sellers" that had made the *New York Times* best-seller list.

Michener was a foundling raised by a Quaker widow in Doylestown, Pennsylvania. He had very warm memories of this woman, who read to him from nineteenth-century novels, especially Charles Dickens. As a teenager, he would later say, "I bummed across the country on nickels and dimes. Before I was 20, I had seen all the states but Washington, Oregon and Florida. I had an insatiable love of hearing people tell stories and what they didn't tell I made up." He then attended Swarthmore on a scholarship, taught briefly, earned a master's degree from the University of Northern Colorado in Greeley, and then joined Macmillan Publishing in New York as a textbook editor. He had not been there long when Pearl Harbor was attacked. He enlisted in the Navy and spent the war on the Solomon Islands. To pass the hours, he wrote what would become *Tales of the South Pacific*, the book published in 1947 that won the Pulitzer, and became a classic musical and a successful film. It was the wild success of the musical that propelled the book's sales from twenty-five thousand books to 2 million.

Never again did Michener gain such critical acclaim. For his subsequent novels, he immersed himself in the local lore and legend and then "wove big, old-fashioned narratives involving generations of fictional families as they moved through expertly documented events in history." Sprawling stories of Hawaii, the Chesapeake region, Israel, and Texas, they began in prehistory and moved steadily to the present. The books became instant blockbusters, were snapped up by book clubs, made into movies, and sold millions of copies. But the critics were cool. And Michener was equally critical: "Writing is hard for me. I'm weak on

TABLE 7-3. *The Apex of Fame: Best-Selling Authors in the Obituary Database*

Name (Age at Death)	Obit Date	Undergraduate College Attended	Higher Degree	Type of Book
1. Roger Tory Peterson (87)	07/30/96	Art school	No	Bird guides
2. James A. Michener (90)	10/17/97	Swarthmore*	M.A.	Novels
3. William L. Shirer (89)	12/30/93	Coe College*	M.A.	History
4. Marjory Douglas (108)	05/15/98	Wellesley*	No	Nonfiction
5. William H. Whyte (81)	01/13/99	Princeton*	No	Nonfiction
6. Leo Rosten (88)	02/20/97	U. of Chicago*	Ph.D.	Nonfiction
7. Carlos Castaneda (72)	06/20/98	Not named	No	Mystical novels
8. Dorothy West (91)	08/19/98	Boston College, Columbia	No	Novels
9. Cleveland Amory (81)	10/16/98	Harvard*	No	Novels and social history
10. Harold Robbins (81)	10/15/97	None	No	Novels
11. Vance Packard (82)	12/13/96	Penn State*	M.A.	Nonfiction
12. Pierre Franey (75)	10/16/96	Not named	Not named	Cookbooks
13. Jerome Weidman (85)	10/07/98	City College of New York	Studied law	Novels
14. Lucille Kallen (76)	01/21/99	None	No	TV writer
15. Jessica Mitford (78)	07/24/96	None	No	Nonfiction
16. Jeffrey Moss (56)	09/26/98	Princeton*	No	TV shows and books

* Graduated from college.

Major Work	Career Note	Obit Length
Field Guide to the Birds	Rejected by four publishers	84"
Hawaii and others	Came up from bottom; became multimillionaire	78"
The Rise and Fall of the Third Reich	Journalist; later life difficult	60"
The Everglades: River of Grass	Preservation advocate in Florida	60"
The Organization Man	*Fortune* editor	59"
The Education of Hyman Kaplan	Social scientist	54"
The Teachings of Don Juan	"New Age" pioneer	50"
The Wedding	Published best-seller at age 88	50"
Who Killed Society?	Became animal welfare advocate	49"
Never Love a Stranger	Hated by critics	47"
The Hidden Persuaders	Former journalist	41"
5 Cookbooks	Also on TV	39"
I Can Get It for You Wholesale	Also playwright	39"
TV writer for Sid Caesar's show	Part of TV writing team	37"
The American Way of Death	Wrote exposés; from eccentric family	35"
Father of Cookie Monster	Developed *Sesame Street* characters	35"

style, plot and form—all things you're supposed to be good at. Also I start a great deal that I don't finish. But I always have a great backlog I want to write about. I can't ever conceive of running out of ideas. They crowd me." His great strength and gift was basic storytelling. He loved to hear stories and then reweave them into far larger canvases. And tens of millions of people loved to read them.

While the sweeping narrative has long been associated with fiction, in recent decades American journalists have developed a novelistic form of nonfiction that depends on great storytelling. J. Anthony Lukas was a Pulitzer Prize–winning *New York Times* reporter who took this technique and used it in *Common Ground*—a book that won him yet another Pulitzer Prize—about three Boston families dealing with court-ordered school busing. Lukas, an intense, driven man, used the stories of the families to consider the issue of race. Maintaining the drama of the story was so important that halfway through the seven-year process of researching and writing the book, he replaced one family that was not proving sufficiently compelling with another.

Born in New York City, Lukas attended the Putney School and then graduated from Harvard, where he worked on the campus newspaper, *The Harvard Crimson*. He served in the Army and then briefly as a political speechwriter before becoming a journalist at the Baltimore *Sun*. After four years, Lukas went on to a brilliant and distinguished career at the *New York Times,* serving first as a foreign correspondent and then as a national reporter, covering such important stories as the trial of the Chicago Eight and Watergate. He was fascinated by the turmoil of the 1960s and won a Pulitzer Prize for an article about a young, privileged Connecticut girl "beaten to death with her hippie boyfriend, in the East Village. The article contrasted her affluent suburban upbringing with her squalid drug-ridden life in New York City, which her family knew nothing about." During much of the 1970s, Lukas worked as a freelancer before embarking on *Common Ground*. He said, "I firmly believe that any good journalist must essentially be temperamentally an outsider. I don't think a full sense of belonging and security is conducive to creativity." When *Common Ground* was published in 1985, it won not only the Pulitzer but also the National Book Award and the National Book Critics Circle Award. It became a critical success that also sold well.

Lukas's next project was another ambitious, sprawling nonfiction tale, *Big Trouble*, described as "a study of America at the start of the [twentieth] century through the spectacular trial of a labor leader for the murder of the former Idaho governor." Lukas, long prone to depression, hanged himself while working on the final revisions. His agent lamented, "He'd convinced himself that it was not good enough, which was crazy because it was brilliant."

While many people buy books to be swept away by a great yarn, fiction or non, for many readers books serve a very practical purpose. Hence, the booming how-to/advice category. In a society dedicated to self-improvement and the pursuit of happiness and success, there was a huge (and often untapped) audience of readers for these new kinds of volumes. Certainly Dale Carnegie and Dr. Spock, with their million-sellers, had demonstrated people's intense interest in doing things right and expanding their skills. How-to books became such a major category in publishing that in the 1980s they were assigned their own separate *New York Times* best-seller list.

Samuel C. Brownstein was a man who loved to teach and, better yet, to tutor. He liked helping those who were having trouble with something get better at whatever they needed to know. And at a time when far more Americans were beginning to pursue higher education, he also helped create a whole new book category. He was "best known as the man who guided millions of high school seniors through the treacherous terrain of the Scholastic Aptitude Test as the coauthor of *Barron's How to Prepare for the S.A.T.*" There are many different routes to authorship; Brownstein's was via the New York public schools, where he and another high school teacher realized in the early 1950s that "mastering subjects in the classroom was not enough to assure admission to the better colleges." So they began to offer after-school classes on how best to prepare for these all-important college entrance exams. By the time they were teaching ten such after-school workshops, publisher Manuel H. Barron heard of them. His young company specialized in educational guides and test preparation, all aimed at a nation ever more dedicated to higher education. In 1952, Barron asked them to put their class into print. Their first book was *Barron's How to Prepare for the College Entrance Examinations*. Said the *New York Times*, "A new industry was born."

Many other companies flooded a market soon overflowing with anxious baby boomers and their parents. But for over forty years Brownstein and *Barron's* would remain preeminent best-sellers. Brownstein's first effort—eventually retitled to focus on the SAT—went into eighteen editions and sold 4 million copies. He had another eighteen titles in print dealing with everything from the Graduate Record Examination to the High School Equivalency Examination.

Another major how-to/self-help category in recent years has been diet books. This is no surprise in a nation where half of us are fat to obese but our popular culture idolizes slender to skinny. And so hope springs eternal that one can shed those pounds (even though reliable research shows that almost all pounds shed will be in time regained—the old yo-yo syndrome). Dr. Stuart M. Berger was a Manhattan doctor who tapped into this yearning as an "author of best-selling diet and health books." Catering to the perennial American fascination with nutrition and diet, he shot to number one bestsellerdom in 1985 (in the advice/how-to list) with *Dr. Berger's Immune Power Diet*. When his book came out, Berger was his own best exhibit, a six foot seven-and-a-half-inch man who had shed 210 pounds, dropping from 420 pounds to 210 by following his own diet. Most of his books, explained the *New York Times*, "advocated healing and dieting techniques based on nutrition and improving the strength of the body's immune system. He also contended that his programs would result in increased longevity." Dr. Berger, educated at Harvard and Tufts, churned out other such books, including *Forever Young—20 Years Younger in 20 Weeks: Dr. Berger's Step-by-Step Rejuvenation Program* and *How to Be Your Own Nutritionist*. All of which would be pretty standard for the diet gurus, *except* that Dr. Berger died at age forty (causes not determined at time of autopsy), weighing 365 pounds. As if all that were not sad enough, the State Board for Professional Medical Conduct had been on his case for several years over allegations having to do with his Central Park West medical practice.

Harvey Penick topped the *New York Times'* how-to/advice best-seller list also, but he did it in 1992 with "the best-selling sports book in history when he was 87 years old." Who was this elderly athlete? A "long-time guru in the golf world," the head pro at the Austin County Club for forty-eight years and the teacher and mentor to such golf greats as Ben Crenshaw and Tom Kite, the latter being the "leading tour money-winner in golf history with more than $9 million." Apparently, for sixty years Harvey Penick had "scribbled in his little red book at the end of the day his thoughts on the course he had been on, anecdotes about the people he coached, and tips on how to play the game better. Example: 'Sit next to good golfers at dinner time; their confidence will help make you a better putter.'" His book, *Harvey Penick's Little Red Book: Lessons and Teachings from a Lifetime in Golf* sold 1.3 million copies. Penick became an author simply because he mentioned his lifelong jottings to a former sports journalist who suggested they collaborate on a book. In such unlikely ways do best-selling books wend their way to the shelves!

What the paperback revolution revealed was a vast untapped audience of people who were not regular book buyers but might be enticed by the right material. Of course, what that material is is the perennial question in publishing, especially when an author or agent is proposing a topic that has no track record: Who will buy this book? Will it sell? Might it even be that hoped-for thing—a blockbuster? Certainly no one was expecting much when an unknown freelance writer named Linda Goodman published an astrology book titled *Sun Signs* with publisher Taplinger in 1968. It became the first such book to make the *New York Times'* best-seller list. Like Brownstein and his SAT prep books, Goodman's work revealed a huge appetite for a field hitherto untouched by publishing, but in her case it was astrology and mystical matters. Ultimately her three astrology books would sell more than 30 million copies in fifteen languages. Moreover, these books have the wondrous quality of being evergreen and still sell a total of 200,000 copies each year! Explained the *New York Times*, "What set Mrs. Goodman's books apart was a combination of her sharp insights and her elegant, accessible style. Writing in the first person and drawing on the lives of celebrities, historical figures and personal friends to illustrate her points, Mrs. Goodman sometimes seemed more psychologist than astrologer."

Born an Aries in Morgantown, West Virginia, Goodman was always a writer and led an itinerant life working at a variety of newspapers and radio stations. She became interested in astrology through reading the little booklets sold in grocery stores. She and her second husband were living in New York City, when his radio job fell through. Goodman began writing *Sun Signs* to make some money. She was forty-three when it was published and hit the best-seller lists. Five years later her daughter committed suicide, but, drawing on astrology, Goodman refused to accept that the dead girl was her daughter, believing that she had simply disappeared. Goodman became so distraught and spent so much money searching for her child that she became homeless for a time, living for several months on the steps of St. Patrick's Cathedral on Fifth Avenue. But she recovered and went on to write her second and third blockbuster books, *Love Signs* and *Star Signs*.

Leo Buscaglia was another blockbuster best-selling writer out of left field, a onetime professor who became "the bearded self-help author and cuddly television guru who preached love with such single-minded fervor that he seemed unable to stop until he had hugged everyone in sight." He wrote fifteen books about the benefits of love, "five of which were once on the *New York Times* best-seller lists at one time, and which together have sold more than 10 million copies."

Dr. Buscaglia was born in Italy and emigrated to Los Angeles when he was five. He served in the U.S. Navy during World War II, returned to California, and attended the University of Southern California, ultimately earning a doctorate in language and speech pathology. He was then a speech therapist in the California school system until he was promoted to administration. He hated being away from the classroom and quit to join his alma mater and teach in the education division. When one of his favorite students committed suicide, Dr. Buscaglia was so distressed that he decided to teach an unofficial course on the joys of life called Love 1. He figured fifty students would enroll, but six hundred appeared. Thus was launched Dr. Love. The course became the most popular at the university and then a favorite on the lecture circuit.

A perspicacious New Jersey publisher of health books sensed a winner when he heard Dr. Love speak at an education conference. He persuaded him to write what became *Love*, the first of the professor's many popular titles. Soon Dr. Buscaglia was picked up by public television, a huge boon to sales. While the love-thy-neighbor philosophy is not new, Dr. Buscaglia felt that humans could never be reminded too often of the power of plain old love. Wrote the *Times*, "If his popularity made him something of a cult hero, Dr. Buscaglia shunned the role. He wasn't a preacher seeking a congregation, he said, but a teacher trying to inspire people to be, and, yes, love, their individual selves." He traced his own loving ebullience to his "sprawling, high-spirited" family, with his mother singing at the stove as she piled steaming spaghetti high on a platter. Sadly, this loving man left only one survivor: his sister.

Books, especially fiction, have an almost magical ability to connect us with places we want to be, situations we want to experience. Is our daily life humdrum? Our spouse a bit wanting? Romance novels can spice it up. Perhaps it should not be surprising, when Dr. Love sells millions of books about being more loving, that an entire gigantic genre has developed to deliver more romance to a vast (female) audience. But today half of all mass-market paperbacks are romance novels. Preeminent among that genre's authors was Eugenia Price, "the South's most popular writer of antebellum romantic fiction," selling 40 million books in eighteen languages.

Price's story was itself fascinating. A dentist's daughter from Charleston, West Virginia, she went off to Ohio University at age sixteen and then dutifully studied dentistry at Northwestern University before throwing it over to become a writer. First she wrote soap operas, moving from Chicago to New York. Then her life took an unusual turn: in the late 1940s, she became an ardent Christian. She wrote two dozen inspirational books, including *Discoveries, Beloved World,* and *The Eugenia Price Treasury of Faith,* that garnered her a large and faithful readership. Then in 1960, while on a promotional tour, she and her longtime companion, an editor named Joyce Blackburn, stopped off in

Saint Simons Island in Georgia. These two Chicagoans "were so enchanted by the beauty and ambiance of the place that they decided they never wanted to leave. It was a measure of their immediate and intense devotion to the island that the two women immediately bought cemetery plots."

Price now embarked on a new writing career—as a novelist. The main characters in her first trilogy were a Saint Simons clergyman and his two wives. As the *New York Times* explained, "her hoop-skirted heroines tended to be too unremittingly beautiful, her handsome heroes a shade too dashing and their problems a bit too easily solved for Ms. Price to have won serious literary acclaim." But meanwhile her Saint Simons trilogy—*Lighthouse, New Moon Rising,* and *Beloved Invader*—sold like the proverbial hotcakes. She went on to pen a Florida Trilogy, a Savannah Quartet, and then a final Georgia series. *Bright Captivity,* part of a seasonal Georgia trilogy, made it onto the *New York Times* best-seller list.

So engaging and true to history were her romances that thousands of tourists descended on Saint Simons Island to visit the houses and countryside she had made so familiar—not to mention the graveyards, where some of the headstones bore the names of real islanders she had given new life to as fictional characters.

Just as American readers turned out to have a great appetite for books about love—whether in self-help books or romance novels—they were also found to be highly motivated to read about all aspects of business: how to be better at it, the lives of the heavy hitters, and so on. One of the earliest signs of this fascination came with the great success of the mystery writer Emma Lathen, whose detective was a New York banker named John Putnam Thatcher. He was "the first fictional sleuth to spring from the world of business and finance, and he became an immediate hit on Wall Street." Naturally, avid readers wondered just who Emma Lathen was that she could create the "authentic, often intricate business deals that produced both the murders and the clues their banker hero used to solve them."

Year after year, as new John Putnam Thatcher books appeared, Emma Lathen's identity remained carefully shrouded. But eventually mystery insiders learned that Emma Lathen was that rare creature, a fiction-writing duo. One was Mary Jane Latsis, a Wellesley grad and Harvard-trained economist who had put in brief stints with the CIA and the United Nations in Rome before returning to Wellesley to teach. She died late in 1997. The other was a Harvard-trained lawyer named Martha Henissart, who had practiced law first in New York and then in Boston. At one time they had been roommates and avid sharers of favorite mystery novels. When she moved back to Boston, Henissart asked Latsis if there were any good new mysteries around. Latsis said no. "Why not," they wondered, "write one ourselves?"

Their system was this: they would agree on a basic outline and characters. Then they would write alternating chapters and exchange and critique them. Latsis always wrote the first chapter and Henissart the last. Explained the *New York Times*, "They would then get together for a final joint rewrite, ironing out inconsistencies and gradually synthesizing a distinctive composite style." Decade after decade, they turned out one mystery book per year. And once they became successful, selling hundreds of thousands of copies, they could afford to quit their jobs and become full-time writers. It was about this time—when their writing would not ruffle their clients' feathers—that the mystery of their identity was revealed. As part of their unusual collaboration, they bought a house together in Warren, New Hampshire, and would contemplate plots while hiking together in the White Mountains. Occasionally, Latsis's forty-year boyfriend would visit, respecting her aversion to matrimony.

For those who prefer something tougher than clever mysteries, there is the hard-hitting genre of crime and suspense. Lawrence Sanders was in the "front ranks of durable and best-selling genre authors" based on the "sure-fire formula of crime, sex, violence and moral high-handedness." Sanders was versatile, said his editor, establishing "classic series in every form: the caper, the thriller, the police procedural and the private-eye novel." When he died, his thirty-eighth novel, *Guilty Pleasures*, was about to be published. By then Sanders had sold 58 million books in the United States and additional millions in thirty other countries. Said his publisher, "I don't go anywhere—on vacation abroad, on the subway—without seeing one of this guy's books."

He hit it big with his first effort, *The Anderson Tapes*, which had an unusual format: it used "fictional documents, primarily police reports and tape transcripts culled from sophisticated surveillance devices." He had acquired the technical know-how necessary to create such a novel from twenty years as a journalist writing for magazines such as *Science* and *Mechanics*. Sanders was born in Brooklyn but grew up in the Midwest, graduated from Wabash College in Indiana, and then served in the Marine Corps during World War II. He was probably best known for his "seven deadly sins cycle," with each book dominated by pride, greed, or another of man's worst foibles.

After all these authors who churned out dozens of books that sell in megadoses, one must turn to Hannah Green, "an acclaimed author who wrote one slender novel of such delicately distilled perfection that she could hardly bring herself to compose another." Her book, *The Dead of the House*, was a classic coming-of-age novel, always a very difficult feat to pull off. Yet it received glowing reviews. The *Times'* reviewer said that he had completely surrendered "my own callowness and smugness to the ecstasy that is fiction, is art." It was—as most coming-of-age novels are—a thinly fictionalized tale of the author's own childhood, "in an Ohio village and on the summertime shores of Lake Michigan." Unlike the other authors in our database, who pounded out a book every year or two, Green spent twenty years perfecting and polishing hers.

She came to the task of writing with outstanding credentials. She had studied at Wellesley with Vladimir Nabokov and then under Wallace Stegner at Stanford, where she got her master's degree. For a time she taught at Stanford; then she moved east to New York, where she taught creative writing part-time at Columbia and then New York University. In Manhattan she met her painter husband. They were traveling in France soon after Green had finally surrendered her manuscript to be published. In a church in the town of Conques, Green saw "the bones of Saint Foy, one of the last martyrs to Roman rule." For the next twenty-five years, Green worked on her second novel, the story of a twelve-year-old girl who refused to give up her Christian faith, was killed for this, and inspired a cult that continues to this day in France. *Little Saint: The Hours of Saint Foy* was finally published in 2000, after Green's death.

Writers like Hannah Green don't sell many books, but they are admired by critics and their few but faithful readers. Like those on our best-seller Apex, the writers who made our Apex of Fame for Literary Authors, as shown in Table 7-4, attended the top schools, four of them attended Harvard, and Ralph Ellison attended Tuskegee. In this table are listed authors who produce the kinds of works that tend to sell thousands or tens of thousands of copies over the years, not millions. Those on this list are poets, cultural critics, and difficult but worthy novelists.

Today children's books merit large, welcoming sections in bookstores and, in bigger cities, entire bookstores dedicated to tots through teens. And why not? They account for $500 million of the $2.4 billion in books Americans buy each year. And like how-to books, the great proliferation came only in recent decades. Longtime children's publisher Charles E. Gates explains that "The small world of juvenile publishing was transformed in the mid-'60s when President Johnson's New Society program suddenly made millions of tax dollars available to the nation's libraries and schools for the purchase of 'supplemental reading materials.' The Johnson administration was determined to cure the 'Why Johnny Can't Read' syndrome by means of government largesse." School libraries were flooded with money to buy books, and "juvenile publishers found themselves inundated with orders." By the time the Reagan administration killed the program, publishers had whole departments dedicated to kids. Fortunately for them, by then the baby boomers were becoming parents and were lavishing every kind of object on their children that might lead to their betterment. Books were important such objects.[5]

Richard Scarry was one who rode that wave of children's books to great success. His colorful illustrated books featured jolly animals (and, of course, the lowly worm) doing all the things people do, but explained in great detail and with much silliness. His wit and style made the books enthralling to children of all ages. In the pages of Richard Scarry's books, children could see how a house is built or how a letter is mailed and delivered or get an idea of what Paris looks like, while meeting a huge gallery of endearing creatures and families. In his fictional Busyworld, exuberant animals played out all the roles of everyday life with charm and verve.

TABLE 7-4. *The Apex of Fame: Critically Acclaimed Authors in the Obituary Database*

Name (Age at Death)	Obit Date	College	Higher† Degree	Type of Book
1. Allen Ginsberg (70)	04/06/97	Columbia*	No	Poetry
2. Alfred Kazin (83)	06/06/98	City College* of New York	M.A.	Literary criticism
3. Diana Trilling (91)	10/25/96	Radcliffe*	No	Criticism
4. Henry Roth (89)	10/15/95	City College of New York	No	Novels
5. Julian Green (97)	08/18/98	U. of Virginia	No	Novels, plays
6. William S. Burroughs (83)	08/04/97	Harvard*	No	Novels
7. May Sarton (83)	07/18/95	None	No	Poetry
8. James Dickey (73)	01/21/97	Vanderbilt*	M.A.	Poetry
9. Brendan Gill (83)	12/29/97	Yale*	No	Articles
10. Ralph Ellison (80)	04/17/94	Tuskegee Institute	No	Novels
11. William Gaddis (75)	12/17/98	Harvard	No	Novels
12. Harold Brodkey (65)	01/27/96	Harvard*	No	Novels
13. J. Anthony Lukas (64)	06/07/97	Harvard*	No	Articles
14. Janet Lewis (99)	12/05/98	U. of Chicago*	No	Poetry
15. Helene Johnson (89)	07/11/95	Boston U., Columbia	No	Poetry
16. Joseph Brodsky (55)	01/29/96	None	No	Poetry
17. Helene Hanff (80)	04/11/97	One year	No	Letters
18. J. F. Powers (81)	06/17/99	Northwestern	No	Novels

* Graduated from college.

† Only two had a higher degree.

Major Work	Career Note	Obit Length
"Howl"	Poet of Beat generation	117"
On Native Grounds	Articles and books of criticism	73"
Cultural and literary criticism	Wife of Lionel Trilling; critic	67"
Call It Sleep	Novel acclaimed after 30 years	62"
Avarice House	Famous in France	62"
Naked Lunch	Writer of Beat generation	60"
Poetry and novels	Popular on campus; feminist	56"
Deliverance (novel)	Also professor	54"
"Man of Letters"	Wrote for *The New Yorker*	54"
The Invisible Man	First novel made his fame	48"
The Recognitions	Novel acclaimed after 20 years	47"
The Runaway Soul	Famous for delay in writing novel	45"
Pulitzer Prize–winning reporter	At the *New York Times* and Baltimore *Sun*	40"
Poetry and three novels	Hundreds of poems as well as short stories and novels	40"
Poet of Harlem	Part of Negro Renaissance in Harlem	38"
Three books of poetry	Poet laureate of the United States	36"
84 Charing Cross Road	Poor at end of life	35"
Morte d'Urban	Wrote about priests	35"

Scarry was born in Boston, studied at the Boston Museum School from 1939 to 1942, and then served in the Army in World War II. When he returned, he began illustrating books, the first of 250 he would eventually illustrate and/or write. His longtime publisher estimated that more than 100 million Scarry books had been sold over the years, both here and abroad. He was the author of eight of the top fifty best-selling hardcover children's books of all time. He clearly had a natural rapport with children, and he appreciated that fact. He once said, "It's a precious thing to be communicating to children, helping them discover the gift of language and thought." Since 1968, Scarry had worked out of the Swiss ski resort of Gstaad.

Margaret E. Rey was another famous and successful children's author. Unlike Scarry, who created hundreds of characters and stories, Rey and her husband, H. A. Rey, who died in 1977, invented one adorable and memorable character—Curious George—and saw this monkey through innumerable adventures. The Reys were Germans who had moved to Paris in 1935 to evade the Nazis. He was an artist, and while they were in Paris a publisher proposed that they create a children's book called *Rafi et les Neuf Singes*. This was the model for Curious George, but then the Nazis invaded France and the Reys fled to the United States. In 1941, Houghton Mifflin brought out the first Curious George book, and over the next twenty-five years the Reys wrote six sequels. Mrs. Rey said of her husband, "We worked very closely together and it was hard to pull the thing apart and say who did what."

Typical of the series was *Curious George Goes to the Hospital*. George has swallowed part of a jigsaw puzzle and must have many tests. Explained the *Times*, "The tale is designed to put at ease children who might face a similar crisis in real life." But many of the stories had no such didactic point but were simply amusing tales of mischief and mishap where all comes right in the end as the Man in the Big Yellow Hat sets his pet, George, straight. After her husband's death, Rey went on to create another twenty-eight Curious George books in collaboration with Alan J. Shelleck. These books were also made into an animated television series, always a major boost to book sales. Children's books offer something few adult books do: myriad merchandising possibilities. Rey always kept control of all the rights to the character. All told, more than 20 million Curious George books were sold in English and twelve other languages.

Our final publishing figure is Jay S. Garon, "a New York literary agent who transformed his career and the world of publishing with a single call to a Mississippi lawyer in 1987." Garon grew up in Falls River, Massachusetts, spent some time in Hollywood as a character actor, and then returned to New York, where he produced shows for radio, television, and theater before opening a literary agency in the 1950s. Some of his early successes were a diet book by actor James Coco, romance novelists, and Hedy Lamarr's memoirs. Then, in 1987, he received—as agents constantly do—three chapters of a first novel. What Garon did not know at the time was that thirty other agents had already turned the material down. But Garon thought it promising and gave the writer, John Grisham, a call. When his new client finished the novel, *A Time to Kill*, and sent it in, Garon liked it but found it very difficult to sell. Finally, after rejections by fifteen publishers, Garon found one willing to bring the courtroom drama out as a paperback original.

But from there on, reported the *New York Times*, "author and agent would make publishing and movie history as Mr. Garon negotiated multimillion-dollar publishing and movie contracts for a string of Grisham legal thrillers like *The Firm, The Client* and *The Pelican Brief*." When *USA Today* issued its list of the top one hundred best-selling books for the five years it had featured the list, books by John Grisham occupied seven of the slots! In the 1990s, brand-name authors such as John Grisham, Danielle Steel, and Tom Clancy came to dominate book sales as never before.[6] In 1994, when 62,000 new titles were published, seventeen titles sold more than a million copies each; thirty-six books sold more than half a million copies each; and forty-seven sold above 440,000 but less than a half-million copies each.

In recent decades the world of books has been getting steadily larger in a number of ways. Looking for greater profits, more and more publishers have merged. In 1977, fifty different publishers produced three quarters of all adult trade books; today seven companies produce that amount.[7] At the same time, the bookselling structure has shifted dramatically. Where once the great majority of adult fiction and nonfiction books were sold through thousands of independent bookstores, today those stores' share of sales is less than a fifth. The big chain bookstores sell a quarter of all books. But today half of all books are sold not by bookstores at all but at discount stores such as Wal-Mart, in warehouse clubs, and by book clubs.[8] Despite all the hoopla about the on-line retailers, they still account for only a small fraction of book sales. But the great dispersal of book sales is in many ways a continuation of the paperback revolution, which democratized books by making them cheaper and more widely available. There is probably no greater proof of the triumph of higher education in America than the great explosion of book sales.

Yet the publishing industry is passing through a period of uncertainty and turmoil as ever-larger conglomerates sell their books through ever more concentrated outlets, whether Borders bookstores or Wal-Mart. Michael Korda, editor in chief at Simon & Schuster, wrote in his recent memoir, *Another Life*, that however big a business publishing has become, it "still rested on imponderables—little old ladies typing away at their novels on kitchen tables; the whims of writers; four-page outlines of books that were sold for hundreds of thousands of dollars, or even millions, on buzz alone."

Notes

1. Betty Ballantine, "The Paperback Conquest of America," in *The Book in the United States Today,* ed. Gordon Graham and Richard Abel (New Brunswick, N.J.: Transaction, 1996), pp. 101–112.
2. Gordon Graham and Richard Abel, eds. *The Book in the United States Today* (New Brunswick, N.J.: Transaction, 1996), p. 241.
3. Albert N. Greco, *The Book Publishing Industry* (Boston: Allyn and Bacon, 1997), pp. 125–127.
4. Charles Kaiser, "Making the Best-Seller List," *Brill's Content,* March 1999, pp.111–115.
5. Charles E. Gates, "Children's Books" in *The Book in the United States Today,* ed. Gordon Graham and Richard Abel (New Brunswick, N.J.: Transaction, 1997), pp. 11–23.
6. "John Gray atop our list of 100: Five Years of Best-Sellers," *USA Today,* February 11, 1999, p. 5–D5.
7. John Blesso, "An Anatomy of Trade Publishing," *Author's Guild Bulletin,* Summer 1998, pp. 10–11.
8. Stephen Horvath, "The Rise of the Book Chain Superstore," in *The Book in the United States Today,* ed. Gordon Graham and Richard Abel (New Brunswick, N.J.: Transaction, 1997), p. 63.

8

Corporate and Financial Titans

IBM's Computing Pioneer

Driven Man Who Putted His Way to Riches

Wall Street Star

As the United States enters the twenty-first century, American corporations straddle the globe, business colossi that deliver goods, services, information, and entertainment. Many a large American company has more assets and revenues than some smaller sovereign states. There are 6 billion people in the world, and every day a billion drink a Coca-Cola-manufactured drink.[1] Here at home, we are in the midst of extraordinary prosperity created by our huge and buoyant consumer economy. The United States experienced a great burst of wealth a century ago, when the nation industrialized. Another period of great growth began after World War II, when the service-based economy took off. Now we are garnering the fruits of the information/computer age. Half of our unprecedented $4 trillion gross domestic product comes from America's eight hundred largest companies, the multinational corporations and financial institutions that employ a good sixth of the nation's 125 million workers. The old saying "The business of America is business" is as true today as ever. Over the decades, corporate America has been a tremendous generator of national wealth, putting to work the myriad advances in technology and knowledge.[2]

Preeminent among corporate leaders stands Thomas J. Watson, Jr., who led IBM and America into the computer age, prompting *Fortune* magazine to call him "the greatest capitalist who ever lived." Watson Jr. was that rare child who outdid his spectacularly successful father on his own terrain. Thomas Watson, Sr., was a giant in big business all through his son's childhood. The press dubbed this autocrat "thousand-dollar-a-day" Watson for his salary, which made him the nation's highest paid executive, and he was described by *Forbes* as an "icon of American success." Watson Sr. had taken over a faltering office equipment company in 1916, renamed it International Business Machines, and turned it into a powerhouse. The marketing strategy was simple: a sales force totally dedicated to understanding its customers' equipment problems and solving them. Those who invested $1,000 in International Business Machines in 1918 saw their investment soar to $148,000 by 1947.[3] Thomas Watson, Jr., joined his father's punch-card-tabulating company in 1939 and, by the time he retired in 1971, had completely transformed it, building it into an international computer giant that was seen "as a symbol of management excellence and technological prowess."

But for World War II, Watson Jr. might well have lived a very different life. Like many offspring of wealthy, hard-driving fathers, he didn't exert himself too much. A rich boy who barely made it through Brown University, he spent his twenties as a dedicated playboy squiring pretty girls around the glamorous nightclubs of New York and Hollywood. He also took up flying, an interesting choice since his father was so afraid of airplanes that he refused to fly. Then came the war. Watson married, went overseas, proved his mettle flying dangerous missions into Russia, and returned home a serious man.

International Business Machines had became a preeminent corporation by catering to the fact that ever-larger American companies and government agencies needed to track mountains of data, whether census figures, inventory, sales, taxes, or payrolls. As business and government went national and then global, they could function well only if they could keep track of all their numbers. Watson Jr. did not fully appreciate the computer immediately. During a visit to Philadelphia in 1946, the two inventors of the first real computer, the ENIAC, showed him their machine. Watson Jr. would later say, "I had no idea what I was looking at" and scoffed at the idea of these two academics pursuing a patent and imagining they might compete with IBM. But a year later, when the inventors got a contract with the Census Bureau, Watson Jr.

took a long, hard look and realized that computers, not IBM punch cards, were the future.

By 1950, Watson Jr. had managed—despite his father's and the old guard's resistance—to expand his engineering ranks from five hundred to four thousand employees, with almost all the new hires being electrical engineers. These were the people who would design and build the new IBM computers, big, hulking machines with flashing lights that made strange grinding noises. Even the first-generation machines could perform calculations a thousand times faster than the old punch-card tabulators. But the new machines were big, expensive, and complicated. Nonetheless, their incredible capabilities made them impossible to ignore.

"Around 1955, 'computer' became a magic word as popular as vitamins," the *New York Times* obit quoted Watson Jr. as saying. "Top executives rightly believed that the companies of the future were going to be computer-run. Everybody wanted one . . . even though precisely how to use the machines was still a mystery, it became the consensus that management ran a bigger risk by waiting to computerize than by taking the plunge." And it was here that IBM commanded an advantage over its rivals. It had a sales force that had traditionally worked closely with customers to determine just what their needs were and then helped them through any ensuing problems in making the machines work. Computers were not just new, they were intimidating. The IBM sales people made the transition far easier, for their forte was knowing their customers well and being helpful. And, as is still true, any company installing a new computer system needs a great deal of hand-holding and assistance.

Forbes Greatest Technology Stories reports, "In 1963, there were about 12,000 computers in the United States. By 1965, that number was closer to 25,000; by 1969, the number was 50,000. Most of those machines were from IBM. In 1965, the company's share of the computer industry was 65 percent, its revenues were $2.5 billion and net earnings totaled $333 million." Before World War II, when IBM was already a highly successful company, its annual revenue was $148 million. By 1955, as IBM plunged into computers, its revenues tripled from

$215 million to $734 million. Within the next decade, the company's revenues would double.[4]

In this chapter we look at some of America's most important and dynamic corporate and financial figures, people who have made the United States preeminent worldwide in computers, information and communications, entertainment, marketing, and finance. Businesspeople make up the biggest single group in the *New York Times* obits, totaling almost 1,700, or nearly 18 percent of the database. The 470 corporate and 276 financial executives make up about a half of that big group, and their obits average twelve and eleven inches respectively, longer than those of small businessmen. About 5 percent of the group are women.

Corporate Executives

The twenty-five corporate executives who received the most coverage in their obituaries—our Apex of Corporate Fame in Table 8-1—reflect the wide range of business opportunities in recent decades: computers, media, airlines, oil, autos, tobacco, food, and drink. And while these are the business executives with the longest obits, as is often the case in this book, we have featured only some of them in this chapter. The people we actually write about are those who we feel were pioneers or illustrate certain important trends.

The education of the business executives in the *New York Times* database is noticeably high end. As shown in Tables 8-2 and 8-3, almost one half of the corporate executives attended an Ivy League or top fifty college, while 60 percent of the financial people did, with a great emphasis on the Ivy League. Thirty percent of the corporate leaders went on to receive an advanced degree as did 33 percent of the financial leaders. In these two tables, we also compared our groups to the eight hundred top CEOs recently featured in *Forbes*.[5]

The *Forbes* list shows how the higher education of CEOs of the eight hundred largest U.S. corporations has changed in the past twenty years. Far more on the *Forbes* list graduated from college—90.9 percent of the eight hundred CEOs, with 32 percent graduating from one of the top fifty colleges—than did those in our database.

What is most striking is what has happened at the graduate level. More than half (57 percent) of the *Forbes* CEOs earned a graduate degree! The most common advanced degree was the master's in business administration (M.B.A.)—over 31 percent, while 10 percent earned a law degree. So the percentage who obtained a law degree among corporate executives has remained constant while the number completing a higher business degree has markedly increased.

And it is there that the elite universities hold sway. Almost half (44 percent, or 111 of 251) of the M.B.A.s were obtained from the top fifty universities. Almost a third, or 31 percent, of the M.B.A.'s were earned at Ivy League universities. A fifth came from Harvard Business School alone! These M.B.A.s were commonly earned two to eight years after college graduation, so they were influential in advancing careers rather than a perk of higher corporate status.

What makes for success in corporate America? First, helping one's company grow—usually through developing new and/or better products, but also through opening up new markets, often overseas. The importance of major technological advancements is obvious. Second is creating value for shareholders. Remember that Thomas J. Watson, Sr., was the highest-paid executive in America, but the IBM shareholders didn't begrudge him that for a moment. Why? Because he was making them all rich, too. Under his regime, the value of IBM stock was soaring. Third, the most successful executives are those who take risks and make decisions, because usually the big growth and profits are in new and unknown territory. Taking risks is an integral part of corporate success. But consequently, so is failure. Businesspeople understand that if you are actively moving ahead, seeking new approaches, then inevitably you will fail—perhaps frequently. Watson Jr. surpassed his father at IBM by making the huge—and at the time dangerous—decision to get behind a completely new product—computers—and then tolerating numerous failures as the company got it right. "Fail, fail until you get it right" might well be a reasonable business motto.

Yet even as executives sing the praises of risk, their own success usually depends upon a long-term commitment to their corporation. We see this in our own group, and it is confirmed by the careers of the

TABLE 8-1. *The Apex of Fame: Corporate Executives in the Obituary Database*

Name (Age at Death)	Obit Date	Company
1. Seymour Cray (71)	10/06/96	Cray Computer Corp.
2. Roberto C. Goizueta (65)	10/19/97	Coca-Cola Co.
3. Leon Hess (85)	05/08/99	Amerada Hess Corp.
4. Thomas Watson, Jr. (79)	01/01/94	IBM
5. J. Gordon Lippincott (89)	05/07/98	Lippincott & Margulies
6. David Packard (83)	03/27/96	Hewlett-Packard
7. Harold S. Geneen (87)	11/23/97	ITT Corp.
8. Daniel E. Provost (78)	10/20/97	Liggett & Meyers
9. Semon Knudsen (85)	07/09/98	GM Corp.; Ford Motors Co.
10. Robert W. Sarnoff (78)	02/23/97	RCA Corp.
11. Jay Pritzker (76)	01/25/99	Hyatt Hotel Chain
12. Alex Manoogian (95)	07/13/96	Masco Corp.
13. Mark Weiser (46)	05/01/99	Xerox Corp.
14. Michael Walsh (51)	05/07/94	Tenneco
15. T. Vincent Learson (84)	11/06/96	IBM
16. Curtis L. Carlson (84)	02/22/99	Carlson Co.
17. Alexander Pregel (91)	06/28/98	Canadian Radium & Uranium Co.
18. David Longaberger (64)	03/22/99	Longaberger Co.
19. Thomas H. Davis (81)	04/24/99	Piedmont Airlines
20. Juan Metzger (79)	09/10/98	Dannon Co.
21. William P. Tavoulareas (75)	01/16/96	Mobil Corp.
22. John Atwood (94)	03/10/99	North American Rockwell Corp.
23. James V. Blevins (87)	04/15/99	Blevins Popcorn Co.
24. Jerry R. Junkins (58)	05/30/96	Texas Instruments Inc.
25. Jheri Redding (91)	03/21/98	Jheri Redding Products; Nexxus

Note: There were 470 executives of major corporations in the database. Most of them were famous for founding or expanding their companies; many developed new products.

Accomplishments and Fame	Obit Length
Created supercomputers	66"
Turned company around	60"
Fuel-oil business; New York Jets football team owner	57"
Pioneer in computer manufacturing	53"
New product designs	51"
Silicon Valley pioneer	46"
Made ITT a global conglomerate	40"
Vice president of tobacco company; promoted product	34"
Restyled new autos	34"
Made RCA a conglomerate	33"
Founder of hotel chain	33"
Developed single-handled faucet	32"
Leading visionary of "ubiquitous computing"	32"
Reorganized company	31"
Helped develop new-generation computer in 1960s	31"
Founder of trading stamp conglomerate	31"
Supplied polonium to Manhattan Project	30"
Business visionary: weaved baskets	30"
Founder of Piedmont Airlines	30"
Put fruit into yogurt, creating a new product	29"
Expanded business	28"
Developed military planes	28"
Founded company; developed a better popcorn	28"
Made company high tech and global	27"
Founder of hair care cosmetics	27"

TABLE 8-2. *Undergraduate Colleges Attended by the Executives in the Obituary Database and by Forbes' Top 800 CEOs*

College	Corporate Executives (N = 470)		Financial Executives (N = 276)		Forbes' Top 800 CEOs*	
	Number	Percent	Number	Percent	Number	Percent
Ivy League	100	28.7	97	43.1	106	14.6
Rest of the top fifty	71	20.4	35	15.6	125	17.2
Other private colleges	69	19.8	45	20.0	273	37.6
Other public colleges	73	21.0	27	12.0	175	24.1
Military academies	5	1.4	5	2.2	13	1.8
Foreign colleges	6	1.7	5	2.2	35	4.8
Religious institutions	1	0.3	2	0.9	0	0
Junior colleges	4	1.2	1	0.4	0	0
Attended, but not named	19	5.5	8	3.6	0	0
Total	**348**	**100.0**	**225**	**100.0**	**727**	**100.0**
Education not stated	122		51		73	

* "Corporate Resumes," *Forbes*, May 17, 1999, pp. 259–286.

eight hundred CEOs reported in *Forbes*. These eight hundred CEOs had a median age of fifty-six years, had been with their present company twenty years, and had been chief executive officer for five years. A similar commitment to a single company has been noted by Andrew Hacker in *Money*: "Among the current chairmen of the one hundred largest firms, forty-four have been on the company's payroll for thirty or more years, and for another twenty-four it has been at least twenty."[6]

TABLE 8-3. *Degrees Attained by the Executives in the Obituary Database and by* Forbes' *Top 800 CEOs*

Degree	Corporate Executives (*N* = 470) (%)	Financial Executives (*N* = 276) (%)	*Forbes'* Top 800 CEO's* (%)
Bachelor's	38.5	43.5	34.4
Master's (M.A., M.S., M.P.A., etc.)	7.2	9.1	9.4
M.B.A.	4.7	8.0	31.4
Ph.D., other doctorates	5.3	4.3	5.0
M.D.	0.4	0	0.4
Law degree	11.7	11.2	10.5
Others: Pharmacy, religion, etc.	0.2	0.4	0
None	31.9	23.6	9.1
Total	**100.0**	**100.0**	**100.0**

* "Corporate Resumes," *Forbes*, May 17, 1999, pp. 259–286.

Note: The percentage of each executive group who attained a higher degree was: corporate executives in the obituary database, 29.6; financial executives in the obituary database, 33.0; *Forbes'* Top 800 CEOs, 56.6.

A perfect illustration of this is the career of T. Vincent Learson, described by the *New York Times*, as "a former chairman of IBM who led the company's gamble on a new generation of computers, a project whose success insured IBM's prosperity for two decades." Just as Watson Jr. had had difficulty convincing his autocratic father that the company should abandon punch-card technology, so Learson had trouble convincing Watson Jr. that they should develop a new computer, the System 360, that could be added onto as a client's needs grew or changed. The impetus was the growing success of Honeywell in selling cheaper machines that could use IBM software. Learson argued that IBM should develop a more powerful computer operating on special IBM software. This would shut out Honeywell, but it also risked deeply alienating longtime customers because System 360 would also make all previous IBM machines obsolete.

Watson Jr. made a large bet, the biggest ever at that time in U.S. business. Six huge plants were built and fifty thousand employees hired. R-and-D expenses ran to $1 billion a year. At first Watson brought his brother, Arthur, back from Europe to manage the project, but that was a disaster that cost the company several years of progress. Watson admitted the failure and gave full power to Learson. Meanwhile, Watson was enraged by the success of upstart supercomputer company Control Data, which had cornered the supercomputer market. After a visit there, he wrote a scathing memo to his people: "There are only 34 people, including the janitor. Of these, 14 are engineers and 4 are programmers. To the outsider, the laboratory appeared to be cost-conscious, hard-working and highly motivated. Contrasting this modest effort with our own vast development activities, I fail to understand why we have lost our industry leadership position by letting someone else offer the world's most powerful computer."

Learson's task was to reclaim that position. He had joined the company in 1936 right out of Harvard, where he had majored in mathematics. He had risen through the ranks in the Watson Sr. years and then become a senior vice president under Watson Jr. All those years as a company man now paid off. He understood what it would take to get this machine, which was designed to allow for a great deal of flexibility, out the door. It took five excruciating years and $5 billion before the System 360 mainframe computer came onto the market. But with the 360, wrote *Forbes*, IBM now had "the most advanced full line of machines anywhere. In addition, the diversity of the software offered by IBM was impressive and could solve an array of business problems. Being able to link software and hardware on a new, and then unique, platform, was an overwhelming advantage. In short, IBM had thrashed the competition." The revenue and profit payoff was huge. The System 360 turned IBM into a billion-dollar corporation. It also gave it huge leverage internationally by becoming widely adopted overseas.

What we have not talked about at all regarding IBM is its long on-again, off-again antitrust lawsuit. In 1952, Attorney General Tom Clark filed an antitrust suit, based on the fact that IBM controlled 90 percent of the punch-card tabulator business. Watson Jr. took several years to convince his stubborn father that IBM should just settle and move on to computers. However, once the System 360 hit the market, IBM was once again heading into monopoly status, this time with computers. Oddly enough, the new attorney general in this era was none other than Ramsey Clark, the son of the very attorney general who had pursued IBM in the 1950s—and who was running IBM now but Watson Jr.?

The System 360 was supposed to be followed by the even better 360/91, and IBM salesmen convinced potential customers of Control Data to hold on until this new, superpowerful computer came out. It never materialized, but its putative coming almost wiped out Control Data, which in 1968 resurrected the antitrust charges. Soon, IBM was once again bogged down in antitrust litigation. Watson Jr. proved as stubborn as his father had been, but he had no son to cajole him into settling and moving on. The case dragged on until 1982, long after both Watson and Learson, his successor, had retired.

The antitrust case highlights a critical aspect of successfully running a business in the United States. Even the biggest, most powerful executives must always be mindful of the applicable rules and regulations. In the United States, the federal government provides an all-important regulatory framework. While business traditionally moans and groans about the overabundance of government regulations and our overactive legal system, without law and order, it is very hard to manage a business, much less make plans for the future. One need only think of the present-day chaos in Russia, which has few functional institutions, to appreciate the centrality of reliable institutions to a flourishing capitalist system. Moreover, as business has become so vast, wealthy, and powerful, citizens and small business depend more and more on government and the courts to represent their interests.

A major global corporation like IBM, which set world standards of managerial excellence, can function as an incubator for its more entrepreneurial employees, who in turn develop new corporations. Witness the career of Kenneth N. Pontikes, the founder of Comdisco, a pioneer in computer leasing and support services. Pontikes was the son of Greek immigrants who ran a grocery store on Chicago's South Side. He got a B.S. from Southern Illinois University and, in 1963, went to work at Data Power Inc., a computer service firm, before signing up with IBM in the heady days when the System 360 was coming out. Pontikes was an IBM salesman for five years, long enough to see that as companies upgraded to better computers something could be done with their old computers. Since many companies now realized they needed computers but not all needed or could afford the latest and the best, there was a ready market niche. Pontikes knew the machines well. So, in 1969, he bailed out, got a $5,000 loan, and set himself up as a broker of used computers. In 1971, he took the company public. To truly appreciate Pontikes's accomplishment, you have to know the venture capitalist's rule that nine out of ten companies fail before even getting to an initial public offering. Pontikes was not only that rare one-in-ten success, he prospered so well that a decade later he was one of the nation's wealthiest men.

Pontikes followed the rule for corporate success of always looking to grow, expand, and develop new markets. For example, he created "centers to provide backup processing power to customers with computers that had been damaged by natural disasters or power failures." When IBM became a major competitor, Pontikes "branched into refurbishing and leasing medical equipment and other high-technology items." There is a great deal of expensive, quickly outmoded equipment in the United States that is still valuable to secondary and tertiary customers. By the 1990s, Comdisco's revenues were up to $2 billion.

One of the most admired feats in corporate America is when a leader rejuvenates an already famous and successful company. Such was the accomplishment of Roberto C. Goizueta, "a Cuban refugee who became chairman and chief executive of the Coca-Cola Company, strengthening its global dominance in soft drinks and building one of the greatest generators of shareholder wealth in corporate history." At first glance, Goizueta appeared to be an amazing immigrant success story. But in fact, he was from a prominent Cuban family that sent him to an American prep school and then Yale, where his photographic memory and voracious intellect helped him graduate tenth in his class. He went home to Cuba but declined to work in his father's construction business, instead signing on with Coca-Cola as a chemical engineer. A year and a half after Castro took power, Goizueta and his wife and children departed to the United States, where in 1960 he began his corporate climb during the reign of chairman and chief executive J. Paul Austin.

Austin was no slouch as a businessman by most people's standards. From 1962 to 1980, when he retired, Coca-Cola went from being a sleepy, one-drink company, with overseas sales accounting for only 30 percent of its $567.5 million in revenues, to a company with numerous soft drink products and $6 billion in revenues, a tenfold increase. Austin had dispatched his sales force to the four corners of the earth to prose-lytize that "moment of pleasure," and by 1980, 65 percent of that $6 bil-lion came from foreigners guzzling Coke and other fizzy drinks. The profit on those billions was $422 million.

When the elegant but hard-driving Goizueta became chairman and chief executive in 1980 (the first non-Georgian ever to hold the job), he saw a company sitting too comfortably on its laurels. He was deeply unhappy that the stock price had been steadily dropping even as the company expanded. And Pepsi-Cola was making inroads. Goizueta announced that a new day had come by telling his managers, "We're going to take risks. What always has been will not necessarily always be forever." The first big risk was Goizueta's decision to "allow the sacro-sanct Coca-Cola brand name" to be attached to a new product, Diet Coke. It came on the market in August 1982 and by late 1983 was "the nation's largest-selling sugar-free beverage and the fourth-largest-sell-ing soft drink, trailing only Coke, Pepsi, and 7-Up."

Meanwhile, Goizueta was focusing on boosting profits by turning around "the moribund bottler network by purchasing underperforming bottlers, replacing management, increasing volume and then spinning the bottling companies off to a subsidiary, Coca-Cola Enterprises, a public company in which Coke retained a 49 percent interest."

Goizueta was, as he promised, shaking things up and taking risks: "You can't stumble if you're not moving. And if you stumble and make a decision that doesn't pan out, then you move quickly to change it. But it's better than standing still." All through the 1980s, Coke enthusiasti-cally introduced its fizzy products into remote overseas cities and boondocks, boosting foreign sales to 75 percent of revenues. But at the same time, it was losing slices of the domestic market to Pepsi and the cheaper generic soft drinks sold by supermarkets. Goizueta felt that drastic steps were needed, and no doubt the huge success of Diet Coke emboldened him. In 1985, one year short of its centennial, after spending $4 million on tests and focus groups, Coca-Cola announced that it was changing its formula to create a sweeter Coke, New Coke. The old Coke would soon disappear.

Mark Pendergrast, in *For God, Country and Coca-Cola,* devotes an entire chapter to New Coke entitled "The Marketing Blunder of the Century." An unparalleled howl of consumer rage arose through the land, growing louder with each passing week. Coca-Cola headquarters was besieged by outraged devotees. One wrote, "The new formula is gross, disgusting, unexciting and WORSE THAN PEPSI!"[7] The media had a heyday, showing distraught Coke lovers stockpiling their beloved traditional drink and decrying this new imposter. Within three months, the company humbly caved in and brought back the old formula as Classic Coke. While New Coke is still around, this despised beverage accounts for "less than one-tenth of 1 percent of all soft-drink sales." This was about as stringent a reminder as one could get that however powerful corporate America is, it remains at the mercy of its customers. A company is only as great as its customer base.

But somehow, what Goizueta himself described as a "blunder and a disaster" had a phenomenal effect on sales. A decade later, the company had increased its volume of cola sales by almost 30 percent. At a time of great and rapid social change, Coca-Cola (in its longtime formula) was, mused Pendergrast, "as much icon as soft drink," and it stood for "traditional values." Moreover, Coke had become so ubiquitous that it was not only a worldwide symbol of America; for many people it had deep personal associations. To see that beloved symbol disappear was more than Americans could stand. They let loose a torrent of consumer fury that could not be ignored. And when Classic Coke returned, they drank it in bigger numbers than ever before.

Goizueta's massive misstep illustrated his philosophy that occasional failure is inevitable when one is making hard decisions and shaking things up, and that one simply needs to rectify those mistakes. But meanwhile, his strategy of focusing on stock value had been spectacularly successful. When Goizueta took over in 1981, Coca-Cola stock was worth a total of $4.3 billion. When he died in 1997, its value had soared to $152 billion. Those who bought $1,000 worth of stock the year Goizueta ascended to chairman saw that stock become worth $65,000. While some were appalled that Goizueta took home a bonus of nearly $83 million in stock in 1991, the shareholders didn't mind at all. As one working-class Coca-Cola millionaire joyfully declared, "Coca-Cola has put my 6 children and 17 grandchildren through college."

One of the most noticeable corporate trends of the postwar era has been the globalization of business. No one exemplified this more than Harold S. Geneen, often viewed as the "architect of the international conglomerate," a feat that in turn made him "the most significant and controversial businessman of the 1960s and '70s." Business is as prone to fads and trends as any other human endeavor, and when Geneen began preaching the beauty of owning dozens, even hundreds of different enterprises all over the world—thereby spreading risk around—he found many converts.

Geneen is an interesting contrast to both IBM's Watson Jr. and Coca-Cola's Goizueta, two blue-blooded Ivy League executives who had lived and breathed only their respective corporations before taking the helm. In 1926, at the age of sixteen, Geneen began his working life with the New York Stock Exchange, was trained as an accountant, and then held numerous managerial positions at the American Can Company, Bell and Howell, and Raytheon. When he went to International Telephone and Telegraph in 1959, it had one business focus: overseas telephone calls. When he became president and CEO in 1959, that was still true and the company's annual revenues were about $800,000 a year.

Geneen's genius was to see the world as ITT's oyster. He spent the next two decades "virtually inventing the international conglomerate," wrote the *New York Times*. "He did it by buying companies. All sorts of companies." Soon ITT was into hotels, home building, auto rentals, insurance, billboards. Geneen presided over the purchase of 350 companies in eighty nations, making ITT the eleventh-largest industrial company in the United States, "a colossus with more than 375,000 employees and $16.7 billion in revenue."

To keep track of this vast international empire, Geneen had more than a hundred managers filing weekly written reports. In his 1984 book, *Managing*, Geneen explained that with his system of overlapping management fiefs, he was hearing from more than one point of view. "I don't believe in just ordering people to do things," he said in a 1977 interview. "You have to sort of grab an oar and row with them." This probably conveyed far too benign a management style for a man featured in *Time*'s "Titans and Builders" issue as one of the "Bosses from Hell." ITT executives were described as "beaten," poor souls who "were regularly grilled and even sickened in large meetings with CEO Harold Geneen." His successor put it this way: "He worked incredible hours and motivated people with fear, kindness, threats, everything under the sun to get the most out of people."

Geneen was an empire builder who was compared to Alexander the Great and Napoleon. But of course, he was not a politician or elected official. His arrogant efforts to sway political events in ITT's favor made the company, in some quarters, a hated symbol of American imperialism at its worst. The *New York Times* reported, "There were also disclosures that in 1970 ITT tried to block the election of Chilean President Salvador Allende Gossens, a Marxist who nationalized an ITT subsidiary and was overthrown in 1973." The company was also in hot water over charges that it had offered congressmen $400,000 in contributions with the hope that an antitrust action could be squashed.

The conglomerate movement, which viewed diversification as the answer to risk, tailed off by the 1970s, hurt by rising interest rates and a hostile federal government. Geneen retired in 1977, and ITT was gradually dismantled as one company after another was sold off. By the time Geneen died in 1997, all that was left was a hotel company.[8] Then that disappeared into a merger, and Geneen's huge creation had melted away. Geneen had certainly invented a new kind of business entity. He had increased shareholder value. He was a much-admired, even feared, chief executive. Yet in the end, unlike IBM with its world-changing computers and Coca-Cola with its beloved products, ITT had nothing long-lasting to show for the whirlwind Geneen years. So while growth and the bottom line are always important components of corporate success, there is also the question of what the company has contributed to society.

All the Americans now yakking loudly on their cell phones in public places and dependent on their beepers would have no trouble recognizing the contributions of William J. Weisz, chairman and chief executive of Motorola. Weisz was "especially influential in Motorola's drive to apply electronics to pagers, portable telephones and two-way radios, all products in which the company [in 1997] has become a world leader." Moreover, he was a mover and shaker who helped improve the radio frequency spectrum and "helped set the stage for global wireless communications." Motorola had started as a maker of car radios and moved on to other nifty technological products. Weisz was manager of a group developing a new portable radio in the mid-1950s, when his executive talents were first recognized.

Weisz grew up in Chicago, where his father was a dentist, graduated from MIT with a degree in electrical engineering, and joined Motorola in 1948. One colleague explained that Weisz had "a remarkable knowledge and understanding of technology, combined with an ability to communicate the possibilities of that technology to customers and decision makers throughout the world." His management style was very easygoing. He and other senior executives in shirtsleeves ate in the company cafeteria every day, creating a corporate culture that made employees feel free not only to discuss things with their top boss but to disagree with him. Weisz was a great exhorter and memo writer. He stressed, "Failure is not falling down. It is failing to get back up—quickly."

As the postwar corporations matured and new rivals materialized—whether foreign firms or new upstarts—great anxiety arose about how to maintain competitiveness. Corporate gurus descended upon the corporate landscape, ready to lead high-level navel gazing. Preeminent among them was W. Edwards Deming, the father of quality management. Deming's career is fascinating for the circuitous manner by which he attained guruhood. He was born in Sioux City, Iowa, his father a lawyer just scraping by. Young Deming worked his way through the University of Wyoming in Laramie, later earning a master's degree in math and physics from the University of Colorado and then a doctorate in physics from Yale University in 1928. From there, Deming went to AT&T's Hawthorne manufacturing plant in Chicago, becoming a protégé of Bell Labs' Walter Shewhart, a pioneer in the "use of statistics to control manufacturing processes."

Then Deming put some time in with the government, working at the U.S. Department of Agriculture and taking a one-year sabbatical to master statistical theory and practice with another pioneer in the field, Sir Ronald Fisher at the University of London. This enabled Deming to help the U.S. Census Bureau develop sampling techniques. During World War II, he worked with military planners applying "statistics to the production of supplies for warfare." After the war, Deming began teaching at New York University's Stern School of Business, preaching the importance of using statistics to get a handle on quality control and then pressing from there to truly improve quality. But at that stage, he could have been fairly described as an "obscure statistician." Then came an invitation from Japanese industrial leaders to give a series of lectures about his ideas, which they knew from his journal articles. Those lectures would transform his whole career.

According to the *New York Times*, Deming's "theories were based on the premise that most product defects resulted from management shortcomings rather than careless workers, and that inspection after the fact was inferior to designing processes that would produce better quality." Deming argued that enlisting the efforts of willing workers to do things properly the first time, "not teams of inspectors," was the real secret of quality improvement.

Japanese businessmen rebuilding their war-shattered economy embraced Deming's approach because they knew they were dependent on the world markets and would have to find some way to differentiate their products. They hoped it would be quality. So Deming first became a revered corporate guru in Japan. American executives had little interest in his message because they viewed better quality as equaling higher prices, which were anathema to their customers. Deming was also a great proselytizer of reducing waste, and he practiced what he preached: "One of his daughters recalled that he had dated the eggs in his refrigerator with a felt-tipped pen so that the oldest would be eaten first and none would go to waste."

But when Japanese electronics and then Japanese automobiles found huge favor with American consumers in the 1960s and 1970s, corporate America got interested in Deming, the darling of the Japanese. The first to seek him out was the Ford Motor Company, which was losing hundreds of millions of dollars as young Americans snapped up reliable, fuel-efficient Toyotas and Hondas. While the heart of Deming's approach was the statistical study of product quality, he also espoused a management philosophy that said that workers should be treated not as adversaries but as associates and included respectfully in all aspects of running a company. He would certainly have approved of Weisz at Motorola, who was already eating in the cafeteria and quite at ease mingling with his workers.

One Ford executive vividly remembered Deming's first foray into this big American corporation: "We were sitting there with our pens poised to write down the prescription for what we should do about quality. The first thing he said was, 'Do you have a constancy of purpose?' We were not quite sure what to make of him." Nor were they thrilled to hear that 85 percent of quality problems were the fault of management, which tolerated underpar results. Despite the early puzzlement, Ford followed through, installing statistical controls in all its factories. As the quality of Ford cars rose, along with the company's corporate fortunes, other American companies were intrigued. Deming showed that management itself was ripe for innovation, an approach that, if properly pursued, could produce higher profits.

One of the great themes of postwar corporate America has been going global, pushing beyond national markets into the potential bonanza of foreign lands. Other great themes have been the importance of providing better service, and expanding and improving communications. John William Berry, Sr., was one who took a quintessential American family business, the Yellow Pages, and made it global. The company dated back to 1909, when his father, Loren, had sold $700 in advertising for an uncle in Illinois who was starting a fledgling phone service. The uncle wanted the ads to underwrite the first list of subscribers. Loren Berry saw the potential and created the Yellow Pages. (The pages were yellow "according to company lore, because Loren Berry deemed it the best background for black type.") The family business flourished as the telephone became commonplace. Son John attended Dartmouth and got a degree in business, joining his father in 1948.

By 1963, John became president, and in 1966 he "entered a joint venture with the International Telephone and Telegraph Company, ITT-World Directories." It quickly grew into the biggest Yellow Pages company outside the United States "except the Europeans call them Golden and the Australians settled for Pink." When he sold the company in 1986 to Bell South, it was a $1-billion-a-year company.

Rene Anselmo was another businessman who saw that the world was getting smaller and launched a Spanish-language television network in the United States. The son of the Bedford, Massachusetts, postmaster, Anselmo graduated from the University of Chicago in 1951, where he was involved with theater. After college, he went on vacation in Mexico and ended up working in local television. After a dozen years south of the border, he came back to the United States, realizing that the country could now sustain a Spanish-language network. By 1987, when it was sold to Hallmark Cards, the Spanish International Network (SIN) consisted of more than four hundred broadcast, satellite, and cable outlets. The *New York Times* reported that Anselmo had made $80 million for his quarter of the business. It was a well-timed sale because the Federal Communications Commission was charging that SIN was partly owned by a Mexican media family, thereby violating federal laws against foreign ownership of American TV networks.

From his Spanish-language network, Anselmo was deeply familiar with the global communications revolution. He announced, to great skepticism, that he was going to create an alternative to the "monopoly on satellite transmission of video images held by Intelsat, which is owned by 120 governments, including the United States." When his company, PamAmSat, launched its first satellites from French Guiana, each was "emblazoned with the company's unofficial logo, which conveyed Mr. Anselmo's views of government-run monopolies. The logo featured a cartoon dog raising its leg, as if to a tree." When Anselmo died in 1995, PanAmSat had three satellites orbiting the earth, beaming signals for such up-and-coming media powers as HBO and ESPN. That year the company earned $18 million on revenues of $63.7 million.

Sales are essential to any business enterprise, and Walter H. Weintz discovered a whole new method of reaching people, for he was "a pioneer of direct mail advertising," described as "one of the most brilliant direct-mail strategists in the country." Weintz realized that Americans always look forward to the day's mail, yet there may be nothing there of interest. His simple but clever idea was to use that moment of expectation to put something enticing into the hands of all those adults sorting through the post. One Rodale Press executive credited Weintz with inventing "many of the strategies and techniques that transformed direct response advertising into today's multibillion-dollar industry."

Weintz, a New Yorker who graduated from Duke University, had a chance to test out many of his ideas when he worked as circulation director at *Reader's Digest* in the 1950s. One of his most memorable was sending 100 million pennies to potential subscribers with the instructions "Keep one penny for bread. Or for luck. Send back the other penny as a down payment on a subscription to the Reader's Digest—a penny to seal the bargain!" The logistics of this were not simple. The U.S. Mint in Denver dispatched the $100,000 in pennies in open flatbed trucks. When they were unloaded at a Long Island warehouse, the floor broke under the tons of copper. Such gimmicks helped the circulation of *Reader's Digest* almost triple from 4.5 million to 12 million by 1959, when Weintz left to open his own company.

In his memoir, *The Solid Gold Mailbox*, Weitz wrote of direct mail, "It is fascinating and exciting because with a good idea you can make a fortune overnight simply by mailing out a few thousand or a few million sales letters—or, with a bad idea, poorly planned and executed, you can lose that fortune with equal ease."

Advertising is one of the most powerful weapons in the business arsenal, and successful ad campaigns can transform a product and even

enter and linger in the national consciousness. Such was the accomplishment of Shirley Polykoff, "a pioneering advertising woman" whose
various ad campaigns for Clairol hair dyes liberated women to have
whatever hair color they pleased. The ads are remembered to this day. It
was Polykoff, herself a bottle blonde, who invented the phrase "Does
she . . . or doesn't she?" for the then-tiny Clairol hair dye division of
Bristol-Myers, with the reassuring final line "Hair color so natural only
her hairdresser knows for sure." In 1956, this was considered a risky and
risqué campaign. *Life* magazine initially turned it down. But Polykoff
huffily suggested that the men at the magazine ask the women (mainly
secretaries) who worked there if there were anything sexual in the
words. She knew women well enough to know that nice girls (the only
kind who worked at a place like *Life)* would never acknowledge any
such thing. And so the ads ran. A *New Yorker* profile of Polykoff noted
that the "Does She or Doesn't She?" print ads "always included a child
with the mother to undercut the sexual undertones of the slogan to make
it clear that mothers were using Miss Clairol, and not just 'fast'
women."[9]

When those words—"Does she or doesn't she?"—first tantalized a
far more innocent and buttoned-up America, only 7 percent of
American women dared use hair dye. It was the province of actresses,
models, and other questionable sorts. However, Polykoff had a more
benign view since she had been dyeing her hair for some time to retain
her teenage status as the only blonde in her family. "Does she or doesn't
she?" was followed by three other Clairol classics. One was, "Is it true
blondes have more fun?" While Polykoff may have been thinking partly
about herself, this was also the era of Marilyn Monroe and other potent
Hollywood blondes. And then there were the memorable "If I've only
one life to live, let me live it as a blonde" and "The closer he gets, the
better you look." Can one be surprised to learn that within a decade half
of all American women felt free to frost, tint, and outright change the
color of their hair? Or that Clairol's annual revenues soared from $25
million to $200 million? Moreover, Clairol captured half of the fast-
expanding hair-dye business, a position it has maintained to this day,
when hair dye sales amount to $1 billion a year. Polykoff showed that

there was a lot of money to be made in conveying the romantic possibilities of a new you.

In a country as wealthy as America today, entertainment and leisure activities, whether movies, sports, or travel, have become very big business. John K. Hanson saw this fact in his own busy life and capitalized on American's innate wanderlust. Hanson was one of those beings obviously destined for business. Born in Thor, Iowa, even as a youngster he was selling things from his pony cart. When he went to the University of Minnesota, he got a practical degree in mortuary science so he could join his father's funeral home. Then he also took over the family furniture and appliance store. Next he founded a bank and took a piece of the local dealerships for International Harvester and Oldsmobile.

But work was not all, and this former Eagle Scout still loved to camp out. So it was right up his alley when he had a chance, in 1957, to invest in a California travel-trailer manufacturer. He then persuaded the company to open a branch in Forest City, Iowa. When the West Coast operation collapsed, Hanson offered to assume the $42,000 in debts and run the company, whose assets amounted to thirty-nine trailers and $100 in the bank. In 1960, he launched Winnebago, the name of which was inspired by a nearby river named for local Indians. He also developed the motor home and set up assembly lines to produce motor homes cheaply enough that many middle-Americans could afford to wander the country for months on end, like so many gypsies. By 1970, the company was so successful that he took it public, holding on to 47 percent himself.

Needless to say, business can be extremely stressful at times—so much so that in 1954 insurance salesman Don Clayton of Fayetteville, North Carolina, was told by his doctor to take a month off to rest his frayed nerves. To relax, Clayton headed off to the local miniature golf courses but became outraged at their crummy designs. He had nothing but scorn for twirling clowns and open-mouthed turtles. He went home and laid out a course that would "reward the same skills demanded of expert putters on the professional tour." Convinced he was on to something, Clayton and his father invested $5,200 to build an elegant eighteen-hole course on a leafy lot. At twenty-five cents a game, they

TABLE 8-4. *The Apex of Fame: Financial Executives in the*
Obituary Database

Name (Age at Death)	Obit Date	Business
8. Bernard Cornfeld (67)	03/02/95	Investors Overseas Services; Fund of Funds
9. Michael von Clemm (62)	11/08/97	Credit Suisse First Boston; Merrill Lynch
10. Mary Roebling (89)	10/27/94	National State Bank
11. Arthur T. Roth (91)	09/21/97	Franklin National Bank
12. Zalman C. Bernstein (72)	01/09/99	S. C. Bernstein & Co.
13. Richard Shinn (81)	03/03/99	Metropolitan Life Insurance Co.
14. Jacques Coe (103)	02/25/97	His own firm; Partner in Cowen & Co.
15. Henry A. Loeb (90)	01/28/98	Loeb Partners Corp.
16. James Fletcher (63)	09/24/98	South Shore Bank (Chicago)
17. Donald Bruckmann (70)	04/25/99	Dean Witter Reynolds International
18. Charles H. Dyson (87)	03/19/97	Dyson-Kissner-Moran Corp.
19. Gilbert Fitzhugh (88)	12/31/97	Metropolitan Life Insurance Co.
20. Charles E. Saltzman (90)	06/18/94	Henry Sears & Co.; Goldman, Sachs & Co.
21. Fischer Black (57)	08/31/95	Goldman, Sachs & Co.
22. Madelon Talley (65)	07/23/97	Dreyfus Leverage Fund; various posts
23. Tristan E. Beplat (85)	12/03/97	Manufacturers Hanover Trust Co.
24. Max H. Karl (85)	04/20/95	Mortgage Guarantee Insurance Corp.
25. Harold Goldberg (68)	01/31/96	Moody's Investment Service
26. Peter W. Eccles (60)	12/23/96	Eccles Associates
27. Bennett A. Brown (68)	08/04/97	Citizens & Southern National Bank
28. W. B. Fitzgerald (65)	04/19/98	Independence Federal Savings Bank
29. Austin Koenen (56)	05/18/98	China International Capital Corp.
30. Ira J. Hechler (80)	04/10/99	Hechler & Associates

Note: There were 276 financial leaders in the database, including Wall Street financiers, bankers, brokers and insurance executives.

presided over major changes that modernized and opened up Wall
Street. He oversaw "the installation of electronic equipment that tripled
the daily trading capacity to 150 million shares." Batten had been a J. C.

Accomplishments and Fame	Obit Length
Started go-go mutual funds (went bankrupt)	28"
Investment banker who pioneered Eurobonds	28"
First woman to head a major American bank	26"
Driving force in consumer banking	25"
Promoted discretionary brokerage accounts	25"
Led company to prominence in insurance	25"
Pioneered technical analysis (oldest active broker)	24"
Investment firm vice chairman	24"
Pioneering lender to poorer neighborhoods	23"
Investment banker	23"
Pioneered leveraged buyouts	22"
Added home and auto insurance to company	22"
New York Stock Exchange vice president	21"
Black-Scholes theory on how to value options	21"
First female fund manager on Wall Street	21"
Aided economic reconstruction of postwar Japan	21"
Founded modern private mortgage insurance	20"
Expert in rating corporate debt	20"
Expert on foreign currency fluctuation risk	20"
Rehabilitated bank	20"
Founder of first minority-controlled savings bank	20"
Public finance specialist	20"
Leader in leveraged buyouts	20"

Penney executive who had transformed that company with a new credit card and a mail-order catalogue and so had a sense of the importance of opening the stock exchange beyond its traditional confines, responding to criticism that Wall Street was "dominated by securities industry insiders."

Michael W. McCarthy was chairman of Merrill Lynch & Company, presiding over "what was the biggest American brokerage firm in a period of rapid domestic and foreign expansion. Merrill, for example, set up an office in Tokyo in 1961, the first American securities firm to do so. Between 1959 and 1964, the firm also opened 21 new offices in the United States, creating a network of 159 offices across the country." As his firm was reaching out to encourage ordinary Americans to invest in stocks and bonds, McCarthy was among those urging the New York Stock Exchange to "get away from the onus of a private club." Why should only insiders make money in the stock market?

One suspects that Merrill chairman McCarthy was committed to opening up the moneymaking potential of the stock market to regular folks because of his own history. He was a small-town boy who but for a stroke of unlikely fortune would never have entered the gilded precincts of Wall Street. He was born in Belle Plaine, Minnesota, the youngest of six children. He graduated from high school in Beach, North Dakota. Then he migrated to the greener pastures of California, where he found work in Oakland at the Mutual Stores Grocery chain. It so happened that several years after McCarthy joined Mutual Stores, the chain was bought by Safeway; Merrill Lynch financed the purchase. Charles E. Merrill, the brokerage firm's founder, got a chance to observe McCarthy's skill as a bookkeeper and came away impressed. Thus, when Merrill needed someone in 1940 to help organize Merrill Lynch's administrative and office systems, he called on McCarthy.

Within four years, McCarthy had become a partner, and by 1957 he was the managing partner who took the firm public. "We sincerely believed public ownership would increase and stabilize the capital positions of the member firms." Two years later, McCarthy was president and two years after that, chairman. A later Merrill chairman hailed McCarthy as a "visionary leader, overseeing expansion in the U.S. and abroad." He was obviously a man who realized—from his own modest beginnings—that most Americans knew nothing about stocks except that they were for rich people and might never consider buying a stock unless a local broker in a local office suggested them. People like McCarthy began the slow process of opening the potential earnings of the stock market to average Americans. Merrill Lynch & Company remains one of the top brokerages, managing $500 billion in private assets. Today 48 percent of Americans own stocks, bonds, or mutual funds.[10]

Investment bankers underwrite new stock and bond offerings for companies and government and provide top-dollar advice on mergers, acquisitions, and other financial matters. Charles Allen was one of the minor legends who quit high school, became "a runner on the New York Stock Exchange, founded the influential investment house of Allen & Company and became the financial speculator known as the shy Midas of Wall Street." Despite his lack of formal education, Allen, who worked with his brothers Herbert and Harold, was a huge and wide-ranging reader, scanning everything from the daily papers to showbiz rags to the *New England Journal of Medicine*. His company underwrote the necessary capital for Syntex Corporation, which "developed oral contraceptives and anti-inflammatory drugs" and also for Teleregister Corporation, "a pioneer in online computer systems."

Charles Allen was very much a banker with a global vision. He provided money for "oil and mineral developments in Libya, Algeria, Morocco and Mauritania, as well as gold mines in the Philippines and the Grand Bahama Port Authority." He and his brothers also saw the coming boom in California and bought and developed the Irvine Ranch, one of the "largest master-planned urban development[s] in the U.S." Allen also sat on the boards of numerous major corporations, lending his financial skill to such companies as PepsiCo, CF&I Steel, Warner Bros., and the Ambac Corporation.

Wall Street is not the only source of overseas capital; so are such quasi-governmental agencies as the World Bank. For many years Lewis T. Preston was the classic investment banker, heading up the prestigious, powerful firm of J. P. Morgan. In 1991, he retired and led the World Bank in the post–Cold War era. Preston remade both institutions in periods of great change and turmoil. He was described by a Morgan colleague as "the architect of the modern J. P. Morgan and the

pre-eminent international banker of his era. He led our firm with pene-
trating vision, formidable intellect and strength of character." These
qualities were not immediately evident, however. In Ron Chernow's *The
House of Morgan*, he describes Preston as a "Harvard graduate from a
rich Westchester family, [who] had started in the Morgan mailroom (as
everybody did) in the early 1950s. He was first viewed by elders as a
playboy, socialite and jock." However, he had also been a Marine, and
he brought charm and toughness to a fast-changing banking scene, one
in which Morgan would not survive if it did not change. Wrote
Chernow, "Preston had to retrain masses of old-time commercial
bankers and credit analysts, making them into risk-taking market
whizzes."[11]

Preston used his power as chairman of J. P. Morgan to "resolve some
major financial problems." First was the chaos created when the Hunt
brothers attempted (but failed) to corner the market in silver, which
imperiled numerous large banking institutions. Morgan led the bailout
that calmed those rough waters. Perhaps more important was his help in
mid-1982 in shoring up the collapsing Continental Illinois Corporation,
a debacle that threatened to destroy the entire holdings of more than
fifty midwestern banks. Preston also boldly addressed the unhappy realities of Third World debt. Poor nations had taken on loans they were
unable to repay, and in December 1987 "Mr. Preston persuaded other
banks to follow Morgan in writing off as much as 50 per cent of the face
value" of these loans.

No doubt those experiences were part of what recommended him for
the presidency of the World Bank, "set up after World War II to provide
loans and technical assistance for the economies of developing countries." Preston felt a sense of noblesse oblige, taking a huge salary cut—
his $285,000 World Bank salary was a tenth of his salary at Morgan—to
exercise his financial talents for the greater good. During his four years
at the World Bank, starting in 1991, he "oversaw the entry of the former
Soviet republics into the institution, sought to give it a larger role in
restructuring the public sectors of client countries, moved to make it
more responsive to prevailing social concerns, and moved to trim its
sprawling bureaucracy." He also insisted that the bank judge itself not

just by how many loans it made. Instead, he asked, how successful were the actual projects funded by the bank?

Wall Street penetrated the consciousness of average Americans starting in the 1980s, when hostile takeover battles made for colorful high-stakes drama. Filmmaker Oliver Stone brought the world of high finance and huge egos to the big screen in *Wall Street,* while author Tom Wolfe skewered these new investment banker "masters of the universe" in *The Bonfire of the Vanities. Barbarians at the Gate,* the tale of the RJR Nabisco buyout, read like fiction but was appalling fact.

The forerunner of all those cigar-smoking red-suspenders guys was Thomas Mellon Evans, Sr., who "earned fame and fortune as a master of mergers and acquisitions, an asset stripper. . . . When Wall Street was as boring as a gray flannel suit . . . [he was] one of its most daring and rapacious characters, waging waves of takeover battles."

Evans was from Pittsburgh, and his remote connection to the super-rich Mellons secured him a clerk's job at a Mellon-owned entity when he graduated from Yale in 1931. He steadily bought bonds in a sinking company, locomotive manufacturer H. K. Porter. When Porter went bankrupt in 1939, Evans was its largest bondholder and became president. During the next ten years, the firm flourished, branching out into construction and hardware. Meanwhile, Evans pursued and acquired Crane Company and began steadily adding companies, following the lead of Geneen at ITT and other conglomerate builders.

"He was a financial guy—a balance sheet buyer," explained his son in 1995. "He would buy something for less than book value and figure that the worst that could happen was he would liquidate it and come out okay." When following this policy led to several firms in New Jersey being shut down, a local politician described Evans as "the corporate embodiment of Jaws, the great white shark."

The next generation of Wall Streeters was even more buccaneering, self-declared stars who actively sought the public limelight. Jeffrey P. Beck was a "flamboyant merger-and-acquisition specialist on Wall Street . . . [who] played a major role in completing two of the nation's largest leveraged buyouts." The first was the purchase of Beatrice Foods by BCI Holdings and the second the buyout of RJR Nabisco by Kohlberg Kravis

Roberts & Company. These were two of the most famous and highest-profile of the "junk bond" deals of that era. The intense media coverage meant that ordinary Americans could observe Wall Street engage in its usual corporate Darwinism. It was not Beck's job to worry about what real companies employing real people might suffer. Wall Street was, as ever, about weighing balance sheets and getting the best dollar out of every deal. When Beck prevailed in these financial battles, reported the *New York Times*, "he would howl through the corridors like a mad dog, earning him the nickname 'Mad Dog.'" Moreover, he had supposedly eaten a "box of dog biscuits" for the benefit of RJR CEO F. Ross Johnson during the buyout. Beck reveled in his wild ways and wild reputation, accepting a cameo role in Stone's 1987 film. He even shopped his own life story around as worthy of a motion picture. When he died at the young age of forty-eight, he was on wife number four.

Raised in Florida, Beck graduated from Florida State University and then earned an M.B.A. from Columbia University in 1971. He was among the Wall Street baby boomers who made a business school diploma an important form of entree to the business world. Part of Beck's notoriety was a $2.5 million bonus given him by Drexel Burnham Lambert just before the firm declared bankrupcy.

Executive compensation remains a hot-button issue. The soaring salary levels, bonuses, stock options, and severance deals known as golden parachutes regularly stun not just ordinary wage slaves but even longtime businesspeople. To some extent one can thank or curse Arch Patton, "one of the best-known management consultants in the post–World War II era." Patton was a director of the one of America's most admired management consulting firms, McKinsey & Company. He had the idea of doing a "multi-industry survey of how top executives were compensated." This became a regular annual feature that ran in the *Harvard Business Review* from 1951 to 1961. Patton's interest was to better advise his clients on how to use the carrot of bonuses and stock options to get executives to deliver maximum performance. He even wrote a book entitled *Men, Money and Motivation*.

Money and how much certain people made was a subject of intense interest in many quarters, and so many variations on his list are now published. The practical effect was for every executive in every field to demand parity with all others. Executives' pay began soaring. While in 1960 American CEOs made about 30 times as much as their average employees, by the 1990s that figure had streaked up to a multiple of 400. Asked how he felt about this, Patton replied, "Guilty." Today, the leading American corporate CEOs make more than $1 million a year, if salary, bonus, perks, and stock options are included. Bill Gates, founder and CEO of Microsoft, does not make a huge salary by industry standards, but in mid-1999 his stock options made him worth a mind-boggling $100 billion. An entire Web site was devoted to monitoring the value of his stock options. As global mergers become commonplace, this soaring executive compensation creates awkwardness, for in no other country are executives paid comparable amounts. In the United Kingdom, top executives earn an average of $645,000, in Japan the number is $420,855, while in Germany it's $398,430. When the German car company Daimler-Benz bought the American Chrysler, the German CEO was making $2 million versus the Chrysler CEO's $11.5 million. But now, as a German company, DaimlerChrysler reports neither executive's salary publicly.

Corporate America and Wall Street have been the traditional high-status business venues for most of this century, attracting those who want to make big money. Today, of course, Silicon Valley has become a third destination. To be successful, executives working in big, competitive organizations must exhibit a flair for creating new businesses or expanding existing ones. Our Apexes of Fame generally feature prominent executives at the top firms—IBM, Coca-Cola, Hyatt, Texas Instruments, J. P. Morgan, Goldman Sachs, and so on. In addition to big-time Apex executives, lesser-known men and women are also influential on the contemporary business landscape. Business involves taking risks and tolerating some failure, while always seeking a better bottom line.

Notes

1. Constance L. Hays, "Global Crisis for Coca-Cola, or a Pause That Refreshes?" *New York Times* November 1, 1998 Sunday Business p. 1.

2. "The Chemistry of Growth," *Economist*, March 6, 1999, p. 72

3. Jeffrey Young, *Forbes Greatest Technology Stories* (New York: Wiley, 1998), p. 32; see the chapter on IBM.

4. Ibid., p. 57.

5. "Corporate Resumes," *Forbes,* May 17, 1999.

6. Andrew Hacker, *Money* (New York: Touchstone, 1996), p. 37. Hacker has a good chapter on CEOs.

7. Mark Pendergrast, *For God, Country and Coca-Cola* (New York: Collier, 1993), p. 354.

8. K. T. Greenfeld, "Voracious Inc." *Time,* December 7, 1998, p. 175.

9. Malcolm Gladwell, "True Colors" *New Yorker*, March 22, 1999, pp. 70–77.

10. Robert D. Hershey, Jr., "Survey Says 78.7 Million Own Stocks in United States," *New York Times,* October 22, 1999, p. C1.

11. Ron Chernow, *The House of Morgan* (New York: Atlantic Monthly Press, 1990), pp. 655–658.

9

Creative Philanthropy

Patrician Champion of Art

Gracious Doyenne of Music

Showered Gifts on Maine

As some Americans became very rich in the past century, there also arose a tradition of creative philanthropy that harkens back to Andrew Carnegie, who gave large portions of his steel fortune for public libraries, and John D. Rockefeller, who bestowed many of his Standard Oil millions on medical research and public health, both unusual charitable endeavors in their day. While getting rich is an honored American pursuit, so is giving one's money away to help society.[1] There were plenty of rich men in Carnegie's time, but we remember him because of his creative philanthropy. Very much in that tradition was Paul Mellon, who gave away about a billion dollars of his Mellon Bank inheritance as an "endlessly inventive benefactor of the nation's cultural life." Above all, Paul Mellon will be remembered for the magnificent National Gallery of Art on the Mall in Washington, D.C., which began as his father's gift to the American people but became his son's great lifework. "Giving away large sums of money nowadays is a soul-searching problem," he once said. "You can cause as much damage with it as you may do good."

In this chapter we look at the philanthropists who gained notice from the *New York Times*. Predictably, they make up a small portion of the database, with fewer than 250 people classified as philanthropists. We spotlight those wealthy men and women notable for their deep personal involvement in how their charitable dollars were spent, pioneers who created significant new cultural, scientific, and civic institutions. While many people give large sums to demonstrate their wealth and importance, only the most successful philanthropists leave a genuine and original mark. Those are the philanthropists who are *not* principally motivated by statements of status but who bring their own personal passions to bear upon their projects. Their personal involvement in their philanthropic enterprises makes the difference. Because they spend time with artists, musicians, scientists, or local citizens, they understand what will help them, what will spark other projects. These successful philanthropists then *stay* involved, providing the stability and continuity that make for success.

The most striking fact about the database philanthropists is that they are almost evenly split between men and women, the only group of which this is true. Their average obit was a little over thirteen inches long. Just over half the philanthropists had a college degree, as shown in Table 9-1. Of those with degrees, 60 percent came from one of the top fifty schools; more than a third had degrees from the Ivy League. One quarter held an advanced degree of some kind. More than 30 percent of the men held law degrees. For almost a third, no educational information was given.

The Apex of Fame, shown in Table 9-2, is topped by Paul Mellon. It is also almost equally divided between men and women. It is dominated by those who have given to the arts, whether museums or opera companies. A handful were major patrons of science. One theater patron, heiress Doris Duke, was big on animal rights and preserving the astonishing collection of mansions at Newport, Rhode Island; while Zachary Fisher backed the Intrepid Sea-Air-Space Museum. What is also noticeable is the source of their fortunes: more than two thirds of the men made their money in business, while the bulk of the women inherited it.

The initial impetus for the National Gallery of Art came not from Paul Mellon but from his father, Andrew Mellon, a Pittsburgh financier whose son described him as having "an astonishing flair for recognizing nascent industrial potentialities." Having built a huge financial empire, Andrew Mellon then served as U.S. treasury secretary from 1921 to 1932. His son dutifully worked in the family bank

TABLE 9-1. *Education of the Philanthropists in the Obituary Database, by Sex*

Education	Men (N = 122) (%)	Women (N = 126) (%)	Total (N = 248) (%)
High school or less	3.5	4.0	3.6
Some college	9.8	13.5	11.7
College graduate (no higher degree)	23.8	32.5	28.2
Master's or equivalent degree	5.7	4.8	5.2
Ph.D.	1.6	0.8	1.2
M.D.	0.8	0.8	0.8
Law degree	30.3	0.8	15.3
Other professional degrees	1.6	0.8	1.2
Not stated	23.0	42.1	32.7
Total	**100.0**	**100.0**	**100.0**
Attended college (%)	73.8	54.0	63.7
Graduated from college (%)	63.9	40.5	52.0
Achieved a higher degree (%)	40.2	7.9	23.8

Note: There were 248 obituaries in the database in which the principal gained fame because of his or her philanthropy. Of these, 51 percent were of women and 49 percent were of men.

after completing his education at Yale and Cambridge in England but concluded that commerce left him utterly cold. Paul Mellon summoned the courage to inform his father that he could not be "an inadequate replica of yourself, or a counterfeit," and to his amazement his father didn't mind. Meanwhile, Secretary Mellon, having decided that Washington needed a world-class art museum, offered to build it and donate his own superb collection of paintings. The collection included thirty-one masterpieces from the legendary Hermitage Museum in Leningrad, sold by a Soviet Union desperate for hard currency. Construction of the National Gallery had just begun in 1937 when Andrew Mellon died.

TABLE **9-2.** *The Apex of Fame: Philanthropists in the Obituary Database*

Name (Age at Death)	Date	College	Degree
1. Paul Mellon (91)	02/03/99	Yale*	B.A.
2. Bernard Cantor (79)	07/06/96	NYU	None
3. Doris Duke (80)	10/29/93	None	None
4. Lucille Lortel (98)	04/06/99	Adelphi	None
5. Betsey Cushing Whitney (89)	03/26/98	None	None
6. Alice Tully (91)	12/11/93	None	None
7. Avery Fisher (87)	02/27/94	NYU*	B.A.
8. Mary Lasker (93)	02/23/94	Radcliffe*	B.A.
9. Zachary Fisher (88)	06/05/99	None	None
10. Lita A. Hazen (86)	10/03/95	None	None
11. Janet Hooker (93)	12/16/97	None	None
12. Elizabeth Noyce (65)	09/20/96	Tufts	None
13. Dorothy H. Hirshon (89)	01/31/98	Bennett Junior College	None
14. Dorothy Chandler (96)	07/08/97	Stanford	None
15. J. Richardson Dilworth (81)	12/31/97	Yale*	Law
16. Milton Petrie (92)	11/08/94	Not named	—
17. Francis Goelet (72)	05/23/98	Harvard*	B.A.
18. Jack Weiler (91)	10/14/95	Not named	None
19. William Rosenwald (93)	11/01/96	MIT*	B.S.
20. Lawrence A. Fleischman (71)	02/04/97	U. Detroit	B.A.
21. Leo Jaffe (88)	08/21/97	NYU*	B.A.
22. Batsheva de Rothschild (84)	04/22/99	Columbia	None
23. Sybil Harrington (89)	09/19/98	Not named	—
24. Catherine Shouse (98)	12/15/94	Wheaton*	M.A.
25. Louise Rheinhardt Smith (91)	07/15/95	NYU*	B.A.
26. Henry A. Loeb (90)	01/28/98	Princeton*	Law

* Graduated from college

Note: More than half of the philanthropists in this table are women. Their contributions included creative support of the arts, music, education, and medicine.

Source of Wealth	Philanthropic Fame	Obit Length
Heir	National Gallery of Art	115"
Financier	Art museumsin N.Y.C. and L.A.; Rodin Collection	80"
Family	Animal rights, AIDS, historical preservation, Duke University	79"
Husband	Doyenne of Off-Broadway Theater	76"
Husband	Museum of Modern Art; Yale; New York Hospital–Cornell Medical Center	65"
Family Inheritance	Lincoln Center, Metropolitan Museum of Art, and other art institutions	53"
Fisher Radio	Arts organizations (Lincoln Center) and universities	44"
Husband	Medicine and urban beautification; Albert and Mary Lasker Foundation	43"
Real estate	Intrepid Sea-Air-Space Museum; Fisher Armed Forces Scholarships	41"
Family	Cold Spring Harbor Lab; medical research and arts	39"
Family	Smithsonian; redecoration of the White House and State Department	35"
Divorce settlement	Promoted economic development for state of Maine	34"
Divorce settlement	Neighborhood children's center; New York City Human Rights Commission; the arts	33"
Family	Modernization of Los Angeles; Music Center of Los Angeles County	32"
Finance	Metropolitan Museum of Art; Yale Art Museum	32"
Petrie Stores Corp.	Charities, museums, and needy people he read about in the newspaper	28"
Goelet Corp.	Metropolitan Opera; New World Records; Atlantic Salmon Federation	28"
Real estate co.	Medicine, education, and Jewish causes	27"
Private investor	Education and the arts; Jewish causes and United Jewish Appeal	27"
Kennedy Gallery	Museums: Getty, Detroit, Cleveland, and others	26"
Columbia Pictures	Education, civic and Jewish causes	26"
Family	Martha Graham School; de Rothschild Foundation for Arts and Sciences	26"
Husband	New York Metropolitan Opera; medical charities	25"
Heiress	Wolf Trap Farm Park for the Performing Arts	24"
Art collection	Museum of Modern Art (New York City)	24"
Finance	Mount Sinai Medical Center; the New School; civic and Jewish causes	24"

Paul Mellon, the son, assumed charge, taking on with great dignity and modesty the mantle of a very powerful and influential philanthropist. Mellon, who loved the English countryside and raising horses, could easily have retreated to the life of a wealthy English gentleman. He had spent much of his childhood in England because his mother and her second husband were English. Instead he had returned to the United States and dedicated himself to using his father's vast fortune to preserve and open up new worlds of art and beauty to the public. He had grown up with a father "seemingly devoid of feeling and so tightly contained in his lifeless, hard shell." But the son embraced all that was beautiful in art and nature and developed a passionate belief in their saving grace. In 1991, he gave to the National Gallery a portrait of a young girl by George Romney that had long hung in his family's house. All those decades later, he could still recall, "In Pittsburgh, that painting was like an oasis in a desert of smog." Art and nature played an almost life-saving role for him, a rich boy whose divorced parents were preoccupied with their own lives. He clearly hoped they would do the same for his fellow citizens. In 1967, he explained that he deeply believed that "There is no intellectual or emotional substitute for the authentic, the original, the unique masterpiece. Just as there is no substitute for the world of direct sensual experience."

Over the years, Paul Mellon served on the board of directors of the National Gallery of Art and was responsible for the addition in 1978 of the spectacular $100 million East Wing. He refused to have his family's name emblazoned anywhere, believing that that would deter other art collectors from donating their works to what he saw as a national museum. Ultimately he himself, who spent many an hour at the gallery seeing to various matters, would give 913 works to the institution, including forty paintings by Degas, fifteen by Cézanne, and five by van Gogh. He also became an ardent collector of unfashionable British art, eventually creating a special and much-admired museum, the Yale Center for British Art, to house that collection. These were his best-known charities, for they had his imprint, but Mellon foundations also supported many other artistic and environmental enterprises over the decades.

After the National Gallery, Paul Mellon's greatest legacy almost certainly was land preservation. He always loved the rural life and was a lifelong horseman. His principal residence was a four-thousand-acre horse farm in Virginia. He and his wife also maintained houses and estates not just in the usual haunts of the superrich, such as Manhattan and Paris, but also in Antigua and Cape Cod. His love of the American seashore and concern about the deteriorating environment led him to give great sums of money to help preserve what would become the Cape Hatteras National Seashore, the Great Beach of Cape Cod, Cumberland Island off the coast of Georgia, and Sky Meadows State Park in Virginia.

But Mellon's true jewel was the National Gallery, and it shone as it did because John Walker III was first the chief curator and then the museum's longtime director; he "shaped the museum into a world-class institution." The *New York Times* described Walker as "a member of a ground-breaking generation of museum professionals who, spurred by a wide-ranging interest in art old and new, left an indelible stamp on this country's art institutions, often inventing them from scratch." It so happened that Walker had grown up in Pittsburgh, also the only son of wealthy parents, and had been Paul Mellon's friend since childhood. Like many of the wealthy boys of his era, he attended Harvard as a matter of course. But there he found *his* passion when he studied art history and museums under Professor Paul J. Sachs, who turned out to be a great influence on a whole generation of cultural leaders. From Harvard, Walker headed to Florence, where he spent six years studying the Old Masters under Bernard Berenson, the great connoisseur and expert on Italian art. Walker's first job was in the department of fine arts at the American Academy of Rome. In 1937, he married the daughter of an English earl, and by 1939 he arrived in Washington to work under the National Gallery's first director, David E. Finley.

Walker arrived as architect John Pope Russell's magnificent Old World structure was being built, which enabled him to have an all-important "hand in the museum's layout," as well as the opportunity to help install the original collection. Later directors would describe Walker as the museum's "unsung hero" and the "art brains behind it." A curator for European paintings at the Metropolitan Museum of Art in Manhattan said of Walker, "His great achievement was in persuading all these American collectors to give their collections to the nation. These enormous collections, which would have been given to their local museums, went instead to Washington. They found his argument irresistible. Exhibitions come and go. It's the great art that remains."

And Walker was always in passionate pursuit of great art. His background gave him easy access to those with money or art. It was not by chance that Paul Mellon and his sister, Alisa, gave hundreds of their best paintings to the National Gallery, nor that the East Wing came to be built. Walker's greatest triumph was landing the Chester Dale collection, with its luminescent French Impressionists. Reported the *New York Times*, "The wooing of Dale, a mercurial stockbroker, was so trying that it turned [Walker's] hair white and left him on tranquilizers for the rest of his life." But Dale not only came through with his fabulous art, he left the persistent Walker a bequest big enough for the gallery director to buy a summer place on Fisher Island, Florida, that he wryly called Will O'Dale.

The National Gallery of Art is just one of the most preeminent of the many new museums that have enriched our national life in recent decades. At a time when the predominance of electronic media—whether movies, television, or recorded music—has removed most of us from firsthand cultural experiences, museums remain places offering the genuinely authentic, art and artifacts that can be experienced in an intimate, personal way. In early January 1999, Museum of Modern Art director Glenn Lowry pondered the extraordinary success of museums, their ascension to "the pre-eminent cultural institutions of our time, a symbol of power, stature and sophistication. In the United States alone there are more than 1,240 art museums, half of which are less than twenty-five years old. . . . Once seen as elite, these institutions enjoy broad popular appeal."[2] In museums, at a time when so much of what we experience visually is through a screen, people can look at art and other artifacts and respond directly. They can observe how paint is laid on, they can scrutinize just how medieval armor is constructed. Museums present actual physical objects. They are also highly democratic, social public spaces, again at a time when many feel atomized, isolated. More Americans go to museums than attend live sports.[3] And so museums have become institutions that answer many contemporary needs: the human need to mingle with others in a neutral public space, the search for knowledge, and the desire to experience something real, not ersatz. And also the chance to move beyond ourselves, whether through art or fascinating objects that transcend the everyday. As Paul Mellon once declared, "What this country needs is a good five-cent reverie."

Like Paul Mellon, Dominique de Menil of Houston believed in the redeeming power of art and beauty. Initially collecting with her husband, John de Menil, she continued on her own after his death in 1973 and in 1987 opened an exquisite museum in their hometown that charged no fees, had no shop, but simply "fostered the contemplation of an astonishingly wide range of objects." Wrote the *New York Times* art critic John Russell, "Everything that was of true quality interested them, from Etruscan art to Cycladic sculptures, Byzantine bronzes, African tribal art, the Surrealist paintings of Max Ernst and the recent work of Cy Twombly, an American painter long resident in Italy."

While on the surface such a museum might suggest a woman and collector removed from the hurly-burly of life, de Menil, the mother of five, was very much a civic activist. After all, despite her family's wealth (based on oil-well technology), she and her husband had had to flee France and the Nazis in 1941. One of her first enterprises in Houston was buying a run-down movie theater in a black neighborhood that became an exhibition space for black artists past and present. De Menil organized and installed the shows herself. She also brought to Houston other unique spaces, including a nondenominational Rothko Chapel. Imposing Rothko paintings dominated, setting a somber tone, along with Barnett Newman's sculpture *Broken Obelisk*. And just before de Menil died in 1998, she preserved a series of Byzantine frescoes on loan from Cyprus in a new Greek Orthodox chapel.

Herbert Waide Hemphill, Jr., was a born collector. As a child in Atlantic City, where his father operated a lucrative fleet of two thousand wicker rolling chairs, Hemphill used to sally forth to bigger cities with his mother as she searched for Dresden china. Hemphill held up his end by collecting marbles, stamps, duck decoys, puzzle jugs, and south Jersey glass bottles. At his various prep schools, he was an art and theater type. He then spent a formative year at Bard College studying with painter Stefan Hirsch, who also collected folk art. When Hemphill moved to Manhattan in 1949, he followed the collecting crowd and began buying serious modern art. But soon he began dabbling in folk art, perhaps because he missed the sort of venues where he had found his childhood treasures: the junk shops and flea markets. By 1956, he was focused exclusively on folk art. His East Thirtieth Street brownstone fast filled with treasures, more than three thousand objects ranging from paintings to bottle-cap animals to fish decoys and whirligigs.

In 1964, Hemphill was one of six founders of the Museum of American Folk Art in Manhattan. He then spent the next decade as the museum's first curator, organizing such shows as "20th-Century Folk Art and Artists," "Tattoo," and "Occult." Two of Hemphill's major contributions were to expand the definition of folk art beyond objects made in New England before 1900 and to include living artists in his collection. Hemphill traveled the back roads and went off the beaten track, ever on the lookout for new talent and new things. He was a dedicated browser of parking-lot flea markets and yard sales. He was also ever prepared to lend his works, and eventually twenty-four museums took advantage of that generosity. In 1986, he donated 427 folk artworks to the National Museum of American Art in Washington, making folk art one of its new strengths. Said the director of the Folk Art Museum, "It is impossible to consider folk art in America without recognizing Hemphill's major contributions."

Another type of museum was started by George C. Dade, who tried to capture and preserve an exhilarating moment in American history with his Cradle of Aviation Museum at Mitchel Field in Uniondale, Long Island. Dade was born in the tiny town of Blackduck, Minnesota, where he spent his childhood through age nine. Then, in 1921, his father, a master woodworker, was enticed east to Glenn Curtiss's airplane factory. He helped turn Sitka spruce into the airplanes that launched early aviation. And so young George Dade found himself "watching the pioneering giants of aviation taking off from his front yard." Hanging around the airport at Curtiss Field, George Dade came to meet Richard E. Byrd, Amelia Earhart, and Charles A. Lindbergh. He was honored when the mechanics would let him set out the blazing kerosene pots that lined the runways at night. As he grew up, he got jobs at Curtiss Field varnishing planes, operating the public address system during air shows, and performing other sorts of helpful chores.

Naturally, Dade wanted to learn how to fly, and by age seventeen he had his pilot's license. He bought a plane for $375 and then crashed it into what he had thought was a haystack but was actually a rock topped with hay. He and his younger brother so expertly retrieved and repaired the wrecked plane that they fell into a whole new kind of business—retrieving wrecks for other pilots—which says something about the pell-mell nature of early flying. Their success came from a "biaxial support system" that kept "fragile planes from twisting during transport." This stumbled-upon business would pay off big-time during World War II, when Dade Brothers made $50 million packing and sending planes overseas for the United States and its allies.

With a fortune in hand, George Dade could begin to collect the old planes of those pioneering days of flight. In 1973, he scored a coup by locating and buying Lindbergh's very first plane. Crashed by a later owner, it was moldering away in "an Iowa hog barn." This plane had great sentimental value for Dade because he had been around when Lindbergh was preparing for his historic solo crossing to Paris. The "hog barn" plane became the centerpiece of Dade's collection of sixty planes, rockets, and missiles. What Dade found enthralling was the romance of human flight. At a time when many take flying for granted (and sometimes even hateful, as inflicted by commercial airlines), Dade wanted to preserve flying's early, perilous days and convey the wonder of its development from then to now.

What all our museum people have in common—both philanthropists and curator-directors—is a great passion for their specialty and the desire to share that with as broad an audience as possible while still presenting what was real. Many people can and do get rich, but those who go on to use their money in a creative way to open new worlds to others are rare.

Our next group of movers and shakers were almost all men and women who viewed live music as an indispensable joy and pleasure and who donated large amounts of time, energy, intelligence, and money to making music a more ordinary part of everyday life.

On the West Coast, Dorothy Buffum Chandler used her status as a power at the *Los Angeles Times* to "transform modern Los Angeles . . . Her greatest single achievement was probably her nine-year drive . . . to finance and build the Music Center of Los Angeles County, which revitalized the city's downtown district." Dorothy Chandler was a powerful force in many arenas, starting with her husband's family's newspaper. But as a philanthropist, her great lifetime work was what came to be known as the Dorothy Chandler Pavilion, a cultural center meant to accomplish numerous things. One purpose was civic: to give southern California a mecca of pop culture, a venue in which to hear fine classical music. Chandler could not imagine an aspiring world-class city minus such a basic accouterment of modern civilization. One *Los Angeles Times* editor described her thus: "She was just really a ball of fire with whatever she set her mind to, whatever she wanted to get done." Her own self-assessment was this: "I think of myself as a catalyst. There are so many people with good ideas and good intentions. They doubtless know more about the arts than I do. But I pull them together. That's my job."

But she was also determined to make wealthy Californians see the possibilities and necessity of philanthropy. Reported the *New York Times*, "One friend recalled how she tore up a $200,000 check from a wealthy businessman and handed it back to him, telling him that it was unacceptably paltry." Unfortunately, her influence was not lasting. When the *Chronicle of Philanthropy* rated cities for charitable giving in the mid-1990s, Minneapolis came in first, New York twenty-seventh, and Los Angeles ranked forty-eighth.

Like any other major endeavor in life, philanthropy requires leaders who will strongly remind those who have reaped that they must also sow. Americans, more than any other nationality, believe deeply in the value and potential of charity. Rich people are *expected* to be generous in giving away their millions. When people are not wondering how

Microsoft ever managed to dominate the computer market with its maddening Windows product, they are speculating about how CEO Bill Gates will disperse his billions in a meaningful way. And indeed, we are entering a whole new era of philanthropy. In 1980, there were 22,000 family and private foundations. By 1997, that figure had more than doubled, rising to 54,000; the Foundation Center estimated the assets of these organizations to be $300 billion.[5]

In mid-1999, the *Economist* reported that Americans had donated $175 billion to nonprofit organizations.[6] Three quarters ($109 billion) came from living individuals, $13 billion came from foundations, $13 billion from bequests, and $8 billion from companies. This tradition of charity and philanthropy has created and funded so many enterprises—everything from universities to symphony orchestras—that nonprofits now account for 8 percent of the gross domestic product and employ a striking 10 percent of the workforce.[7]

How do we know these facts and figures? Because of the work of Ralph L. Nelson, an "innovative Queens College professor . . . widely regarded as a father of the economic study of philanthropy." Until Professor Nelson became interested in and demonstrated the economic importance of charitable giving, economists had no interest in it. In 1984, Nelson crowned two decades of work on philanthropy with a "complex economic model based on survey data and other variables to produce annual estimates of current donations." The development of reliable figures on philanthropic giving then made possible a whole new branch of economics that has established that tax rates, the state of the stock market, and which political party is in power all affect charitable giving.

The importance of major philanthropy in a community cannot be overstated. In a society like ours that has made a collective decision that the arts in particular will not get much government funding, if the local rich are not willing to ante up for local colleges and cultural institutions, their communities will be the poorer in many ways. Truly clever philanthropists with big ambitions will always try to leverage their donations. Thus, Dorothy Chandler, for example, first raised $19 million and then figured out how to raise another $13.7 million through bonds that would be guaranteed by the county. In the course of that venture, she taught Los Angelenos that they could come together and create something big and important. She herself was a young transplant from Illinois whose family prospered in the Golden State with the Buffum Department stores. She met Norman Chandler, scion of the family that owned the *Los Angeles Times*, while at Stanford and married him soon thereafter. She was a woman with a strong sense of noblesse oblige and the will to motivate others to her point of view.

On the East Coast, another department store heiress, this one a Filene living outside Washington, D.C., led the way in creating a new and major venue for the performing arts. Catherine Filene Shouse was the philanthropist who donated Wolf Trap in Virginia, an outdoor national park for the performing arts. Catherine Filene Shouse was unusual for her time, a Boston heiress who was given a top-notch education. In an era when the rich generally preferred their daughters to attend finishing school, make their social debut, and then marry, Catherine Filene earned a B.A. at Wheaton College and then a master's in education from Harvard. She then became active in national politics. President Calvin Coolidge appointed her the chairwoman of the First Federal Prison for Women.

In 1930, she bought Wolf Trap Farm, across the Potomac River and fifteen miles west of the capital. There she would become a serious dog breeder in the 1940s. After the end of her first marriage, she remarried, this time to Jovett Shouse, a former member of Congress and lawyer, and they were very much fixtures on the Washington social scene. In 1949, she became seriously involved in Washington's musical life—such as it then was—serving in various capacities on the board of the National Symphony Orchestra. She was instrumental in getting the Kennedy Center built. But while the Kennedy Center was fine for a certain kind of esthetic experience, Mrs. Shouse was clearly thinking of something that combined the pleasures of music or dance, lovely summer evenings, and picnics on the grass with friends and family. So she took a hundred acres of Wolf Trap Farm and gave it to the U.S. Department of the Interior. At the same time, she set up the Wolf Trap Foundation "to manage the park, arrange programming and raise money," a unique partnership between the public and private sectors for managing an arts center. One suspects that only a longtime Washington insider could have pulled off such an arrangement.

Wolf Trap opened in 1971 and quickly became a cherished part of summer in the capital. When the main amphitheater was destroyed by a fire in 1982, Mrs. Shouse led the drive to rebuild it, and also to build an additional seven-thousand-seat Filene Center. She helped raise $9 million and then persuaded Congress to put up a matching sum. In 1984, Wolf Trap reopened, and once again the audiences returned, delighted to sup on fried chicken while fine music wafted through the sultry summer night. Each year, half a million people go to enjoy themselves at Wolf Trap, thanks to the philanthropy of Catherine Filene Shouse.

Our remaining trio of musical philanthropists are all associated with Lincoln Center in Manhattan, one of the world's premier venues for the performing arts. Alice Tully was a singer of average talent whose late-life philanthropy turned her into a major and beloved force in music, a name familiar to many from Alice Tully Hall at Lincoln Center. Born in Corning, New York, where her mother's family owned Corning Glass, Alice Tully's family moved to New York City when her lawyer father went there to work for the Metropolitan Life Insurance Company. By her teens, Tully had decided to dedicate herself to a musical career. Though she played piano, her real love was singing. She studied voice in New York for three years, then sailed to Paris for seven more years of study. She made her professional debut there in 1927 singing works by Gluck, Franck, and Faure. Six years later, she returned to New York for her operatic debut, singing Santuzza in *Cavalleria Rusticana.* Long after she had retired from performing, she would say, "It may not have been the biggest career, but it was a good one. I was always concerned with the best in music, and I think I had something individual to offer."

During World War II, Alice Tully settled in New York City, where she put her skills as an aviator to use, flying along the coast looking for signs of enemy submarines. She also worked as a nurses' aide at the French Hospital in Manhattan, tending war wounded. She would continue to sing professionally until 1950. Then, in 1958, her mother died and Alice Tully inherited the huge Corning Glass fortune. She now embarked on a new role as philanthropist. After decades as a passionate musician, she knew firsthand the many ways money could make a difference in the arts. Above all, musicians need a performing space that showcases their skills, while the audience needs a listening space that allows them to savor the artistry. Two of the theaters at Lincoln Center were considered acoustic disasters, and so initially Tully balked when approached about underwriting a new chamber-music hall at the Juilliard Building. But when Lincoln Center brought in a top-flight acoustician, Tully agreed to pay most of the $4.5 million cost. With the sound problem firmly in hand, Tully looked to the issue of patron comfort. "I had spent so many, many hours cramped in narrow spaces, both here and in Europe," she explained to the architects, determined that for once there would be adequate legroom. When the architects objected, saying this would cost three rows of seats, Tully went to the president of Lincoln Center and said, "Do let us have one comfortable hall in New York City." After prevailing in the battle of the legroom, Tully focused on the creation of a resident Chamber Music Society and was its board chairwoman for many years. When the new hall opened in 1969, it was hailed as "a superb setting for chamber music, both acoustically and visually."

While she would be most associated with Lincoln Center because of her hall there, Tully also gave generously to such dance organizations as the Martha Graham Dance Company and Elliot Feld, and was always an important patron of Manhattan's many premier museums. Much of her money was donated anonymously. One pianist who made playing for the disabled and for people in state mental institutions one of his special projects did not know for years that it had been Alice Tully who was underwriting him. Said one friend of hers, "She wouldn't know herself how much money she had donated. She did what she thought was best, where she thought it would do the most good."

Like Alice Tully, Avery Fisher also had a minor musical career. He was "an influential figure in New York musical circles, an amateur violinist whose love of music led him to build his own high-quality radios and phonographs." That early tinkering developed into a highly profitable high-fidelity business. With that fortune, Avery Fisher became a major philanthropist. He, too, underwrote a hall at Lincoln Center, now named for him.

Avery Fisher was born in Brooklyn into a large family where music reigned. His father had a huge record collection, and parents and children all played musical instruments. Though he thought about becoming a professional musician, Fisher did not. Instead, he earned a degree from New York University in biology and English. He worked for a while in advertising and then in 1932 entered publishing as a book designer. Long after, he would still describe book design as his "first love," saying, "Looking at a beautiful typographical design is like listening to music." Even as he designed books by day, once home he was busy tinkering, improving the sound quality of radios. By 1937, that hobby had become a company Fisher called Philharmonic Radio. In 1945, he sold that company and then began another, Fisher Radio. He lured numerous European engineers to the United States with far higher salaries than they could make in Europe: "Those fellows turned out superb equipment." Nor did the Fisher Radio folks rest on their laurels of turning out the Rolls-Royce of audio equipment. Fisher and his engineers were always on the cutting edge, incorporating the latest technical improvements. But by 1969, Fisher was ready to retire, and he sold his company for almost $31 million.

In 1976, Avery Fisher gave $10.5 million to Lincoln Center. Four fifths was to go to maintaining Philharmonic Hall and another fifth to one of Avery Fisher's favorite creations, a program that gave cash awards to young musicians. But then Lincoln Center came to him asking to use $4 million of the maintenance gift to try once again to rectify the famously bad acoustics in the Philharmonic. Fisher agreed and took "an active if unofficial hand in the process." Reopened as Avery Fisher Hall, the renovation did not deliver acoustical perfection but was "generally agreed to have solved many of its original problems."

Fisher was a generous donor to the arts who served on numerous boards of directors and also gave money to NYU, his alma mater. But closest to his heart were his awards to young musicians. He knew how difficult and competitive the life of an aspiring musician was. And as a constant attender of musical performances, he had seen some young musicians developing. The Avery Fisher Career Grant provided $10,000 for the many expenses struggling musicians encountered. For better-established American instrumentalists, there was the prestigious $25,000 Avery Fisher Prize. "Music has been my life, and my family's, too," explained Fisher in 1986, on the tenth anniversary of the establishment of the prizes. Many of Fisher's friends were musicians, and he enjoyed inviting them to his Park Avenue apartment: "It's a busman's holiday for them and we have a grand old time."

Francis Goelet was from an old-line Manhattan family of great wealth. And like Alice Tully and Avery Fisher, he was a deeply involved patron of the city's classical musical life. A longtime member of the board of the Metropolitan Opera, Goelet made his mark as a philanthropist by commissioning "dozens of new musical works, many opera productions and an important contemporary music recording project."

Born in Bordeaux, France, Francis Goelet grew up there and then went to the United States to attend prep school and Harvard. He eventually became chairman of the Goelet Corporation, "a private company that oversaw his family's interests and investments in mining, oil and gas businesses." The Goelets, wealthy people who had served on many boards, had long been active in New York's cultural life. But Francis Goelet went beyond the usual noblesse oblige to become personally involved in ensuring that these musical venues would have fresh, innovative material. He paid for all or some of the staging of seventeen new operas for the Met. Three were world premieres: Samuel Barber's *Vanessa* and *Antony and Cleopatra* and John Corigliano's *Ghosts of Versailles.*

A longtime member of the Metropolitan Opera's board, Goelet then joined the board of the New York Philharmonic Symphony Society in 1959 and was active on its music policy committee. From this vantage point, he began commissioning new music. The *New York Times* noted that "several of these have become 20th century landmarks, among them Toru Takemitsu's 'November Steps,' Elliott Carter's 'Concerto for Orchestra,' Roger Sessions's 'Symphony No. 8' and Aaron Copland's 'Inscape.'" In 1992, he paid for thirty-six new works to celebrate the Philharmonic's 150th anniversary. The pieces were written by a wide range of composers, from Alfred Schnittke to Steve Reich. Then, in 1975, in an effort to reach beyond performances, Goelet undertook his most significant endeavor: creating New World Records. Inspired by the nation's bicentennial, this anthology of recorded music aimed to document the full variety of American music, whether jazz, cowboy songs, or early rock. This was a massive, ambitious enterprise running to one hundred discs. He would remain the label's chairman until his death in 1998. It is probably hard to overestimate the impact of this one generous man on the world of new music.

Mary Lasker was a philanthropist who thoroughly understood the concept of leverage. In 1944, she and her husband, an advertising executive who knew something about how to gain people's attention, began bestowing the Albert Lasker Awards for "outstanding contributions to clinical and basic medical research." The point of the award was to spotlight major diseases and the need for more research money. But the awards also acted to recognize and support promising work, thereby influencing medicine. To ensure that the awards were bestowed on the truly worthy, not just an admired elder or someone's friend, nominations were solicited from the top people at medical schools and research institutes. Then a separate jury reviewed the nominations and voted. Decade by decade, the Lasker Awards accrued more and more prestige, for they consistently highlighted truly important work. By 1995, 52 of the 275 Lasker Award winners had gone on to win Nobel Prizes.

Even as the Lasker Awards were attracting attention to important medical work, Mary Lasker was lobbying government officials to underwrite more research. "I am opposed to heart attacks and cancer and strokes," she used to say, "the way I am opposed to sin. Without money nothing gets done." She particularly focused her efforts on getting Congress to support the National Institutes of Health. "The N.I.H. has flowered," said Dr. Michael E. DeBakey, for thirty years chairman of the Lasker Prize jury, "because in many ways she gave birth to it and nursed it. It was in existence, but it was she who got the funding for it." Lasker was a frequent visitor to Washington, D.C., where she lobbied not only for more NIH funding but also for the creation of new research centers dedicated to specific diseases. She was a highly effective lobbyist, said

Dr. DeBakey: "She went with ideas and what might be called humanitarian concerns and it was very difficult to oppose that." She also understood the importance of scientists meeting legislators and arranged these sorts of encounters. It certainly helped that she had what Robert Moses once rhapsodized were "the blend of many essences in the beautiful package: intelligence, vision, generosity, charm, kindness—Mary has them all."

Mary Lasker was born in Watertown, Wisconsin, the daughter of a banker. Her mother was an activist who founded two parks. (Her mother's influence was evident in Mary's great love for public beautifying through landscaping and planting flowers.) Mary went east to Radcliffe, graduating cum laude before putting in a brief stint at Oxford. She then returned to enter the Manhattan world of art and art galleries, working at the Reinhardt Galleries. As she engaged in acquisitions, loans, and benefit shows, she also began to build her own art collection. For a time, she was married to the gallery's owner, Paul Reinhardt. In 1940, some years after she left the world of art, she met and married Albert Lasker, a wealthy and successful retired advertising executive. He encouraged her in her passionate interest in helping medicine, an interest apparently inspired "partly by illnesses of people around her and by her own health." Five decades of medical activism made Mary Lasker a real force in the world of science and medicine, a woman who could persuade Congress of the value of major funding for medical research both basic and applied: "I couldn't cut up a frog, and I certainly couldn't perform surgery. I'm better at making it possible for other people." Dr. DeBakey thought her loss a great blow to medicine: "Mary Lasker is an institution unto herself. Asking what her importance has been is like asking what Harvard has meant to this country." In 1985, her devotion to the gardening world earned her a pink tulip named in her honor.

Lita Annenberg Hazen was another major philanthropist who was active mainly in the scientific world. While Mary Lasker's great legacy was the blossoming of the NIH, Lita Hazen's was the Cold Spring Harbor Laboratory on Long Island and the Mount Sinai School of Medicine in Manhattan. "Lita Hazen was a wonderful patron of pure science, who enjoyed bright and unusual people who would say things that she wouldn't expect," said Dr. James Watson, a Nobel laureate and director of Cold Spring Harbor.

Lita Hazen was one of eight children of Sadie and Moses L. Annenberg, a family made very rich through media holdings. Like many rich girls of her time, Lita had no college education but married an entertainment lawyer/Hollywood producer. While all the Annenberg children were generous to charity, several became renowned philanthropists. Lita Hazen's daughter recalled, "Medical discoveries were the most exciting and important things that she could imagine, and I don't remember her ever thinking differently or anything that competed with that. She always envisioned that someone would have a better answer." Like many of the philanthropists we have written about, Lita Hazen had personal relationships with many of the scientists and doctors whose work she admired; thus, she had a good sense of how money could help foster better medicine and medical research. Over the years, she endowed professorships in such fields as immunochemistry and molecular biology. She also endowed a research foundation that brought together scientists in varying fields to cross-fertilize their ideas. She founded a biomedical workshop at the Aspen Institute that enabled junior scientists to meet Nobel laureates. She understood the importance of ideas flowering and flowing.

Another major philanthropist of science was Howard B. Keck, who used his Superior Oil Company fortune to finance the M. Keck Observatory, "a highly sophisticated telescope built by the California Institute of Technology and the University of California on top of Mauna Kea, an extinct volcano on the island of Hawaii." The telescope, which began operating in the 1980s, was built in the hope that it could begin answering "fundamental questions about the origins and nature of the universe." Other areas of science that the W. M. Keck Foundation funded were oceanography, pharmacology, and genetics, and research into uses of lasers for surgery.

Howard Keck was the son of William Keck, who had built Superior Oil into one of the nation's largest oil-and-gas-producing companies. Howard had numerous interests besides business and liked fast things, fielding winning cars in stock racing and winning horses in the Kentucky Derby. After his father died in 1964, Howard Keck turned Superior Oil into a leading "independent company for energy exploration and production." After Keck had a fight with his sister, who wanted the company sold, Mobil paid $5.7 billion for Superior.

Well-thought-out philanthropy that is also directed at specific problems can be very influential and quite effective. Dana C. Creel was a major force behind the Rockefeller Brothers Fund from 1950 to 1975, when he was president and director, presiding over $150 million in funding. "Dana Creel was an innovative giver who directed money to places that were not particularly prominent or popular at the time," said one Rockefeller adviser. What that meant was backing groups such as the Southern Regional Council, which was promoting integration in the South in the 1950s, or the National Urban League, giving money to create a Skills Bank that would recruit blacks to work in government and private business. Individual grants went to members of minority groups attending law school. Creel probably had more than the usual concern because he himself had grown up in the Deep South in Smyrna, Georgia, and earned a law degree from Emory University Law School in 1939. He was briefly a financial adviser to the Rockefeller Brothers Fund, attended Harvard Business School, and then joined the Army in World War II. Time spent serving in Asia during the war made him aware of the crushing nature of Third World poverty.

Creel also funded women's education when this was not terribly popular, not to mention birth control. "These were not the typical interests of wealthy people and he helped change the focus of giving," said the Rockefeller aide. At a time when cancer was spoken of mainly in whispers, Creel arranged a $6 million donation to create the Memorial Sloan-Kettering Cancer Center. These funding decisions and his low-key style apparently made him a maverick in his day.

Our final philanthropist is Elizabeth Bottomley Noyce, "a microchip millionaire's scorned first wife who showed as much imagination and verve in deploying her half of his Silicon Valley fortune as he had in making it." Born in Auburn, Massachusetts, Elizabeth Bottomley was the child of a working-class family. While attending Tufts University, she met and married a graduate student at MIT, one Robert N. Noyce. In the course of their marriage, they had four children, and they moved often as Robert Noyce helped pioneer the computer age and founded several important companies, including Intel Corporation. California, their ultimate destination, was not to Mrs. Noyce's liking, and she preferred spending summers at their fifty-acre Maine estate. When her husband divorced her to marry another Intel executive in 1975, Elizabeth Noyce consoled herself with half of his vast computer wealth and a new life in Maine, where she gave away $75 million.

While she gave to traditional sorts of places, such as the Portland Museum of Art and the Maine Maritime Museum, Noyce made her mark engaging in what she called "catalytic philanthropy," investments intended to improve the local economy. One of her most famous efforts came in response to the widespread closing of local bank branches as big out-of-state banks bought and consolidated local institutions. Concerned that local businesses would have trouble getting loans from these new institutions, in 1992 she created a new bank in downtown Portland, the Maine Bank and Trust Company. Over the next several years, it prospered enough to open fourteen branches across the state. When Maine's biggest bakery was about to be bought and shut down, throwing twelve hundred people out of work, Betty Noyce stepped in and bought it herself.

She also poured quite a bit of money and energy into brightening up Portland. When the city's downtown area began to look shabby, she acquired almost 10 percent of its run-down retail and office properties and spruced them up. This attracted new tenants such as L.L. Bean. At the time of her death in late 1996, Noyce had provided almost $10 million to build a big glass-and-wood public market, inspired by the famous Pike Place Market in Seattle. The idea was to create a lively spot in downtown Portland that would also provide a bona fide outlet for local farmers and fishermen.

Along the way, Noyce endeared herself to the state's yacht builders by commissioning two large and luxurious boats, and she helped shore up a lagging home building industry by building five homes. Yet throughout all this, she declined ever to append her name to any of her benefactions. The president of her philanthropic foundation said, "She never wanted any kind of memorial. People wanted to name scholarship funds after her, and buildings, and she always said no." However, on the second floor of the public market, there is a statue of an elderly woman pushing a cart of vegetables and feeding corn to a crow. Friends have nicknamed it, "Betty Sharing the Bounty."[8]

Perhaps as befits a woman whose fortune came from Silicon Valley, Betty Noyce was very much on the cutting edge of philanthropy, acting on the idea that money can be helpful beyond the traditional philanthropic venues of culture and medicine. As tens of thousands of newly wealthy people want to exercise their philanthropic urges, the field is presently in great flux. The president of the National Center for Family Philanthropy said in wonder in late 1998, "It's become the Wild West. The changes are seismic. It's the numbers of people involved, the diversity of interests and opportunity, with new foundations being created every day." There are even consulting firms that do nothing but advise these new rich. The president of one such firm, Philanthropic Initiatives, described a client who proposed to "throw $300 million" at finding and then nurturing brilliant minority students. Another client has taken the tack of awarding $25,000 to six "unsung heroes" each year. Some West Coast venture capitalists decided to apply their business model to philanthropy, putting money into community projects they think have promising social prospects. Another family foundation decided to focus on young fathers who are not involved with their children, feeling that reconnecting them will have a significant social payoff.[9]

One suspects that Paul Mellon would have approved of all this. He saw money mainly as a means to an end. "I think that's the usefulness of private wealth," he once explained. "Foundations and individuals can make decisions to act on things that are slightly controversial faster than governments because the machinery is less."

Notes

1. "Philanthropy in America," *Economist,* May 30, 1998, pp. 19–21.
2. Glenn D. Lowry, "The State of the Art Museum, Ever Changing," *New York Times,* January 10, 1999, sec. 2, p. 1.
3. Judith H. Dobrzynski, "Art Museum Attendance Keeps Rising in the U.S.," *New York Times,* February 1, 1999, p. D1.
4. Judith Miller, "In L.A., a New Generation Discovers Philanthropy," *New York Times,* December 8, 1997, p. 14.
5. Anne Adams Lang, "The $20,000 Surprise and Other Foundation Shakers," *New York Times,* November 18, 1998, p. 8.
6. "Philanthropy in America," p. 29.
7. Ibid, p. 19.
8. Sara Rimer, "An Idea + a Philanthropist = a Market," *New York Times,* January 1, 1999, p. A10.
9. Lang, "The $20,000 Surprise."

10

Leading Judges,
Politicians, and Lawyers

Americans pride themselves on being a people ruled by law. But they also bemoan how litigious U.S. society has become. Each year U.S. colleges turn out as many new lawyers—40,000—as new Ph.D.s. In 1950, the country had 220,000 lawyers; a half century later it has almost a million![1] In recent decades, Americans have increasingly sought out the legislature and then the courts to solve their woes and right their wrongs. In 1970, 87,300 civil cases were filed before U.S. District Courts. About 8,000, or 10 percent, of the cases came to trial. By 1996, the number of civil cases had soared to 273,000, with 7,500, or 3.1 percent, going to trial![2] And indeed, as both government agencies and businesses have grown vastly larger and more powerful, the courts have come to serve more and more as the avenue for ordinary citizens to seek justice and redress—or as a vehicle of expression for the aggrieved and vengeful.

Perhaps no judge better exemplifies this expanding vision of the law than U.S. Supreme Court Justice William J. Brennan, described in his *New York Times* obituary as "a towering figure in modern law who embodied the liberal vision of the Constitution as an engine of social and political change." In the course of thirty-four years on the highest court in the land, through eight presidential administrations, Justice Brennan authored 1,360 opinions, all of which were aimed at guaranteeing, he said, "the essential dignity and worth of each individual." Brennan's most important judicial legacies were the one-person, one-vote doctrine that "ended the established order in the nation's legislatures," numerous rulings that "transformed the Constitution's equal protection guarantee into a weapon against sex discrimination," and the enshrinement of due process, "the simple requirement that government officials meet a citizen face-to-face before taking adverse action." The *National Review*, which was no fan of Brennan's, concluded in 1984 that "There is no individual in the country, on or off the Court, who has had a more profound and sustained impact upon public policy in the United States for the past 27 years."

In this chapter we look at judges, politicians, and lawyers, three very powerful groups who create and shape our legal and legislative systems and thereby our whole society.

Judges

The four Supreme Court justices in our database, including Brennan, are all in the Apex of Fame shown in Table 10-1, each with a long front-page obituary. Federal judges preside atop the legal hierarchy not only because they wield great power but also because their legal peers know they have given up a huge income to engage in important public service. To insulate federal judges from worldly pressures, they have lifetime appointments to the bench and can be removed only by impeachment. All told, there are almost 900 federal judges in the United States. In our database, there are 174 judges, including federal, state, and local judges. The judges' obits averaged just over sixteen inches. Predictably, the vast majority held a law degree, but a few—presumably local justices—did not. Almost 30 percent attended one of the top fifty schools, with twenty-eight holding Ivy League degrees.

Not surprisingly, almost two thirds of those in the Apex of Fame were federal judges, whose cases and decisions tend to be the most important. The remainder were state and local judges who made high-profile rulings. Of the thirty-four Apex of Fame judges, half were graduates of one of the top fifty law schools. Seven, including two of the four Supreme Court justices, had a degree from Harvard Law School. Another seven had a degree from one of the other Ivy League law schools.

The lifetime tenure of the federal judges is in vivid contrast to those of the politicians, many of whom are also lawyers (see Table 10-2), who retain their jobs only on the sufferance of the voters. Moreover, there are far fewer federal-level politicians, or members of Congress: only 535 at any given time. However, for both groups—federal judges and politicians—success means having a significant impact on the nature and shape of our laws. Success also usually means moving up their respective career ladders to the more important and powerful positions—from local judge to federal district judge and from there to the appellate system and perhaps the ultimate, the Supreme Court. Politicians often start locally, achieve statewide office, go to the U.S. House of Representatives and then the Senate, where a few join the many large egos eyeing the White House.

For practicing lawyers, the law has many possible forms, anything from solo practitioner to government lawyer to corporate law. Like doctors, lawyers must acquire a professional degree. To obtain a license, lawyers must pass their state bar exam. For the many lawyers who practice in big firms, generally at the end of seven years as an associate, they are promoted to partner. If not, they are expected to leave. But whatever form practice takes—corporate, criminal, class action—success means winning cases. What is striking in recent decades has been the growth of the big national and multi-national law firms[3]. While the average income for an American lawyer has been about $75,000, top partners in big firms in cities like New York and Washington can now expect to earn more than a million a year. Moreover, the *American Lawyer*'s annual review of top law firms shows that gross revenues of the 100 largest firms doubled from 1988 to 1998 from $10.6 billion to $23.1 billion.

Justice William Brennan was viewed as highly successful not only because he was the author on so many important Supreme Court decisions but because he was able to build majorities no one thought possible as the Supreme Court gained more conservative members in his

TABLE 10-1. *The Apex of Fame: Judges in the Obituary Database*

Name (Age at Death)	Obit Date	Jurisdiction	Undergraduate College Attended
1. Warren E. Burger (87)	06/26/95	U.S. Supreme Court	U. of Minnesota (night)
2. William Brennan, Jr. (91)	07/25/97	U.S. Supreme Court	U. of Pennsylvania
3. Harry A. Blackmun (90)	03/05/99	U.S. Supreme Court	Harvard
4. Lewis Powell, Jr. (90)	08/26/98	U.S. Supreme Court	Washington and Lee
5. John Minor Wisdom (93)	05/16/99	U.S. Court of Appeals	Washington and Lee
6. Elbert P. Tuttle (98)	06/25/96	Federal appeals judge	Cornell
7. Robert Wilentz (69)	07/24/96	New Jersey chief justice	Harvard
8. A. Leon Higginbotham, Jr. (70)	12/15/98	U.S. Court of Appeals	Antioch
9. Harold Rothwax (67)	10/23/97	New York Supreme Court	City College of New York
10. Juanita K. Stout (79)	08/24/98	Philadelphia Municipal Court	U. of Iowa
11. Irving Ben Cooper (94)	09/20/96	New York and U.S. judge	U. of Missouri
12. Marie Lambert (76)	03/30/97	Surrogate Court, New York City	Brooklyn College
13. Helen B. Burnham (81)	02/14/98	Salina town judge	Utica school
14. Giles S. Rich (95)	06/12/99	U.S. Court of Appeals	Harvard
15. Thomas Murphy (89)	10/31/95	Federal judge	Georgetown
16. Owen McGivern (87)	07/08/98	New York Supreme Court	Holy Cross
17. John R. Bartels (99)	02/15/97	New York federal judge	Johns Hopkins

Law School Attended	Accomplishments and Fame	Obit Length
St. Paul College of Law	Chief justice for 17 years: position and influence	158"
Harvard	Gave Court liberal vision	152"
Harvard	Author on abortion right	150"
Washington and Lee	Crucial centrist; corporate lawyer	119"
Tulane	Helped end segregation in the South	60"
Cornell	Pro civil rights in South; judge at age 98	58"
Columbia	His court aided women and poor	49"
Yale	Only the third black appointed to the position; liberal judge	48"
Columbia	Stern criminal court judge	40"
Indiana U.	First elected black woman judge	37"
Washington U.	Judge for 60 years; various famous cases	36"
New York U.	Elected judge; "patronage queen"	35"
None	Won five terms; had no legal training	33"
Columbia	Patent court; drafted patent laws	32"
Fordham	"99% conviction record" as prosecutor	30"
St. John's	Tammany man; 14 years on the bench	30"
Harvard	Various cases: Willowbrook, Gotti, Labor	27"

(continues)

TABLE 10-1. *The Apex of Fame: Judges in the Obituary Database*

Name (Age at Death)	Obit Date	Jurisdiction	Undergraduate College Attended
18. Charles R. Richey (73)	03/21/97	U.S. District Court	Ohio Wesleyan
19. Haydn Proctor (93)	10/05/96	New Jersey Supreme Court	Lafayette
20. Lawrence D. Duke, Sr. (86)	04/01/99	Court of Fulton County, Georgia	Oglethorpe
21. Homer Thornberry (86)	12/13/95	Federal Appeals Court	U. of Texas
22. T. F. Gilroy Daly (65)	07/12/96	Federal judge	Georgetown
23. James J. Leff (77)	04/09/98	New York Supreme Court	New York U.
24. William Ringel (97)	06/01/99	New York criminal court	City College of New York
25. J. Edward Lumbard, Jr. (97)	06/07/99	U.S. Court of Appeals	Harvard
26. Charles Stewart, Jr. (78)	10/31/94	New York City federal judge	Harvard
27. Jacob D. Fuchsberg (82)	08/28/95	New York State appellate judge	Not named
28. James Yeargin (86)	12/04/95	New York City judge	Shaw
29. Walter J. Cummings (82)	05/02/99	U.S. Court of Appeals	Yale
30. Domenick Gabrielli (81)	03/28/94	New York State judge	St. Lawrence
31. Walter E. Hoffman (89)	11/24/96	Federal judge	U. of Pennsylvania
32. Ronald N. Davies (91)	04/21/96	Federal judge	U. of North Dakota
33. Nathan R. Sobel (91)	05/21/97	New York Supreme Court	Not named
34. T. Emmet Clarie (84)	09/27/97	U.S. District Court	Providence College

Note: There were 174 judges in the database. Of these, 92 percent were men and 8 percent women.

Law School Attended	Accomplishments and Fame	Obit Length
Case Western	Watergate cases and civil rights cases	27"
Yale	New Jersey Senate president; in all three branches of government	26"
Atlanta Law School	Prosecuted Klansman as assistant attorney general	26"
U. of Texas	Voice for racial justice; man of integrity	24"
Yale	Effective judge in high-profile cases	24"
Harvard	Presided at sensational homicide trials	24"
New York U. (night)	Zesty figure with headline cases	24"
Harvard	Made changes in court management	24"
Harvard	Numerous criminal and civil cases in 22 years	23"
New York U.	"Liberal judge of defense"	23"
St. John's U.	Effective prosecution as district attorney	23"
Harvard	Wrote more than 2,700 opinions	23"
Albany Law School	"Scores of major rulings"	22"
Washington and Lee	Spiro Agnew case; pro civil rights	22"
Georgetown	Integration in Little Rock High School	21"
Brooklyn College (night)	Tried 2,000 jury cases	21"
U. of Connecticut	Presided over Connecticut's most complex criminal case	21"

TABLE 10-2. *Career Characteristics of the Judges,*
Members of Congress, and Lawyers in the
Obituary Database

Characteristics	Judges (N = 174)	Members of Congress (N = 86)	Lawyers (N = 349)
College graduates	98.8%	85.5%	100%
Law degree	94.3%	51.2%	100%
Position: How obtained	Appointed*	Elected	Law degree and bar examination
Length of career	Often for life	Various	Lifetime
Mean age at death	81.7 years	79.9 years	76.5 years
Obituary Length (Column Inches)	17.6"	25.0"	11.1"

* Some local judges are elected.

later years. Some credited Brennan's time as a labor lawyer with his consensus-building skills. Said one judge, "Justice Brennan's great success on and off the Court has been achieved because he is an ebullient, generous, charismatic human being. The point is not that Justice Brennan has always been right. Rather, it is that the human qualities of the man have placed him at a formidable advantage."

Justice Brennan was born in Newark, New Jersey, the second of eight children. His parents were Irish immigrants, and his father was active in Democratic politics and the labor movement, ultimately serving as Newark's commissioner of public safety. William Brennan graduated from the Wharton School of Finance and Commerce at the University of Pennsylvania, married, and then headed off to Harvard Law School, where he graduated in the top of his class. He returned home, joined a top-level law firm, and specialized in representing management in labor disputes. He also distinguished himself in helping to lead court reform in New Jersey. In 1949, New Jersey's Republican governor asked this much-admired, well-paid, Democratic lawyer to become a poorly paid trial judge. To the amazement of the members of the local bar, Brennan agreed. Within three years he had been appointed to the state's Supreme Court, where he continued to impress people with his court reform efforts. In the spring of 1956, at a speech at the Department of Justice in Washington, D.C., on the problems of court congestion, he won notice from judicial insiders.

That fall, Brennan was asked to go to Washington to meet President Eisenhower. Brennan later said, reported the *New York Times*, that he had assumed he was being invited to head a group on court administration, a position he did not want. He was surprised to find the attorney general waiting for him at the train station in Washington and flabbergasted when informed that President Eisenhower, a Republican, wanted to name him to the Supreme Court. . . . No Catholic had served on the Court since . . . 1949, and with the 1956 Presidential election only weeks away, [it was believed this appointment] would be beneficial."

Chief Justice Warren E. Burger served as the fifteenth chief justice for seventeen years, retiring in 1986. President Richard M. Nixon appointed Burger specifically to rein in the liberal activism that had characterized Chief Justice Earl Warren, another Eisenhower-era appointee. (No doubt Nixon had noted approvingly Burger's frequent question "Why is this case in the courts? Isn't this a matter for the legislature to address?") And in marked contrast to Brennan, he liked to admonish lawyers, "If we get the notion that courts can cure all injustice, we're barking up the wrong tree."

Of course, the irony was, as the *New York Times* noted, that Chief Justice Burger's Supreme Court was "in its way as activist . . . creating new constitutional doctrine in areas like right to privacy, due process, and sexual equity that the Warren Court only hinted at." Concluded one Supreme Court expert, "the Court today is more of a center for the resolution of social issues than it has ever been before."

Chief Justice Burger was one of seven children growing up modestly outside Saint Paul, Minnesota. An all-around star in high school, he pursued the rest of his education at night, first at the University of Minnesota and then at Saint Paul College of Law, while selling insurance. He then joined one of Minnesota's oldest firms and taught part-time at the law school. He specialized in appellate cases, arguing more than a dozen before the Supreme Court. He was active in civic affairs and politics and a firm backer of Harold Stassen's early presidential bids. At the 1952 presidential convention, Burger "helped swing the Minnesota delegation and gave Eisenhower the votes that put him over the top." His reward was a job in Washington, D.C., as the assistant attorney general in charge of the civil division. Two years later, in 1956, he was appointed to the U.S. Court of Appeals and then, in 1968, nominated to become chief justice of the Supreme Court by President Richard M. Nixon.

Chief Justice Burger was not viewed as having a strong intellectual influence on the Supreme Court. His greatest energy went into judicial administration. This certainly won him plaudits from a beleaguered judiciary. Said one gratefully, "He has invested the prestige of the Chief Justiceship in efforts to make the American judicial system function more efficiently." For instance, he insisted that his fellow justices use computers to write their opinions as far back as 1981, long before most Americans had mastered these now-commonplace machines.

Like Brennan, Burger came to the notice of the White House through a speech. He had been sitting on the U.S. Court of Appeals for the District of Columbia circuit for thirteen years and had a reputation as a conservative, law-and-order judge. He had also become fascinated with the legal system in such European nations as Norway, Sweden, Denmark, and the Netherlands. In the speech that so impressed Nixon, he said, "I am sure no one will take issue with me when I say that these Northern European countries are as enlightened as the United States in the value they place on the individual and human dignity." He pointed out that they did not waste time with anything like the Fifth Amendment, which allows an accused person to avoid testifying: "They go swiftly, efficiently and directly to the question of whether the accused is guilty."

On the U.S. Supreme Court, the presence of such strong personalities as Justice Brennan and Chief Justice Burger made Lewis Powell a "crucial centrist." Justice Powell mediated between the increasingly split liberals and conservatives, becoming "the court's master of compromise and coalition-building." Take the 1978 case of Allan B. Bakke, a white student turned down for medical school who was challenging the school's practice of setting aside sixteen spots for minorities. The Court was predictably split four to four between its two wings. Powell agreed with the conservatives that excluding anyone, including whites, on the basis of race from those sixteen spots was wrong. However, he then agreed with the liberal four that race and ethnicity could be considered when universities were admitting students.

Justice Powell was unusual in that he had never been a judge at any level before joining the Supreme Court; he was a highly successful Richmond lawyer, a senior partner in one of Virginia's oldest firms. Powell was born near Richmond, where his father was a furniture company manager. He had a private education and then attended Washington and Lee University, where he was very much a Big Man on Campus. After majoring in commerce, he enrolled at Washington and Lee's law school, where he graduated first in his class. He then headed north and earned a degree from Harvard Law School. There one of his classes was taught by later Supreme Court Justice Felix Frankfurther, who "impressed the young lawyer with a pragmatic approach to legal issues that was very different from the more formal and unskeptical approach of the professors at Washington and Lee." Powell declined an offer from a prestigious Wall Street firm and returned to Richmond. He started with a small firm and was one of the partners who developed it into a major national firm. He distinguished himself in World War II and was a highly active member of the American Bar Association, the American Bar Foundation, and the American College of Trial Lawyers.

At age sixty-four, when Powell expected to start winding down his busy law career, giving him more time for his wife and grandchildren, the Nixon administration approached him for the second time with an offer to serve on the Supreme Court. He declined, changing his mind only when President Nixon called and "said it was Mr. Powell's patriotic duty to serve." He went onto the Court under duress, sorry to leave his beloved Richmond and his practice. He would say, "The truth is that I'd rather be a lawyer than a judge. I really prefer to be competitive rather than neutral, detached and disinterested."

Powell's judicial pragmatism was noticeable in certain decisions. For example, he joined the liberal bloc in a decision requiring the state of Texas to provide free public education to the children of illegal aliens. He noted first of all that the children were "innocents" who had no influence on their parents' illegal activities and should not be punished for them. Moreover, he wrote, "it can hardly be argued rationally that anyone benefits from the creation within our borders of a subclass of illiterate persons."

While most Americans understand abstractly the incredible power of the U.S. Supreme Court, certain decisions have driven home just how deeply it can affect us. Certainly one of the most famous and controversial Supreme Court decisions ever was *Roe v. Wade,* which made abortion legal. When Justice Harry A. Blackmun died, he was identified, as he knew he would be, as the "author of abortion right." As the justice who wrote the seven-to-two opinion, he became the symbol of this historic law—hated by some and revered by others—and the recipient of tens of thousands of letters, many vitriolic. The decision reflected his growing conviction that the Court should act "as an essential voice for the vulnerable and powerless."

Justice Blackmun was a low-key Republican who referred to himself as "Old Number 3," a deprecating reference to the circumstances of his appointment. President Nixon had tried and failed twice to get a southerner appointed to the Court. Chief Justice Burger suggested his childhood friend from Saint Paul, the well-respected Judge Blackmun on the U.S. Court of Appeals for the Eighth Circuit. And so, on his third try, President Nixon prevailed in filling a year-old vacancy on the Court. Blackmun had indeed grown up and been close friends with Burger, but while Burger had attended the state university, the Harvard Club of Minnesota had given Blackmun a scholarship. At Harvard College, Blackmun worked as a janitor and tutor for extra income. Though drawn to medicine, in the end he opted to attend Harvard Law School. Upon Blackmun's return to Minnesota, he clerked for an appellate judge whose job he would assume twenty-seven years later. After his clerkship, Blackmun spent sixteen years with a large corporate firm that had among its clients the Mayo Clinic of Rochester, Minnesota. He left that firm to spend a decade as Mayo's general counsel before moving on to the bench.

Justice Blackmun was regarded as a man whose worldviews changed considerably during his twenty-four years on the Supreme Court. One law professor who had clerked for him explained why: "Paradoxically, by donning the robes of high office, Justice Blackmun became less isolated from the everyday world and more aware of the human beings behind the cases. He took his job seriously and did his own work. The Court's sprawling docket exposed him to a broader, more brutal slice of life than he had ever known." For many years, Justice Blackmun supported the death penalty, trying to fashion rules that would make it fair. But just before he retired, he was confronted by a death row case where the prisoner had murdered a man in a barroom brawl. This made him wonder why this man, rather than any other one of thousands of brawlers, had been condemned. Blackmun concluded that applying the death penalty fairly was impossible: "It seems that the decision whether a human being should live or die is so inherently subjective, rife with all of life's understandings, experiences, and prejudices and passions, that it inevitably defies the rationality and consistency required by the Constitution."

While the Supreme Court has the difficult task of sorting out the fundamental meanings of our laws, those sitting in the lower courts then have to apply these rulings. The great challenge for judges is rendering opinions that respect the intellectual requirements of the Constitution while acknowledging the realities of human beings and daily life. Judge Elbert Tuttle was called "perhaps the most influential civil rights judge in southern history" by the *Atlanta Constitution* for the "pivotal role" he played in "extending civil rights to black Southerners in the 1950's and 60's." He would write more than fourteen hundred opinions in almost forty years on the bench.

Judge Tuttle liked to tell the story of his 1954 appointment to the Fifth Circuit Court of Appeals, encompassing the six states of the Old Confederacy: Georgia (his home), Alabama, Florida, Louisiana, Mississippi, and Texas. Apparently when Tuttle told a Washington friend that he was leaving his job as general counsel to the Treasury

Department, he cavalierly explained, "I'm going home to retire on the Fifth Circuit Court of Appeals." The friend asked incredulously, "Have you seen what the Supreme Court did last week?" meaning its historic decision in *Brown v. Board of Education,* ending school segregation.

Judge Tuttle said he wasn't at all worried, predicting that the wisdom of the Court would quickly prevail: "They'll fall into line." Years later, after presiding over several decades of tough, contentious segregation cases, he smiled when he told this story and said, "Famous last words."

Judge Tuttle was the quintessential peripatetic American: born in California; spending some time in Washington, D.C., where his father had a job with a federal agency; and then growing up in Hawaii when his father worked in the sugar industry. Young Tuttle went back east to attend Cornell College, served in the Army, worked on newspapers, and then attended Cornell Law School. Upon his graduation, he and his brother-in-law decided to open a law firm in Atlanta, Georgia, which they saw as an up-and-coming city. Though well established as a successful tax lawyer, Tuttle occasionally stepped out of his specialty to take on cases of racial injustice, including defending a black man he had saved from a lynch mob. Tuttle led a pro-Eisenhower delegation to the Republican National Convention, and his reward was appointment to the Treasury Department.

Probably Tuttle's most famous cases as a judge had to do with the desegregation of southern schools. These included the historic integration of the University of Georgia by Hamilton E. Holmes and Charlayne Hunter, whose story was told in chapter 4. One of the odd charms of the *New York Times* obituaries is that over time one can read about numerous participants in the same historic events, following very different lives until they intersect—in this instance in a courtroom. In this case, a lower court judge had ordered the university integrated but then delayed the carrying out of his own order, meaning the college students might miss another semester. Judge Tuttle nullified the postponement, and the two students were able to enroll in time for the spring semester. The riots set off by that act finally made Judge Tuttle aware of the depth of resistance to it. Thus the next year, when his ruling enabled James H. Meredith to become the first black student to integrate a white

Mississippi school, he urged the Justice Department to deploy soldiers to ensure peace. Instead, several hundred U.S. marshals were dispatched and were overwhelmed by the rampaging mob. Two people were killed, twenty-eight marshals hit by gunfire, and scores of others were hurt.

Judge Harold J. Rothwax was a New York State Supreme Court justice who began his legal career as a dedicated legal aid lawyer and also vice chairman of the American Civil Liberties Union. A native New Yorker who graduated from Columbia Law School, during the 1960s he was a central figure representing numerous liberal and radical causes, from Black Panthers to welfare rights. Then, in 1971, New York City Mayor John V. Lindsay appointed Rothwax to a judgeship in the criminal courts, where he heard felony criminal cases. Presiding over hundreds of "gruesome" trials turned out to be an intensely radicalizing experience for Judge Rothwax. He now concluded that many of the Supreme Court decisions of the 1960s that he had so supported while at Legal Aid and the ACLU had been "too complex for the police to understand and allowed murderers and other violent criminals to go unpunished."

After twenty-five years on the bench, Judge Rothwax published *Guilty: The Collapse of Criminal Justice.* He concluded that there was too great a disconnection between the intellectual ideals of the highest court of the land and the nitty-gritty of the streets. According to the *New York Times,* "he proposed that Miranda warnings against self-incrimination should be abolished, that 10-to-2 jury verdicts instead of unanimous decisions should be permitted and that the police and prosecutors should be given more leeway to seize evidence and to use it against defendants at trial." His tough stance in his courtroom earned him the nickname "Prince of Darkness."

Even the smallest American hamlets have local justices, and a surprising number of these are not lawyers but simply citizens with common sense. Helen Billings Burnham was a "part-time, round-the-clock town justice in Salinas, N.Y." for twenty-two years. Judge Burnham came to know the law by serving as the court clerk for her husband, who was indeed a lawyer. Their court handled myriad demands: traffic infractions, small-claims disputes, and misdemeanor cases with penalties no greater than a year in jail. This small-town court also presided over arraignments of accused killers and others charged with felonies. When her husband died in a motorcycle accident in 1971, Burnham was appointed to fill out his term. The town Republicans did not see this as a job for a woman and put up a man when the next election came around. Burnham ran as a conservative and won, as she would for another five terms.

Reported the *New York Times*, "Over the next two decades she dispensed justice with such consistent compassion, good humor and common sense that in 1989 the National Judges Association named her the outstanding non-attorney judge in the United States." In the middle of many a night, the sheriff's office would call, and Judge Burnham would get out of bed, put her black robe on over her nightgown, and preside over a felony arraignment in the family room of her house. But her job had a happy side, too and that was weddings. She performed more than three thousand marriage ceremonies, or almost three per week!

Politicians

Judges are generally remembered for certain outstanding decisions and influential cases. Politicians' reputations derive from both their overall worldview and specific stands they have taken on important national issues. Successful politicians are those who attain (and retain) positions of power long enough to leave a significant imprint. We were surprised to discover, when looking at our database, which of the many occupations merited the longest average obit: members of Congress, at twenty-five inches. There are eighty-six former U.S. senators and representatives in our *New York Times* obituary database, fifty-three Democrats and twenty-seven Republicans. Eighty-five percent of these onetime members of Congress had graduated from college, and half held law degrees. Fifteen of them, or less than a fifth, graduated from one of the top fifty colleges, with eight going to Ivy League schools.

The Apex of Fame for members of Congress, shown in Table 10-3, shows how important longevity is in making one's mark in politics. The

Apex features twenty-four men and three women, ten of whom were U.S. senators, with three quarters Democrats and one quarter Republicans. The mean time served in Congress was an impressive twenty years. While 63 percent of those in the Apex had a law degree, three had never been to college.

House Speaker Thomas P. "Tip" O'Neill, Jr., fifth in the Apex of Fame, was a gregarious, cigar-smoking New Deal liberal who embraced politics and government as offering solutions for the problems of ordinary people. The *New York Times* described him as viewing the Democratic Party with "near-religious fervor, the party [that] was the one of the cities, the working people, the poor, the needy, the unemployed, the sick and the disinherited." And certainly in much of the Cold War era, many Americans embraced this vision of government as the solver of society's problems.

Speaker O'Neill was a professional politician who went way back, a working-class Boston Irish Catholic lad who campaigned for Al Smith during his 1928 presidential bid against Herbert Hoover. O'Neill's father was a longtime member of the Cambridge City Council. While still a senior at Boston College, the younger O'Neill made his inaugural run for the council, which he lost, having taken for granted the votes in his own neighborhood, where he didn't bother to campaign. Hence, he didn't get those votes. His father told him, and Tip would always repeat this advice, "All politics is local"; in other words, don't take your own constituents for granted. In 1936, at the young age of twenty-four, Tip O'Neill was elected to the Massachusetts House of Representatives and had risen to Speaker by the time he ran in 1952 for the congressional seat vacated by John F. Kennedy. O'Neill's constituents were not only the blue-collar workers of his lifelong neighborhood but the nations' leading academics and intellectuals at Harvard University and MIT. O'Neill's wife and five children remained in Cambridge, keeping him well rooted.

In Washington, D.C., O'Neill became the protégé of Congressman John W. McCormack of Massachusetts, who ascended to Speaker of the House in 1962. Through McCormack, O'Neill became a regular at informal gatherings of important Democrats, developing friendships

TABLE 10-3. *The Apex of Fame: Members of Congress in the Obituary Database*

Name (Age at Death)	Obit Date	Education	Party-State	Position Held (Years)
1. Barry Goldwater (89)	05/30/98	Attended college	R.-Ariz.	Senate (30)
2. J. William Fulbright (89)	02/10/95	Law degree (George Washington U.)	D.-Ark.	Senate (29)
3. Bella Abzug (77)	04/01/98	Law (Columbia)	D.-N.Y.	H. Rep. (2)
4. Edmund S. Muskie (81)	03/27/96	Law (Cornell)	D.-Maine	Senate (18)
5. Thomas O'Neill, Jr. (81)	01/07/94	College graduate	D.-Mass.	H. Rep. (40)
6. Abraham A. Ribicoff (87)	02/23/98	Law degree (U. of Chicago)	D.-Conn.	Senate (18)
7. Barbara Jordan (59)	01/18/96	Law (Boston U.)	D.-Tex.	H. Rep. (6)
8. Morris K. Udall (76)	12/14/98	Law degree	D.-Ariz.	H. Rep. (30)
9. Sonny Bono (62)	01/07/98	High school dropout	R.-Calif.	H. Rep. (4)
10. Margaret Chase Smith (97)	05/30/95	High school graduate	R.-Maine	H. Rep. (8); Senate (24)
11. John C. Stennis (93)	04/24/95	Law (U. of Virginia)	D.-Miss.	Senate (41)
12. Paul Tsongas (55)	01/20/97	Law (Yale)	D.-Mass.	H. Rep. (4); Senate (6)
13. George W. Crockett (88)	09/15/97	Law (U. of Michigan)	D.-Mich.	H. Rep. (11)
14. John E. Moss (84)	12/06/97	Attended college	D.-Calif.	H. Rep. (26)
15. Charles C. Diggs, Jr. (75)	08/26/98	Attended college	D.-Mich.	H. Rep. (26)

Elections Lost (No.)	Accomplishments and Fame	Obit Length
1	1964 presidential nominee; icon of modern conservatives	119"
1	Helped shape U.S. foreign policy	109"
6	Feminist and activist known for belligerent, exuberant style	92"
2	Vice-presidential candidate in 1968; governor of Maine	88"
1	Speaker of the House, 1977–87; favored liberal legislation	85"
1	Governor of Connecticut; member of JFK's Cabinet	84"
2	First black elected to Congress from Texas since Reconstruction	74"
0	Fiercely liberal; advocate for environment and political reform	72"
1	Singer and TV star who became mayor, then congressman	57"
1	Long career in both House and Senate	55"
0	Senator influential on military affairs	50"
2	Ran for U.S. president in 1992	35"
0	Civil rights advocate as judge and congressman	33"
0	Freedom of Information Act; Consumer Safety Acts; incorruptible	33"
0	Founded Black Congressional Caucus; censured for accepting kickbacks	33"

(continues)

TABLE 10-3. *The Apex of Fame: Members of Congress in the Obituary Database*

Name (Age at Death)	Obit Date	Education	Party-State	Position Held (Years)
16. Carl Elliott (85)	01/12/99	Law degree	D.-Al.	H. Rep. (16)
17. Jennings Randolph (96)	05/09/98	College graduate	D.-W.V.	H. Rep. (14); Senate (26)
18. Albert Gore, Sr. (90)	12/07/98	Law degree	D.-Tenn.	Senate (18)
19. Hamilton Fish, Jr. (70)	07/24/96	Law degree (New York U.)	R.-N.Y.	H. Rep. (25)
20. Seymour Halpern (83)	01/11/97	Attended college	R.-N.Y.	H. Rep. (14)
21. Chalmers Wylie (77)	08/15/98	Law degree (Harvard)	R.-Ohio	H. Rep. (26)
22. Dante B. Fascell (81)	11/30/98	Law degree (U. Miami)	D.-Fla.	H. Rep. (37)
23. Mike Synar (45)	01/10/96	Law degree (U. of Oklahoma)	D.-Okla.	H. Rep. (16)
24. Coya Knutson (82)	10/12/96	College graduate	D.-Minn.	H. Rep. (4)
25. Donald S. Russell (92)	02/25/98	Law degree (U. of Michigan)	D.-S.C.	Senate (1)
26. William Natcher (84)	03/31/94	Law (Ohio State U.)	D.-Ky.	H. Rep. (40)
27. Dean Gallo (58)	11/07/94	Attended high school	R.-N.J.	H. Rep. (10)

Note: Of the 27 members of Congress in this table, 20 were elected to the House of Representatives and 10 to the Senate; 3 served in both houses of Congress. There were 86 members of Congress in the obituary database.

and connections that would aid his steady rise to the leadership. His natural ebullience and charm served him well, especially as the nation headed into the terrible travails of the Vietnam War and Watergate.

Elections Lost (No.)	Accomplishments and Fame	Obit Length
2	Sacrificed political career for principles of social justice	32"
1	Present at creation of the New Deal; lowered voting age to 18	31"
2	Liberal Southern Democrat; father of Vice President Al Gore, Jr.	30"
0	Leader in House on civil rights legislation	29"
1	Civil rights and medicare legislation	29"
0	GOP stalwart; federal bailout of savings and loan industry	28"
0	Chairman of House Foreign Affairs Committee; arms control; drug war	27"
1	Reformer and maverick; killed Gramm-Rudman Bill	26"
2	Student loan legislation; career thwarted by husband	26"
2	Governor of South Carolina; federal judge for 30 years	26"
0	Long career in House; 18,401 continuous roll-call votes	25"
0	Elected to Congress five times; environmental legislation	25"

Early on, Congressman O'Neill came out against the war, concluding that the war in Vietnam was a civil war and we had no business being there. In his autobiography, *Man of the House*, he described President

Lyndon B. Johnson calling him to the White House over his Vietnam stance but accepting his opposition if it was for moral reasons.

O'Neill's ten years as Speaker were spent under two presidents — Jimmy Carter and Ronald Reagan, both elected on anti-Washington platforms. Decades of expanding government had sparked a backlash. O'Neill was aghast at this trend and the rising middle class that wanted to rein in the very programs he believed had benefited them. He opposed, for instance, balancing the budget, believing that doing so would "dismantle the programs that I've been working for as an old liberal." President Reagan was even more distressing to him than Carter. Explained the *New York Times*, "the Speaker regarded government as the solution to many social problems, as an agent of social change; Mr. Reagan regarded it as a problem in itself, interfering in the lives of Americans and impeding economic and social progress." Speaker O'Neill was puzzled by the tremendous popularity of a president whom he described as "a cheerleader for selfishness." But of course, unlike Carter and Reagan, O'Neill had never engaged in any professional activity except politics, and he had been a Washington insider for decades. He was not even a lawyer, as were most of his congressional colleagues. His success as Speaker was due to his ability to keep the relations among otherwise warring factions cordial.

While O'Neill's obituary limns the general outlines of his long and successful career as a liberal Democrat, that of Texas Senator Ralph Yarborough relates more specific legislative legacies. It also conveys the extraordinary power that a national politician has to change society. Yarborough grew up on a farm, the seventh of eleven children. He had worked in some humble jobs before becoming a lawyer and legislator. "Aside from a brief period at West Point, he "taught school, toiled in a wheat field, helped build oil tanks and worked his way on a freighter to Europe, where he studied for a year." After graduating from University of Texas Law School, Yarborough began his political ascent: assistant attorney general for two years, state judge for five, and then three tries for governor before winning a U.S. Senate seat in 1957.

During his fourteen years in Washington, Senator Yarborough "fought to expand the role of the Federal government in assisting veterans, workers, the poor and the infirm." As chairman of the Senate Labor and Public Welfare Committee, he increased health care, raised the minimum wage, and extended education benefits to 5 million new veterans. Certainly, one of his most influential and long-lasting contributions was the National Defense Education Act of 1958. With this, for the first time, the federal government began making loans and grants to universities and their students, stimulating the huge expansion of higher education and making it accessible to those who otherwise would not have been able to afford it.

In 1968, Senator Yarborough backed presidential peace candidate Eugene McCarthy. This was too much for his Texas constituents, and two years later he was defeated. His subsequent efforts to get back to the Senate also failed. So he returned to lawyering in Austin, specializing in oil and gas business.

While politicians such as O'Neill and Yarborough were hugely influential in domestic politics, affecting the lives of millions of Americans, Senator J. William Fulbright "left a lasting imprint not only on foreign affairs but also on education, as creator of the Fulbright fellowships for international study." In three decades in the Senate during the Cold War, fifteen of those as chairman of the Foreign Relations Committee, Fulbright made his mark as the leader of the anti–Vietnam War forces and those who believed in détente with the Soviet Union. "The biggest lesson I learned from Vietnam," he would say, "is not to trust government statements. I had no idea until then that you could not rely on government statements." This skepticism would affect ensuing generations of Americans, who came to question the truthfulness of officials and viewed Washington with an increasingly jaundiced eye. At the same time, Senator Fulbright could also claim credit for widening the horizons of the 250,000 individuals who would go abroad or come to the United States as Fulbright scholars.

This Arkansas Democrat, who was very bright and supercilious, ruffled plenty of feathers. The son of a wealthy Arkansas businessman and a newspaper columnist, Fulbright entered the University of Arkansas at fifteen and conquered all—as a football star, student body president, and captain of the tennis team. But his great epiphany was when he received a Rhodes Scholarship to Oxford University in England, where he spent three years. "Oh, God, it was wonderful," he enthused decades later. "I used the language in the most primitive manner, as you can imagine; the University of Arkansas in those days was not that impressive." Upon his return, Fulbright enrolled at George Washington University Law School so he could court his future wife. After working for several years in the Justice Department, he was called back to Arkansas to become president of the university. A new governor ousted him two years later, and Fulbright gained some revenge by winning a congressional seat sought by the governor's ally. Two years later, when that same governor ran for the U.S. Senate, Fulbright also entered the race and won. Once in the Senate, his great interest was foreign affairs and his great concern was keeping out of wars.

Senator Fulbright remembered that all politics is local. He was an opponent of all civil rights legislation: "First, because I doubted its efficacy; second, because my constituents wouldn't have tolerated it." Nonetheless, eventually his age made him vulnerable and in 1974 the sixty-nine-year-old incumbent was defeated by Arkansas governor Dale Bumpers, forty-eight. Fulbright's other legacy was President William Clinton, who was very much a protégé of the senator. Clinton would say, "If it hadn't been for him, I don't think I'd be here today. He was a great inspiration to thousands and thousands of us who were young when he was Senator and serving."

While high-profile Washington politicians are known for their influence and power, there are large numbers of influential but anonymous inside-the-Beltway experts who toil away on federal and congressional staffs. These are the bright, dedicated worker bees who can bring profound change and make government go round. Dorothy Fosdick was one such, a "foreign policy expert who helped fashion the United Nations, the Marshall Plan and NATO in the 1940's, advised Adlai Stevenson in the 1952 Presidential campaign and then spent nearly three decades as Senator Henry M. Jackson's chief cold war strategist."

Fosdick was not an obvious hard-liner, child as she was of the famous pacifist minister of Manhattan's Riverside Church, Dr. Harry

Emerson Fosdick. But she was deeply influenced by her famous neighbor and later mentor Reinhold Niebuhr, a theologian "whose belief that evil is a palpable world force that must be resisted and overcome became the geopolitical creed of a generation of cold war theorists." And then there was also her uncle Raymond B. Fosdick, an international lawyer and proponent of the original League of Nations.

Dorothy Fosdick graduated from Smith, earned a doctorate in public law at Columbia University, and became an academic. But not for long; in 1942, she was recruited by the State Department to become a top-level thinker. She helped lay the groundwork for the United Nations and by age thirty-four was one of nine strategic planners working under the legendary George Kennan. She helped "shape the Truman Doctrine, the Marshall Plan, and the North Atlantic Treaty Organization." She backed Adlai Stevenson, wrote some serious books, and then, in 1954, signed on with Senator Henry Jackson. She was not just his top aide but his alter ego. Reported the *New York Times*, "She wrote his speeches, helped develop his strategic positions and political initiatives and orchestrated his legendary informational hearings." Famous among those who knew government, she was offered ambassadorships and college presidencies, but she turned down those high-profile positions. Explained her sister, "She had no personal ambition. She only wanted to save the world."

Equally unknown to the outside world, but certainly important in political Washington, D.C., was Louis E. Martin, "whose work behind the scenes as an adviser to three Democratic Presidents and whose efforts to bring more blacks into government earned him the sobriquet 'the godfather of black politics.'" A native of Savannah, Georgia, Martin graduated from the University of Michigan. He worked briefly at the *Chicago Defender*, and then moved to Detroit to edit another black newspaper, the *Michigan Chronicle*. Unlike other influential Detroit blacks, who were Republicans, Martin decided the Democratic Party was where labor's best interests lay, and therefore it was his choice, too. He also understood the value of organizations as vehicles of power and influence and founded the National Newspaper Publishers Association, a group of black publishers.

Martin first went to Washington under the auspices of the Kennedys to work in John F. Kennedy's first campaign. He stayed on as an adviser and, unlike most of the Kennedy group, had little trouble when Lyndon B. Johnson became president. In fact, here his influence was most evident, for Martin pressed hard to get Thurgood Marshall named as the first black justice on the Supreme Court. Martin was a man, said his friends, who was "able to wield considerable influence inconspicuously." Clifford L. Alexander, a White House counsel under Johnson, viewed Martin as his mentor.

In 1970, Martin founded yet another group, the Joint Center for Political and Economic Studies, to help black politicians and scholars advance in their careers by offering networking and solid advice. Martin was chairman for eight years, thereby meeting and nurturing ambitious, bright members of his race from all over the nation. He became familiar with a talent pool that could be drawn on as opportunities arose. Martin, for instance, recruited Vernon E. Jordan to become head of the National Urban League. In time, Jordan became one of Washington's leading power-broker lawyers and one of President Clinton's closest advisers.

Another Martin, this one David B. H. Martin, was a unique Washington type. Unlike the "black godfather," who took the art of mentoring, networking, and advising to new heights, this Martin was a different kind of creator, a "lawyer creator and sometime government official whose inveterate legal tinkerings have been credited with the creation of the Cape Cod National Seashore, government-backed student loans and other innovative Federal, state and municipal programs."

Martin was a New Yorker, son of the first editor of *Time* magazine. He went off to Yale at sixteen, entered the Navy when he graduated, then earned a law degree from Harvard. He spent a decade in private practice in Boston and came up with his first "social invention" while commuting back and forth on the train. His idea was government-backed, low-interest student loans. Through a lawyer friend in government, this ingenious idea became a Massachusetts program in 1957, the model for the federal program that was enacted (thanks to Senator Ralph Yarborough) a year later.

Martin now realized that government offered creative possibilities and went to work as a legislative aide to a Massachusetts senator. Working with a colleague in Senator John F. Kennedy's office, the two came up with the "mechanism that allowed the preservation of Cape Cod's natural seashore while allowing private citizens to maintain their property within the protected area." The Cape Cod National Seashore, enacted in 1961, became the model for similar projects elsewhere.

Martin was a man who held many, many jobs, according to his obit, moving on from the Senate to the Department of Health, Education, and Welfare, and then to Yale University, then executive director of the Massachusetts Housing Finance Agency, back to Congress, and various other stops along the way before settling in the very Cape Cod that he had helped to preserve.

Lawyers

While politicians and judges make and interpret the laws that shape our society, lawyers act as the intermediaries between the world and those laws. What with the explosion in the number of lawyers, laws, and people, Americans have increasingly sought out the nation's nearly 1 million lawyers to solve their woes and right their wrongs. Much of the early civil rights movement was fought in the courts. That highly visible success caused many other unhappy groups and endless individual underdogs to look to judges and juries for redress. Nonetheless, rare is the person who emerges from our legal system beaming with happiness and gratitude. Writer Ambrose Bierce summed it up for many with his definition of a lawsuit: "A machine which you go into as a pig and come out of as a sausage."

For practicing lawyers, law careers have many possible forms, from solo practitioner to government lawyer to corporate law. Like doctors, lawyers must acquire a professional degree. To obtain a license, lawyers must pass the state bar exam. Many lawyers who practice in big firms are promoted to partner, usually at the end of seven years as an associate. If not, they are expected to leave. But whatever form their practice takes—corporate, criminal, class action—success means winning cases. What has been striking in recent decades is the growth of big national and multinational law firms.[3] While the average income for an American lawyer is about $75,000, top partners in big firms in cities such as New York and Washington can now expect to earn more than a million dollars a year. Moreover, *The American Lawyer*'s annual review of top law firms shows that the gross revenues of the hundred largest firms more than doubled from 1988 to 1998 from $10.6 billion to $23.1 billion.

A great many of the 349 lawyers who received obits in the *New York Times* practiced corporate law, which is no doubt lucrative, prestigious within the field, and necessary to the ongoing march of capitalism. But these toilers in the corporate vineyards receive but perfunctory send-offs unless they have some other compelling clients—say, a Jackie Kennedy Onassis—or accomplishments. Almost 40 percent of the lawyers attended one of the top fifty schools, with almost a third—ninety-eight—coming out of the Ivy League. The Apex of Fame for Lawyers, shown in Table 10-4, features thirty people—including one woman—who have made their mark in the legal field in a variety of ways: They represented famous clients, advised presidents as well as mobsters, and broke significant legal ground in creating new civil and legal rights for minorities, the disabled, the poor, gays, and children. Clark Clifford, with far and away the longest obit, was the classic Washington lawyer and power broker, a grand old man who knew everybody but had the misfortune to end his career tainted by an international banking scandal. John Ehrlichman was notorious not as a lawyer but as a major figure in the Watergate scandal. The remaining top ten lawyers were all master litigators, formidable figures in the courtroom throughout their careers. Thirty percent of the Apex lawyers attended one of the top fifty colleges as undergraduates, with a comparable number attending highly selective law schools.

The biggest stars of the bar are, without doubt, trial lawyers. With their name clients, juicy cases, best-selling books, and media play, they become celebrities themselves. And they get long obits. Melvin Belli, number six in the Apex of Fame, was identified as "an impresario of a lawyer who pioneered new techniques and huge settlements in personal injury cases. . . . In a profession storied as much for its histrionics as for its seriousness of purpose, Mr. Belli was a superstar." Above all, in his fifty-three years of practice at the bar he was known for defending Jack Ruby, the man who killed Lee Harvey Oswald. But Belli also represented other infamous sorts: gangster Mickey Cohen, movie stars Mae West and Errol Flynn, comedian Lenny Bruce, and televangelists Jim and Tammy Faye Bakker.

A native Californian, Belli graduated from the University of California at Berkeley and then Boalt Hall Law School. No great star in law school, he began to gain notice with his creative courtroom tactics on behalf of people who had sustained various injuries. One of his earliest and most famous cases involved a woman who had lost a leg to a San Francisco trolley. The jury awarded her $65,000, whereupon the company appealed, feeling the award was too high. Belli came into the court for the appeal with an L-shaped bundle but did not touch it until his summation. He unwrapped what turned out to be his client's new artificial leg. "Ladies and gentlemen of the jury," he said, "this is what my pretty young client will wear for the rest of her life. Take it." He laid it in the lap of the first juror and went on eloquently about the inadequacy of this stiff limb compared to the original, lost leg. This time the jury awarded $100,000.

Belli, acclaimed by *Life* magazine in 1954 as the "King of Torts," clearly understood that good tort is also good theater, from the opening curtain to the final bow. Thus, he dressed flamboyantly, met with clients in a lavish San Francisco town house ablaze with brocade, velvet, and crystal chandeliers, and worked in a luxurious office decorated with a skeleton, braids of garlic, an impressive bar, and walls of books, all visible to passersby through a huge picture window. Away from the courtroom, he cultivated the persona of bad-boy bon vivant, ever in pursuit of wine, women, and song. (He was on wife number five when he died.) Yet, through all his colorful living and controversial cases, his firm racked up one huge victory after another: $19 million for sixteen families whose servicemen sons died in an air crash, $32 million from California crematoriums that failed to handle dead people properly. In 1987, he estimated that, all told, his firm had won $350 million through winning or settling cases. If the usual one third fee held, his firm would

TABLE 10-4. *The Apex of Fame: Lawyers in the Obituary Database*

Name (Age at Death)	Obit Date	College	Law School
1. Clark M. Clifford (91)	10/11/98	Washington U.	Washington U.
2. Paul O'Dwyer (90)	06/25/98	Fordham	St. John's
3. Arthur L. Liman (64)	07/18/97	Harvard	Yale
4. John D. Ehrlichman (73)	02/16/99	U. of California at Los Angeles	Stanford
5. William Kunstler (76)	09/05/95	Yale	Columbia
6. Melvin Belli (88)	07/11/96	U. of California at Berkeley	U. of California at Berkeley
7. Simon Rifkind (94)	11/15/95	City College of New York	Columbia
8. Louis Nizer (92)	11/11/94	Columbia	Columbia
9. Spottswood W. Robinson III (82)	10/13/98	Virginia Union	Howard
10. Ben Margolis (88)	02/08/99	Not named	Hastings Law
11. Robert J. Morris (82)	01/02/97	Not named	Fordham
12. Milton S. Gould (89)	03/24/99	Cornell	Not named
13. Thomas Stoddard (48)	02/14/97	Georgetown	New York U.
14. David W. Belin (70)	01/18/99	U. of Michigan	U. of Michigan
15. Sidney Korshak (88)	01/22/96	U. of Wisconsin	DePaul
16. Ralph S. Abascal (62)	03/19/97	Not named	U. of California at Berkeley
17. Arthur Krim (84)	09/22/94	Columbia	Columbia

Specialty/Position	Career and Fame	Obit Length
Government positions	Secretary of Defense; adviser and friend to four presidents	116"
Civil rights	"Liberal battler for underdogs and outsiders"	71"
Corporate	Master litigator; Iran-*contra* affair; Attica	66"
Zoning and land use	Nixon aide jailed for involvement in Watergate	56"
Civil rights	Defended social outcasts	49"
Personal injury	Flamboyant style and huge settlements	48"
Corporate and trust	Lawyer to corporations, Jackie Kennedy, Holocaust survivors	41"
Entertainment	Lawyer to the famous	39"
Civil rights and property	Desegregation of public schools	38"
Entertainment	Defense of blacklisted Hollywood figures	34"
Chief counsel	Senate Judiciary Subcommittee on Internal Security	33"
Prominent litigator	Represented major businesses and Ariel Sharon, Israeli defense minister	33"
Gay rights	Director of Lambda Legal Defense	32"
Corporate and litigation	Served on Warren and Rockefeller Commissions	30"
Labor	Chicago Mob's man and Hollywood fixer	29"
Legal services	Worked for the poor, farmworkers, welfare recipients, and immigrants	29"
Entertainment	Chairman of Orion Pictures and United Artists	28"

(continues)

TABLE 10-4. *The Apex of Fame: Lawyers in the Obituary Database*

Name (Age at Death)	Obit Date	College	Law School
18. Jerry Cohen (70)	01/01/96	Wayne State U.	Wayne State U.
19. Noel Keane (58)	01/28/97	E. Michigan U.	U. of Detroit
20. Charles Schinitsky (80)	02/22/97	St. John's	St. John's
21. Louis L. Redding (96)	10/02/98	Brown	Harvard
22. Bernard G. Segal (89)	06/05/97	U. of Pennsylvania	U. of Pennsylvania
23. Evan J. Kemp, Jr. (60)	08/14/97	Washington and Lee	U. of Virginia
24. Ernest C. Stiefel (89)	09/07/97	U. of Heidelberg	U. of Heidelberg
25. Philip Davis (90)	04/06/98	Not named	Fordham
26. Robert Cooley III (58)	08/03/98	Not named	Howard
27. Leonard F. Rothkrug (68)	11/20/96	Not named	Brooklyn
28. Dorothy Frooks (100)	04/19/97	Not named	Hamilton
29. Charles A. Horsky (87)	08/24/97	U. of Washington	Harvard
30. Paul G. Hearne (48)	05/10/98	Hofstra	Hofstra

Note: There were 349 lawyers in the database. Of these, 325 (93 percent) were men and 24 (7 percent) were women.

thus have earned at least $100 million. And that did not even include the sixty books he wrote or coauthored. All in all, over the years, Belli assuaged a great deal of anger and heartbreak with the balm of victory and money. While he certainly had his famous clients, he also made a

Specialty/Position	Career and Fame	Obit Length
Labor and class action	Sexual harassment and labor cases	28"
Surrogate motherhood	"Baby M" case; arranged more than 600 births	27"
Children's rights	Revolutionized juvenile court system	27"
Civil rights	Cases that led to school desegregation in 1954	26"
Corporate	Civil rights lawyer for the rich and poor	25"
Government positions	Denied job by 39 firms; wrote disability law	25"
Corporate and German law	Chronicled achievements of Holocaust refugee colleagues	25"
Wills and estates	Twice sued for a passenger's right to sit on trains	25"
Military and private	Sought link as descendent of Thomas Jefferson	25"
Zoning expert	Filed the most New York City zoning variance applications	24"
Suffragist	Aided dependent children; conceived the idea of small-claims court; recruiter for Navy	24"
Solicitor general's office	Helped redevelop Washington, D.C.	24"
Disabled rights	Led many organizations for the disabled	24"

great many ordinary people realize they had a chance to seek justice for their wrongs.

William Kunstler was equally famous, but for different reasons. The *New York Times* described him as making "not just a career but a life out of representing people and movements that were disliked, even despised. His clients' unpopularity seemed to inspire Mr. Kunstler, who was recognized by admirers and detractors alike as a lawyer who embraced pariahs." His motivation was simple: "My purpose is to keep the state from becoming all-domineering, all-powerful."

The son of a prominent New York doctor, Kunstler was a French major at Yale, earned a Bronze Star in the Pacific during World War II, and then returned to attend Columbia Law School. He engaged in run-of-the-mill law work until the 1960s, when he became involved in civil rights work for the ACLU, representing Martin Luther King, after which he increasingly came to public notice. Wrote the *New York Times*, "Admirers saw him as a brilliant lawyer, and a skillful and courageous litigator, while his critics saw him as a showoff and publicity seeker." His most famous case was that of the Chicago Seven, seven youthful political activists charged with helping foment the riots at the 1968 Democratic National Convention. The trial became a circus, with the white middle-class defendants calling the judge rude names, wearing judicial robes in mockery, and generally misbehaving. Kunstler's own lack of respect for the judge earned him a contempt of court sentence of more than four years, which was overturned on appeal.

But Kunstler did not limit his clients to civil rights activists and members of the political opposition. He also took on deeply reviled murderers, whether Wayne Williams, who was convicted of killing children in Atlanta, or Colin Ferguson, who shot six people to death on the Long Island Railroad. And when Kunstler died, he was defending some of the terrorist suspects in the 1993 World Trade Center bombing. While he acknowledged enjoying the spotlight, Kunstler clearly had higher motives than sheer fame or notoriety. In 1962, he published a book titled *The Case for Courage: The Stories of Ten Famous American Attorneys Who Risked Their Careers in the Cause of Justice*. For the fact remains that every defendant, however unpopular, needs a lawyer. Lawyers who take on those clients play an important and necessary part in our legal system.

There are numerous kinds of respectable legal practice. None of these attracted Manhattan lawyer Harry Lipsig. Wrote the *New York Times*,

"Energetic, flamboyant, and driven by a passion for perfection, Mr. Lipsig lifted ambulance-chasing to a new level and became known for a string of huge settlements in seemingly long-shot cases." If we wish to blame (or credit) any one lawyer for our mania for trivial and/or bizarre personal injury suits, Harry Lipsig is surely one candidate. A graduate of Brooklyn Law School, he was the lawyer who convinced a jury that a man had been "frightened to death by a car that rolled on to his lawn." The award? $740,000 to the grieving family of this heartattack victim. Then there was the suit against an Acapulco hotel: Mr. Lipsig argued that the hotel had been to blame when a guest was attacked by a shark because it had not notified anyone that it dumped its garbage into the ocean, thereby attracting sharks. What with the money to be made in these sorts of cases, it's little wonder that thousands of lawyers began clogging the courts with even less promising personal injury cases.

In 1988, when Mr. Lipsig won a $25 million civil judgment against the murderer of a young woman, he was featured in *Forbes* magazine as making $6 million a year, placing him fifteenth on its list of America's highest-paid trial lawyers. His secret? "Bore a jury and you've lost the case." As easy as it is to poke fun at a Harry Lipsig he and his colleagues remain the champions of the small guy ill-treated by a big company or just plain fate. In his vivid way, Lipsig described a potential client as "some poor devil torn to shreds or living in that vilest of prisons one can conceive, helpless on a hospital bed, paralyzed." Of course, his point was that lawyers—via the courts—help retain the balance of power between small folks and bigger, more powerful entities.

At the other end of the respectability scale was Simon Rifkind, the senior partner at one of New York's great corporate firms, Paul, Weiss, Rifkind, Wharton & Garrison. The firm is described as having ninety partners and three hundred other lawyers, who specialize in corporate law, "including mergers and acquisitions, and a variety of litigation as well as trusts and estates and real estate law. It has offices in Washington, Paris, Tokyo, Beijing and Hong Kong." Rifkind himself was a general practitioner of great versatility, helping sort out New York City's looming bankruptcy, allocating water rights out in the American West, and representing numerous celebrity clients. Even a Jackie

Kennedy Onassis needed the courts to fend off overly aggressive paparazzi who were invading her privacy.

The child of Russian immigrants, Rifkind came to New York with his family when nine years old. He graduated from City College and Columbia Law School, then served as legislative secretary to U.S. Senator Robert F. Wagner, helping draft New Deal measures. He was also the senator's law partner until the start of World War II. Then he served as a Federal District Court judge until 1950, whereupon he joined Paul, Weiss. While he liked being called "judge," he was much admired as a trial lawyer. Wrote the *New York Times*, "Mr. Rifkind's strengths included the ability to master vast quantities of data in new fields and to cut to the heart of the issues involved. He was so esteemed by the Supreme Court that it chose him in 1956 for the epic task of sorting out Western States' rival claims to water from the Colorado River."

All in all, Rifkind worked as a lawyer for seven decades, advising and representing some of the most powerful politicians and businessmen of the times—everyone from President John F. Kennedy, who had him study railroad labor troubles, to New York governors concerned about electoral apportionment to the heads of Pennzoil Corporation. Rifkind himself described the lawyer's task: "Like an usher in a dark movie theater, holding the client by the hand, the lawyer guides him through the maze of law and regulation which now enmeshes all our lives." For his own firm, he was what is known as a "rainmaker," meaning that he generated many new clients and much income.

While Rifkind generally worked for the upper echelons of the establishment, lawyer Jerry S. Cohen of Washington, D.C., became one of the deans of class action litigation, representing American workers and small-business people. For fifteen years, Cohen was chief counsel to Cesar Chavez and the United Farm Workers of America during the bitter but successful fight to organize tens of thousands of farmworkers, mainly in California. He won such important legal victories as preventing the use of trespass laws to keep union organizers away from the growing fields.

Cohen broke legal ground in 1976, when he successfully represented a public relations worker in the U.S. Justice Department who disputed her dismissal, saying her boss had fired her after she had refused his sexual advances. This was the first time sexual harassment was recognized as illegal under Title VII of the 1964 Civil Rights Act. This ruling truly touched a nerve in the workplaces of America as thousands of women began filing cases, forcing companies to establish new rules of conduct in the office and on the shop floor.

Cohen was a Michigan native who served in the Marines during World War II, then returned home to earn a B.S. from Wayne State University and then a law degree. He worked for a few years in his father's law firm in Detroit, joined the Michigan attorney general's office in the criminal division, and then moved to Washington, D.C., as staff counsel to the U.S. Senate's Antitrust and Monopoly Subcommittee.

When he went into private practice, Cohen made a name for himself as a class action litigator. In the 1970s, he represented hundreds of small businesses that charged paper companies with price-fixing. He won more than $1 billion for his numerous clients in that case. In this era, he also coauthored two books with *Washington Post* reporter Morton Mintz: *America Inc.: Who Owns and Operates the United States?* and *Power, Inc.: Public and Private Rulers and How to Make Them Accountable*. At the time of his death he was the co–lead counsel in the *Exxon Valdez* oil spill case. All told, 34,000 plaintiffs—Alaskan fishermen, environmentalists, residents, and seafood businesses—had brought 150 lawsuits, all seeking compensation for their losses. Cohen's side won $5 billion in punitive damages from Exxon in 1994 for his clients, but the case went to appeal.

While lawyers like Cohen gave high-quality legal representation to the little people of this world—farmworkers, secretaries, fishermen—Stephen Meyers targeted a different group. According to the *New York Times*, "Realizing that both the very rich and the very poor had ample access to the legal profession, the two lawyers [Meyers and his partner, Leonard G. Jacoby] set their sights on the vast middle ground of America. The storefront legal clinic they established in Van Nuys, Calif., in 1972 created an immediate local sensation." Soon these two graduates of the UCLA law school had three hundred lawyers in 150 offices in six states. However, others recognized a good idea when they saw it, and with lawyers now allowed to advertise, others flooded into the same arena: walk-in law firms. The Jacoby-Meyers vision revolutionized the legal profession, opening it to millions of clients who had felt intimidated about walking into a standard law firm. Walk-in storefronts, these were comfortable. To distinguish themselves from the hundreds of competitors, the Jacoby & Meyers firm soon began to specialize in personal injury cases.

This demystifying of the legal profession by hard-sell television ads, storefronts that invited ordinary people to contemplate legal actions, and fixed prices for certain kinds of legal services was profoundly unnerving to the great bulk of lawyers. But it also opened the legal process and the courts to many people who had previously felt they could not afford them.

Successful men and women in America live in a society that honors and fosters both individual and institutional advancement. This encouragement of career accomplishments takes place in a democratic society with a free enterprise economy. But the society also has rules, regulations, and a value system that provide for stability and orderly change. The democratic government not only fosters freedom and civil rights for citizens but provides an infrastructure within which educational and other institutions operate. Consequently, the free enterprise system is regulated, and this regulation takes place via a governmental process that is fundamentally democratic. So the society is one in which individual freedom and initiative is valued but, at the same time, enterprise and freedom are circumscribed by the rule of law.

Notes

1. Andrew Hacker, *Money* (New York: Touchstone, 1997), p. 130.
2. *Statistical Abstract of the United States, 1998*, Table 367.
3. Richard L. Abel, *Lawyers: A Critical Reader* (New York: New Press, 1997), p. 21.

11

Criminals

Fabled Fixer for the Chicago Mob

Soviet Spy Who Passed Atom Plans

1930s "Trunk Murderess"

Seven hundred years ago, Dante's *Inferno* gave the Western world a vividly imagined tour of the many layers of Hell. Guided by the poet Virgil, Dante observed the great variety of human wrongdoers and sinners, all condemned to punishment tailored to their transgression. Dante's system serves quite well even today as we consider the tiny number of poor souls whose *New York Times* obits fall into the dreaded category of criminals, spies, murderers, and thieves. Yes, amidst all the success, fame, and head-spinning accomplishment that daily grace the obituary pages, several dozen among the nine thousand–plus Americans in our database were misguided and sometimes outright evil folks whose lives merit mainly obloquy.

Here, as in the *Inferno*, some are on the wrong side of history, as witness our first group, spies from the Cold War era. Had the Communists won, these traitors would have been heroes. Then a fair number of our criminals succumbed to the age-old temptations of money. Here we find the white-collar criminals, people who were outwardly successful when they began stealing money, exploiting the natural trust others felt for them. And so, while hard work, education, talent, and perseverance are key qualities in achieving success, achieving ignominy generally flows from serious character flaws. Our third group consists of professional criminals and members of organized crime who preyed on our affluent society in a systematic way. But the Mafia members depended on violence or murder to back up their activities. Our final group among the criminals is killers, those who wantonly take human life. In some cases their victims were famous, in some cases their crimes horrific. In addition, there were four other criminals in the database who committed assorted other crimes.

While the *New York Times* generally celebrates the successes in American life, we are a society with a deeply violent streak and we seem to be enthralled by crime and murder. Most other industrialized nations have lower annual homicide rates. In the past decade, however, the U.S. homicide rate has declined by some 12 percent.[1] At the same time, the number of people in prison and under legal supervision in the community remains high: over 1 million prisoners in state and federal incarceration[2] and some 4 million people who are under legal supervision in the community.[3]

While one would not necessarily connect the words "education" and "crime," it is an interesting exercise to look at the educational levels of those in this category. For half of these folks, we have no data. Of the remainder, six were high school dropouts and four had some college. A quarter of the overall group, or ten, completed college. Four of those attended one of the top fifty colleges. All but one of the college graduates went on to take a higher degree; six held a law degree, one a Ph.D., and one a medical degree. The average obit for the criminals was almost twenty-three inches long. If being a criminal were a bona fide U.S. Census–style occupation, this group would have had the second longest average obits in the database, right after members of Congress.

While Dante began his journey at the top of Hell and then descended through ever-worse sins, we will begin at the frigid bottom of the netherworld and work our way up. In Dante's world, the darkest, iciest circle of hell, the frozen Lake of Cocytus, was reserved for traitors. There they were eternally encased in ice up to their necks. Here we would find Morris Cohen, "Soviet Spy Who Passed Atom Plan in '40s." Born and raised in New York, Cohen became a Communist in 1935 and went to fight in Spain with the Abraham Lincoln Brigade. While recovering from a war wound, he was recruited by Soviet intelligence. Said *Pravda* in *its* obit, "Thanks to Cohen, designers of the Soviet atomic bomb got piles of technical documentation straight from the secret laboratory in

Los Alamos." Cohen was probably more important than the far more famous and vilified British scientist Claus Fuchs. When Cohen and his wife heard of their impending arrest, they fled to Moscow and assumed new identities. By 1954, they had resettled in London and taken on a new (Hitchcockian) cover as rare book dealers, and once again they began to spy for the Soviets. Arrested by British intelligence in 1961, they spent eight years in prison before being exchanged. To this day, we do not know which American scientist collaborated with Cohen.

Joel Barr, an electronics engineer linked to the Julius and Ethel Rosenberg spy ring that gave atomic secrets to the Soviets, was never arrested or even indicted for any espionage. Nonetheless, he defected to the Soviet bloc in 1950, when he felt arrest was imminent. According to the book *The Rosenberg File*, Barr provided important information about radar technology that he had access to while working at Western Electric and Sperry Gyroscope.

Once in the Soviet Union, Barr and another American defector helped develop "the whole microelectronics and computer industry in the Soviet Union." Barr was the child of Russian immigrants. He attended City College of New York, where he met Julius Rosenberg and became active in the Young Communist League. Late in life, in 1992, he gave an interview to the *Los Angeles Times* in which he expressed great remorse: "The real revolution for mankind that will go down for many, many years was the American Revolution. Knowing what I do now, it was a tremendous mistake to have done what I did." For twenty years he was married to a Russian woman who thought he was a South African. He retained his American citizenship, which enabled two of his four Russian children to defect to the United States. When Barr went to visit them, he applied for and received Social Security benefits!

But of course the most infamous of all modern spies was Alger Hiss, "the erudite diplomat and Harvard-trained government lawyer who was convicted of perjury in an espionage case that became one of the great riddles of the Cold War." In 1948, Hiss was accused of having been a Communist spy while an employee at the State Department in the 1930s. During congressional hearings and two trials, he denied this but was "convicted of perjury in 1950 and served 44 months in prison. He spent the rest of his life trying to clear his name." Hiss could not be convicted of spying because the statute of limitations had expired. The political classes were "bitterly split over whether he was guilty, innocent or something in between." Hiss has one of the longest obits in the whole *New York Times* database and the longest among the criminals. The *Times* explained that the case "became a source of obsessive fascination, a tangle of conspiracy theories and lingering doubts that inspired the kind of interest later seen among Kennedy assassination buffs and followers of the O. J. Simpson murder case."

There are so few criminals in our *New York Times* database that all forty-one of them are listed in Table 11-1.

Above the *Inferno*'s frozen netherworld that was the lot of traitors, Dante described the Eighth Circle with its ten levels (or trenches), each providing dreadful and fitting punishments. The ten levels begin with falsifiers in the bottommost pit and move on up to panderers. All our white-collar criminals—their reputations permanently sullied by scandal or bad behavior—would have been consigned to these trenches. In level seven we find the Circle of Thieves. There would be Dave Beck, once the powerful president of the International Brotherhood of Teamsters in the mid-1950s. He served thirty months in prison for embezzlement, specifically for "stealing $1,900 from the sale of a union-owned Cadillac." What he would not answer—invoking the Fifth Amendment 117 times—was what had happened to $322,000 missing from the union's treasury.

Mr. Beck joined the union as the driver of a laundry truck. The penniless son of a carpet cleaner and a laundress, he ended up a millionaire. What exactly he might have done with the stolen money remained unclear. A solid Presbyterian, apparently "he never drank, smoked or gambled." And "Despite his wealth, he lived quietly in the basement of a house he built for his mother and sister 20 years ago."

While Beck was a union crook, who stole from the workingman, Congressman Daniel Flood was a political crook, stealing from U.S. citizens. One suspects that each felt he had "delivered" so much to his constituents that he deserved a juicy cut. In the halls of Congress, Flood was always viewed as a colorful character, a onetime Shakespearean actor and "sartorial dandy who was known for his waxed mustache and often referred to as 'Dapper Dan.'" Yet as a powerful House chairman, he funneled billions of dollars' worth of pork into his central Pennsylvania district in the forms of highways, schools, an airport, a VA hospital—and unknown quantities into his own pockets. His first bribery trial ended in a hung jury. In 1980, as a retrial loomed, Flood pleaded guilty and resigned from the House. In Dante's *Inferno*, such thieves suffered eternally among "a mass of serpents, so diverse and daunting, / My blood still turns to water when I think of it. . . . Amid this cruel and repulsive crop of / Monsters, naked men ran terrified." This being modern America, our thieves received no such terrible punishments; Dave Beck received a presidential pardon from Gerald R. Ford, and Flood served a year's probation.

Another ostensibly respectable citizen caught stealing was C. Arnholt Smith, a much respected California banker in San Diego who owned the local baseball team and was a big Nixon backer. A self-made man, he was a high school dropout who first worked as a grocery clerk but then became interested in banking while working for Bank of America as a messenger. With his savings and a loan from his brother, Smith bought a controlling interest in the United States National Bank. A major civic leader, he always sported a tan, Buster Brown shoes, and a brown suit. Eventually his empire "included the Westgate-California Corporation and its vast real estate developments, seafood canneries, silver mines, transportation companies and the Padres." Then, in 1973, his bank collapsed, mired in $400 million in debt. He was convicted of embezzling almost $9 million himself. When the time for sentencing came, a medical report to the state asserted that Smith had only five years left to live, and so he was given a one-year sentence "served in the 'county honor camp.'" There his job was tending roses. He was released after seven arduous months and lived another eleven years.

On the eighth level of Nether Hell one finds the "counselors of fraud." In a certain symmetry, one of these white-collar crooks was Dr. Murdock Head, a highly educated doctor, dentist, and lawyer who served time for bribing—none other than Congressman Daniel Flood! Dr. Head was an active and respected professor of medicine for almost

TABLE 11-1. *Forty-one Criminals in the Obituary Database and Their Type of Offense*

Name (Age at Death)	Occupation	Crime	Prison Sentence
Spies and Political Crime:			
1. Morris Cohen (84)	Soviet spy	Spy	20 years (U.K.)*
2. Joel Barr (82)	Engineer	Defected spy	Foreign fugitive
3. Alger Hiss (92)	Diplomat	Perjury	5 years
4. M. Halperin (88)	Professor	Accused spy	Never arrested
5. C. Conrad (50)	U.S. Army sergeant	Treason	Life in prison[†]
6. I. Rodriques (69)	Puerto Rican Nationalist	Attacked U.S. Congress	Life in prison
7. O. Collazo (80)	Puerto Rican Nationalist	Attacked President Truman	Life in prison
White-Collar Crime:			
8. Dave Beck (99)	Union official	Tax, embezzlement	5 years
9. Daniel Flood (90)	Congressman	Contract fraud	1 year's probation
10. C. A. Smith (97)	Banker	Embezzlement	3 years
11. Murdock Head (70)	Medical professor	Bribery	4.5 years
12. Sonny Bloch (61)	Radio show host	Investment fraud	21 months
13. Charles Givens (57)	Business	Investment fraud	None[‡]
14. R. Schermerhorn (67)	NY State senator	Tax, obstruction	Prison (term not stated)
15. H. Friedman (74)	Union official	Racketeering, embezzlement	4 years' probation
16. Elizabeth Adams (60)	Hollywood madam	Prostitution	1.5 years' probation
Organized Crime, Mafia:			
17. Benny Ong (86)	Chinatown godfather	Murder	30 years
18. James Burke (64)	Mafia	Lufthansa theft	Life in prison[†]
19. S. DeCalvacante (84)	Mafia in NJ	Gambling network	5 years
20. Peter Savino (55)	Mafia associate	6 murders	Life in prison[§]
21. Sidney Korshak (88)	Mafia leader	Organized crime	Never convicted
22. N. Bianco (62)	Mafia in New England	Racketeering	11.5 years[†]
23. Frank Ragano (75)	Mafia lawyer	Tax evasion	2 years

Name (Age at Death)	Occupation	Crime	Prison Sentence
Murderers:			
24. M. Chenault, Jr. (44)	Criminal	Killed mother of Dr. King	Death Penalty[†]
25. James E. Ray (70)	Criminal	Killer of Dr. King	99 years[†]
26. J. Chagra (50)	Lawyer	Linked to killing of judge	10 years
27. J. Kallinger (59)	Cobbler	Killer	Life in prison[†]
28. Winnie Judd (93)	Medical secretary	"Trunk murderess"	Death penalty
29. T. Coleman (86)	GA State engineer	Killed 2 civil rights workers	Never convicted
30. J. Oliphant (71)	Rancher and paramilitary	White supremacist bomber	8 years
31. Akil Al-Jundi (56)	Criminal, then advocate	Murder	Life in prison
32. H. Blyden (61)	Career criminal	Murder	10–15 years
33. R. Brown (66)	Career criminal	Murder	Life in prison
34. M. Burnett (67)	Career criminal	Murder	Life in prison[†]
35. R. Wikberg (51)	Criminal, then journalist	Murder	Life in prison
36. M. Metzger (57)	Lawyer	Murder of wife, threats	None[#]
37. A. Cunanan (27)	Criminal	Murder of Versace	None[#]
Other Crime:			
38. W. Spann (51)	President Carter's nephew	Armed robbery	28 years
39. H. Huncke (81)	Criminal hustler	Various crimes	22 years
40. A. Ulasewicz (79)	New York City policeman	Watergate burglar	1 year's probation
41. F. Sturgis (68)	Policeman, paramilitary	Watergate burglar	1–4 years

[*] Exchanged with the Soviets for a British political prisoner.

[†] Died in prison.

[‡] Ordered to repay customers.

[§] Informer who died while in witness protection program.

[||] Found mentally insane and was institutionalized.

[#] Committed suicide immediately after crime.

twenty-five years at George Washington University Medical Center. Not long after he joined the GW faculty in 1957, Dr. Head bought a large farm near Warrenton, Virginia. This he cleverly transformed into the Airlie Foundation conference center, a delightful retreat for bureaucrats, think-tankers, all manner of important institutional folks, and members of Congress who needed to think deep thoughts in a luxurious setting. Reported the *Times* in its obit, "In 1981, Dr. Head was convicted of conspiring to bribe Representatives Otto E. Passman, Democrat of Louisiana, and Daniel J. Flood, Democrat of Pennsylvania, to obtain lucrative contracts for the Airlie Foundation conference center . . . the prosecution charged that Dr. Head had paid $49,000 in bribes to the two." Dr. Head spent a year in prison, and emerged to practice medicine and law again.

Another "counselor of fraud" was Irwin "Sonny" Bloch, "a radio show host who persuaded hundreds of listeners to invest in worthless securities, bilking them of $21 million." Bloch had a very unusual life; he started out in Chicago, then headed south to put in some time at the University of Miami before quitting "in 1958 to sing and play the drums and trombone with the Coralairs, a local band." Then, hearing that Disney World was coming, he snapped up a thousand acres of land around Orlando at a cheap price and made his first million dollars. His next move was to Palm Beach, where he modeled and acted in community theater. "He got his start in radio, he said, after listening to a host give bad mortgage advice on a tiny Florida station. He complained to the manager, who hired him to be the radio's financial adviser. 'I was hooked,' he said. 'I fell in love with radio.'"

That was in 1977. Over the next fifteen years, his show came to be carried nationwide on two hundred radio stations and had 1.5 million listeners. Initially, he gave good, solid advice. One eighty-nine-year-old widow who lost $35,000 in Bloch's nefarious schemes had listened to him for years. "Everybody simply adored him," she said. "He gave some wonderful, wonderful advice. He made a lot of money for people." This very successful radio personality also stole millions from them, too, finding his mass audience through the modern technology of the airwaves. His fans were often retirees who entrusted all or much of their savings to the scheme Bloch promoted relentlessly on his show. They were exhorted to invest in what turned out to be worthless "investments in failed wireless cable and radio stations in four states and Venezuela." Many were left penniless as Bloch and his ten cohorts bilked them of millions. Bloch died of lung cancer before completing his first prison term, and apparently "He seemed to think the cancer was retribution for what he'd done," said one prosecutor.

Another smooth operator was Charles Givens, a poor Illinois boy who built a multimillion-dollar empire on "how-to-get-rich infomercials, books and motivational speeches." Givens not only wrote the usual books, such best-sellers as *Wealth Without Risk*, he figured out that cable TV was a cheap and effective (and essentially unregulated) new medium for reaching many a sucker. According to the *New York Times*, this guru of easy wealth arrived at his lectures "in a chauffeur-driven white limousine trimmed with gold. His mantra was 'Be all you can be.' He charged people $400 to $900 to learn his 'secrets' of becoming wealthy." In a society that puts such a premium on money, Givens had no shortage of people interested in his message. But by the 1990s, the circularity of it all was catching up with him.

In 1996, a California class action suit found that he had defrauded 29,000 people and he was ordered to refund $14.1 million. The lawyer for the winning plaintiffs said, "The way he made his money was not by using the strategies he sold but rather by selling the strategies themselves." With that court verdict hanging over him, Givens declared bankruptcy. The lesson never learned by the gullible is: If it sounds too good to be true, it probably is. Givens spent no time in prison.

And so on up to the final circle of Nether Hell, the trench of panderers and seducers. There we place Elizabeth Adams, AKA Madame Alex. A native of Manila, Alex operated a "Beverly Hills prostitution ring for two decades." This was obviously no ordinary madam. After she was arrested, local detectives helped reduce her sentence when they "testified Mrs. Adams had provided important information on murder suspects, drug dealers and terrorists." Though she complained that Heidi Fleiss was horning in on her, Mrs. Adams continued her business "most recently from a house abutting the parking lot of the West Hollywood sheriff's office—no doubt passing along much useful information on local and international terrorism." In the *Inferno*, Madame Alex would find herself pursued by "horned fiends with heavy whips . . . crying 'Away, Pander! There are no women here to coin.'" In America she received a sentence of eighteen months' probation.

From here we move upward to Middle Hell, the assigned place for those who engage in violence, which almost certainly encompasses all our mafiosi. Here we find Dante's City of Dis, a "vast and reeking mire . . . filled with ill woes and torments desolate." Some of our mafiosi were known murderers; others depended on the threat of murder to pursue their corrupt activities.

Benny Ong, eighty-seven, is one of those characters seemingly out of a bad film noir, the sort who never saddles his violence with ideology or political baggage. He was "the leader of the most powerful organized crime group in [New York's] Chinatown over the last 20 years." Starting in 1935, he spent seventeen years in jail for murder, though this was to "protect someone higher in the organization." By 1974, he was head of the Hip Sing, which engaged in crimes ranging from "extortion and theft to gambling, smuggling drugs, prostitution and murder, using international contacts and employing notorious street gangs to carry out many of their activities." Oddly, in the obit, someone describes him as "a very nice man."

James "Jimmy the Gent" Burke was a gangster made "legendary" by Nicholas Pileggi in *Wiseguy,* which then spawned the film *Goodfellas.* His major claim to fame was being "the suspected mastermind" of the huge 1978 Lufthansa heist. As reported by the *Times*, a "team of hooded gunmen invaded the airline's cargo terminal at Kennedy International Airport and stole $5.8 million in untraceable American currency being returned to the United States from Germany. The cash, a record amount . . . was never found." Nor was Burke ever prosecuted for that crime or the numerous murders of other suspected participants that followed.

Closely linked to top gangsters in the Lucchese crime family, Burke was known to participate in "loan sharking, extortion, gambling, drug trafficking and murder." He was a "criminal savant" who delighted in all things illegal. Said one colleague in crime, "If you ever offered Jimmy a billion dollars, he'd turn you down and then try to figure out how to steal it from you." And if that meant murdering you, well, so be it. All this did eventually catch up with him; in 1982, he went to prison for organizing college basketball gambling. While there, he was convicted for the murder of a drug dealer who had stolen $250,000 owed in a cocaine deal. The victim had been "found frozen in a Brooklyn trailer." As for Burke, he died in prison.

Now, Dante in the *Inferno* consigned murderers to a river of boiling blood: "The bank of the bubbling crimson flood / Whence the shrieks of the boiled rose shrill and desperate." That river rose and fell depending on the heinousness of the murder. One suspects that Dante would consign to a deeper part of that boiling river of blood the Mafia types who directed cold-blooded murder from afar or personally engaged in it for money, while those who might kill in a fit of passion would be less immersed.

Simone DeCalvacante was the classic Mafia don, a fastidious man who wore expensive suits, white shirts, and ties and insisted that he was an upstanding businessman running a prosperous plumbing and heating company in Kenilworth, New Jersey. Then, in 1969, the FBI released "2,000 pages of secretly recorded tapes of conversations between him and his henchmen and with several New Jersey politicians . . . [that] disclosed some of the Mafia's preferred methods of murder." His group specialized in "labor rackets, illegal gambling, and loan-sharking" in mid–New Jersey, "devising rackets to milk union funds and extort money from legitimate companies." But all the government could ever pin on him was running a gambling ring and for that he served five years.

Peter Savino was no don, just a low-level Mafia thug, not even a full or a "made" member of New York's Genovese crime family. Savino became famous as an informer who brought down the long-elusive Vincent "The Chin" Gigante, head of the Genovese crime family, who for decades claimed to be just a crazy guy wandering Greenwich Village in his pajamas. Savino agreed to become an informant after "Federal agents confronted him with evidence that he had participated in several murders." He actually admitted to having taken part in six murders. The Mob managed to insinuate itself into all sorts of unlikely rackets. Savino testified that for a decade, "the mob skimmed millions of dollars in Government funds from the window-installation contracts in New York City public housing." Savino went into a witness protection program and testified via videotape because he was so gravely ill with cancer. This made for great drama as "the gaunt, often profusely sweating figure" appeared on television monitors in the courtroom, obviously in great pain as he spoke. Though Savino delivered a great deal as an informant, he was, one was glad to learn, still facing "a possible sentence of 20 years" for the murders when he died.

And then there was Sidney Korshak, who "used his reputation as the Chicago mob's man in Los Angeles to become one of Hollywood's most fabled and influential fixers." This was certainly one of the odder obits in the *New York Times,* reporting as it did that "It was a tribute to Sidney Korshak's success that he was never indicted, despite repeated Federal and state investigations. And the widespread belief that he had in fact committed the very crimes the authorities could never prove made him an indispensable ally of leading Hollywood producers, corporate executives, and politicians."

What exactly was the allure of this man, a lawyer who had no actual office in L.A., had no license to practice law in California, and was never seen to take a note or read a brief? And who often talked on pay phones where he knew no tape recorders were rolling? Well, back in his Chicago days, before he had headed west, "a department store chain faced with demands for payoffs from rival unions engaged Mr. Korshak and the problem almost magically disappeared." Soon he was in great demand as "a labor lawyer who could stave off demands from legitimate unions by arranging instant sweetheart contracts with a friendly union, often the teamsters." Hollywood was apparently delighted to have a fixer who could deal with the Mob, and corrupt union leaders were delighted to have a major connection with the legitimate world. While there is no direct mention of murder, Korshak was a Mob lawyer, and the Mob has always used murder as needed. The *Times* even notes that "Mr. Korshak seemed to lead a charmed life. That was partly because his mansion was protected by extensive security measures . . . and partly because he was careful to distance himself from the fruits of his own activities."

The number of American homicides, though large, still represents only a tiny fraction of total offenses: one tenth of 1 percent. As with most crimes, males predominate; the rate of homicide per 100,000 is three times higher for males than for females. The homicide rate for blacks is markedly higher. For white males in 1995, it was 7.8 per 100,000 population, while for black males it was a staggering 56.3 per 100,000, or seven times higher. For white females, the homicide rate was 2.7 per 100,000, a fourth of the rate for black females.[4]

For the Mafia, murder is largely a tool of terror to effect compliance. For our group of murderers, killing human beings was not just a business proposition. Half of the murderers were career criminals who then committed the ultimate crime. But others fit no profile, committing murder for a variety of reasons. M. W. Chenault, a nice boy from a middle-class black family, went to Ebenezer Baptist Church in Atlanta one Sunday in 1974, drew two pistols, and began firing, killing the mother of Martin Luther King. She was playing "The Lord's Prayer" on the organ. He actually meant to kill her husband, the minister of the church, for he had decided "months earlier that black ministers were a menace to black people and must be killed. . . . He said he acted out of hatred for Christianity and because his god had told him to. His lawyers said he was insane." Chenault was only forty-four when he died of a stroke in prison, where he was serving a life sentence.

When James Earl Ray, a longtime drifter, petty criminal, and jailbird, assassinated Martin Luther King, Jr., in 1968, it was out of "passionate hatred of blacks and especially of Dr. King, who had become the nation's pre-eminent civil rights leader." Dr. King was in Memphis to support garbage workers on strike when he was shot and killed. Ray disappeared from the motel room from which he had fired the fatal shots but was found two months later after an international manhunt. In the interim, more than a hundred American cities were hit by riots.

Ray pleaded guilty, thereby avoiding the electric chair, but soon thereafter began to assert that "he had been 'set up,' used as a decoy by shadowy conspirators who included a mystery man he knew only as

Raoul." However, several other panels established to investigate these assertions concluded that Ray had committed the crime and done so on his own. Some members of the King family embraced the conspiracy theory and were making further inquiries when Ray died.

Ray was the classic sad American drifter. He was the oldest of nine children born into a poor family where criminality was commonplace and the mother was of "very limited intelligence." They lived on the wrong side of the tracks in Alton, Illinois, and when Ray entered school he wore rags and had no shoes. Not surprisingly, this boy had a fierce temper. He dropped out in tenth grade, tried the Army, but could not accept the rules and authority. Thus he headed west to what would be a life of inept crime, which landed him in prison numerous times for a total of thirteen years. He was a pretty good escape artist and was on the lam from a Missouri prison when he shot King. While in prison he became enraged whenever he saw King on TV. "Somebody's got to get him," he was quoted as saying. "If I ever get to the streets, I am going to kill him." He did—and spent the rest of his life in prison for it.

As one of Texas's highest-paid lawyers, Joseph Chagra was an unusual defendant in a murder trial, but he admitted his "complicity in the first assassination of a Federal judge in more than a century." In 1979, Judge John H. Wood, Jr., an avowed enemy of drug traffickers, was shot in the back as he walked onto the driveway of his San Antonio, Texas, town house. Joseph Chagra and his ne'er-do-well drug-running brother, Jimmy, were immediate suspects because Jimmy was to have gone before Judge Wood on a trafficking charge that very day.

What made the case odder and more lurid was that the hired hit man was the father of Hollywood star Woody Harrelson. Apparently Jimmy Chagra paid the elder Harrelson $250,000 to knock off the judge. Charles Voyde Harrelson's wife was indicted as part of the conspiracy, too. Ultimately, lawyer Chagra plea-bargained ten years in jail and served six before going home. He would die at age fifty in an automobile accident. Charles Harrelson was sentenced to life. Drug trafficker Jimmy was looking at a number of decades.

The remaining two murderers made the obits because theirs were extremely notorious cases in their eras. That of Joseph Kallinger was notably gruesome. His crime spree terrorized East Coast suburbs from Thanskgiving 1974 until shortly after January 8, 1975. Kallinger, a Philadelphia cobbler, would appear with his thirteen-year-old son at a house posing as salesmen. Once in the house, they savagely "beat, robbed, and terrorized" those inside. They struck in places as peaceable and far apart as suburbs of Baltimore, Maryland; Harrisburg, Pennsylvania; and Camden and Dumont, New Jersey. In Leonia, New Jersey, they brutally slit the throat of a young woman and left her to die in the basement. Kallinger was finally caught when "a blood-stained shirt left by one of the intruders in Leonia was traced by a laundry mark."

This cruel and vicious man had six children, who complained of his abuse and then recanted. One of those sons "was found dead in the rubble of an old building in Philadelphia." Ultimately, Kallinger was convicted of that murder, as well as the murder of another boy only nine years old. Kallinger's own lawyer would say, "He was sick. He was an evil man, and the evilness was a manifestation of the illness." He died in prison at age fifty-nine from a seizure. His son, who was his accomplice in crime, was "confined for a time in Pennsylvania and is believed to have changed his name. His whereabouts, and those of what remains of the Kallinger family, are not known."

Winnie R. Judd was that rare creature: a famous female murderer. Back in the 1930s, the United States was a less homicide-prone nation, and so gruesome murders were national news. Known as the "Trunk Murderess," Judd's case was infamously bizarre, a tabloid sensation of the 1930s. Mrs. Judd, twenty-six, had just arrived at Los Angeles's Union Station in the fall of 1931 when a porter noticed "what appeared to be blood dripping from one trunk." She declined, when asked, to open the trunk and drove off in a car with her brother. Police tracked her down and "inside the larger trunk . . . found the body of Agnes Anne LeRoi, 32. What they found in the smaller trunk catapulted the case into headline news around the country. It contained remains of Hedvig Samuelson, 24, her body neatly cut into three pieces to make it easier to pack. A few days later, a valise left behind by Mrs. Judd was found to contain a fourth body section."

Apparently Winnie Judd knew these women and had sneaked into their house and shot them "out of jealousy over attentions paid to them by her married boyfriend." She became so infamous overnight that when she was returned to Phoenix in those pre-TV days to face trial "thousands lined the streets for a glimpse, and the owner of the home where the murders occurred sold 10-cent tickets for tours." Two years later Winnie Judd was convicted of the crimes and sentenced to hang, which set off a great public debate on capital punishment. But in the end she was deemed crazy and sent off to the Arizona State Hospital for the Insane. Over the next three decades she escaped on six occasions, usually only for a short time. But in 1962, she disappeared and was not seen again for seven years. During this time she was in San Francisco working as a housekeeper for a wealthy elderly woman. Star attorney Melvin Belli stepped forward to fight her extradition. Judged sane, she was sent to the penitentiary, where she remained until 1971, whereupon she returned to her old employer. She moved around a bit in her final years before she died at age ninety-three. She claimed to the end that she had shot the women in self-defense but wrote, "I've asked God many times to forgive me."

The criminals in our database lived beyond the rule of law; they were people who transgressed society's boundaries *and* got caught. Crime is a high-risk occupation that can, however, be very lucrative and, for some, even glamorous.

Notes

1. *The New York Times Almanac, 2000,* p. 319.
2. In 1996, 1,136,819 persons were incarcerated; see *Statistical Abstract of the United States, 1998,* Table 377.
3. John J. Dilulio, Jr., "Federal Crime Policy," *Brookings Review,* Winter 1999, p. 21.
4. *Statistical Abstract of the United States, 1998,* Table 151.

12

Hollywood & TV People

"Sweater Girl" and Sultry Star

Master of Unsettling Low-Budget Films

Originator of *Meet the Press*

The power and reach of American movies and television are immense. A popular film or TV show will be seen by hundreds of millions of people all over the world. A small but telling example: *The Flintstones,* a highly popular cartoon series that ran from 1960 to 1966 in the United States, then went into syndication in eighty countries around the world. Now at any hour of the day someone somewhere on the planet is watching Fred and Wilma handling the dilemmas of prehistoric life. When it comes to glamour and money, few other industries can rival Hollywood. However, television is certainly the more pervasive medium, with its amazing penetration of everyday life, its cultural and political influence and international scope, and its incredible ability to generate wealth. Each year, the average American attends five movies, while the average American household logs three thousand hours in front of the tube.[1]

In this chapter we meet a cross-section of successful and influential people who have played important roles in the rise of movies and TV. Some are the stars, a group that gets a big play in the *New York Times* when each dies. Our database has 271 actors and 157 actresses, or 428 in all. These actors and actresses had the sixth longest obits, at an average of sixteen and a half inches. If higher education is important to one's development as an actor, it is not obvious. Only a fifth, or eighty-six, had a college degree, while 3 percent had advanced degrees. It is very likely that the actual rates are higher, since we have no educational data at all for just over half the group. Forty-four, or almost half, of those who were college grads went to one of the top fifty schools, with nineteen holding an Ivy League degree. Since a successful acting career requires no formal credentials, it makes sense that so few stars hold college degrees. Our different chapters on predominant high-status professions underscore the different requirements. For instance, when Betty Grable said, "There are two reasons I am successful in show business, and I am standing on both of them," this was a simplification, but it did make the important point that most actors and actresses begin with accepted physical beauty.

The Apexes of Fame for the actors and actresses, shown in Tables 12-1 and 12-2, show that Hollywood movie stars dominate both lists. However, with television now the reigning medium, one suspects that in coming decades, those who make their careers primarily on the small screen will eventually predominate on such lists. As Hollywood makes fewer movies and studios no longer promote their own stables of stars, it becomes harder and harder for anyone to become an enduring star of the magnitude of a Ginger Rogers or a James Stewart. Those active in the studio era typically worked in sixty, seventy, or eighty films, leaving a large body of work behind.

Many stories in this chapter are about the behind-the-scenes people, the producers and executives who developed new kinds of entertainment or formats. Through the lives of some of these folks, we can follow the growth of Hollywood and the extraordinary rise of television in its now-varied forms as a powerful medium of information and entertainment.[2]

Success in Hollywood and TV can be either critical or popular or both. A successful actor is one who is admired for his or her talent and leaves behind a significant body of work, including some films or television shows important enough to be considered classics. Generally, stars make a reputation based on certain strengths—a talent for comedy or for playing tough guys or sexy women. Yet the best actors and actresses are those who transcend their usual roles to convincingly play someone unexpected. Those who can exert some control and are innovative can expect to have a longer, richer career and more possibilities for success than others. Academy Awards and other such prizes are certainly validations of careers, as are salary levels. The movie star pecking order is based to some degree on money. Ginger Rogers in her heyday was the highest-paid woman in America. Today, top stars (mainly men we should note) can command $20 million a picture and also demand a percentage of the profits.

For producers and directors, success usually means hit films and huge incomes. In 1938, Louis B. Meyer, head of MGM, made the nation's highest salary, $1.2 million.[3] In the 1999 *Forbes* list of wealthy Americans, filmmakers George Lucas, Steven Spielberg, and Jeffrey Katzenberg were all on the list as billionaires, as was Michael Eisner, CEO of Disney.[4] However, Hollywood is by no means measured just by money. Hollywood cares a great deal about making films that are admired or are huge box-offce hits. Also, a particular artistic vision or the creation of a new and popular genre will build a reputation. Woody Allen, for example, has made only two movies that were popular successes, but his distinctive work is admired and supported year after year.

In the early Hollywood years, a handful of studios controlled the careers and destinies of dozens of directors and hundreds of actors and actresses. For almost four decades, the studios churned out several hundred movies a year, most of them long since forgotten. To get a flavor of the old Hollywood studio star system, one need look no further than sultry sweater girl Lana Turner, one of MGM's biggest female stars from the 1930s to the 1950s. She explained in 1969, "It was all beauty and it was all power. Once you had it made, they protected you; they gave you stardom. The ones who kept forging ahead became higher and higher and brighter and brighter and they were *stars*. And they were treated like stars. We had the *best*."

Of course, what is most striking about Lana Turner's early career is the overriding role of luck and sheer beauty. Turner's own life story was about as amazing as any movie plot. She was born in Wallace, Idaho, but her miner father then moved the family to San Francisco, where he was mugged and murdered. His widow became a beautician and relocated to Los Angeles. In one of the most famous bits of Hollywood lore,

TABLE 12-1. *The Apex of Fame: Actors in the Obituary Database*

Name (Age at Death)	Obit Date	Undergraduate College Attended	Type of Acting
1. James Stewart (89)	07/03/97	Princeton*	Film, TV
2. George Burns (100)	03/10/96	None	Radio, TV, film, club show
3. Burt Lancaster (80)	10/22/94	New York U.	Film
4. Red Skelton (84)	09/18/97	None	Radio, TV, film, show
5. Gene Autry (91)	10/03/98	None	Radio, TV, film
6. Henny Youngman (91)	02/25/98	None	Show, TV, film
7. Robert Mitchum (79)	07/02/97	None	Film
8. Don Ameche (85)	12/08/93	Loras College*	Radio, play, film
9. Burl Ives (85)	04/15/95	E. Illinois State Teachers College	Musical, play, film, TV
10. Dean Martin (78)	12/26/95	None	Film, TV
11. Phil Hartman (49)	05/29/98	California State University at Northridge	Film, TV
12. Burgess Meredith (89)	09/11/97	Amherst	Play, film, TV
13. Robert Young (91)	07/23/98	None	TV
14. Flip Wilson (64)	11/27/98	None	TV, show
15. Joseph Cotten (88)	02/07/94	None	Play, film, TV
16. E. G. Marshall (84)	08/26/98	Carleton	Play, film, TV
17. Richard Kiley (76)	03/06/99	None	Radio, theater

Accomplishments and Fame	Obit Length
National icon; won Oscar for *The Philadelphia Story*; made more than 80 movies	120"
Comedian team with wife Gracie Allen and others; won Oscar for *The Sunshine Boys;* began second career at age 79 after major heart surgery	86"
Circus acrobat turned Hollywood star in more than 70 movies; *The Killers*	75"
Clown prince on his own TV and radio show; made 4 films; had his beginning in rural vaudeville shows	66
Singing cowboy in movies; multimillionaire who owned radio and TV stations, oil wells, and baseball team; songwriter with 300 songs	66"
Comedian known as "King of One-Liners"; performed at any occasion	63"
Actor in more than 100 movies; *Cape Fear, The Story of G.I. Joe*	62"
Won Oscar for *Cocoon*; made more than 40 films	60"
Folk singer who won an Oscar for *The Big Country*; made 32 movies, 13 broadway productions, and more than 100 record albums	60"
Teamed with Jerry Lewis and the Rat Pack; comic on TV show and in films	58"
Stand-up comedian, *Saturday Night Live, NewsRadio,* and movies	56"
Virtuoso in various roles; Broadway; *Of Mice and Men, Rocky,* TV	53"
Played wholesome characters in *Father Knows Best, Marcus Welby, M.D.*	53"
Comic on many shows and TV host on his own show	50"
Versatile Actor in *Citizen Kane* and more than 60 other movies	46"
Character actor in *The Defenders, The New Doctors*	45"
Won Tony Award for *Man of La Mancha,* three Emmys and two Golden Globes for *The Thorn Birds, A Year in the Life, Picket Fences*	44"

(continues)

TABLE 12-1. *The Apex of Fame: Actors in the Obituary Database*

Name (Age at Death)	Obit Date	Undergraduate College Attended	Type of Acting
18. Buddy Rogers (94)	04/23/99	U. of Kansas	Film, TV, stage
19. Raul Julia (54)	10/25/94	U. of Puerto Rico*	Play, film
20. Lloyd Bridges (85)	03/11/98	U. of California at Los Angeles*	Film, TV
21. Wenceslao Moreno (103)	04/21/99	Not named	Show, TV
22. Lew Ayres (88)	01/01/97	U. of Arizona	Film
23. Emil Sitka (83)	01/25/98	None	Play, TV, film
24. Roddy McDowall (70)	10/04/98	None	Film, TV, play
25. Ellis Rabb (67)	01/13/98	Carnegie Technical Institute*	Theater
26. Harry Blackstone, Jr (62)	05/16/97	Not named	Magic show
27. George Fenneman (77)	06/06/97	San Francisco State*	TV
28. Jack Lord (77)	01/23/98	New York U.*	Play, film, TV
29. Dane Clark (85)	09/16/98	Cornell U.†	Play, film, TV
30. Cesar Romero (86)	01/03/94	Not named	Play, film, TV
31. St. John Terrell (81)	10/20/98	Columbia	Play
32. Bill Ballantine (88)	05/19/99	Art Institute of Pittsburgh	Circus show

* Graduated from college.

† Received law degree.

Note: There were 271 actors in the obituary database. These top 32 in length represent 11 percent of them.

Accomplishments and Fame	Obit Length
Bandleader who starred in *Wings, My Best Girl*	44"
In classic plays and Hollywood movies; father in *The Addams Family*	42"
Starred in *Sea Hunt, Airplane,* and his own TV shows	42"
Ventriloquist for more than eight decades on TV and in shows	41"
Career guided by conscience; *All Quiet on the Western Front*	40"
Foil of the the Three Stooges; appeared in 450 movies	38"
Child star who became versatile actor; *Lassie Come Home, How Green Was My Valley*	38"
Actor and director; founder of Association of Producing Artists	36"
Illusionist on Broadway; son of the "Great Blackstone"	34"
Actor-Announcer on *You Bet Your Life;* films and commercials	33"
Starred in *Hawaii Five-O; Dr. No,* an early James Bond film	32"
Starred in World War II films; *Go, Man, Go, The Glass Key,* 30 other films	31"
The Joker in *Batman* TV series; gigolo in films	30"
Reenactment of Washington Crossing the Delaware River became a tradition	30"
Clown, artist, and writer; Ringling Brothers and Barnum & Bailey Circus	29"

TABLE 12-2. *The Apex of Fame: Actresses in the Obituary Database*

Name (Age at Death)	Obit Date	Undergraduate College Attended	Type of Acting
1. Jessica Tandy (85)	09/12/94	None	Play, film, TV
2. Ginger Rogers (83)	04/26/95	None	Show, film, play
3. Claudette Colbert (92)	07/31/96	None	Film, play, TV
4. Greer Garson (92)	04/07/96	U. of London*	Film, play
5. Myrna Loy (88)	12/16/93	None	Film, play, TV
6. Shari Lewis (65)	08/4/98	Columbia	Show, TV
7. Lana Turner (75)	07/01/95	None	Film, TV, play
8. Audrey Meadows (71)	02/05/96	Not named	TV, play
9. Dorothy Stickney (101)	06/03/98	Drama school	Play, musical
10. Ann Corio (85)	03/09/99	None	Play, show
11. Dorothy Lamour (81)	09/24/96	None	Film
12. Alice Faye (83)	05/10/98	None	Film, play, radio
13. Martha Raye (78)	10/20/94	None	Show, TV, film
14. Butterfly McQueen (84)	12/24/95	City College of New York*	Film, play
15. Violet Carlson (97)	12/08/97	None	Play, musical
16. Maureen O'Sullivan (87)	06/24/98	None	Film, TV
17. Susan Strasberg (60)	01/23/99	None	Play, film, TV

Accomplishments and Fame	Obit Length
Won Oscar for *Driving Miss Daisy,* Tony Award, National Medal of Art	112"
Won Oscar for *Kitty Foyle*; made more than 70 movies; humble upbringing	87"
Won Oscar for *It Happened One Night*; made more than 60 films; *Cleopatra*	77"
Won Oscar for *Mrs. Miniver*; seven Oscar nominations; *Auntie Mame*	55"
Honorary Oscar; *The Thin Man, The Best Years of Our Lives*	50"
Ventriloquist and puppeteer in children's shows; won 12 Emmys; wrote 60 books for children	46"
They Won't Forget, The Postman Always Rings Twice	43"
The Honeymooners, Top Banana, The Bob and Ray Show	42"
Life with Father, Longest-running non-musical on Broadway	41"
A burlesque queen on Broadway; East Coast burlesque queen	41"
Made more than 50 films; 7 "Road" pictures with Bob Hope and Bing Crosby	40"
Left Hollywood at the height of her fame; *Tin Pan Alley, Hello, Frisco, Hello*	38"
Entertained World War II troops; clown in burlesque shows before Hollywood	35"
Gone With the Wind; Became Harlem community worker	35"
A Soubrette in musical comedies; *The Red Robe, The Student Prince*	35"
Jane in Tarzan movies; *The Thin Man*; made more than 60 movies	34"
The Diary of Anne Frank; later life a failure	34"

(continues)

TABLE 12-2. *The Apex of Fame: Actresses in the Obituary Database*

Name (Age at Death)	Obit Date	Undergraduate College Attended	Type of Acting
18. Dinah Shore (76)	02/25/94	Vanderbilt*	Radio, TV, film
19. Marion Bell (78)	12/24/97	None	Musical, opera
20. Rosina Lawrence (84)	07/06/97	None	TV, film, play
21. Ida Lupino (77)	08/5/95	None	TV, film
22. Julie Haydon (84)	12/29/94	None	Play
23. Betty Bryant (76)	01/25/99	None	Showboat
24. Annabella (86)	09/21/96	None	Film, play, radio
25. Nancy Claster (82)	04/27/97	Goucher*	TV
26. Audra Lindley (79)	10/25/97	None	TV, film, play
27. Vivian Blaine (74)	12/14/95	None	Film, TV, play
28. Minnie Pearl (83)	03/06/96	None	Radio, TV, show
29. Mildred Natwick (89)	10/26/94	Bennett Junior College	Play, TV, film
30. Mary Frann (55)	09/25/98	Northwestern	TV

* Graduated from college.

Note: There were 157 actresses in the obituary database. These top 30 in length represent 19 percent of them.

a reporter first spotted the luscious Miss Julia Turner in 1937 while she was sipping a soda in a Hollywood ice-cream parlor, skipping her high school secretarial class. The director-producer Mervyn LeRoy became her mentor, advising a new first name (she chose Lana) and acting lessons. What really mattered was that the camera loved her

Accomplishments and Fame	Obit Length
Hosted variety and talk shows; appeared in 7 movies	32"
Brigadoon, her only New York musical; *A Night at the Opera*	29"
Our Gang, Little Rascals, Pick a Star; began as a dancer	28"
Made more than 50 films; *The Untouchables, Alfred Hitchcock Presents*	27"
Played Laura Wingfield in *The Glass Menagerie, Widow of George Nathan*	26"
Long Career on Ohio River showboat; wrote about career in 1994 book	26"
Le Million, July 14, Seventh Heaven; French-born	24"
Miss Nancy of *Romper Room* who educated children before *Sesame Street*	24"
Sex-starved wife in *Three's Company*; made more than 100 TV dramas	24"
Guys and Dolls; child singer who became actress by chance	23"
Queen of country comedy; worked at the Grand Ole Opry for more than 50 years	23"
Excelled at eccentricity; *Barefoot in the Park, The Snoop Sisters*	22"
Wife in *Newhart; Days of Our Lives, Kings Crossing*	22"

silky sexiness, for she exuded that unique quality, star power on the silver screen. The *New York Times* described her first role (in *They Won't Forget*) thus: "Wearing a skintight sweater and skirt, she sauntered along a street, spoke not one line, was murdered in the first reel and began a quick climb to stardom." While "her acting was often barely passable," she played a sex symbol in dozens of forgettable movies with such titles as *The Bad and the Beautiful* and *These Glamour Girls*. But she also played in such film noir classics as *The Postman Always Rings Twice.*

Her personal life was even more lurid than her on-screen persona. She married and divorced seven men: bandleader Artie Shaw, a restaurateur (father of her one child) twice, a sportsman, actor Lex Barker (one of the Tarzans), a businessman-rancher, and even a nightclub hypnotist. Yet the most sensational episode was in 1958, "when her lover, the reputed mobster Johnny Stompanato, threatened to disfigure her and was stabbed to death" by Turner's fourteen-year-old daughter. A jury exonerated the daughter for justified homicide.

While Lana Turner was a classic Hollywood studio star, her route to success was very unusual: Hollywood found her sitting on a soda fountain stool looking gorgeous. She was not, like most successful actresses, working hard on the vaudeville circuit or taking lessons in singing, dancing, acting, and getting the small roles that snag important people's attention. It was her extreme good fortune that the camera ate her up. However, once discovered, she worked to acquire the fundamentals (if not the finer points) of acting.

Contrast Lana Turner's movie career with that of Jessica Tandy, "who enhanced the American theater and enriched the American screen as few actresses have." Jessica Tandy was a stage actress of great talent who played opposite her equally talented husband, Hume Cronyn, for fifty years in numerous theater productions. Yet she became truly famous only late in life, when she appeared as a wise old lady in two popular Hollywood films, *Driving Miss Daisy* and *Fried Green Tomatoes*. The mass audience of movies (as well as the even more mass audience of TV, when the movies were shown there) made her known to millions. Her route to success in the movies was the complete opposite of Lana Turner's.

One of the surprises of Tandy's obit—the longest of any actor or actress in our database—is that she came from England as war loomed in 1940, having just divorced her actor husband of eight years. She was a seasoned, much-admired stage actress who had never wanted to do anything with her life but act. In London, she performed in dozens of contemporary plays, as well as such sought-after roles as Ophelia in *Hamlet* opposite the legendary John Gielgud. Yet once in New York, she found it was "such a struggle to make ends meet that she almost abandoned the stage." Her marriage to the wealthy Hume Cronyn transformed her life in many ways, giving her a theatrical soul mate as well as money and family. Together they moved to Hollywood. Hume got some decent roles, but Tandy, neither voluptuous nor sexy on-screen, found herself endlessly cast as a lady's maid saying, "Yes, Mum, No, Mum."

She would recall, "I was in the doldrums in Hollywood. It was not a happy position. I began to feel I had no talent and it was all a pipe dream. It was Hume who got me out of it." Cast by him in a Tennessee Williams play "Portrait of a Madonna," Tandy received rave reviews. Then there was the part in *A Streetcar Named Desire* with Marlon Brando that would mark her 1947 Broadway triumph. One suspects that as a young actress she did not fill the big screen, for when the film version of *Streetcar* was made, Vivien Leigh was chosen to play her part. The Hollywood of the studio system did not have a place for Tandy. Only very late in her career was she able finally to return to Hollywood as the star she certainly was.

While we remember Tandy for certain choice roles, she, in fact, was always working, often in mediocre productions. She was a big talent who worked hard to always be working. "You are richer for doing things," she would advise. "If you wait for the perfect part or for what sends you, you will have long waits, and you deteriorate. You can't be an actor without acting." One was amazed to learn that all her life she suffered from "stage fright that had got worse rather than better."

When we think of Hollywood's most important contributions to movies, musicals are right up there. One of the genre's giant talents was Gene Kelly, "the dancer, actor, director and choreographer who brought a vigorous athleticism, casual grace and an earthy masculinity to the high romance of lavish Hollywood musicals." His is the second longest actor's obit, after Jimmy Stewart's. Like Lana Turner, Gene Kelly had no particular early aspirations to become a performer. Years later he would muse, "I don't really know why I clicked. I didn't want to be a dancer.

I just did it to work my way through college. But I was always an athlete and gymnast, so it came naturally."

But for the Depression, Hollywood would almost certainly never
have been graced by Gene Kelly. Born in Pittsburgh, Pennsylvania, he
was one of five children whose mother (part owner of a dancing school)
insisted they all study dance and music. Kelly was also a boy who liked
to play football and hockey. He went off to Pennsylvania State College,
and when hard times hit he had to leave school to teach gymnastics.
When he did complete college and get his degree in economics, the lack
of jobs sent him back to his mother's dancing school for work. Soon it
was his school: then he and his brother developed a dance act; and by
1938 Kelly, twenty-seven, had departed for New York to get serious
about his career as a dancer. A small Broadway part led to a big part and
notice by Hollywood. Here was a very handsome young man who could
sing, dance, *and* act! Legendary Hollywood producer David O. Selznick
signed Gene Kelly to an exclusive contract but then "lent" him to
MGM, studio home of over-the-top musicals.

Gene Kelly's first movie, *For Me and My Gal* with Judy Garland in
1942, was a huge hit. Kelly made several more films before he could
influence the choreography and content of *Cover Girl* with Rita
Hayworth. "For once," wrote a film critic, "a dance on the screen is not
merely a specialty but actually develops character and advances plot." Of
course, Kelly would go on to make such classics as *Singing in the Rain,
On the Town,* and *An American in Paris.* He brought a uniquely
American-guy style to dance, making it both more playful (by dancing
with cartoon characters) and more profound. At a time when Hollywood
tended to view its stars as mainly screen talent, Kelly showed that performers often had much more than that to offer. Rather than stick with a
tried-and-true formula, he was always trying to stretch the possibilities.

Burt Lancaster was one of the durable Hollywood stars. He arrived
as the studio system was on the wane, coming to movies rather late in
his own life. Born in East Harlem, he grew up knowing how to fight
with his fists but was also a member of his church choir and an amateur
actor at the Union Settlement House. He was a good enough athlete to
get a scholarship to attend New York University. But after two years he

dropped out to form an acrobatic team with a boyhood friend. Soon they had hooked up with a small circus and were earning three dollars a week. All through the Depression, they toured with various traveling groups, including Ringling Brothers and Barnum & Bailey Circus. Then in 1939, a finger injury ended Lancaster's days as an acrobat. He then took a variety of jobs, including lingerie salesman and firefighter in a meatpacking plant, before being drafted for World War II. He met and married a USO entertainer, returned to New York with her, and through her job with a producer ended up on stage as an actor for the first time at age thirty-four. Seven movie producers stepped forward with offers, and by 1946 he was on the big screen playing tough guys.

Lancaster was always a risk taker. And very soon after he entered movies, he saw the value of forming his own production company. In this he was a pioneer, and it was a deliberate move so "I can do things that will help me as an actor " While he continued to play tough guys and swashbucklers in other people's films, in the ones he made for his production company, he played a wide range of characters. He explained to one interviewer, "I took a $50,000 salary loss on the picture *All My Sons*, in which I starred as the idealistic son of a war profiteer, because I believed in it, and I've never been sorry. O.K., it didn't make money; it was too talky, too preachy. But we took a chance, we tried. Why, I'd still be the same punk kid I used to be back in East Harlem during the Depression if I was afraid to take a chance." His production company also made Paddy Chayefsky's *Marty*, an unlikely love story about a Bronx butcher, and saw it win the Oscar for Best Picture in 1955.

Burt Lancaster's strategy of starring first in a mass-market movie and then in a more artistic film clearly paid off. *New York Times* critic Vincent Canby wrote, "As one looks back over his career now, one can see that something was really happening, that the young circus performer who came to movies comparatively late in life in *The Killers* was slowly but unmistakably evolving from movie star into a first-rate actor of unexpected qualities." Burt Lancaster made some exceptional films, including a star turn as the Sicilian prince in Luchino Visconti's *The Leopard* and his late-in-life role as the over-the-hill criminal in Louis Malle's *Atlantic City*.

In their heyday, Hollywood films were the major source of entertainment for much of America.[5] In the 1930s, the average American went to the movies every two weeks, meaning that she (the bulk of the audience was women) saw at least twenty-five movies a year, if not more, since double features were commonplace. Two thirds of the nation's entertainment dollars were spent on Hollywood films. Moviegoing peaked during World War II, when 82 million Americans went to a movie each week! They almost certainly saw and enjoyed some of the films of Hollywood producer Pandro S. Berman, a talented filmmaker who flourished in the four decades of the studio era. The son of a Universal Pictures general manager, Berman grew up with Hollywood, starting as an assistant film cutter at RKO Studios and then serving as an assistant to Tod Browning and other directors. In 1930, RKO made him a producer.

What exactly is a producer? In *Hollywood Cinema*, authors Richard Maltby and Ian Craven quote producer Jesse Lasky's amusing description: "The producer must be a prophet and a general, a diplomat and a peacemaker, a miser and a spendthrift. He must have vision tempered by hindsight, daring governed by caution, the patience of a saint and the iron of a Cromwell . . . his decisions must be sure, swift, and immediate, as well as subject to change, because conditions change continuously in the motion picture industry. . . . In his hands lies the supervision of every element that goes to make up the finished product [i.e., the movie]. These elements are both tangible and intangible, the control of human beings and real properties as well as the control of the artistic temperament, the shaping of creative forces and the knowledge of the public's needs for entertainment."[6]

Harvey Weinstein, cofounder and cochairman of the successful Miramax Films, has his own thoughts on the Hollywood producer, the hands-on person who pulls together the financing for a film and organizes all the production details. He says, "You have to taste the sweat. You have to know film grammar, history, think and be a producer, work it from top to bottom."[7] Because Hollywood has set up a system where production costs often seem to equal profits, the bottom line—so critical to judging the success of most businesses—cannot serve that usual function. Considering that production costs in Hollywood can include such luxuries as private planes for directors, round-the-clock nannies, bodyguards, and so on, profits can be elusive. Entertainment writer Judith I. Brennan says that lacking a meaningful bottom line, film studio executives have been judged by "an ever-shifting, loosely defined set of intangibles—taste, instinct, connections, a talent for schmooze, show-biz knowledge."[8]

In our database we have 167 producers, of whom 25 are women. Just over a third have a college degree, while almost 14 percent have a higher degree. What's striking about the producers is that half of them have a degree from a top fifty school and a third from the Ivy League. Their obits average almost twelve and a half inches, placing them in thirty-first place in the list of dominant high-status professions.

Our database also contains 137 directors, 20 of whom are women. Directors are the people who have the artistic vision, who are on the set every day. Forty percent have a college degree, and 10 percent an advanced degree. Of those who have degrees, just under half went to one of the top fifty schools, with just under a fifth having an Ivy League diploma. Their average obit lengths are almost fifteen column inches, putting them in thirteenth place in the list of dominant high-status occupations. Their greater fame than producers reflects the fact that few successful movie producers are known to the general public, while many successful movie directors have ardent followings.

The Apex of Fame for producers (see Table 12-3) shows the specialization among the various formats. While an actress might well appear on Broadway in a play as well as in films and on TV, a theatrical producer generally sticks to that terrain, while the movie folks stick to movies and the television producers stick to TV. While the theatrical producers dominate the top of the list, the movie producers dominate overall, getting far more coverage than television producers. One suspects that this is partly a case of the greater prestige and fame connected to films versus TV.

The Apex of Fame for directors, shown in Table 12-4, is heavily dominated at the top by Hollywood movie directors, although the list also includes luminaries from the worlds of opera, theater, and dance.

TABLE 12-3. *The Apex of Fame: Hollywood and Other Producers in the Obituary Database*

Name (Age at Death)	Obit Date	Undergraduate College Attended	Type of Art
1. George Abbott (107)	02/02/95	U. of Rochester*	Theater, film
2. Lucille Lortel (98)	04/06/99	Adelphi	Theater
3. Bernard B. Jacobs (80)	08/28/96	New York U.‡	Theater
4. Jean Dalrymple (96)	11/17/98	None	Theater
5. Dawn Steel (51)	12/22/97	New York U., Boston U.	Film
6. Shirley Clarke (77)	09/26/97	Not named	Film
7. Lillian McMurry (77)	03/29/99	Not named	Blues music
8. Joseph Green (96)	06/22/96	None	Film
9. Julius Monk (82)	08/22/95	Not named	Cabaret shows
10. Jon Stone (65)	04/01/97	Williams†	TV
11. Anne Hummert (91)	07/21/96	Goucher*	Radio, musical
12. William Githens (92)	11/22/98	Columbia†	Film
13. Robert Saudek (85)	03/17/97	Harvard	TV
14. Don Simpson (52)	01/21/96	U. of Oregon*	Film
15. Stanley Garfinkel (67)	09/21/97	Harvard†	Film
16. Henry Hampton (58)	11/24/98	Washington U.*	Film
17. Pandro Berman (91)	07/15/96	None	Film

Accomplishments and Fame	Obit Length
"Mr. Broadway"; involved in more than 120 productions and 11 movies as playwright, director, actor and producer	90"
Patron of Off-Broadway; produced 500 plays; *The Threepenny Opera*; owned the Lucille Lortel Theater and started the White Barn Theater	76"
President of Shubert Organization; pillar of Broadway; *A Chorus Line, Nicholas Nickleby, The Gin Game, Amadeus*	61"
Brought theater to City Center as its publicist; *Hope for the Best, Brighten the Corner, Burlesque*	58"
Paramount studio chief; *Cool Runnings, Fallen, City of Angels*	52"
The Connection, Robert Frost (Oscar winner), *The Cool World*; champion of independent filmmaking	32"
Founded Trumpet Records; recorded Sonny Boy Williamson, Elmore James; unlikely producer of black music	30"
Creator in Yiddish film heyday; *The Jazz Singer, Yidl with a Fiddle*	29"
Host of clubs and cabarets: Ruban Bleu; Downstairs, Upstairs; Plaza 9	28"
Creator of *Sesame Street* as writer, producer, and director; 18 Emmys	28"
Creator of radio soap operas: *Just Plain Bill, Waltz Time*	27"
Newsreel pioneer; training films for the Navy	27"
TV executive; a pioneer of culture on TV; *Omnibus, Profiles in Courage*; 11 Emmys and 7 Peabody Awards	26"
Top Gun, Flashdance, Beverly Hills Cop II; known for blockbuster movies and excessive lifestyle	25"
Historian; documentary film *Completely Dior*	25"
Civil rights documentaries; *Eyes on the Prize* won 4 Emmys	25"
Hunchback of Notre Dame, Butterfield 8; more than 100 movies	24"

(continues)

TABLE 12-3. *The Apex of Fame: Hollywood and Other Producers in the Obituary Database*

Name (Age at Death)	Obit Date	Undergraduate College Attended	Type of Art
18. Carlton Moss (88)	08/15/97	Morgan State U.	Film
19. Owen Bradley (82)	01/09/98	Not named	Country music
20. Ben Bagley (64)	03/27/98	None	Theater
21. Ross Hunter (75)	03/12/96	Not named	Film
22. Albert Broccoli (87)	06/29/96	Not named	Film
23. Joseph Cates (74)	10/12/98	New York U.	TV
24. Florence Greenberg (82)	11/04/95	Not named	Pop music
25. Jim Copp (85)	04/26/99	Stanford, Harvard	Children's music

* Graduated from college.

† Received master's degree.

‡ Received law degree.

Note: There were 168 producers in the obituary database. The 25 longest obituaries represent 14 percent of them.

Leading the filmmaking pack is the reclusive Stanley Kubrick, best known for *2001* and *Dr. Strangelove.* This apex also includes designers, whether lighting designers like Abe Feder, or Dorothy Jeakins, who won three Oscars for her movie costumes.

Producer Pandro Berman produced a series of frothy Fred Astaire-Ginger Rogers musicals (including *Top Hat* and *Shall We Dance?*) that were huge hits, as well as more serious fare such as *The Hunchback of Notre Dame.* Berman brought great glory to many of his stars. Elizabeth Taylor won an Academy Award for his 1960 film *Butterfield 8,* while Bette Davis achieved stardom in 1934 in his *Of Human Bondage.* Katharine Hepburn also won an Academy Award acting in his 1933 film

Accomplishments and Fame	Obit Length
Filmed the black experience; *Negro Soldier*; writer, scholar, and critic	24"
Worked with Patsy Cline, Loretta Lynn, Brenda Lee, Bill Monroe	24"
The Shoestring Revue, The Littlest Revue, Revisited series	24"
Pillow Talk, Airport, more than 60 movies	23"
James Bond films: *Dr. No, Goldfinger, Thunderball*	23"
Innovative TV specials; 2 Emmys; more than 1,000 productions	23"
Housewife who discovered the Shirelles; lost everything by 1977	21"
Playhouse Records; *East of Flumdiddle, Gumdrop Follies, Thimble Corner*	21"

Morning Glory. Yet, few Americans would recognize Pandro Berman's name.

After a decade of making films at RKO, a place where, Berman said, "none of the owners ever agreed on anything," he moved on to MGM, the Tiffany's of Hollywood studios, where he would remain for the next twenty-seven years. Berman was the producer of more than one hundred films, including *Gunga Din* with Cary Grant and *Room Service* with the Marx Brothers. Later films included *The Blackboard Jungle* with Sidney Poitier. The *New York Times* described Berman as being admired for "producing films that were entertaining and technically masterful." While working, he never personally won any awards for his

TABLE 12-4. *The Apex of Fame: Directors, Managers, and Designers in the Obituary Database*

Name (Age at Death)	Obit Date	Undergraduate College Attended	Type of Career
1. Jose Quintero (74)	02/27/99	U. of California at Berkeley*	Play director
2. Lincoln Kirstein (88)	01/06/96	Harvard*	Ballet director
3. Rudolf Bing (95)	09/03/97	Not named	General manager
4. Stanley Kubrick (70)	03/08/99	None	Film director
5. Louis Malle (63)	11/25/95	U. of Paris	Film director
6. Garson Kanin (86)	03/14/99	None	Director, writer
7. Robert Lewis (88)	11/25/97	City College of New York	Director, teacher
8. Oliver Smith (75)	01/25/94	Queens College	Set designer
9. Samuel Fuller (85)	11/01/97	None	Film director
10. Abe Feder (87)	04/26/97	Carnegie Institute of Technology	Lighting designer
11. Alan J. Pakula (70)	11/20/98	Yale	Director, producer
12. Ben Edwards (82)	02/16/99	Feagin School	Set designer
13. Dorothy Jeakins (81)	11/30/95	Otis Art Institute*	Costume designer
14. Emile Ardolino (50)	11/22/93	Pennsylvania State U.*	Set designer
15. Ardis Krainik (67)	01/20/97	Northwestern*	General director
16. Margo Rose (94)	09/16/97	Not named	Puppeteer, designer
17. Jean Louis (89)	04/24/97	Not named	Costume designer

Accomplishments and Fame	Obit Length
Revived Eugene O'Neill plays: *The Iceman Cometh*	88"
Cofounder of New York City Ballet	80"
"Titan of the Met": Led Metropolitan Opera for 23 years	75"
Spartacus, Lolita, Dr. Strangelove, Paths of Glory, The Shining	74"
U.S. and France: *Pretty Baby, My Dinner with André*	65"
Films and plays: *The Diary of Anne Frank, Born Yesterday*	64"
Founded Actors Studio; directed Broadway plays and musicals	62"
West Side Story, Camelot; over 250 productions	60"
Master of low-budget films: *The Big Red One, White Dog*	56"
"Unchallenged Master"; 300 Broadway shows	51"
More than 20 films: *The Sterile Cuckoo, To Kill a Mockingbird*; an actor's director: 4 actors and actresses won Oscars with him	46"
Broadway plays by Eugene O'Neill, William Inge, Shakespeare	42"
Won 3 Oscars designing costumes for films: *Joan of Arc*	40"
Theater: "One of the most prolific and imaginative designers"	35"
Rescued and established the Lyric Opera of Chicago	33"
Helped design Howdy Doody	31"
Dresses for Marilyn Monroe, Rita Hayworth and more than 200 other stars; designed costumes for 60 films	30"

(continues)

TABLE 12-4. *The Apex of Fame: Directors, Managers, and Designers in the Obituary Database*

Name (Age at Death)	Obit Date	Undergraduate College Attended	Type of Career
18. Frank Perry (65)	08/31/95	U. of Miami	Film director
19. Robert Parrish (79)	12/06/95	Not named	Editor, director
20. Peter E. Obletz (50)	05/04/96	Hamilton College*	Manager
21. Marvin Rothenberg (79)	10/02/97	City College of New York	Director
22. Saul Bass (75)	04/27/96	Brooklyn College	Graphic designer
23. Chet Forte (60)	05/20/96	Columbia*	TV director
24. Gilbert Moses (52)	04/18/95	Oberlin	Stage director
25. Peter Adair (53)	06/30/96	Antioch*	Film director
26. Norman Rene (45)	05/26/96	Carnegie Mellon U.*	Theater and film director
27. Gene Fowler, Jr. (80)	05/17/98	None	Director, editor

* Graduated from college.

Note: There were 137 directors, managers, and designers in the obituary database. The 27 longest obituaries represent 19 percent of these behind-the-scenes men and women.

films, but in retirement he was honored with lifetime achievement awards both at the 1977 Academy Awards ceremony and in 1992 from the Motion Picture Producers Guild of America. Berman spent his last three years as a producer at 20th Century Fox, where his final film was a 1970 drama with Elliott Gould called *Move.*

Samuel Fuller came onto the Hollywood scene as a director in 1948, and proceeded to make two dozen films over the next thirty-five years. Unlike Pandro Berman, whose work could only be characterized as well-made and "entertaining," Fuller was more of an auteur who had a

Accomplishments and Fame	Obit Length
David and Lisa, Diary of a Mad Housewife, Mommie Dearest	29"
Films: won Oscar for *Body and Soul, All the King's Men*	26"
Alwin Nikolai Dance Company; Murray Louis Dance Company	24"
Made some of the most memorable commercials of 1950s, 1960s	24"
Made art of movie titles: *The Man with the Golden Arm*	23"
Sporting events; made *Monday Night Football* a ratings force	22"
Plays, musicals; cofounder of Free Southern Theater	21"
Gay documentaries: *Word Is Out, Absolutely Positive*	21"
Prelude to a Kiss, Reckless; founded the production company	20"
Directed *I Was a Teen-Age Werewolf*; won Oscar for *Seeds of Destiny*; more than 100 movies and shows	20"

definite style and vision that marked all his films. They were distinguished first by his frugality (hence his *New York Times* designation as "the reigning virtuoso of low-budget films") and speed. All were made in black and white. But most striking was their subject matter. One critic noted Fuller's "great originality in seeing the constant criminal element in life, whether in the American city, on the range, or in every theater of war. . . . His central characters are invariably psychotics, chronically hostile to organization, thriving on double-cross and resolving doubts through brutality."

Fuller viewed such intellectual admiration of his work (widespread especially in France) as rather amusing. He just saw himself as telling tough-guy stories. Fuller was born in Massachusetts but lost his father when he was eleven. His mother moved the family to New York, where Fuller first sold tabloid newspapers ("I learned early that it was not the headline that counts, but how hard you shout it"), then ascended into the newsroom at thirteen as a copyboy. Then, at seventeen, he signed on at the *New York Evening Graphic* as a reporter.

While Fuller was at the movies one day, the newsreel showed movie star Mary Pickford playing tennis with her husband. She looked so tan and glamorous in her tennis whites that Fuller decided then and there to head to the West Coast. He got a job as the crime reporter for a San Diego paper and by the mid-1930s had started writing dime-store novels with titles like *Burn Baby Burn, Make Up and Kiss,* and *Test Tube Baby.* Having pulled off those books, he threw over journalism and headed to Hollywood and those glamorous tennis togs. He began flogging his own scripts. His breakthrough was the 1938 film *Gangs of New York.*

World War II broke out, and Fuller served as an infantryman in the absolute thick of the fighting, landing on Omaha Beach on D-Day. He memorably described the beach as "lined with the intestines of men." At the end of the war, he published another novel, *The Dark Page.* Fuller was yearning to direct his own stuff, and a producer agreed to back him if only he could provide a cowboy script. So Fuller came up with *I Shot Jesse James.* Now he really showed his mettle, thrilling the producer by making the film in a mere ten days for $118,000, which included Fuller's $5,000 directing fee. Thus was Fuller launched on a career in which he cranked out interesting black-and-white films for small sums while always putting in for a hefty part of the profits. When he made the first Korean War movie, *The Steel Helmet,* in 1951 in ten days for $105,000 and it grossed $6 million, he earned more than $400,000 the first year alone. (Of course, keeping costs down meant that when you needed a tank in a war movie like this, instead of shelling out for a real one, you just painted a cheesy-looking one on cardboard). Yet Samuel Fuller had loved being a reporter, he often said, and "If only a reporter could get a thousand dollars an hour the way a director does, I'd be in it today."

Two of Fuller's more celebrated films were made in the mid-1960s while he was at Allied Artists: *Shock Corridor,* described by the *New York Times* as "a disturbing work in which a reporter has himself committed to a mental institution to track down a murder suspect but loses his mind in the process," and *The Naked Kiss*, in which "a prostitute tries to rehabilitate herself in a small town, only to find that the philanthropist she falls in love with is a child molester." One is not too surprised to learn that the latter "failed miserably at the box office." Working in Hollywood was not easy, and over the years, "producers berated Mr. Fuller, recut his movies and ruined his work." Finally, though, he convinced the Lorimar studio to let him make *The Big Red One,* a World War II movie drawing on his own experiences. This $6 million film (his biggest budget yet) became his best known, though it, too, was forcibly cut down from four hours long to make it commercially viable. While Fuller did not have any big hits, he did have a distinctive style and an *oeuvre* that earned him much admiration. He developed a real following as "his films began showing up at film festivals in Europe and in colleges and revival houses in the United States."

Notice that while Samuel Fuller and Pandro Berman had similar career spans, Berman's role as a reliable and versatile studio producer enabled him to make four times as many films. With the demise of the studio system,[9] moviemaking became a far riskier business. Hollywood began to depend on a few big hits—the blockbusters—to carry the 75 percent of all movies that do not recoup their production costs. Hollywood movies are generally extremely expensive investments—currently up to an average of $40 million per movie—whose reception and box-office receipts are very hard to predict. The merchandising income from tie-ins to movies like *Star Wars* or *Jurassic Park* can far exceed the box-office receipts. But few movies lend themselves to such commercial tie-ins.

Those who could generate Hollywood blockbusters became the new venerables. Don Simpson, the wild half of a producer team with Jerry Bruckheimer, made "blockbuster films adhering to what had been called a high-testosterone, low-subtlety formula." These included the 1987 *Beverly Hills Cop II* and the 1986 *Top Gun*. Twice, in 1985 and

1988, the two were named Producers of the Year by the National
Association of Theater Owners. Don and Jerry, as they were known,
made monster hits and monster money. The *New York Times* reported
that their "films reportedly reaped more than $2 billion in theater rev-
enue and sales of record albums and videocassettes by 1991."

Don Simpson was "popular and well respected . . . a brilliant devel-
oper and analyst of scripts, with a knack for zeroing in on a flaw in a
screenplay." Simpson's life trajectory was a dramatic story. He was born
in Seattle to "poor, sternly religious parents." He actually grew up in
Anchorage, Alaska, graduated from University of Oregon and then
headed south to Los Angeles, where he was soon writing screenplays
for Warner Bros. In 1975, he became an executive at Paramount, rising
to president for worldwide production in early 1981. Sometime in the
1980s, Simpson developed a reputation as a troubled party animal way
too involved in drugs, sex, and rock 'n' roll, a man with "a reputation
for high living and personal excesses." He had come a long way from
his straitlaced childhood. But his and Bruckheimer's films were box-
office smashes, and in 1988 they signed a big multimillion-dollar production deal. But when they stumbled badly in 1990 with *Days of
Thunder* (about stock car racing), Paramount wanted to renegotiate and
they left for Disney. In 1994, a somewhat humbled Bruckheimer said of
the pair, "Our purview was too narrow. We pigeonholed ourselves into
making these blockbuster movies, when we never set out to do that in
the first place." When they hit some hard years, their Midas touch suddenly gone, they vowed, "Let's just do what we started to do when we
came here: make movies we like." However, Don Simpson was dead
soon after at age fifty-two, found in a bathroom in his Bel Air home. He
apparently died of natural causes.

While Hollywood remains tremendously influential as a medium of
popular culture, it cannot compare with television. There was very little
understanding at first of how pervasive the medium would become. By
1958, there were three networks: ABC, NBC, and CBS (DuMont had
folded in 1956). Most had been radio enterprises that had segued into
television, bringing along many familiar formats: soap operas, quiz
shows, comedies, drama, news, and sports. By 1953, almost half of

Americans owned a TV. Today 97 million households have not just one but 2.4 television sets. With the rise of public, cable, and satellite TV, the networks have seen their vast audience share fall by half, along with their portion of national advertising revenue. Today 70 million households subscribe to cable TV, while 85 million have VCRs,[10] which allow them to watch movies at home. So movies continue to play a major role in American entertainment, but they are often not seen in movie theaters.

Among the early pioneers of TV was Dennis James, an on-air personality who figured out in 1938 that TV was a very cool medium even at its most primitive. Pleasant, relaxed, and amusing, he became a fixture, "a ubiquitous game show host, announcer, actor and commercial spokesman" for the next fifty years. He was, his family said, the first person to do a television commercial (for Wedgwood china), the first sports commentator (for play-by-play professional wrestling), and the first to run an audience participation show (called *Okay, Mother*).

Dennis James was a native of Jersey City, New Jersey, who graduated from St. Peter's College and then set out to become an actor. He attended the Theater School of the Performing Arts at Carnegie Hall, sold dog supplies at Abercrombie & Fitch, and then wangled a job at a small radio station. From there he ended up at Allen B. DuMont's experimental TV station in Passaic, New Jersey. Dennis perfected his TV persona as he engaged in all manner of host and announcing duties before heading off to serve in World War II. When he returned to DuMont, television was starting to attract audiences. In 1946, James became one of TV's first stars as the hilarious commentator for professional wrestling. Explained the *New York Times*, "Knowing nothing about professional wrestling . . . he made up names for holds he didn't recognize and used a rubber dog bone from his Abercrombie days to create crunching sounds of bones breaking while stripping his fingers down a balloon to create the effect of blood-curdling screams."

James quickly evolved into a highly adept host or announcer of game, quiz, and variety shows, including *Ted Mack's Original Amateur Hour*. Just as the movie camera loved Lana Turner, so television embraced James. He was handsome in a pleasing way; everything about him was easygoing, and he made people feel good. But he in no way

eclipsed the guests or interfered with the proceedings by taking too
much limelight. He had an on-air personality that flowed along perfectly in this intimate yet cool new medium. By the 1950s, James was
doing thirteen live shows a week and earning more than $500,000 a
year. Then, like Burt Lancaster, he realized that with his own production company he could better control his destiny and make more money.
And so he moved west to Los Angeles in the 1960s and joined what had
by then become the heart of television production. He would be the
longtime host of the syndicated version of *The Price Is Right* and then
Name That Tune. And he remained in demand for commercials till the
end: one for Physicians Mutual Insurance Company of Omaha was running when he died.

James was always a much-sought-after host for televised charity
fund-raisers. Every year he presided over the United Cerebral Palsy
telethon, ultimately helping to raise more than $700 million. His pleas-
ant, witty touch helped other charities running other telethons raise
more than $300 million. These large figures convey the reach and power
of television as opposed to any other medium.

Much of early television was really just radio shows transferred to
a small black-and-white screen.[11] Thus, there were quiz shows and
variety hours, but also the ensemble comedy shows that followed their
characters' woes and triumphs week after week. But once television
began to develop, it created new material and formats. Audrey Meadows was one of the early great television actresses. She was also a
precautionary tale of how actors who do not control the means of production can be eternally typecast in one role. It was Meadows's "por-
trayal of a working-class housewife on *The Honeymooners* [that]
placed her in the pantheon of television comedy's grandes dames." If
she ever had any subsequent acting triumphs, they merited no mention
in her obit.

Born in China into a missionary family, she grew up in Sharon,
Connecticut, aspiring to be a singer. And she indeed made her debut at
age sixteen, in Carnegie Hall. However, she was steered into acting and
spent World War II touring in a USO production. In 1951, she joined the
televised version of *The Bob and Ray Show*, two venerated New York

radio comics. On the side, she played opposite Phil Silvers on Broadway in *Top Banana*. Then rumor came that Jackie Gleason, a new big deal in TV, was looking to replace his ailing female lead. Meadows appeared and was dismissed as too pretty. She went home, remade herself into a frump, and sent photos of the redone her to Gleason, who then hired her. She, Gleason, Art Carney, and Joyce Randolph played two couples: Ralph and Alice Kramden and Ed and Trixie Norton. Said the *New York Times*, "Miss Meadows superbly held her own by remaining the calm sarcastic center around which the brilliant comedy of Gleason and Carney swirled. Listening to Ralph's hare-brained get-rich-quick schemes, Alice would stand with arms folded and eyes disdainful." *The Honeymooners* set a standard and a style for TV comedy that has stood the test of time. The show is still endlessly watched in reruns on cable and airline flights.

To appreciate the odds of making it as an actor or actress, much less a successful one, consider these earnings figures: In 1997, the Screen Actors Guild had 25,300 members in its New York branch. Almost a third, or 8,300, earned nothing from screen acting that year. Another 6,000, or almost a quarter of the whole membership, made less than $1,000. Another 5,390 made more than $1,000 but less than $7,500. Only 900, or 3 percent, made more than $100,000 that year. That leaves another 4,710 members of SAG making somewhere between $7,500 and $100,000.[12]

Robert Young was an actor who started under the old studio system, where he forged a respectable career playing in dozens of films but then became a major star in two classic TV shows, *Father Knows Best* and *Marcus Welby, M.D.* He explained his career thus: "I am a plodder. My career never had any great peaks. But producers and directors knew I was reliable. So when they couldn't get really big stars, they'd say, 'Let's get Bob.' As a result I always kept working, each time a little higher."

A Los Angeles native, Young always wanted to act. He was in his high school's drama club and after graduating worked part-time so he could study and act at night at the Pasadena Community Playhouse. He had an attractive and winning manner and got his first role in a Charlie Chan mystery, *The Black Camel.* He was signed by MGM and proceeded to be the fallback choice of male lead, playing with such great female stars as Greta Garbo, Katharine Hepburn, Jean Harlow, and Greer Garson.

In 1949, Young played the strong, humorous father in the radio series *Father Knows Best,* which was "a classically wholesome and idealized portrait of family life in the Midwest." The show debuted on television in 1954 but was not seen by the fledgling CBS as particularly successful and so was canceled. But viewers demanded its return, so in 1955 NBC picked up the show and gave it a more family-friendly slot in midevening. The show would continue for another five seasons, ending at the peak of its popularity because Robert Young had tired of the role. Even as he was playing this wholesome role, he was battling with alcoholism, regularly attending AA meetings.

After a period of semiretirement, which Young said he hated, he heard about an upcoming new series on NBC featuring a doctor. Though another actor was slated for the part, Young went to Grant Tinker, then a TV executive at Universal Studios, and convinced him to let him have the role. Said Tinker, "There was a very sympathetic quality to Young as an actor. You can easily confuse him with a kindly doctor. He was also a guy who had backbone. He was very determined." The show premiered in 1969 and became the biggest hit ABC had had up until that time. Unlike *Father Knows Best,* which was just fun entertainment, *Marcus Welby* dealt with "serious problems like autism, blindness, LSD side effects, drug addiction, and leukemia. . . . [Dr. Welby] treated not only physical ailments but the fears and family issues of each person." The medical show, like the sitcom, would be an enduring staple of television, with the compelling drama of illness and accident a surefire way of capturing big audiences.

Probably no aspect of television has been as influential as television news, which has dramatically reshaped the nature of politics and public life. Whereas once Americans got their news from newspapers, which provide quite long and detailed articles, today most Americans get their information about the world from television, which provides far less factual information in its news reports and stresses stories and personalities with good visuals. Mastering the TV news sound bite has become absolutely necessary for anyone hoping to convey information and influence people.

Lawrence E. Spivak was the "originator of the NBC News program *Meet the Press* and one of the first broadcasters to use panels of reporters to interview national and international leaders." Moved from radio to TV in 1948, *Meet the Press* remains the longest-running program on television and has been the inspiration for other similar shows of what we now call pundits and "talking heads." The show immediately began making news, establishing itself as a high-profile forum for those wanting to catch the nation's attention. Thus, it was on *Meet the Press* in 1948 that Whittaker Chambers first accused Alger Hiss of being a Communist, a story that still provokes passionate discussion to this day. The likelihood that the Soviets possessed atomic bombs was first revealed by a military general on *Meet the Press*. And New York Governor Thomas E. Dewey disclosed on the show that he would not run for president and instead endorsed Dwight E. Eisenhower. By 1951, the show was being called "easily the most provocative program discussion show on the air."

Major political leaders of all kinds—whether King Hussein of Jordan, a U.S. senator, or a cabinet officer—found it to their advantage to appear on *Meet the Press* and submit to reporters' grilling. Said Spivak, "Television has an awesome facility for showing up sincerity as well as insincerity. So if a man is honest and knows his stuff, he'll emerge with his proper stature. By the same token, so will a phony." Spivak was a New Yorker who attended Harvard, where he loved to box (perhaps good preparation for the rough-and-tumble of his future show). For a decade, he helped run some hunting and fishing magazines. Then, in 1935, he bought *The American Mercury*, an important magazine of public opinion. In 1945, he began *Meet the Press* on radio, and once it became a success on TV, he sold his money-losing magazine in 1950. He saw his own role as "nothing more than a devil's advocate after a story." Such Sunday-morning panel shows still play an important role in showcasing politicians addressing the issues of the day.

Fred Friendly, like many television pioneers, started off his career in radio. Even as a neophyte in his hometown of Providence, Rhode

Island, Friendly always had a noble vision of what these mass media could do, as evidenced by his earliest radio enterprise: a series of biographical shows detailing the lives of such geniuses as Thomas Edison and Harvey Firestone. He then served in World War II and returned to Manhattan, where he joined NBC Radio. There he met the world-famous war correspondent and broadcaster Edward R. Murrow. The little-known Friendly suggested that the two make "an album of recordings of world leaders and other newsworthy people speaking in the recent past." *I Can Hear It Now* was a huge success and launched a partnership that would shape the fledgling field of television news. Probably Friendly's greatest legacy was inventing one of the most powerful informational formats this new medium offered, the "news documentary." Friendly pioneered "such techniques as the use of original film clips, live, unrehearsed interviews, and the use of field producers who supervised reporting on location." One of his and Murrow's first documentaries examining Senator Joseph McCarthy showed how much of his anti-Communist crusade was lies and cruel bullying, helping to bring McCarthy down.

Friendly always had an acute appreciation for TV's unprecedented power. In 1966, he said, "TV is bigger than any story it reports. It's the greatest teaching tool since the printing press. It will determine nothing less than what kind of people we are. So if TV exists now only for the sake of a buck, somebody's going to have to change that." Friendly was an intense, high-minded journalist whose vigorous pursuit of stories about "hotly debated issues including civil rights, government secrecy and tobacco's role in causing lung cancer" fueled an ongoing clash between the corporate interests of the network owners and the news division. Nonetheless, Friendly rose to the presidency of CBS News in 1964. He did not last more than two years before the news-versus-money clash came to a head. The occasion was a Senate hearing on Vietnam that Friendly believed was important enough to be carried live. His boss disagreed and stuck with the scheduled rerun of *I Love Lucy.* An outraged Friendly resigned and would later write that this had been "a choice between interrupting the morning run of the profit machine—whose only admitted purpose was to purvey six one-minute commercials every half-hour—or electing to make the audience privy to an event of over-riding importance taking place in a Senate hearing room at that very moment."

Having quit the networks, Friendly then entered a career phase as a journalism professor and Ford Foundation broadcast consultant. These provided a platform from which he could function as a high-profile goad to and conscience of the broadcasting industry. In many ways, much of the higher-minded coverage he believed television should deliver now comes via cable. C-Span, for example, provides continuous coverage of Congress, along with many other important Washington-based events. Ironically, television news documentaries remain a staple of the networks, in part because they are so cheap compared to enter-tainment shows. But Friendly was a much-respected gadfly because he spoke up about the networks' constantly diminishing commitment to quality news. One wonders what he would have made of NBC's enter-tainment division producing a two-hour special, *Confirmation: The Hard Evidence of Aliens Among Us?* that looked just like a normal usual documentary. Presented with the usual serious tone of those enterprises, it purported to "explore reports of alien visitation from mind-altering implants to abductions."

Charles Kuralt was another CBS News legend, the youngest CBS correspondent ever, reporting from Vietnam and throughout Latin America and the familiar host of many a special broadcast and docu-mentary. But where he really made his mark was in his cross-country meanderings, which allowed him to "interview the overlooked and explore the underappreciated." While most journalists were avidly pur-suing stories about the doings of the powerful (mainly on the East and West Coasts), from 1967 to 1980 Kuralt wandered America with *On the Road* in a motor home looking for the small but delightful: a ninety-three-year-old brick maker or the Mississippi sharecropper who put nine children through college. "I have resolutely pursued irrelevance out there on the back roads," he said modestly. But a longtime president of CBS said of Kuralt, "He achieved texture in television news not seen before, a blending of pictures and words that illuminated the country in a remarkable way." His longtime cameraman said of him with great admiration, "The simplest thing was put under his microscope, and it became something beautiful, hopeful, encouraging."

Like most of his peers, Kuralt did not begin his career in TV. He started as a reporter and columnist at the *Charlotte News* in North Carolina, his home state. He was always restless, and one suspects that he saw TV as his ticket to a life of wandering. "I have always had the travel itch," he said, remembering his social worker father taking him on his widespread rounds. "I looked forward to those trips. God, I loved it. And he would tell me little bits of history, try to interest me in what was passing by down there in eastern North Carolina. Maybe that's where it began." CBS News executive producer Don Hewitt hired Kuralt because he was a wonderful writer: "He had a reverence for words rare in an industry obsessed with pictures. But television news, like any other, is and always will be about telling stories and not about showing pictures." While he could cover a big story as well as anyone, Kuralt's gift was finding the little story and telling it just right.

Once commercial network television was up and running, it did not take long to see that it would always pursue the largest possible audience. So avidly did the networks cater to low- and middlebrow tastes that FCC Chairman Newton Minow once described it as a "vast wasteland." Many cities and states responded by establishing educational television channels. The cleverness of Ralph Rogers, a Dallas businessman, was to see in the late 1960s that if all these local independent stations could be linked together, a new network could be created. Thus was born the Public Broadcasting System, whose mandate was the finer things in life, not just milking every hour for its six minutes of lucre. For the adults who watched TV for the typical four hours a day and the kids watching a typical three hours a day, PBS might supply some better alternatives.

Rogers served as chairman of this new and important broadcast entity, PBS, from 1973 to 1979. Nor was he mere window dressing, for during this time he "was widely credited with resisting efforts by the Nixon Administration to push public television out of public affairs broadcasting and cut its financing." Jim Lehrer, longtime PBS news anchor, said, "He basically saved our bacon. He carried the water for all of us." Decades later, Rogers was still outraged: "People like me couldn't believe that any President of the United States could say to the people of the United States, who own the air, that they could not discuss public affairs on the air."

Rogers's personal history was rather astonishing. A native of Boston, he was a natural businessman, running many prosperous companies. But then, in his early thirties, he was suddenly stricken by rheumatic fever, which at the time was often fatal. He survived but was warned the problem would recur, eventually destroying his heart. Unwilling to accept this death sentence, Rogers set out to find a cure. Wrote the *New York Times*, "He raised money, enlisted the support of drug companies and laboratories, and found scientists who would accept his financial help to work on the disease. Eventually this effort led to the discovery that the disease was linked to strep throat. Through the development of antibiotics, rheumatic fever was all but wiped out." This can-do attitude characterized Rogers's whole life, making him a major business and philanthropic leader in Dallas.

As the father of four and grandfather of sixteen, Rogers also championed the Children's Television Workshop and was one of the first backers of *Sesame Street*. Presumably he understood how grateful parents would be to have an alternative to all the network cartoon shows with their huge blocks of commercials exhorting children to eat sugary cereals and buy this or that new toy. And if you follow the *New York Times* obits closely, there you will find Jon Stone, the "Emmy Award-winning writer, producer and director who helped create *Sesame Street* and such beloved characters as Cookie Monster, Big Bird and Oscar the Grouch." Stone had hoped to become an actor when he graduated from Williams College and obtained a master's degree from the Yale School of Drama. We don't know what became of those aspirations, but he ended up as a producer of CBS's classic children's show *Captain Kangaroo*. Then he retired to Vermont at a rather young age of thirty-some. But he was enticed back to write the pilot script for *Sesame Street*, which debuted on November 10, 1969. One of Stone's brilliant strokes was to bring in Jim Henson, creator of the beloved Muppets. Stone would stay on for three decades as head writer and producer for an acclaimed children's show today seen by about 120 million children in 130 countries. "We set out to make a show that children and adults could watch together and children could ask questions."

Of course, the big story in the past couple of decades in TV has been cable and the incredible proliferation of new options beyond network, all of which have steadily eroded the networks' audience and profits. CNN showed that there was real interest in a twenty-four-hour-a-day news operation of international scope. In recent years, the networks have begun spinning off their own cable news channels. Where once accredited print journalists outnumbered TV and radio reporters on Capitol Hill, today the ratio is reversed at three to two. People whose houses are plugged into the Internet are already watching eight fewer hours of television per week. One of those who saw early on that viewers might pay for choices beyond the networks was B. J. Magness, "a onetime cottonseed salesman who mortgaged a cattle ranch to start a business that grew into Tele-Communications Inc., one of the nation's biggest cable companies."

A native of Oklahoma, Magness started his first cable company in 1956 in Memphis, Texas, stringing the wires himself. His first wife ran it out of their kitchen. At that early stage, people were just looking for better reception. But the idea of additional programming soon followed. Then the Magnesses moved to Bozeman, Montana, and linked up with another group that was creating a new station through microwave transmissions. In 1968, those combined enterprises were renamed Tele-Communications. Magness served as chief executive from 1968 to 1973, when John Malone took over. Magness also held large stakes in ninety-one cable programming companies, including Turner Broadcasting and Home Shopping Network. All this made him fabulously wealthy; in 1996, *Forbes* estimated his assets to be $960 million. Certainly, the late 1970s marked the true beginning of cable television's steady erosion of the networks' longtime monopoly. In 1972, when 6.5 million people subscribed to cable, the networks were not too worried. But by 1996, Tele-Communications alone would have fourteen million subscribers, a hefty chunk of the 72 million households that now have cable TV. VCRs certainly played a role in the diminishing watching of network TV. Though they were a luxury in 1980, 8 million households now own them. Owners of video stores bought 641 million tapes of movies and old TV shows in 1996, while citizens who understand how to tape bought 392 million blank tapes!

The 1980s were the last decade when the networks really had the stage to themselves and could blithely ignore cable. It was also the decade when Brandon Tartikoff made his reputation as "one of the most successful showmen in the history of network television, who brought to NBC such hit series as *Hill Street Blues, The Cosby Show, Miami Vice,* and *Cheers.*" As one longtime friend said of Tartikoff, "At the last great moment when network television was a communal experience for America, Brandon was the one in charge of delivering the programs that created that experience." Not only did Tartikoff dominate the eighties, he was also the man who signed on the little-known Jerry Seinfeld, whose show became NBC's most successful series in the 1990s, after Tartikoff left.

From an early age, Tartikoff was interested in television and stories. Wrote the *New York Times,* "At 10 he began telling his parents that he thought the lead actor in his favorite show, *Dennis the Menace,* was miscast. Later, at Yale, in a writing seminar given by the author Robert Penn Warren, he suggested that a D. H. Lawrence story needed a better plot. Mr. Warren told him, 'You should probably think of a career in television.'" So, after graduation, Tartikoff went to an ABC affiliate in Chicago. He caught the attention of the network with his inventive promotions of old movies.

In 1977, he joined NBC in New York at a time when the network was in a state of chaos and its ratings were in the basement. Within three years and at the tender age of thirty-one, Tartikoff was head of network programming. When Grant Tinker arrived a year later, he said, "In the midst of NBC's floundering, Brandon looked like an island of sanity." Through all this stressful time, Tartikoff was undergoing treatment for a recurrence of Hodgkin's disease. Nor were his triumphs yet obvious. Tinker tells of a 1982 meeting with network affiliates where the station owners demanded that Tartikoff, who was sitting outside looking sick as a dog, be fired. Tinker refused, and within the following year, Tartikoff's new shows began to rack up the ratings. Subsequent seasons saw the introduction of such hit shows as *L.A. Law, Family Ties, The Golden Girls,* and *St. Elsewhere.*

Through all these early travails, said one friend, "He never took himself too seriously. He always won with grace and with style and with humor." He was much admired for his handling of his illness—never missing a day of work—and his spirited embrace of life. Most Saturdays he played softball. He drove a beat-up VW and never noticed if he had holes in his shoes. Wrote the *New York Times,* "Throughout his career he built a reputation as one of the best-liked executives in Hollywood." In 1991, he and his daughter were in a serious car accident. Tartikoff then left NBC to briefly become chairman of Paramount Pictures. But he soon resigned to concentrate on helping his child recuperate. His great strength in TV, said one friend, was that "he believed in everything he was doing and more than that he believed in the medium and the people who watched it."

Leonard Katzman was "a television producer, director and writer who produced more than 350 episodes of *Dallas,* one of the most popular series in television history." The CBS show revolved around the machinations of a larger-than-life, filthy-rich Texas oil family, the Ewings. The paterfamilias, J.R., was everyone's vision of the hard-driving double-dealing businessman, determined to get his way both in the office and in the bedroom. The show, which began in 1978 and folded in 1991, in many ways captured the Reagan eighties-excess zeitgeist. Katzman denied any great social commentary: "All we were ever trying to do was entertain the audience. There was never any real deep meaning to it. We weren't trying to do a documentary every week." People ate it up. Reported the *New York Times,* "Its Nov. 21, 1980, episode, revealing the solution to the mystery of who had shot the dastardly J. R. Ewing, was the most widely watched single program in television history until then."

Katzman was a New Yorker who began in movie serials like *Superman* and then moved into television in 1960 with the CBS series *Route 66.* Before *Dallas,* he worked on such successful shows as *Gunsmoke, The Wild, Wild West,* and *Hawaii Five-O.*

The days of mass-audience network shows such as *Dallas* and *Miami Vice* are over. With the growing proliferation of other options, such as cable, pay television, and the Internet, audiences have become fragmented and niched as advertisers look for the biggest value for their dollar. One longtime network executive who recognized that trend was Paul L. Klein, "an executive who helped pioneer new forms of pay television," a service familiar to many staying in chain hotels. In the 1960s, Klein worked for NBC in its audience measurement office, and there he developed something of a reputation for his theory that viewers usually turn on the TV just looking for, "the least objectionable program," or LOP. He left NBC for a time to develop his Pay-Per-View company, which he then sold to Time Inc. He returned to NBC and was a big proponent of "event programming," or running big specials during a Sunday evening slot. Some of the more memorable offerings were *Holocaust, Shogun,* and *Centennial.* But then Klein left the networks again and in 1982 founded the Playboy Channel, "the first to produce, license and broadcast adult programming on pay television."

Movies and television are a high-glamour, high-risk, top-money world where only the most successful have lifelong careers, becoming wealthy and internationally famous.[13] This is an extraordinarily influential group, shaping as they do not only our popular culture but also the image of the United States overseas.

Notes

1. *The Wall Street Journal Almanac, 1999,* p. 675.
2. Howard J. Blumenthal and Oliver R. Goodenough, *This Business of Television* (New York: Billboard 1998), chap 1.
3. Richard Maltby, *Hollywood Cinema* (Cambridge, Mass.: Blackwell, 1995), p. 79.
4. Jonothan T. Davis, ed., *Forbes Richest People* (New York: John Wiley & Sons, 1997), pp. 309–318.
5. David A. Cook, *A History of Narrative Film* (New York: W. W. Norton & Co., 1996), chaps. 6–8.
6. Maltby, *Hollywood Cinema,* p. 82.
7. Judith I. Brennan, "Hollywood Roulette," *New York Times Magazine,* January 17, 1999, p. 22.
8. Ibid.

9. Geoffrey Nowell-Smith, *The Oxford History of World Cinema* (New York: Oxford University Press, 1997), "The Studio Years," pp. 220–234.
10. *The Wall Street Journal Almanac, 1999,* p. 675.
11. Blumenthal and Goodenough, *This Business of Television,* pp. xv–xvi.
12. Maltby, *Hollywood Cinema,* pp. 471–478.
13. Ibid., p. 12.

13

Inventors Who Changed Our World

Orderly Mind Behind Rolodex

Solver of the Damp Diaper Problem

Pioneer of the Internet

By the 1940s, Arnold Neustadter's Zephyr American Corporation had already marketed such useful items as the Autodex, a "spring-mounted personal phone directory that popped up at a given letter of the alphabet," the Swivodex, "a spill-proof inkwell," and the Clipodex, "a device secretaries could clip to the knee as an aid in taking dictation." And then came his big breakthrough, "the cylindrical rotating alphabetical card file he called the Rolodex." Who could be surprised that this handy gadget swiftly became a desktop necessity in every busy office? But the Rolodex would become far more. According to the *New York Times,* the Rolodex ultimately reached "the status of a cultural icon . . . the lasting symbol of the art of networking." The executive with five Rolodexes was showing the world she was, well, well connected.

Neustadter, a Brooklyn boy who attended Erasmus High School and then New York University before working briefly for his father's box company, ran American Zephyr almost single-handedly for thirty years. "He was a very organized man," said his wife. "He was always one for advancing things that he thought were done in a clumsy way." In 1961, Insilco Corporation of Ohio bought his company, renamed it Rolodex, and by the 1990s was selling 10 million units around the world each year.

Neustadter is that almost mythical being: a lone inventor whose unique idea turns into a unique product used worldwide, bringing him much fortune and some fame. (With the exception of Thomas Alva Edison, inventors don't generally become famous.) In this chapter we will meet more such mythical beings. But we also meet equally impressive—but more typical—inventors, the people who worked (often as part of a bigger team) for major corporations such as DuPont, IBM, or Motorola, or at prestigious universities. Bell Laboratories, one of the great American research institutions, alone holds twenty-five thousand patents and, according to the *Economist,* adds three new patents *each day*! IBM holds twenty-one thousand. In 1997, IBM received thirty-two new patents each week. All these American inventors helped create and advance new technologies, launch new products, and start new businesses and even whole new industries.[1]

In this chapter we look at some of the nation's most influential and fascinating inventors, people whose products many of us use or depend on every day. Some of them had a few dozen patented inventions, which may be as simple to understand as a Rolodex. Others had several hundred patents, often in a far more complex field—say, optics, sound, or computers. A good portion of our inventors worked within the realm of major corporations. Yet there are also a striking number of inventors of entrepreneurial bent who started their own companies and became wealthy. To fully appreciate the dimensions of these inventors' accomplishments, it helps to know that only 2 percent of all patents are ever licensed to major corporations and only one of every one hundred patented products makes money. Success for inventors is measured in the number of patents gained, plus the ability to get their inventions out into the world. Fame is another matter: many inventors' products are very famous, but not the people who invented them.

The twenty-nine inventors who received the most obituary coverage during the past six years—our inventors' Apex of Fame in Table 13-1—were a varied group, including electrical, mechanical, and aeronautical engineers, chemists, physicists, mathematicians, professors, computer scientists, businessmen who founded or expanded companies, corporate executives, a professional athlete, a police officer, and independent full-time inventors. Almost half of them were employed by a major corporations such as DuPont, B. F. Goodrich, or IBM, but the others were in academia or smaller businesses. Then there were the few brave souls who operated independently.

There were 108 inventors in our *New York Times* database, four of them women. Theirs obits averaged fifteen and a half inches long. As for the inventors' education, a fifth held a Ph.D. or other advanced degree, half were college graduates, a fifth had no education information in their obit, while the remainder had either a high school degree or some college. Where did they get their degrees? Fourteen from an Ivy League school, another fourteen from one of the other top fifty schools, eight from foreign universities, and the rest at a wide variety of state and private schools.

The education of the twenty-nine most famous inventors was as various as their occupations. Two attended high school but never went to college; four attended college but did not graduate; for two others their education was not stated. Of the twenty-one college graduates, eight went to one of the top fifty colleges (three of them to an Ivy League school). Of the twenty-one college graduates, nine earned a doctorate, 3 earned a master's degree, and one earned a law degree, while eight earned no higher degree.

Rarely are inventors' career trajectories as simple and straightforward as that of the Rolodex inventor, who had a major brainstorm and successfully promoted it most of his life. In contrast, Luther G. Simjian, for instance, who held two hundred patents for products as diverse as a self-focusing camera and the automatic teller machine (ATM), would found three different companies to handle them all. Simjian emigrated to America from Turkey as a teenager, finished high school, and then spent a decade working at Yale Medical School. There he became director of a new photography department and got his first patents. In 1939, he left to launch Reflectone. "Disturbed by the deaths of many contemporaries and friends during World War II," Mr. Simjian invented the first flight simulator to train pilots and tail gunners. Decades later, that company would be sold for about $90 million to British Aerospace.

TABLE 13-1. *The Apex of Fame: Inventors in the Obituary Database*

Name (Age at Death)	Obit Date	Company and Career
1. Seymour Cray (71)	10/06/96	Control Data Corp.; Cray Research: electrical engineer
2. Victor Mills (100)	11/07/97	Procter & Gamble: chemical engineer
3. David Evans (74)	10/12/98	U. of California at Berkeley, U. of Utah: professor
4. J. Presper Eckert (76)	06/07/95	U. of Pennsylvania: electrical engineer
5. Russell Colley (97)	02/08/96	B. F. Goodrich Co.: mechanical engineer
6. Hazel Bishop (92)	12/10/98	Hazel Bishop: varied career
7. Jerome Murray (85)	02/11/98	Murwood Labs (his own company): engineer
8. Joseph Sobek (79)	03/31/98	Professional athlete: tennis, racquetball
9. Robert Gallati (82)	02/02/96	New York City police official
10. Gino P. Santi (81)	04/09/97	Air Force: engineer
11. Robert Switzer (83)	08/29/97	Day-Glo Color Corp.: chemist
12. Waldo Semon (100)	05/28/99	B. F. Goodrich: chemist
13. Marion Donovan (81)	11/18/98	Housewife; sold patents
14. Edward Lowe (75)	10/06/95	Kitty Litter Co.: owner
15. Jerome H. Lemelson (74)	10/04/97	Independent inventor
16. Luther Simjian (92)	11/02/97	Reflectone: owner inventor
17. Jonathan Postel (55)	10/19/98	U. of Southern California: computer scientist
18. Gary Kildall (52)	07/13/94	Digital Research Co.: computer scientist/ professor
19. Richard Hamming (82)	01/11/98	Bell Labs: mathematician
20. Harold Osrow (80)	03/28/97	Osrow Products: owner (went bankrupt)
21. Karl E. Prindle (95)	10/22/98	DuPont Cellophane Co.: chemist
22. Elmer Wavering (91)	11/27/98	Motorola Inc.: rose to president

Accomplishments and Fame	Obit Length
Father of supercomputer	66"
Father of disposable diapers	40"
Computer graphics pioneer; taught future leaders	40"
Coinventor of early computer, ENIAC; 87 patents	36"
Designed space suits, plane deicer, etc.; 65 patents	33"
Made lipstick kissproof	33"
Electric knife, heart surgery pump, etc.; 75 patents	32"
Invented racquetball (lost money)	29"
Designed first computerized fingerprint ID system	28"
Developer of pilot ejection system	28"
Coinventor of Day-Glo paint	28"
Developed vinyl and synthetic rubber	27"
New type of baby diapers—forefunner of disposables	26"
Discovered Kitty Litter on a hunch	25"
Inventor advocate; second to Edison in patents, more than 500	25"
Invented flight simulator, ATM, etc.; more than 200 patents	24"
Internet pioneer: address system	24"
Created first popular operating system for PC	23"
Pioneer in digital technology	23"
Built better broom and automotive items; more than 30 patents	22"
Made cellophane marketable	22"
Pioneer in auto electronics: built first commercial car radio	22"

(continues)

TABLE 13-1. *The Apex of Fame: Inventors in the Obituary Database*

Name (Age at Death)	Obit Date	Company and Career
23. John V. Atanasoff (91)	06/17/95	Iowa State College: physicist
24. Benjamin Eisenstadt (89)	04/10/96	Cumberland Packing Co.: owner
25. Arnold Neustadter (85)	04/19/96	Zephyr American Corp.: owner
26. Reynold Johnson (92)	09/18/98	IBM: engineer
27. Marvin Camras (79)	06/28/95	IIT Research Institute: electrical engineer
28. W. E. Hanford (87)	01/31/96	DuPont; Kellogg; Olin: chemist
29. Roy J. Plunkett (83)	05/15/94	DuPont: chemist

Note: Inventing is not a well-defined or specialized occupation. As the above table shows, some inventors were corporate owners or executives, engineers, chemists, and other professionals.

Meanwhile, Simjian, whose forte was electronics and optics, was busy working on the inventions (twenty patents' worth) that would go into making the ATM, all the while wondering whether people would be willing to put money into a machine with "no proof of what they had put in other than a printed receipt." But a big New York bank gave it a try. Wrote Simjian in his autobiography, "It seems the only people who were using the [first experimental] machines were a small number of prostitutes and gamblers who didn't want to deal with tellers face to face. And the bank said there were not enough of them to make the deal lucrative." But those early doubts were overcome, and convenient cash machines are now available all over the world.

A prolific and varied inventor, Simjian would say, "One thing I discovered about myself in the early days of my life is that I can't stick with just one idea for too long." He invented a computerized indoor golf practice range, an exercise bike that also massaged the torso, and a special swivel chair whose prototype he sent to his stockbroker. "It allowed you to sit at a dressing table and look at your hair from four different angles," he explained.

Accomplishments and Fame	Obit Length
Designed first electronic digital computer	21"
Developed Sweet 'N Low and paper sugar packets	21"
Invented Rolodex and other organizers	18"
Invented computer hard disk drive; more than 90 patents	18"
Father of magnetic tape recording; more than 500 patents	16"
Developed polyurethanes; more than 120 patents	15"
Accidentally discovered Teflon	14"

The number of patents awarded annually in the United States has more than doubled since 1950, when it was 43,040. In 1996, the Patent and Trademark Office at the U.S. Department of Commerce issued 109,646 patents. This included 48,741 patents to U.S. corporations, 923 to the U.S. government, 13,729 to U.S. individuals, 41,476 to foreign corporations, 259 to foreign governments, and 4,518 to foreign individuals.[2]

Successful inventors often see what (in retrospect) seems obvious long before anyone else and then make that product a reality. New Yorker Harold Osrow's father, a garment business owner, invented and patented a simple dishwasher gizmo, a plastic brush on a hose that fit over a faucet. The son showed his special genius (and launched his company) by expanding the concept into a full-fledged car-wash contraption, the sort with "soap dispensers and swirling brushes that made Osrow a mainstay in the automotive products field."

Most of Harold Osrow's thirty patents and products, however, were for "novel household items he had helped tinker into being." Probably the best known and ubiquitous in cold-weather states was the plastic windshield ice scraper and snow brush. Simple, necessary, and cheap, it sells by the millions every year. And it was one of two products to emerge from Osrow's original quest to invent a portable plug-in windshield defroster: "He tested a prototype plug-in model in the freezer unit of his home refrigerator one night. When all the ice melted away in a matter of minutes he repackaged his idea as a defroster that proved popular until the advent of self-defrosting refrigerators." By the early 1980s, Osrow Products had 350 employees at its Long Island factory and sales of about $10 million a year on everything from cordless irons to a talking ice-cream machine.

But Osrow's story also shows how high-stakes this field can be. For in the mid-1980s, another company proved that one of Osrow's most popular products—a pasta-making machine—infringed on its own patent. Losing this suit pushed Osrow Products into bankruptcy. Undaunted, the founder began yet another company. Just before Osrow died, he was "working on his latest brainstorm, a coffee table that rises and converts to a full-size dining table."

Because patents can be so incredibly valuable, lawsuits over who really invented what and when are commonplace. An independent industrial inventor such as the brilliant Jerome H. Lemelson became a "hero to fellow inventors" because of his lifelong (highly litigious) crusade to get the patent royalties due him, often from big corporations. Lemelson had a flair for complex inventions as varied as bar-code scanners, video camcorders, and whole automated warehouses, and his five hundred patents put him into the august company of Thomas Alva Edison, who is still the all-time inventing genius with 1,093 patents. But, reported the *New York Times,* Lemelson "spent most of his life struggling to make ends meet."

Like that of many inventors, Lemelson's gift appeared early, when he developed an "illuminated tongue depressor for his physician father." Before he ever went to college, Lemelson "was designing weapons and other systems for the Army Air Corps in World War II. After obtaining three engineering degrees from New York University and working on a Navy project there to develop rocket and pulse jet engines, he had a brief career as an industrial engineer before striking out on his own as an independent inventor."

Lemelson always had a notebook with him, and whenever inspiration hit, he would scribble away and then ask all those present to date and sign his ideas. While this might strike outsiders as odd, it is standard procedure to protect oneself from idea poachers. And the brilliant Lemelson constantly felt preyed upon by those who were ready to steal his ideas without proper compensation. He excoriated the U.S. Patent Office because "it dragged out the patent process for years, sometimes forcing him to divide a single idea into numerous separate—and expensive—applications covering different industrial processes before he would be legally entitled to collect royalties, often years after products and processes based on his ideas were in widespread use."

However, eventually revenge was his, and very sweet it was. In 1992, Lemelson won a $100 million lawsuit against Japanese automakers, forcing them to pay him for the use of "automated manufacturing systems based on refinement of the 'machine vision device' that he had invented almost 40 years earlier." By the time numerous European and American carmakers had ponied up, too, Lemelson had won $500 million! He and his wife set up a foundation to increase the public's appreciation of—what else?—inventors.[3] And in a brilliant stroke of public relations, Lemelson established an annual $500,000 award given out by MIT to the inventor most underpaid for a lucrative invention. In 1997, the winner was Douglas Engelbart, the man who had invented the computer mouse. He had originally been given only a $10,000 bonus by his company, which holds the patent.

Jerome Murray was a New York inventor with seventy-five patents whose ideas, he said, "came from observation and trying to find a better way." In 1951, he was sitting at Miami International Airport watching people descend from planes on movable stairways in the tropical rain and getting soaked as they rushed to the terminal. People in wheelchairs were brought off the plane with forklifts. Says the *New York Times*, "His invention, a covered walkway between the plane and the terminal, is now in airports all over the world."

Inventing seems to require a certain cast of mind, a unique way of looking at the world and figuring out how it can be improved upon. "I've never seen courses in inventing," Murray once said. "Science and marketing can be learned, but inspiration comes from within." At the age of fifteen, he sold his first invention—a new kind of windmill that powered a small generator. It was successfully marketed to farmers without electricity as a means of powering their radios. With that promising start, Murray attended MIT, where he earned a degree in aeronautical engineering. During his first job, with a Cleveland company, he invented sixteen products and was awarded $1 for each. After World War II, he got smart and started his own company, Murwood Laboratories.

Over time Murray brought onto the market an electric carving knife, the audible pressure cooker, and the television antenna rotator, a simple product that generated $40 million in sales over a number of decades. But he felt that his most important contribution was the pump that made open-heart surgery possible, because it saved lives. When he ran out of money to work on it, he donated the device to Johns Hopkins Hospital, which completed its development. Called a peristaltic pump, it moves "fluids in a wavelike motion of contractions and expansions similar to the way that peristalsis moves the contents of the digestive tract." This breakthrough for open-heart surgery is also helpful for kidney dialysis and "assembly-line injection of vegetable soup into cans without crushing the peas and carrots."

While inventors like Jerome Murray created an eclectic range of useful things, others specialized. Inventor Robert Switzer stuck to weird paints and dyes, products we know under the heading of Day-Glo, a company he launched with his brother after World War II. Switzer's unique fascination began inauspiciously. He was at Berkeley on a scholarship and working unloading crates from railcars when he fell down and hit his head so hard he was in a coma for months. He spent his long recuperation in a darkened room, which sparked his interest in ultraviolet light. When his brother Joseph was home from college they "took a black light into the storeroom of their father's drugstore looking for naturally fluorescent organic compounds." Their mission was to jazz up Joseph's amateur magic act by creating a glow-in-the-dark dancer's costume and mask that would travel in opposite directions, giving the audience the illusion that the dancer had separated in two.

They got a chuckle out of all that but also saw the myriad commercial applications. They began creating numerous products, "including bright fabric panels that troops in North Africa used to identify themselves as friendly to Allied dive bombers. The material also allowed warplanes to operate at night from aircraft carriers in the Pacific, a capability not enjoyed by the Japanese Navy, whose planes had to land on their carriers before nightfall." After the war, the brothers moved to Cleveland, Ohio, and created the Day-Glo-Color Corporation, whose products were eventually glaringly visible on bathing suits, detergent packages, and Hula Hoops. They also served a multitude of more serious purposes, such as the Day-Glo–colored penetrants that helped "to find hidden flaws in machined parts, such as engine pistons." Switzer was "a serious unassuming man who despite his wealth often wore the same checked coat with pants that didn't match and a bow tie, and he didn't care." A dedicated environmentalist, he used some of the money from the sale of the company in 1985 (he wanted to retire) to establish fellowships that would produce "practical problem-solvers" for environmental science.

Like Switzer, electrical engineer and inventor Marvin Camras spent his career largely focused on one (very big) technical problem. Ultimately, he was awarded more than five hundred patents "for the invention and refinement of technology that is the basis for audio and video recording and computer data storage." What Camras did was invent and then develop and refine the magnetic coatings that have made possible video and cassette tapes, as well as the hard drives and floppy disks that store computer information. "Marvin Camras is a legend, and we are all grateful for what he did," said Ray Dolby, chairman of Dolby Laboratories, a manufacturer of noise reduction equipment.

Camras was a very early bloomer: at age four, he built a flashlight, and in first grade he built a transmitter! He loved classical music (as do many scientists) and wanted to help a cousin studying opera record her singing. So he built "a magnetic wire recorder. . . . A short time later he discovered that making the recordings on magnetic tape greatly eased the process of splicing and storing the recordings." His tinkering caught the attention of a professor at the Illinois Institute of Technology, and he was offered a job at the Armour Research Foundation (now the IIT Research Institute) to develop his invention. In 1944, he got a patent for the "method and means of magnetic recording," the beginning of modern tape recorders. He would work and teach at IIT for more than fifty years. In that time his patents were licensed to more than one hundred manufacturers, including such giants as General Electric and Eastman Kodak; but, reported the *Times*, "Mr. Camras did not realize great wealth from any of his inventions." Presumably, he was an inventor whose great passion was music, not money. Improving recorded sound was a high priority for this man, and he forever changed what we heard from machines, even as he was also fashioning the most old-fashioned of instruments, high-quality violins and violas. While owning his own company appeared to be of no interest to him, it also meant that someone else got rich from his genius.

The importance of an inventor having either his own company or major institutional backing is underscored by the experience of Marion Donovan, a woman with a great idea but no way to develop it. As with Harold Osrow, inventing seemed to run in her family. Donovan's father and uncle had invented "the South Bend lathe, an ingenious device that proved so useful for grinding automobile gears and the like that the brothers made a fortune turning them out in a factory in South Bend, Indiana." As if that were not enough, they then wrote a book, *How to Operate a Lathe*, that sold 1.5 million copies in seventy-eight languages! Marion Donovon grew up in this world because her mother died when she was seven and her after-school hours were spent at the family's factory.

After college, Donovan did a stint in Manhattan as an assistant *Vogue* beauty editor. After World War II, she married and moved to the Connecticut suburbs to raise a family. Confronted with babies in cloth diapers that seemed to become wet as soon as she put them on, she knew there had to be a better way. Explained the *Times*, "Mrs. Donovan was in the bathroom one day when the shower curtain caught her eye and a lightbulb went off in her head. Before you could say waterproof material, the curtain was missing a panel and Mrs. Donovan was up in the attic at her sewing machine. Three years and many shower curtains later she came up with the Boater, a re-usable diaper cover made of surplus nylon parachute cloth." Moreover, she had used snap attachments, replacing the dreaded safety pins. In 1951, she sold the patents for a cool $1 million.

Now she was ready to move on to Phase 2 of the diaper revolution: the altogether disposable paper diaper. But while Donovan, a great beauty, had no trouble getting in to see executives at paper companies to pitch her idea, these male chauvinists laughingly dismissed the absurd notion of throwaway diapers. So she gave up on that and moved on to other useful things, eventually getting a dozen-plus patents for such clever things as the Big Hangup, a hanger that neatly stores dozens of skirts, and a wire soap holder that did away with grungy buildup.

But because Donovan lacked corporate backing, it was another inventor, Victor Mills, who went down in history as the Father of Disposable Diapers. Mills was a chemical engineer who worked for thirty-five years at Procter & Gamble, and his story is far more typical of how most new products are developed and go onto the market. All the inventors we have looked at so far were not just highly creative, they were also—with the exception of Marion Donovan and Marvin Camras—entrepreneurs and businesspeople who started their own companies, often after working for someone else. If you are manufacturing a relatively simple product—a Rolodex or an ice scraper—you don't need the deep pockets of a corporation for research and development to get to market. But when you work in more complex fields where your inventions are part of a complex continuum, then you need institutional support, whether by IBM or a major university.

Mills, wrote the *New York Times*, led "an engineering team that invented the first mass-market disposable diapers and changed the way millions of parents attend to infants. . . [The disposable diaper] became a symbol of the culture of convenience that permeates most modern, time-pressed societies."

Mr. Mills had been at Procter & Gamble in Cincinnati almost thirty years when he took on the diaper problem in the 1950s. Up to that time, he had worked on a wide variety of products. "I was a guinea pig all through my childhood," recalled his daughter. "I remember a tooth liquid, Teel. You'd drip a few drops on a toothbrush. It was cherry red. I liked

the taste, but it was not a success." At another point, the family tested
endless versions of Duncan Hines cakes—"until they came out of our
ears." By the time Mills started working on what would eventually
become Pampers, he had young grandchildren. "While driving his
daughter's three children home from a vacation in Maine, Mr. Mills
tried out Pampers prototypes on one of them." Apparently they did the
job. When the first Pampers were test-marketed in Peoria, Illinois, in
1961, they still required safety pins and cost ten cents apiece, pretty
pricey for that era. With steady improvements in design and price, disposable diapers became the norm not just in America but in many foreign countries. In the United States alone, 95 percent of babies use
them, and they are a $4-billion-a-year market.

Sometimes an inventor, whether independent or working for a corporation, sets out to solve a specific problem, such as making a better diaper. But other times, major inventions come about by serendipitous
mistakes. Such was the case with Roy J. Plunkett, the "scientist whose
accidental invention of Teflon 50 years ago not only changed the way
Americans cook but also helped develop a multibillion-dollar plastics
industry." Plunkett was a research chemist with a doctorate from Ohio
State working in a New Jersey laboratory for E. I. du Pont du Nemours
& Company. He was specifically looking for new kinds of refrigerants
and one day observed with marked disappointment what had developed
in one of his laboratory cylinders: some kind of white, waxy material.
But he decided to check it and found it "resistant to heat . . . chemically
inert . . . [and unable] to stick to anything." It wasn't what he had been
looking for, but it might, he thought, be something better. In 1941, he
secured a patent for what was trade-named Teflon, a nonstick substance
that most of us know from cooking pots but that also has thousands of
other industrial applications. While much of his forty-year career at
DuPont was spent in management, Plunkett's discovery was important
enough to get him into the National Inventors Hall of Fame in 1985. He
always enjoyed the fact that Teflon "has been of great personal benefit to
people—and not just indirectly, but directly to real people whom I know."

Another DuPont chemist, Dr. William E. Hanford, was a prolific
inventor whose early groundbreaking work with other chemists produced

polyurethanes, laying the foundation for thousands of commercial applications ranging from building insulation and varnishes to tough coatings for machine parts, films, foams, high-performance sneakers, and most artificial body parts installed in humans. The chairman of MIT's chemistry department told the *Times*, "It was a tremendous breakthrough. Today the applications are monumental."

And while Dr. Plunkett was the inventor who discovered Teflon, it was Dr. Hanford who made Teflon "commercially viable by directing the research that found ways to form it into sheets and produce it in large quantities." Dr. Hanford seems to have been a restless (or maybe difficult?) sort, for he worked at numerous corporations, directing teams of researchers and bringing out such diverse products as Glim, the first liquid household detergent, and a new shotgun shell. At one point he supervised the building of a synthetic fuel plant in Johannesburg, South Africa, an effort that led to low-cost production of ammonia. By the time he retired, he had been awarded 120 patents.

There is no question that there is "better living through chemistry," and that these inventions and advances have been extraordinarily important. But for many people, they are harder to grasp and appreciate than, say, the inventions of Elmer Wavering, a "pioneer of auto electronics." Here was a man whose early love affair with the radio led him to transport the delights of music into that other American passion, the car. "While still in high school in Quincy, Missouri, he worked in a radio parts store run by Bill Lear, who went on to found the Lear Jet Corporation. They helped customers build their own radios." There Mr. Wavering tinkered into being a radio that "could withstand the rigors of bumpy roads and severe climate changes." The first commercial car radios were cumbersome luxuries, costing $80 when cars sold for $700, but eventually they became standard equipment, allowing music and news to enter the driver's universe.

One of the corporations that made that possible was Motorola, where Wavering spent his career. With the car radio well launched, he worked with a team of engineers to make "the first automotive alternator that could be mass produced . . . [and that] produced steady and reliable electric power." Wavering, who would rise to become president and

CEO of Motorola, said, "The radio may have made the car more fun," but the alternator "made everything else possible." Once cars had a reliable electrical system, Detroit automakers could begin to pile on all kinds of improvements: power windows, steering, and brakes and then air-conditioning, all now fairly standard features on American cars. So whether we're cruising along in our autos or stalled in traffic but cool and entertained, we have Elmer Wavering to thank.

Wavering took an existing American icon—the automobile—and made it better. The group of inventors we're looking at next created and developed something completely new, one of the great inventions of the late twentieth century, the computer—a machine that has launched numerous new industries and whose full implications and potential are still unfolding. After all, in 1977, someone as smart as Ken Olsen, founder and chairman of Digital Equipment Corporation, said, "There is no reason for any individuals to have a computer in their home." Well, today 42 percent of American households have just that.[4] What is striking but not surprising about the computer inventors and pioneers is how well educated they were compared to our first inventors. This is generally not a field that a self-taught tinkerer can excel in.

For many decades, one of the earliest pioneers of the computer was forgotten. Dr. John V. Atanasoff was a young physicist teaching at Iowa State in the late 1930s who was frustrated by the slow calculators of the day. To help in working out certain math problems, he collaborated with Cliff Berry, a young engineer, to build a better, faster calculator that he dubbed the Atanosoff-Berry Computer, or ABC. The *Times* described it as "two knobby rotating drums that contained capacitors. An electrical charge held by the capacitors was ABC's memory, and data was entered using punch cards. To print out the results, an electric spark was passed through other cards; the arrangement of burned spots represented answers, which could be fed into the computer again for further analysis." While the ABC was very primitive, it is now regarded as "the first electronic digital computer of any kind."

During World War II, Atanasoff worked at the Naval Ordnance Laboratory in Washington, D.C., and was involved in atomic testing.

Then, in 1952 he set up his own company, which he sold almost a decade later to Aerojet Engineering. But his early, pioneering work was ignored for many decades.

War has always been one of the great incubators for new technologies, and World War II proved especially so. Many of the *New York Times* inventors made important contributions to the war effort, whether Lemelson and his rocket engines or Switzer and his Day-Glo paints. By the same token, J. Presper Eckert and Dr. John W. Mauchly, the two men who invented the first electronic digital computer, were tackling a vexing military problem: how to calculate the trajectories of artillery shells. Obviously, mistakes could be disastrous. "For centuries, artillery officers labored over those calculations. . . . Many variables, including wind, humidity, target elevation, distance and shell weight, made the calculation extremely complicated and caused the Army to issue volumes of hand-compiled tables." It was this long-standing problem that the two men working at the University of Pennsylvania hoped to address with their "30-ton Electronic Numerical Integrator and Computer, or ENIAC." It featured "18,000 vacuum tubes that received instructions through hundreds of cables resembling an old-time telephone switchboard . . . [and had] stacks of punched cards providing the data." Assembled in 1945, ENIAC was a spectacular success, completing in thirty seconds artillery projections that had typically taken clerks twenty *hours*! The ENIAC was crucial to the Manhattan Project and the success of the atom bomb.

When World War II was won, Eckert and Mauchly left the University of Pennsylvania amid squabbles about patent rights and started their own company. While they proved quite capable of developing better, faster computers—including the UNIVAC—they lacked capital and business acumen. They were soon rescued from looming bankruptcy by James Rand of the office products company Remington Rand. In this era, before organized venture capital, inventors of complex products often had little choice but to work at large corporations with deep pockets. No one else could supply the money and support to get complicated enterprises to their potential markets.

Forbes Greatest Technology Stories tells how America first learned about UNIVAC and computers. During the 1952 presidential election, CBS News wanted to forecast the winner based on exit-poll numbers. Remington Rand offered UNIVAC on the condition that the behemoth with all its flashing lights, rumblings, and tubes be shown on TV. As CBS's on-air pundits confidently predicted a tight race between Adlai Stevenson and General Dwight D. Eisenhower, Eckert became panicky about the UNIVAC. Wrote *Forbes*, "[The UNIVAC] was predicting that Eisenhower would sweep Stevenson in a landslide. . . . Eckert feared he would be the laughingstock of the country" and refused to go on air. CBS had the grace to admit that the UNIVAC had predicted the 20 percent victory margin early on, but that "no one trusted it. . . . When the news got out, the powers of the invincible, omniscient, and mysterious computer reached mythic status. UNIVAC instantly became a household name." [5]

By 1989, when Eckert retired from Unisys, the giant computer company that evolved out of Remington Rand, he had eighty-seven patents to his name and had won a presidential honor for his work. He was also rather bitter that a 1973 patent case had credited the otherwise forgotten John V. Atanasoff, whose lab he had visited so many decades before, for being a computer pioneer. Eckert wrote angrily to his students that Atanasoff had "never really got anything to work. He had no programming system. Mauchly and I achieved a complete workable computer system. Others had not."

The computer is such a complex machine that many inventors were eventually involved in its many-layered advances. And while World War II was the impetus behind Eckert and Mauchly and the ENIAC, the Cold War provided as much pressure for subsequent advances, with U.S. military and intelligence agencies largely footing the bill. Seymour Cray, "father of the supercomputer," came out of the University of Minnesota in 1951 with a bachelor's degree in electrical engineering and a master's in mathematics. His first job at Engineering Research Associates (ERA) involved contract work for the Navy in cryptography. Located in a converted wooden glider factory in Minneapolis, ERA was in the forefront of further developing the digital computer. Thus began a legendary career. Wrote the *Times*, "Known as an idiosyncratic and quirky computer wizard, Mr. Cray had a remarkable ability to focus on a single challenge: the need to extract more and more speed from each new machine he designed."

Cray's great breakthrough was to abandon bulky, balky vacuum tubes in favor of transistors. But he disliked the very corporations that made possible his work. One boss at Control Data recalled that a five-year plan requested of Mr. Cray had read as follows: "Five-year goal: Build the biggest computer in the world. One-year goal: Achieve one-fifth of the above." He convinced Control Data to let him take a thirty-four-person team to his hometown of Chippewa Falls, Minnesota, and work from there. The CDC 6600 they created had a processing speed of 3 million instructions per second, a new record. This and subsequent Cray supercomputers "permitted researchers to simulate nuclear weapons explosions and crack enemy codes. They were soon turned to tasks like weather prediction and oil exploration." In the early 1970s, Mr. Cray left Control Data to begin his own firm. After a promising first decade that saw the successful introduction of the Cray 1, Cray Computer spent several hundred million dollars developing a super-computer that never made it to the market, undercut "by the arrival of cheap and powerful microprocessor chips . . . and the end of the Cold War." Cray Computer declared bankruptcy in March 1995, and about eighteen months later Cray died in an auto accident.

While Cray was trying to develop bigger, faster machines, others were working on smaller, faster machines, the kind that would work well in offices "as opposed to the Pentagon or the C.I.A. International Business Machines was at the forefront of the computer mainframe business, and it was always busy looking for leaps forward." In 1932, another Minnesota native, Reynold B. Johnson was teaching high school science in Michigan when he decided to make his life easier by inventing an "electromechanical device for automatically checking and grading pencil-marked multiple choice tests." He was impressed enough with his invention to approach IBM, but Big Blue was not interested. Two years later, IBM changed its mind, hired Johnson, and put him to work in one of its labs. "He produced hundreds of inventions," reported the *Times*, "many relating to the handling, punching and reading of keypunch cards, then the primary means of storing computer data."

Then, perhaps remembering Cray's great breakthroughs while off with a small team, IBM sent Johnson out to San Jose, California, to start a West Coast lab. His task? To figure out a more efficient way of storing and retrieving data. The solution: the computer hard drive, which used magnetic platters to store memory, making it possible to find any of the stored material at any time. This was a huge step forward over a magnetic tape drive or a stack of punch cards, each of which had to be dealt with sequentially. The Random Access Memory Accounting Machine (RAMAC) had "50 24-inch diameter double-sided aluminum magnetic disks; it weighed a ton and stored 5 megabytes of data." It cost $189,950 or rented for $3,200 a month. (To put subsequent progress into perspective, at the end of the 1990s, IBM introduced a new hard drive with a 1-inch diameter disk that weighed several ounces and stored 340 gigabytes of data!)

While Cray was pursuing speed and Johnson was intent on storing ever more data, Gary Kildall was "the pioneering computer scientist who created the first popular operating system for personal computers." Of course, one might add that in the 1970s only the savviest of nerds even had such an object as a personal computer and it would have been one they had put together themselves, an object the *Times* called "a hobbyist microcomputer." These were "generally programmed with a punched paper tape reader or by laboriously entering information by programming toggle switches."

A Seattle native, Kildall had a Ph.D. in computer science from the University of Washington and was teaching at the U.S. Naval Postgraduate School in Monterey when he wrote a program that "controlled the way the central processing unit stored and retrieved information from a floppy disk drive." He named the program Control Program/Microcomputer, or CP/M. Kildall and his wife then founded a company to sell this operating drive, and it soon became the standard operating system in the first generation of personal computers. By the early 1980s, some 600,000 personal computers had been sold. Kildall's company had $6 million in sales, and business was booming.[6]

And so when IBM appeared at his door in 1980 looking to license CP/M for its entry into the personal computer market, Kildall felt he could call the shots. IBM decided to buy not just Kildall's CP/M-16 but an operating system called PC-DOS from a far more eager unknown named Bill Gates. With CP/M-16 priced at $240 and PC-DOS priced at $40, PC-DOS became the industry standard within five years. The *New York Times* noted, "Many people in the computer industry argued that Microsoft's MS-DOS infringed on CP/M patents, but Mr. Kildall decided not to sue." He said, "In those days everyone was imitating everyone else. That's why I didn't do anything about CP/M; it never occured to me." Kildall was an easygoing fellow who apparently disliked the cutthroat aspects of business and avoided many of the more aggressive tactics employed by his competitors." In 1991, Kildall sold his company to Novell.

David Evans was a much-hailed "pioneer in computer graphics" who spent his career in academia. After receiving a doctorate from the University of Utah, he went to Bendix, where in the late 1950s he was the project manager on two big computers. But sensing that Bendix was not going to survive in computers, he left to teach, first at the computer sciences department at University of California at Berkeley, briefly at Harvard, and then at the University of Utah. Professor Evans concentrated on computer graphics, and his great technical contribution was "the insight that each individual point in a computer image— each pixel—differs only incrementally from the pixels adjacent to it. By computing only these differences, rather than creating an entirely new pixel in each instance, a computer can reserve tremendous amounts of processing power." This allowed for far more complex computer graphics.

But Evans's greatest contribution to the field of computers was clearly as a professor and mentor. As the *Times* noted, he "oversaw the education of some of the computer industry's most influential figures." And indeed his students make up an incredible Who's Who of important figures. Among them: Butler Lampson, who coined the phrase "personal computer" and designed and built the first machine—at a bargain

$20,000—at Xerox's Palo Alto Research Center (PARC) in 1973; Alan Kay, another leader in the development of the PC at PARC; Jim Clark, a founder of Silicon Graphics as well as Netscape Communications Corporation, which helped open the World Wide Web to ordinary individuals; John Warnock, cofounder of Adobe Systems, whose "printing software helped create the desktop publishing industry"; Edwin Catmull, cofounder of Pixar, a computer animation studio; and last but not least, Alan Ashton, cofounder of WordPerfect Corporation.

Alan Kay, the PC pioneer, would say, "All of us were misfits and late bloomers. But if your résumé looked at all interesting, he would let you in and give you two years of support." Professor Evans was obviously a natural nurturer, for he was also a Boy Scout scoutmaster for twenty-seven years and the father of seven children, who went on to have thirty-nine children and grandchildren.

Once computers became more readily available, a myriad of new applications was developed. Dr. Odo J. Struger, for instance, invented what was known as a rugged computer that controls machinery. It would change the way factories all over the world operate, not to mention roller coasters and the fabulous stage effects of modern musicals. This became a billion-dollar-a-year business.

Dr. Struger developed the idea in his dissertation written at the Technical University of Austria, and then went to Allen-Bradley in Milwaukee in 1958 and led the team that created what are known as programmable logic controllers (PLCs). Explained the editor of an engineering journal, "[PLCs] are used to control a wide range of equipment, everything from heating, ventilation, air-conditioning, to plastic injection molding machines to commercial washing machines." PLCs also have a fun side, controlling sets of shows such as *Phantom of the Opera* and rides at places such as Disney World. Dr. Kruger spent his career at Allen-Bradley, earning fifty patents along the way.

Dr. Robert R. J. Gallati did something completely different with the computer. Described as "a visionary New York City police official," Gallati "designed the first computerized fingerprint identification system." Gallati came out of law school in the late 1930s, saw that the Depression offered little work for attorneys, and joined the "over-qualified rookie class of 1940." He served in a variety of capacities, walking a beat, supervising security for the United Nations, commanding the Manhattan North uniformed force, and running the Police Academy. But the life-changing event for him was the 1957 Appalachian meeting of high-level mafiosi. The ensuing hue and cry showed the abysmal state of police identification. Wrote the *Times*, "It took state police two years to assemble the full arrest records of the Appalachian suspects, one of whom was found to have 200 separate police files."

The federal government was appalled and made available large sums to address the problem of keping track of criminal files. In 1964, Governor Nelson A. Rockefeller appointed Gallati to tackle the job. He then spent eight years developing "a rapid-response computerized system of fingerprint identification that became a model for computerized systems later adopted by the Federal Bureau of Investigation and other states." No longer would a cop have to spend days going through index cards trying to match a suspect's prints. When he retired, Gallati had established a computerized fingerprint file of 3.5 million criminals.

Today, one of the fastest-growing uses for computers is the Internet, a technology still in its infancy. Among its pioneers was Jonathon B. Postel, "who played a pivotal role in creating and administering the Internet." Like much else in the computing world, the Internet's early purpose was military, a network supported by the U.S. Department of Defense. In 1969, while at the University of California at Los Angeles, where he was working on his doctorate, Postel helped install the communication switch for Arpanet, the government-operated predecessor of the Internet. As a computer scientist at the Information Sciences Institute, part of the University of California, for thirty years, Postel handled the burgeoning task of administering Internet addresses. Said one colleague, "As mundane and simple as it seemed, he set policies that made it very easy for the network to grow. He minimized bureaucratic delay and at the same time kept silly and nonsensical things to a minimum."

Inventors are incredibly creative people who are constantly driven to design new and useful products. Theirs is the ultimate high-risk field, with very few patented inventions ever actually being manufactured or succeeding. Inventors can hope to get rich from their own companies, but the vast majority work in the security of corporations or big universities.

Notes

1. "A Survey of Innovation in Industry," *Economist*, February 20, 1999, pp. 1–27.
2. *The New York Times Almanac, 1998*, p. 777.
3. There is a good Web site on Lemelson and his Inventors Center at the Smithsonian at www.si.edu/lemelson.
4. *The Wall Street Journal Almanac*, 1999, p. 350.
5. Jeffrey Young, *Forbes Greatest Technology Stories* (New York: John Wiley & Sons, 1998), chap. 1.
6. Ibid., pp. 221, 253.

14

Revolutionaries of Fine Food and Drink

Solomon of Bistro Seating

Dean of Wine Merchants

"Guru" of Restaurant Design

In the last couple of decades, as Americans have become busier and more prosperous, they have developed a great love affair with eating out, embracing all kinds of savory new cuisines and fine wines. By 1991, salsa had displaced ketchup as our number one condiment! And in 1993, the Food Network on TV began offering twenty-four hours of food and cooking shows. Joseph Baum was among the food pioneers, a "tirelessly innovative restaurateur" who helped create the legendary Four Seasons restaurant in Manhattan, along with dozens of other much-admired eating establishments. Said one food critic of Baum, "He transformed the American restaurant industry, which was slightly seedy and tawdry. He saw that a restaurant could be sophisticated and refined, the equal of anything in Europe in quality, and that it could also be exciting. He saw that the restaurant business could be sexy and glamorous."

In this chapter we look at the men and women who changed the way many Americans eat, introducing them to new pleasures of the palate. Here are some of the important restaurateurs, chefs, wine producers, and merchants, as well as food writers who preached the gospel of fresh, joyful cuisine and fine wines. Through their passion for better eating and more stylish living, they transformed Americans' experiences of dining out and dining in. While the most successful food folks do become wealthy, most people enter this field because they are fired with a love of cooking, food, and wines. And the most successful and admired are those who somehow expand or improve upon that world. The high-end restaurant business is high-intensity, high-glamour, high-risk. In this chapter, we spotlight both stars and lesser-knowns who brought more sophisticated, healthier eating to America.

Chefs and Restaurateurs

Joseph Baum was a hugely influential figure. Wrote the *New York Times*, "More than any other restaurateur, he operated in the conceptual territory where food and theater overlapped." Food writer Mimi Sheraton explained, "He was the Cecil B. DeMille of restaurateurs— everything was a big production." In the 1960s, Baum was an executive at Restaurant Associates ruling over "a dining empire whose far-flung possessions included airport restaurants, freeway rest stops, snack bars in Central Park, popular chains like Zum Zum and top-dollar trend-setters like the Four Seasons." Baum was interested in presenting the best food in all these spots, often with a great sense of fun and spectacle. When his firm took over a restaurant in the Hotel Lexington in New York City, it "transformed it into a gaudy tropical paradise with an island menu sprinkled with Polynesian pidgin." Diners loved the amusing, exotic feel of the room and the chance to drink silly colored drinks. The place was a huge hit.

Baum was born into the hospitality business. His parents ran a hotel in Saratoga Springs in upstate New York. He worked for a couple of years as a busboy and waiter to earn tuition for Cornell, where he acquired a degree in hotel administration. He served in the Navy during World War II and then, not long after the war, took a job with a company that did accounting for hotels and restaurants. He spent the next few years managing hotels. It was not until he went to work for Restaurant Associates that he began to make his mark. The big moment was when he decided to open a luxury restaurant with a big-name Swiss chef at the unlikely Newark Airport Terminal, a definite backwater locationwise. The Newarker became famous for its cuisine, as well as for always including an extra oyster with its plump half dozen and a third lobster claw with every lobster. After a painful first year of losses, the word of mouth generated hungry crowds and big profits. Baum was launched.

He was a perfectionist who often did not know what he was looking for until he or someone else found it. When conjuring up a new restaurant, he and his firm hired top designers, food consultants, and decorators. "He always reminded me of Merlin," said one food editor. "His eyes would narrow, he'd roll these things around on his tongue, and in a low mysterious voice he would let loose these fragments that were very haiku-like; sometimes enlightening, sometimes puzzling." While figuring out which china and silverware to use could take weeks, Baum was also quite willing to fly anywhere to do "field research" for new menus. And when home, he thought nothing of visiting a dozen of his restaurants in one night to make sure seamless production was the order of the evening. In the course of his career, he opened one spectacular restaurant after another: the Forum of the Twelve Caesars, with an imperial Rome theme; the Fonda del Sol, with a Latin slant; Windows on the World at the top of New York City's World Trade Center, romantic dining in the heavens; the Rainbow Room, a trip back to the glamorous Manhattan of the 1930s. A longtime associate remembered Baum as a maestro who always pulled off astonishing feats: "The only thing he failed to do was build a two-story replica of the Statue of Liberty out of chopped liver. He wanted to put it in Rockefeller Center to kick off Restaurant Week in 1995."

While Baum ran a huge dining empire that fed and entertained tens of thousands on a regular basis, Karen Hubert Allison represented the artisanal aspect of the revolution in eating. She and her husband, Len Allison, owned a small three-star Manhattan restaurant and "were among the pioneers who advocated exploring America's own ingredients and traditions." Never formally trained in cooking in any way, the pair came to running a celebrated restaurant by accident. They wanted to make a documentary about a Brooklyn clothing shop, but they needed $10,000 to buy a camera. They decided to raise the money by serving meals to their friends out of their home. This went so swimmingly that in 1979 they opened their first Huberts, a twelve-table place in Boerum Hill, and soon gained notice in an era when fine cooking was still largely French. They ventured into Manhattan, where their preference for locally grown and produced ingredients helped create a fresh, inventive menu. Their sommelier would later recall, "There were people coming from all over the globe who were either cooking there or sharing food thoughts, and you saw this riot of tastes and flavors settle down into this kind of signature cuisine."

Karen Hubert was a native New Yorker with degrees from City College and Columbia University. After she had her first child in 1987, she began to withdraw from actively running the restaurant, just as a much bigger Huberts opened further uptown. Unfortunately, the Wall Street crash of 1987 took a big bite out of high-end eating, and Huberts had to shut its doors after two years. That such admired pros could not survive underlines the extraordinary difficulty of launching a new restaurant and making it work. (A full half of new restaurants fail within the first year.) The Allisons tried again in 1991 but again could not make a go of it. The couple retreated to teach at the nation's oldest and best-regarded cooking school, the Culinary Institute of America in Hyde Park, New York. (It is a measure of the growing national fascination with food that when the Allisons were there, CIA was one of 360 cooking school programs in the United States. Over the next decade, that figure would more than double, to 740.[1]) When Karen Hubert Allison became ill, they moved to Hawaii. Before she had gotten caught up in the food world, she had been a writer, and in 1997 she published a novel, *How I Gave My Heart to the Restaurant Business*. A cookbook, *The Vegetarian Compass*, came out in 1998, after her death.

Patrick Clark was another influential New York celebrity chef of the 1980s. Running the kitchen at the Odeon, one of the early hip downtown eating spots, Clark surprised people who did not expect to find a twenty-five-year-old black man turning out fine but easygoing French nouvelle cuisine. As restaurant going became a popular pastime, Clark emerged as one of the innovative chefs developing the new American cooking. As with Baum, food ran in Clark's family. His father had been a chef, and Clark attended the culinary program of the New York City Technical College, where his father had trained. Clark also spent time in Britain and then in France working under the legendary Michel

Guérard. Making it as a celebrated chef represents a real triumph of talent and sheer physical stamina and, according to food writer Marion Burros, involves "years of physically demanding work for 12 to 15 hours a day under stressful conditions. In exchange, cooks on the way up are paid comparatively little—$20,000 to $60,000 a year—and have virtually no outside life. . . . During serving hours, a high-powered kitchen resembles a crisis center at full throttle" with fires and flames, fast-moving knives, and numerous large egos crammed into a broiling-hot, crowded space.[2]

Having earned great praise and high ratings as the executive chef at Odeon and Cafe Luxembourg, Clark longed to open his own place. And in 1988, he did: the luxurious Metro on the Upper East Side. But like the Allisons and their bigger, fancier Huberts, Clark was afflicted by bad timing—he did not survive the tight times following the crash of 1987. After two years, he closed his doors and never again ventured to run his own place. Clark moved briefly to Los Angeles and then to Washington, D.C., where his cooking at the Hay-Adams Hotel made a huge impression on President Clinton. In 1993, after tasting Clark's Moroccan barbecued salmon and his smoked-and-seared venison loin with butternut squash ravioli, the president offered Clark the top chef's job at the White House. But with five children to put through college, Clark declined. By 1995, Clark was back in Manhattan, having taken on the tough (but very highly paid) job of running the kitchen at the vast Tavern on the Green, presiding over 1,500 meals a day. There he remained an inspiration to up-and-coming chefs. Said one, "He lived the flavor that he grew up on and he spread that flavor. He was very demanding, sometimes harsh, but he was constant. And the flavor never wavered." While waiting in the hospital for a heart transplant that never took place, Clark was so appalled by the meals that he began sneaking in food and preparing it for himself and his fellow patients. Once again, the fans lined up.

Sam Lopata was another of the stars of the great food revolution. He was a restaurant designer whose signature look was exuberant whimsy. He burst onto the scene in 1978 with a sprawling café called Joanna in New York's Flatiron District that quickly became a magnet for "dreamers with artsy ambitions." During the 1980s, he designed a whole series of of-the-moment Manhattan restaurants: Café Seiyoken, Pig Heaven, Safari Grill, Lox Around the Clock. The *New York Times* described the unusual methods behind his artistic madness: "He wanted what he called a disheveled, love-in-the-ruins look for Lox Around the Clock, [and so] he built a perfectly finished dining room and then hired a wrecking crew to destroy it. The subsequent crumble, replete with dangling electrical wires and occasional glimpses of plumbing pipes and metal supports, remained his favorite dining room."

Lopata was a child of the Holocaust, a Parisian Jew whose family was rounded up by the Nazis. His father, a milliner, died in Auschwitz. For some reason, the rest of the family was released. "He grew up, he said, poor and carefree on the streets of Paris. Because the worst had already happened, he said, there was nothing left to worry about except having fun." From the start, it was clear that his true love was spectacle. While studying at the École Nationale des Beaux-Arts, he was a great organizer of "parades and marches, parties and theatrical installations." In 1971, he moved to the United States, where he supported himself for a while by sculpting prosthetic breasts until he convinced his first client to let him design a restaurant. His high-visibility projects in Manhattan gained him clients in Europe, Japan, and Thailand. His philosophy? "People are either living in a fantasy or looking for a fantasy. Build it and they will come." In 1986, *Time* magazine named him Restaurant Designer of the Year. He was thrilled; "That means the country is ready to laugh." The one complaint about his work? He was "damned as the man who turned up the volume in restaurants." Also, some found his restaurants not so much fun as bad-taste theme parks.

Restaurants serve many functions, and many of the most successful are not so much about food as about being part of a scene. Certainly this was true of Mortimer's, an Upper East Side bistro that was long almost a private club for "Manhattan socialites, glitz folk and achievers." When a food critic came in anonymously to write the place up, she found a welcome equal to that "normally given to bill collectors." Mortimer's was a small, ordinary space with nineteen tables jealously presided over by owner Glenn Bernbaum. Reported the *New York Times*, "Through the years, Mr. Bernbaum spent hours each day juggling seating arrangements." His maxim: "The trick in seating is not where they are but who they are surrounded by." The "they" included people such as Jackie Kennedy Onassis, Bill Blass, and Brooke Astor. "Diners of faint accomplishment [or fame]," explained the *Times*, "were exiled to tables near the kitchen."

The food was as plain as the setting. The house specialties included twinburgers, rice pudding, chicken hash, and mashed potatoes. The prices were low. "The rich don't like to spend money," Mr. Bernbaum said, "and they like to spend money here less than anyplace else." Perhaps it is not so surprising that during World War II, Bernbaum served in the Army's psychological warfare department—relevant training, no doubt, for a place like Mortimer's. But early on, Bernbaum seemed in no way destined to run such a famous restaurant. He was a Philadelphia native whose father was in the retail business, and whose mother was a dedicated fashion plate. He earned a B.A. at the University of Pennsylvania and then followed his father into retail clothing. For twenty years, he was an executive vice president of the Custom Shops, a New York men's clothing chain.

Mortimer's opened with great affray. Bernbaum had not been long in business when the police arrived and arrested his Greek maître d'. Apparently, Bernbaum's employees had learned that he had put them into his will, and this had incited the Greek to plan his new boss's murder. Fellow employees had notified the police. The man spent several years in prison. But Mortimer's soon found a loyal clientele, and after several years, Bernbaum retired from retailing to preside over his daily social rankings. Just before he died in 1998, there arose another mystery: the fate of his beloved pug, Swifty, a dog whose constant presence around Mortimer's added to the homey feeling. Entrusted to a wealthy patron while Bernbaum made a quick trip to Europe, Swifty was reported to have wandered away. His fate never was known.

Food Writers

While the chefs and restaurateurs were frontline promoters of the idea that eating should be delicious, festive, and fun, the food writers were equally important in fomenting and spreading the revolution in tastes and expectations. William Koshland was president of the publishing house of Alfred A. Knopf when he accepted a cookbook that had been rejected elsewhere, *Mastering the Art of French Cooking*, by the then-unknown Julia Child, Louisette Bertholle, and Simone Beck. Published in 1961, "That first volume kindled a revolution in American kitchens as well as a lasting relationship with Julia Child and one of publishing's longest-running and most lucrative success stories."

Koshland was a low-key Harvard graduate who joined Knopf in 1934 and got along well enough with Alfred A. and Blanche W. Knopf that he was able to help them develop a powerful list of quality writers. Koshland clearly took a chance on Child. An American who had been living in Paris for some time, Child and her coauthors had labored six long, hard years to produce a thorough but reasonably simple book on French cooking techniques and recipes. But when the manuscript arrived at Houghton Mifflin, which initially had the contract, the Boston publisher rejected it, saying it was too vast and difficult. The three cooks went back to work for two years to pare down their first effort. Once again, Houghton Mifflin rejected their work, feeling it was too arcane for American home cooks.

But in 1961, Jackie Kennedy was giving the dowdy White House a stylish makeover, which included hiring a French chef. Also by the 1960s, many Americans had traveled in France and were eager to reexperience its delicious food, whether in the fledgling French restaurants popping up in American cities or in their own kitchens. How, Americans wondered, did the French conjure up that perfect fluffy omelette, that aromatic coq au vin, that sinfully rich mousse au chocolat? Looking back many decades later, Julia Child marveled in a magazine interview at the perfect timing of her seemingly ill-fated endeavor: "It was absolutely pure luck that things fell into place as they did."[3] That is a bit too modest. For *New York Times* food writer Craig Claiborne raved about the book, writing, "It will probably remain as the definitive work for nonprofessionals." While the specific techniques were all very helpful, it was Julia Child's spirit that propelled a million home cooks (many watching her drop chickens and gulp wine on public television) to embrace a *joie de vivre* that viewed food as just one part of a more passionate approach to daily living.

Far less well known to the American public but a huge influence in the world of cooking was Richard Olney, whose two early books published in the 1970s, *The French Menu Cookbook* and *Simple French Food*, presented French country cooking to a whole new American audience. Wrote the *New York Times*, "Mr. Olney's most important disciple was Alice Waters, who keeps a jacketless, food-stained copy of *Simple French Food* in the kitchen of her celebrated restaurant, Chez Panisse, in Berkeley, California. But many others also came under his influence, including Deborah Madison, perhaps the country's leading vegetarian chef."

Olney was an Iowa native who studied briefly at the state university before heading to New York to train as a painter at the Brooklyn Museum of Art School. During that time, he made his first visit to Paris. He recalled vividly his first meal there at a "glum little dining room." The mashed potatoes, however, were a *coup de foudre,* "the best I had ever eaten, pushed through a sieve, buttered and moistened with enough of their hot cooking water to bring them to a supple, not quite pourable consistency—no milk, no cream, no beating." By 1951, Olney had moved to France for good. He would eventually write thirty-five books on food and also wine. In addition, he edited the Time-Life Books cookbook series. His ideal was a life where there was "a sort of convergence of all the senses, an awareness of food not only through touching but also through smelling, hearing, seeing and tasting."

The *New York Times* explained in its obit that he had a "notably prickly personality that grated on some people, like Mrs. Child. 'I think he enjoyed being difficult," said Julia, "But on the other hand, he could be absolutely charming if you treated him like the genius he considered himself to be.'"

Pierre Franey was one who spanned all the roles from chef to writer, rising "from pot scrubber in a Paris bistro to executive chef of the legendary Pavilion restaurant and later to a career as a *New York Times* food columnist and cookbook author."[4] This was a man whose certain life's work was food. Franey grew up southeast of Paris in a small village in

Burgundy. By the age of five, he was known as Pierre le Gourmand for his enthusiasm for local cheeses, snails, and other delicacies. While he was still a teenager, his family sent him to Paris to begin his apprenticeship as a chef. Within a year he had advanced to the famed kitchen of Drouant. In 1939, with France descending into political chaos and war, Franey leaped at the offer of a job at France's New York World's Fair pavilion in New York. And when the acclaimed Pavilion restaurant moved into a permanent berth in Manhattan, Franey went along, soon to be chief chef there, as well as at the fabled La Côte Basque and the Hedges, a summer restaurant in East Hampton, New York. During World War II, he fought in the U.S. Army, afterward returning to the Pavilion.

In a dispute about money, Franey left the Pavilion in 1960 and went into the unlikely employ of Howard Johnson's as vice president. This nine-to-five job meant he was free to hang out with his friend Craig Claiborne, the *New York Times'* restaurant critic. In his memoir, *A Chef's Tale,* Franey wrote, "We would go from place to place, making our judgments. For all my life I had been confined to one kitchen or another. But here I was suddenly getting in to see an entirely different world." In the early 1970s, Claiborne left the newspaper for a few years and collaborated with Franey on a restaurant newsletter. When Claiborne returned to the *Times* in 1976, he insisted that Franey be hired, too. The two immediately made a great splash. Claiborne had put in the winning bid at a fund-raising auction for a dinner anywhere in the world, price no object. Claiborne and Franey headed off to Chez Denis in Paris and worked their way through thirty-one courses and many expensive wines, and American Express found itself paying an almost-$10,000 bill. Claiborne described the meal on the newspaper's front page, stirring up both envious fascination with and outrage at such excess.

But Franey's real role at the *Times* was to write the column "The 60-Minute Gourmet," which offered the harried home cook easy-to-understand and highly simplified classic French cooking—and not just one main dish but also side dishes or salads that together would create a pleasing dinner. Said one *Times* editor, "Before Pierre Franey, haute cuisine was confined to the palates of the privileged. In partnership with

Craig Claiborne, he popularized it, leading the way in making it understood and relished by the general public." For the many aspiring chefs who did not read the *New York Times*, Franey wrote numerous well-regarded cookbooks with various collaborators. When he retired from the *Times*, Franey pursued the life of a celebrity chef, appearing on PBS in his own show, *Cuisine Rapide,* and touring around to do cooking demonstrations and promote his cookbooks.

As this chapter makes clear, New York City in the 1970s and especially the 1980s was a hotbed of food innovation and enthusiasm. Evan Jones was a writer who first became famous for the meals he cooked with his wife, Judith Jones, a highly regarded Knopf editor who happened to edit many of that publisher's celebrated food writers, including Julia Child and James Beard. The Joneses met in Paris right after World War II. They worked together on Evan Jones's magazine for American tourists and fell in love with each other and French food. Jones, a Minnesotan whose family had long been in the newspaper business, had been raised on stolid leek-and-potato fare. Now he and Judith roamed the incredible outdoor food markets of France, marveling at the delectable selection of perfectly ripe fruits and vegetables, the freshness of the seafood, the varieties of pungent cheeses. Shopping and cooking became a shared passion. Their East Sixty-sixth Street apartment became, in the opinion of some well-traveled friends, "the best restaurant in New York."

By the mid-1970s, Evan Jones combined his true passion—food and cooking—with his talent as a writer to publish *American Food: The Gastronomic Story.* Coming as it did, when there was such a growing interest in what Americans had eaten before canned and frozen food had sapped much of the taste and texture out of our daily meals, the book served to fuel the food revolution. The next year Jones published *The World of Cheese,* considered the "definitive work." Then, in a natural development, he and his wife collaborated on *The Book of Bread.* Evan Jones often retreated to the couple's Vermont home to write. Sometimes his wife would arrive on Friday evening to find that "her husband had spent his time preparing a dozen dishes for her to savor."

The food revolution was very much about enjoying freshness and new flavors, so it was natural that herbs were rediscovered. Adelma

Grenier Simmons was an authority on herbs who used her Caprilands Herb Farm in Coventry, Connecticut, to promote the use and appreciation of many forgotten varieties. All told, she wrote thirty-five books and many pamphlets on the lore of herbs and their potential culinary and medicinal uses. After *Herb Gardening in Five Seasons* came out in 1963, Simmons found herself and her farm a place of pilgrimage for gardeners and chefs. A big woman who liked to wear a cape, she gave a one-hour lecture to her visitors most days and then invited them to an herbal-themed lunch. The farm eventually featured three hundred herbs grown in thirty-three gardens. There was the Saints Garden for medicine and food herbs: the Shakespeare Garden, with the herbs known from the plays; and the Silver Garden, with pale, shimmery plants. As aspiring chefs—whether amateur or professional—came to be interested in growing and using their own herbs, Simmons proved to be an expert and genial guide, whether through her many writings or through Caprilands.

A native of Shelton, Vermont, Simmons moved to Hartford, Connecticut, to be an international buyer with Albert Steiger department stores. Her parents joined her but felt homesick for rural life. In 1929, they bought a fifty-acre abandoned farm together. The initial plan was to raise goats and vegetables. But after a bad year with the veggies, Simmons focused on the far hardier herbs, plants that could be sold either live or dried. Soon she had created an imaginative herbal world that allowed visitors to be inspired firsthand by a wide range of plants and their possible uses. One young neighbor boy, David Bouley, would go on to run such much-admired New York restaurants as Montrachet and Bouley. Even after becoming a chef, he would return every year to cook a five-course herb-inspired meal for Simmons and her family and staff.

Wine Producers, Merchandisers, and Writers

While the New York food revolution was unfolding on the East Coast, on the West Coast the great wine revival was in progress. Inevitably, the two would soon enliven each other. Maynard Amerine was "widely acclaimed as the father of American wine who helped revive the California wine industry after the repeal of Prohibition." Brought up in Modesto, California, on the family fruit farm, he loved chemistry and found that the reviving wine industry needed hard information. He earned a Ph.D. at the University of California at Davis by researching the basic problem of how climate affects grapes. He was the first researcher hired by his alma mater's new Department of Viticulture and Enology. Over the next sixty years, Amerine helped create a science of grapes and then had the unique personality to communicate that knowledge to academics, as well as vintners, wine makers, and governments.

By closely measuring "the effect of climate on different varieties of grapes," Amerine and his colleague Dr. Albert Winkler explained in a classic 1944 article the advantages of growing appropriate vines in the right microclimates. They showed that the proper match of grapes and climate would yield outstanding grapes and wine and became gurus for many in the fledgling California wine industry: "The grafting and replanting that the two researchers recommended eventually helped California move beyond jug wines to become one of the world's premier wine producing areas." Robert Mondavi, chairman of one of California's major wineries, said, "I still wouldn't plant anything without consulting that [1944] paper." He also read Amerine's 1980 book, *The Technology of Wine Making*, at least once a year.[5]

While Amerine brought a rigorous scientific approach to grape growing, he always understood that fine wines should be bottled bits of poetry. And some of his advice reflected that artistic bent. He advised, for instance, that "the best way to determine when to pick Gewurztraminer grapes is to camp next to the vines in the vineyard and breathe the air." Moreover, while understated and correct in his role as expert, Amerine loved the romance and fun of fine cooking, especially for the many famous people he met as a world-class wine authority. At his Sonoma County home, he "took pride in putting people together, M. F. K. Fisher and James Beard met at his table, where he routinely entertained his students as well as legendary musicians, actors and heads of state."

One of the more exotic and important figures who helped make California wines world class was Andre Tchelistcheff, a White Russian who spent his childhood on the family estate near Moscow. He fought in the White Russian army and upon its defeat went to Czechoslovakia to study agronomy at the University of Brno. By 1930, he was in Paris studying grapes and winemaking, and was then employed in the cellars of Moët et Chandon in the Champagne region. In 1938, longtime California winemaker Georges de Latour came to France looking for a winemaker to help him make truly great wines at his Beaulieu Vineyards in the Napa Valley. For the next thirty-five years, Tchelistcheff presided over Beaulieu, turning Georges de Latour Private Reserve Cabernet Sauvignon into one of the nation's outstanding red wines.

In Hugh Johnson's *Story of Wine*, he describes how when Tchelistcheff "arrived in California he was thunderstruck to see that wineries grew grapes for every sort of wine in the same vineyard. At Beaulieu there were twenty-eight different sorts of wine being made."[6] But gradually, the need to adapt to microclimates began to push vineyards to plant what they could grow best.

In this golden era, Beaulieu Vineyards also attracted Legh Knowles, a former trumpet player in the Glenn Miller Orchestra who became one of the great promoters of California wines at a time when many still scoffed at them. Knowles was hired straight out of the Air Force after World War II by the California Wine Advisory Board: "I didn't know anything about wine, but they wanted someone who could stand up before large crowds. I'd done a lot of that." He moved constantly and was a road warrior, either promoting California wines or selling them, for E. and J. Gallo Winery and then Beaulieu. When Heublein bought Beaulieu, Knowles stayed on and rose to become chairman of the vineyard, even though he disdained the East Coast–based owners as "bean counters." In 1987, the Napa Valley Vintners Association named him one of its "living legends."

Jack Davies was a Los Angeles executive with a Stanford degree and a Harvard M.B.A. who threw it all over to move with his wife to the lovely Napa Valley to grow grapes and make wine. They were on the leading edge of those abandoning professional careers to become part of a new generation of wine makers. In 1965, the Davieses bought the old and derelict Schramsburg estate on Diamond Mountain with the intention of making their mark with sparkling wine: "They restored the crumbling Schram mansion, drove the bats out of five caves that had once been cellars for aging wine, bought wine-making equipment and replanted forty acres of vines with true Champagne grapes, some of the first ever in California."

Writes wine expert Hugh Johnson, "Those first years in the '60s [were] the turning point in modern wine history. A radical new idea was born in many places at once: that wine was not an esoteric relic of ancient times that was disappearing even in Europe, nor just a cheap way to get drunk, but an expression of the earth that held potential pleasure and fascination for everyone."[7] By 1970, California's few dozen wineries of the 1950s had expanded to 220. By 1980, there were more than 500 California wineries.

The great break for Schramberg and the Davieses came in 1972 when California's Richard M. Nixon, who liked the wine, began to serve it in the White House. He really put them on the map when he took twenty-five cases of 1969 blanc de blanc to China to toast the United States' restored diplomatic relations with Premier Chou En-lai. From 1970 to 1980, the company's sales and production soared from a thousand to twenty thousand cases a year. The Davieses were thriving because they had "raised the standards of American sparkling wine production higher than anyone in the industry had believed possible."

Meanwhile, the Davieses understood early on that as sophisticated city folk began to visit the newly thriving vineyards, real estate developers would eye the surrounding hills and dales for their possibilities. Thus, Jack Davies was one of the first to propose that the Napa Valley be made a state-protected agricultural preserve, the first of its kind nationwide. For two decades, this designation was bitterly contested, with Davies always fighting hard to maintain the area's rural character. He was at the forefront of a successful battle to stop the state from widening Highway 29, the valley's main artery.

Louis P. Martini, the longtime chairman of the Louis M. Martini Winery, was another pivotal figure in the Napa Valley. His family had owned the company since 1922 but had actually moved to the Napa Valley in 1933. Martini spent his boyhood among the vines, graduated from the

University of California at Berkeley, served in the Army Air Corps during World War II, and then rejoined the winery. He became the company's wine maker in 1954 and soon showed his creativity and leadership.

While others viewed the Carneros district as fit only for sheep, Martini began growing pinot noir grapes there. Today the district is prized for producing the best of that type of grapes. He also helped address the manpower issue by pioneering mechanical grape harvesting. In the quest to gain respect and new audiences for California wines, he founded the Wine Institute and was a charter member of the American Society of Enologists.

The decades of close attention to microclimates, the development of controlled fermentation techniques, and the discovery that aging wine in French oak caskets imparted a subtle flavor—all these things gradually brought California wines up to a high standard. The astonishing proof of this revolution came at the famous 1976 Bataille de Vins, sponsored by a British wine merchant in Paris. The judges were French, including leading wine growers, famous restaurateurs, and a top official in France's wine-licensing establishment. They tasted French and California wines in unmarked bottles. To the chagrin and amazement of the judges, both the red and white winners were California wines from the Napa Valley. The rising quality of American wines did not go unnoticed. In 1980, for the first time in their history, Americans drank more wine than hard liquor.

On the East Coast, Sam Aaron became the "dean of New York wine merchants and a seminal figure in developing America's taste for wine." Aaron had trained as an educational psychologist, but during the Depression there were no such jobs. He teamed up with his brother, who was buying the Sherry-Lehmann liquor store at Sixty-second and Madison from a onetime bootlegger who had decided that legal sales were not for him. The Aaron boys were all Brooklyn kids. When they opened, recalled Sam Aaron, "It was just another liquor store at first. Then one day a man walked in and changed the future for the shop and for us." This life-changing person was a onetime *New Yorker* writer turned wine importer named Frank Schoonmaker. In 1937, he took young Sam under his wing and escorted him through the vineyards of

Europe. The war came, and Aaron found work as an Army psychologist, but at war's end he returned to Sherry-Lehmann. Now he discovered a great flair for describing wines that made each sound so enticing and desirable that buyers flocked into the store to buy by the case. For instance, "The little town of Sauvigny-les-Beaune, in a fold in the hills between Beaune and Corton, produces what are perhaps the pleasantest medium-priced Burgundies of the whole Côte d'Or."

Several years after Aaron's death, New York Times wine writer Frank J. Prial was still describing Aaron as "probably the greatest wine sales-man I've known. . . . Whatever he was flogging, he would add this to his catalogue: 'When this is gone there will be no more.' The Rothchilds' best or Romanian plonk, it didn't matter: the people came, waving money, demanding one of those precious last bottles."

Sam Aaron's wine-buying trips to Europe found him luxuriously installed in a suite in one of Paris's best hotels, the Hôtel Crillon. With chilled champagne flowing, he played genial host to a steady stream of wine makers and château owners from all over la belle France. If you wanted to sell wine in America, you started with shelf space at Sherry-Lehmann. And as Americans began to pay more attention to and drink more wine, Aaron put his expertise between covers, editing the wines and spirits volume in a Time-Life Books series on food. With literary luminary Clifton Fadiman, he compiled The Joys of Wine, and then, in the role of all-round bon vivant, he and James Beard wrote How to Eat Better for Less Money.

Just as food had its celebrated writers whose knowledge and exper-tise opened up cooking for many, so did wine. Leon D. Adams was "the seminal wine historian in the United States." His 1973 Wines of America was a major history and survey of wine and wineries all over the United States. "With the first edition of his book," explained one major Napa Valley wine maker, "Leon gave the wine industry a hard-as-nails, unsentimental look at what was happening nationwide. We were in the dark about wine growing in the U.S. He organized our sense of who was growing what and where."

A lifelong Californian, Adams was one of the founders of the Wine Institute. Noted the New York Times, "For Mr. Adams, wine was more than a beverage, it was a cause. In his writing and speeches—friend and foe alike often found him inspiring and usually crusty—he said that wine was a civilizing force." Despite this, he was no wine snob, heaping as much enthusiasm on obscure upstate New York wines as he might a renowned Napa brand. His goal was simply to make sure not only that every American understood the importance of drinking wine but also bought it. Said the longtime wine editor of *Gourmet*, "He always said that wine should be as cheap as milk. He had a point."

Fast-Food Pioneers

While we have concentrated thus far on the more laudable changes in our eating habits, of far greater impact for the time-pressed masses has been the vast expansion of fast food. We met Richard McDonald, the man who invented the Golden Arches, in our chapter on millionaires. Our database also includes J. W. McLamore, a cofounder of Burger King, McDonald's longtime rival. Just about the time that McDonald was selling off to Ray Kroc, the man who took McDonald's national and then global, McLamore was creating "a small hamburger shop, called Insta Burger King, in Miami in 1954." Like Joseph Baum of Four Seasons fame, McLamore had a degree in hotel administration from Cornell. The Insta Burger King had been up and running for about three years when McLamore and his partners developed a flame broiler, dropped the Insta, and created the Whopper. This was a huge success, and after that, the chain expanded rapidly. In 1967, the company was sold to Pillsbury.

With life speeding up and many people on the move, fast and familiar food was instantly popular. Murray Riese was one half of a brother duo who "wrought a succession of revolutions in the Manhattan restaurant business" that brought fast food to many a New York corner. They started at the bottom in the Depression, working as dishwashers and saving for several years to pull together a $500 down payment to buy a luncheonette on East Fortieth Street for $8,500. Four years later, they sold the place for $38,000, including $10,000 cash. Murray Riese wondered, "Why sell a sandwich for a 10-cents profit when you can sell a restaurant for $10,000?" With that, they began buying, improving, and selling all kinds of restaurants—five thousand, all told, over the next dozen years!

But then the IRS ruled that they had to own and operate a place for at least three years to qualify for the more profitable capital gains tax category. So they became restaurant operators just as the fast-food industry took off, offering sites in bus and train terminals and numerous prime locations. The Rieses created a great deal of unhappiness with their ideas about mixing and matching rival fast-food chains. Reported the *New York Times*, "When Marriott, which then owned the Roy Rogers chain, learned that the Rieses planned to shoehorn a Pizza Hut and a Häagen-Dazs ice cream outlet into a Roy Rogers restaurant the Rieses were opening in Times Square in 1982, Mr. Riese recalled, 'They sued us.'" But the Rieses won, and soon the food court became a commonplace of shopping malls across the United States.

The combination of prosperity, far more enticing foods everywhere we turn, and the triumph of the automobile have all contributed to ever-fatter Americans. And so it seems appropriate to end this chapter with Albert Lippert, a "once pudgy garment executive who stumbled on a diet program that made him both svelte and rich." The diet program? None other than Weight Watchers.

Albert Lippert was happily living the good life in Long Island after World War II, married to Felice, with two sons. He held a degree in business administration from City College of New York and had done some graduate work at Baruch College. He worked in retail as a buyer of women's coats and suits. On Friday nights, the Lipperts got together with friends and took dance lessons. But the good life was taking a toll. In a decade of marriage, Albert Lippert, who was six feet tall, "had seen his weight balloon to 216 pounds, while his once willowy wife had gone from size 12 to a 16 or 18."

Felice Lippert had heard of a local woman who was teaching weight loss. They decided to substitute this Jean Nidetch for the usual dance instructor one Friday night. She gave them an inspiring pep talk and a sheet that explained the diet developed by a New York City obesity clinic. Within the week Albert had lost seven pounds and Felice four.

Impressed by the program, the Lipperts proposed to the Nidetchs that they become partners. To test out grassroots dieting, Albert rented a room above a Little Neck movie theater. Charging the same amount as the movie, $2, they attracted twenty-two folks worried enough about their weight to show up and pay. The next week sixty-six people appeared, and Weight Watchers was launched. Within the year, the Lipperts had shed a total of a hundred pounds on the Weight Watchers diet, testimony to its initial effectiveness. They also began selling franchises. The franchises were relatively cheap, but the holders had to return 10 percent of their gross to the Lipperts. Reported the *New York Times*, "Within a decade or so, franchises that sold for as little as $2,000 were returning $100,000 a year." By 1978, H. J. Heinz paid $72 million for the company, with $15 million going to the Lipperts. Albert Lippert stayed on a few years as chief executive and then served on the Heinz board of directors. He was a Weight Watchers success story himself, remaining slender his whole life.

Notes

1. Amanda Hesser, "Too Many Cooks? Not Nearly Enough," *New York Times*, October 25, 1998, sec. 3, p. 1.
2. Marian Burros, "Missing: Great Women Chefs in New York," *New York Times*, February 10, 1999, D1.
3. Jennifer C. Wilkinson, "Mastering the Art of Julia Child," *Traditional Home*, March 1999, p. 54.
4. Michael and Ariane Batterberry, *On the Town in New York* (New York: Routledge, 1999), p. 289.
5. Hugh Johnson, *The History of Wine* (London: Reed Consumer Books, 1989), pp. 449–450.
6. Ibid., pp. 448–450.
7. Ibid., p. 452.

15

People with Utterly Unusual Lives

Diarist of 22 Million Words

Master of Erudite Nonsense

Anthropologist and Partygoer

Throughout this book, we have looked at people from our *New York Times* obituary database who were successful in important and influential fields, beginning with business and moving on to the professions, government, academia, and so forth. In this final chapter, we look at people who were also successful, but in far less conventional fields and endeavors. These are the rare few who blazed their own unique path and still made a mark. The beauty of this group is that they are really unclassifiable. Each is an individual who succeeded largely on his or her own terms outside the usual paths followed in our society. (Several operated out of the tolerant world of academe.) Most of these men and women passionately pursued highly unusual talents, interests, or causes.

Some of these fascinating folks could probably be fairly described as bon vivants who honed their vision of living the good life to a fine art. These were people who reminded the strivers and movers and shakers that sometimes we should slow down and savor the way the morning light hits the trees or delight in the pleasure of a dining companion who tells wonderful stories. High in that pantheon stands J. Blan van Urk, who "spent the better part of a century riding happily to the hounds . . . [becoming] a widely recognized authority on fox hunting and lunch." Jack van Urk was a man who did everything from digging ditches to writing advertising to making and losing a million dollars in Florida real estate. But earning a living could probably have been classed as a necessary evil, a tiresome activity that interfered with Jack's real passions in life. And according to the *New York Times,* "These included playing polo, breeding and training dogs and horses, pursuing foxes and other prey, among them tigers in India, jackals in Africa and hares in Australia and having lunch in grand style "

Jack van Urk embodied all that was suave and debonair. He was a picture of elegance in a three-piece tailor-made suit and jaunty boutonniere. Anyone making a movie of his life would surely cast the incomparable David Niven to play him. The film would begin in Indiana, where his surgeon father sent him to the Culver Military Academy. There young Jack would be shown discovering his affinity for horses. Brief scenes at Princeton would follow, depicting his triumph as college heavyweight boxing champion, and then New York in the Roaring Twenties, with Jack fully launched as a convivial man-about-town. Probably the film would be something of a comedy, with van Urk passing through a dizzying array of jobs decade after decade. What would remain constant was his utter devotion to lunch at "21," the legendary midtown Manhattan watering hole and restaurant. Van Urk always occupied table 9, to the left of the entrance, where he would eat chicken hash. Keeping him company might be such people as Howard Cosell or Humphrey Bogart.

Jack's dedication to lunch was equaled only by his passion for foxhunting. Ideally, in any given week he'd tallyho at least twice, sallying forth to the glorious countryside to leap fences, ditches, and hedges as he followed the hounds. Van Urk became that unlikely being, a world authority on his subject, publishing his two-volume *Story of American Fox Hunting* just before World War II. The *Encyclopaedia Britannica* then tapped him as its hunting expert. He wrote the histories of specific local hunts; he claimed, over the years, to have ridden with 141 different hunt clubs all over the world. There was time in all this conviviality to be married to a well-to-do widow. Eventually, the van Urks moved to the Brandywine hunt country near Wilmington, Delaware. True to his principles, Jack van Urk held court each midday lunch at the Hotel Du Pont's Green Room, while continuing to follow the hounds until he was eighty-eight, an example to us all.

David Kidd lived the dream of every child who ever yearned to escape from blandest America into a more mysterious, exotic world. Growing up first in Corbin, Kentucky, where his father ran a coal mine, and then in Detroit, where his father became an auto executive, Kidd longed for something more soulful and enthralling. In the dull world of prewar suburbia, only Stravinsky's *Rite of Spring* lent hope, like some sign of life from a distant planet peopled by lovers of beauty. And so, not long after he completed his degree at the University of Michigan, Kidd went to China as an exchange student. He sailed to the Peking of 1946, an ancient imperial city awash in international intrigue. Kidd, a handsome young man with wavy blond hair, quickly adopted the trappings of the dandified aesthete, down to the silk ascot and the cigarette held just so. He spent the next four years teaching English at various local colleges and fell in love with Chinese art and an aristocratic Chinese girl. As the new son-in-law to the former chief justice of the Chinese Supreme Court, Kidd lived with his wife in a "101-room palace, a labyrinth of courtyards and corridors packed with ancient treasures, including two dozen Yu relatives." With the Communists steadily consolidating their power, Kidd realized that his father-in-law's elaborate Chinese funeral would be the last for a doomed elite. The boy from Kentucky who had longed for magnificence and drama stood in Tiananmen Square and watched the Communists formally take power from an imperial throne that went back thousands of years.

He wrote of these rare and poignant experiences in a memoir, *All the Emperor's Horses*. In that memoir, Kidd described the Yu family's large and elegant garden with its many exquisite rarities: "stones of every type, shape, and size," the more fantastic ones were lavalike, gray-blue, and green, filled with holes and hollowed into whirls and arabesques by wind and water. "Heaped up in piles [they] looked from a distance as huge and wild as primeval mountains." And then there was the grove of ancient cedars, all that had survived a fire at the Ming-era temple that had preceded the four-hundred-year-old Yu palace: "Twisted and bent with age, some ten of them were huddled close together." The garden was an ancient work of art featuring massive entwined wisteria, rare plum trees that shimmered on moonlit spring nights, serene ponds that had once flashed with golden carp, lustrous peonies, and chrysanthemums, all to be contemplated from the Temple of Harmonious Virtues. When the newly poor family had to sell its palace, it was assured by the buyer that he would preserve the garden. But within months this ancient, enchanting landscape was no more, and in its stead was a huge parking lot for trucks.[1]

In 1950, with the Communists about to spread terror and dullness over China, Kidd and his wife fled to the United States. They divorced, and Kidd sought solace in Oriental art circles in Manhattan while teaching at the Asia Institute. But the New York of the 1950s was a gray place. By 1956, Kidd was again an eccentric expatriate, happily ensconced in a three-hundred-year-old mansion in Ashiya, Japan, and teaching at Kobe and Osaka universities. Postwar Japan was a collector's paradise as exquisite art and furniture were cast aside to make way for the new and Western. Kidd hired a Japanese student to help him pursue treasures and bargains that transformed his mansion into a veritable museum. The two evolved into life partners, as Kidd became a devotee of such traditional Japanese arts as the tea ceremony and calligraphy. When the landlord informed him that the mansion would be razed to build a high-rise, Kidd got permission to dismantle the house and then moved it to Kyoto, Japan's cultural heart.

Thanks to his friends in New York, Kidd had become famous among Americans traveling to Japan. He took advantage of this to open a school in Kyoto to teach the tea ceremony and other fading Japanese traditions to Americans. The sponsor was the Oomoto Shinto sect, whose motto, "Art is the mother of religion," captured Kidd's aesthetic sense. But soon Japanese students were enrolling in the school, too, trying to recapture the culture they had too blithely tossed overboard. While Kidd disdained the idea that he might sell any of his treasures, he in fact did so, and therefore many an American collector stopped by. Wrote the *New York Times*, "As a tourist attraction, Mr. Kidd did not disappoint. To sit on a cushion before his throne, listening to his erudite patter, and seeing him sitting cross-legged on his kang, a divided Chinese sofa, rustling his silken gown as he gestured extravagantly with his inevitable cigarette, was to be in the presence of a presence."

Thus, David Kidd had fulfilled his dream of living somewhere far away from coal mines and car factories, a place where beauty and the exotic prevailed. His only regret was that his pal David Bowie never made the movie he said he would of Kidd's youthful years as witness-participant in the death throes of the ancient Chinese empire.

Daniel J. Crowley was, like David Kidd, a boy desperate to escape his ordinary origins, in his case Peoria, Illinois. But while Kidd became an expatriate aesthete who mastered such complex Japanese arts as the tea ceremony and calligraphy, Crowley became an international reveler at carnivals and festivals, preferably in warm tropical locales. All this was done under the rubric of anthropology, for Crowley, like most mortals, had to earn a living. He was a well-regarded professor at the University of California at Davis, author of 350 scholarly papers and several books, all devoted to his specialty, "the arts and culture of Africa and African outposts in the New World, with an emphasis on Mardi Gras and other eruptions of annual excess in the Caribbean and South America." In the course of his firsthand fieldwork into celebratory folklore, Dr. Crowley said he had "circled the globe nine times . . . [visiting] 295 of the 311 political and geographic entities . . . generally finding a party at each stop." What made his assiduous devotion to hands-on fieldwork so impressive was that he was confined to a wheelchair as a result of having contracted polio in the Navy during World War II. In the course of his partying peregrinations, Professor Crowley wore out a dozen wheelchairs. His travel companions were his Trinidadian wife and students provided by University Expedition Projects. Along the way, he filled many notebooks with his scrawled field observations.

Not only was Professor Crowley frequently off engaged in fieldwork in exotic climes, he arranged to get temporary teaching assignments at colleges as far-flung as Trinidad, Australia, and India. He enjoyed a wide range of native cuisines and was renowned for "inventing exotic new cocktails." He once ventured to Iceland to study a carnival there, but found revelry in parkas not as fascinating as Mardi Gras in say, Brazil, where a few strings, beads, and bangles qualified as a costume. However, Professor Crowley did prefer to view most festivities from a balcony: "When they come at you in Rio de Janeiro after snorting amyl nitrite and drinking quantities of liquor, you'd better get out of the way. They have left footprints on my forehead." He often imagined that he would die notebook in hand out in a party. He envisioned an obit that said, "He died as he lived, crushed by 50,000 Brazilians doing the samba." And while it was true he was at yet another Mardi Gras, this one in Oruro, Bolivia, when he died, all that really happened was that he went to sleep and didn't wake up.

Suzanne Railey did not, like Kidd and Crowley, have to invent herself; she merely adopted one of the customs of her class and shaped it into a high art. She was a child of privilege whose family owned a department store in Rochester, New York, but who often, while growing up, spent time in New York, Paris, and Washington, D.C. During her twenties, she lived in Manhattan, and, as her uncle explained, "She did what popular young girls do. She traveled and went to parties." When World War II came, Suzanne moved to Washington, D.C., and began Overcoats for Britain, a charity that supplied warm coats to the people of that beleaguered country. After the war, she met and married Howard Barclay Railey, described as "a businessman attached to the American Embassy in Paris."

It was now that Suzanne Railey found her true calling in life. With a "romantic apartment overlooking the Seine in Paris" as her studio, she began developing her own kind of artistry, dinner parties. Collecting was her other passion, and her Paris apartment bedazzled with its eclectic paintings and treasures, a special setting for her gatherings. "She was a born brilliant hostess," said one Paris friend. "She was always friends with all the ambassadors." When her husband died, Suzanne Railey moved back to Manhattan to a two-bedroom apartment in the East Sixties and began holding dinner parties there. One frequent guest, jewelry designer Kenneth Jay Lane, said, "You never knew who you'd be seated next to. She always had good people." And the setting still dazzled. Said Lane, "Her apartment was amazing, with more objects than you could count on every table and mirrors on the ceilings." A typical gathering featured "diplomats, society doyennes and fashion designers." She explained her philosophy simply: "It all depends on who's in town and what I'm thinking of." She just loved to throw dinner parties:

"It's just so much more attractive to entertain at home. You can actually sit and talk."

In March 1985, Christie's auction house hired her for one sole purpose: to "hold a black-tie dinner party at her home each month, drawing on her long list of wealthy and influential friends, many with extensive art collections. The idea was to generate good will, and eventually business, for the auction house." So here was a woman, a bon vivant who had parlayed her talent for entertaining and her love of dinner parties into an actual job of sorts, one that she held for more than a decade! And while this was not a woman who advanced medicine or created an important business, one imagines that she provided a great deal of pleasure and fellowship to the thousands who over the decades dined in her lovely apartments.

Steven Slepack was a Brooklyn lad who seemed destined for a life of science, having won a full scholarship to the University of Hawaii in marine biology. But once out in those lush islands, he found he preferred to repair to the beach to contemplate the ocean and the rainbows as he played his banjo. After two years, he formally left school and returned to New York. There this natural free spirit discovered he had a talent for street entertaining. First he was a straight banjo player, but gradually he developed a persona, Professor Bendeasy. As the *New York Times* described him, "One of New York's most visible and colorful entertainers for two decades, he was the man in the beribboned tuxedo jacket who delighted a generation of schoolchildren by twisting balloons into animals in Central Park and elsewhere." Often stationed near the wondrous bronze Alice in Wonderland creatures in the park, Slepack could, in mere seconds and with a deft turn here and there, magically turn a limp balloon into a plump pink exotic bird or a blue flower.

Before settling in as a beloved Manhattan character, Steven Slepack traveled here and there, putting in a long sojourn in San Francisco, where he taught his balloon tricks to a local comedian, Steve Martin. But always Slepack returned to New York. And one day in 1990, as he was standing down in the East Village next to his conveyance—a onetime ambulance—he noticed a lovely young woman. Soon she joined him in a tuxedo and harlequin tights. Now it was Professor Bendeasy

and Princess Oulala, working together to create menageries and bou-
quets for delighted children and their smiling parents. In the summer,
this whimsical husband-wife duo worked Central Park; in the winter,
F. A. O. Schwartz. At a dollar a balloon, they could make enough in a
day to live for weeks in their home in Vermont, where they passed the
time reading and listening to music. This "street balloon virtuoso"
understood that his colorful creations generated a childish joy in both
kids and adults, as the inevitable crowd gathered and lingered, oohed
and aahed, a small island of magic in a busy, stressful metropolis.

Our next group were not so much bon vivants and free spirits as men
and women who lived unusual lives because they had unique talents.
John Fulton, for instance, was the first American "to qualify as a matador in Spain." But not only would he engage in the artistry of the bullfight with his cape and sword, he would gather the blood of the bulls he
had killed and use it to paint pictures of them! The seeds of this unlikely
career were planted in Philadelphia in 1945 when twelve-year-old
Fulton saw *Blood and Sand,* a movie starring Tyrone Power as a doomed
bullfighter. Then and there, afire with the "gallantry and romance" of it
all, he decided that bullfighting was his destiny. Unlike most such dec-
larations, this one was carried out. While in high school, Fulton learned
flamenco dancing. His dance teacher knew a local barber who had once
been a bullfighter. The barber took young Fulton, who was now attending the Philadelphia Museum College of Art, under his wing. Fulton
then wangled a year at an art school in Mexico in San Miguel de
Allende, which was also a bullfighting center.

An Army stint served near the Mexican border gave Fulton a chance
to fight bulls in nearby towns. By 1956, he was ready to head to Spain.
Other Americans had preceded him with the same dream, but only he
managed "to be elevated and confirmed as a matador. . . . He had to
endure years of fighting lesser bulls, though, often without pay, in
remote arenas before he became a full matador in 1963." Nonetheless,
though he fought some good fights and had his ardent followers, he was
"never more than a competent journeyman."

But Fulton had no regrets. "It is the most difficult art form in the
world," he explained. "You are required to create a work of art

spontaneously with a semi-unknown medium, which can kill you, in front of one of the most critical audiences around. And it all leaves only a memory." But a properly composed bullfight culminates in the thrilling moment when the sword plunges straight into the animal's heart. With that, explained Fulton, "The skies look bluer, the birds sound better, the food tastes better, the wine is better, friendships deepen."

Despite being perennially hard up, Fulton filled his large house in Seville with other aspiring matadors and was always hospitable. He had some bit parts in movies and served as James A. Michener's guide when the great writer was in Spain to research *Iberia.* Along the way Fulton rescued and adopted a gypsy boy. And he certainly lived his dream.

Alice Greenough Orr was a woman who had a unique "career that took her from the wilds of Montana to Madison Square Garden and the capitals of Europe. Mrs. Orr was always at home on a horse. If it was bucking, so much the better." For more than twenty years, she reigned as "the rodeo queen of the bronc riders." Her talent became apparent early on. Born and raised on a ranch near Red Lodge, Montana, she loved riding wild horses, and her father was soon giving her the horses that needed breaking in. She was the best known of a group of fearless, talented siblings, including a younger sister and two brothers. Alice Orr was good at trick riding and bull riding, too.

At age fourteen, she left school to work as a mail carrier, delivering letters on horseback along a thirty-five-mile rural route, through baking Montana summers and snowdrifts in winter. Her real dream then was to become a forest ranger. But the government did not want any female rangers. She then married her first husband and had two children. About ten years later, in 1929, she was working in a rooming house when she read an ad looking for bronc riders for a Wild West show. She and her sister auditioned and were hired immediately. The rooming house became a distant memory as Alice Orr took Europe by storm in the 1930s. She had tea with the queen of England and amazed the Spaniards by riding fighting bulls into the arenas and then leaping gracefully off their backs.

During the 1940s, she and her second husband operated their own rodeos, with Orr the big star of the saddle bronc riding. Along the way, she was inducted into the Cowboy and the Cowgirl Halls of Fame. Though she retired in 1954, she still did occasional movie work. Few of us could ever think of living such a life, yet such unique and fearless physical prowess is something we can all admire from a distance.

Rudolph Walter Wanderone was the quintessential hustler, a man who played by his own rules in a society where few have that luxury. Starting in the 1920s, this gigantic (five-foot-ten, three-hundred-pound) man made a living shooting pool, "crisscrossing the country and taking on all comers." This brought him great latitude to roam and organize his days as he would. It also brought a minor measure of renown among the other pool hustlers and the suckers who took up their challenges. Then came the terrific 1961 movie *The Hustler,* in which Jackie Gleason played a pool hustler named Minnesota Fats. Wanderone knew a main chance when he saw one and stepped forth into the media limelight to proclaim himself the real Minnesota Fats, the model for the movie character. The movie had in fact been based on a novel by Walter Tevis, who said he'd never heard of this interloper. But neither the newly proclaimed Fats nor the media really cared. He played his character to the hilt, and a good time was had by all.

Wanderone was born in New York, in 1900 or maybe in 1913. In a 1966 biography, he was quoted as saying, "I've been eating like a sultan since I was two days old. I had a mother and three sisters who worshiped me, and when I was two years old they used to plop me in a bed with a jillion satin pillows and spray me with exotic perfumes and lilac water and then they would shoot me the grapes." His was an expansive personality, and he basked in his celebrity, claiming that in the course of his pool-playing career he had "sailed around the world six times, survived two shipwrecks and hobnobbed with the claimed likes of Clark Gable, Arnold Rothstein, Damon Runyon and Al Capone." Perhaps. Once he had anointed himself Minnesota Fats, he became a large and familiar presence on television, always equipped with autograph cards proclaiming his greatness as a pool player. As commercial offers came his way, he could not always resist. He actually took a job flogging pool equipment in grueling cross-country tours. The stress made him so hard to get along with that his wife of forty-four years divorced him.

Wanderone was not only an outstanding pool player but an outstanding character, a man whose excesses and inventions endeared him to a society that does not have much room for the lovable rascals anymore.

When it comes to unusual talents that lead to unusual ways of making a living, Harry Stanley stands out. The *New York Times* described him as "a vaudevillian turned lecturer who was such a subtle master of philolillogical orotundity and frammatical linguistation that when he got wound up it took a while before it became apparent that nobody had the foggiest idea what he was talking about. . . . He had been a leading exponent of double talk for the better part of the century."

Stanley was an ordinary, nerdish fellow sporting a mustache, a serious suit, and the pince-nez that made him look the expert he pretended to be when introduced at business conventions and professional get-togethers. After all, at such events having a guest speaker is standard procedure, and he looked very much the part. He might, for instance, be solemnly introduced as a onetime presidential adviser on foreign affairs. One can imagine the audience settling in to pay close attention to the wise man's words. He would begin with a few statesmanlike generalities, again par for the course. But then would come the solemn declaration "But I for one feel that all basic and sadum tortumise, all the professional getesimus and tortum kimafly will precipitously aggregate so that peace shall reign. I want to make that perfectly clear." At this stage, no one would dare admit they did not understand, afraid they just were not up to the great man's exalted vocabulary. But each successive sentence contained more and more gibberish until his listeners realized that it was tomfoolery. When the laughter subsided, he would introduce himself as "Professor Harry Stanley, Harvard '39, Rutgers nothing."

Stanley arrived in the Lower East Side of Manhattan from Poland when just six years old. He was part of a generation of famous comedians who came up through the New York vaudeville theaters. He developed a successful comedy routine that featured himself and a buxom blond showgirl. He practiced his double-talk not so much on the stage as before a regular lunch group at Wolpin's Restaurant that included George Burns, Milton Berle, and George Jessel. The idea was to torment the waiters. After World War II, Burns and Berle took a flyer on

the brand-new medium of television, becoming wildly famous and successful. Stanley wrote off television as a flash in the pan and instead,
with vaudeville theaters closing left and right, developed double-talk
into a new comedy routine that would play on the straight lecture circuit when audiences needed an icebreaker. Stanley obviously regretted
not making the big time like his old lunch pals, but he was very much
in demand, a serious-looking man who was profoundly and cleverly
silly.

Thus far, most of our unusual people have had to earn a living. And
we have admired the ingenious ways they have done so and still managed
to cling to their passions and dreams. Winthrop K. Edey had no need to
support himself, for he was an heir and grandson of Morris W. Kellogg,
an engineer who had made a huge fortune in oil refineries. Young
Winthrop received an excellent education at a prep school, followed by
Amherst College and the Institute of Fine Arts at New York University.
From the time he had been a boy, he had had two all-consuming interests: disassembling and reassembling clocks and writing in his intensely
detailed diary. And now, as an adult living in Manhattan, he continued
to dedicate himself to these two passions. Over the years, he became
"an internationally known expert on antique clocks, and collected them
with such a discriminating eye that when he helped the Frick Collection
assemble an exhibition of French clocks in 1982, nine of the finest
specimens were from his own collection." Ultimately, he acquired sixty
fine horological specimens, thirty-nine of which were bequeathed to the
Frick.

His daily life had a clockwork aspect to it. Reported the *New York
Times*, "He got up at 5 in the afternoon, and after an evening out with
friends (dinner for them, breakfast for him), Mr. Edey would return to
his West 83rd Street town house and work through the night studying
clocks, pursuing a separate and abiding interest in ancient Egypt and
writing in his diary." His fascination for the past was evident in his own
brownstone, which appeared unchanged since the nineteenth century.
Light was still provided by gas jets and the original tapestries were still
on the walls. And when Winthrop developed an interest in photography
(he gathered a nice collection that included works by Man Ray), he of

course used a "huge wooden turn-of-the-century view camera complete with tripod and eleven-by-fourteen-inch glass plates."

But many of Winthrop Edey's friends, who included "prominent gallery owners, museum officials and collectors," believed that his multivolume diary, which he also gave to the Frick, might well be his greatest treasure, "an important document of New York life." Apparently Edey was a gifted writer and social observer likened by some to Marcel Proust, capable of devoting "several pages to the ramifications of a friend's failure to return a phone call." Perhaps one might think of Edey as an urban Thoreau, recording the habits and movements of Manhattan's human flora and fauna, leading the ultimate in the "examined life." Or perhaps a New York Samuel Pepys, leaving for posterity a detailed record of particular city and society.

Francine Katzenbogen's wealth also allowed her to live life on her own terms. Unlike Winthrop Edey, she was no heiress but one of those rare people who won a New York State lottery jackpot—in her case, for $7 million. Long before her lucky day, she and her family were famous in their Brooklyn neighborhood for collecting and sheltering stray cats. Soon after Francine's lottery windfall, she headed to the West Coast, buying a $1 million Studio City estate in Los Angeles. But then her mother fell ill, and she returned east to be with her. When her mother died after several years, Francine was ready to return to her new life in California. Just as Winthrop Edey's wealth allowed him to dedicate his life to his clocks and diary, Katzenbogen's wealth meant she could lavish care on her cats as never before. Taking all twenty of her beloved strays along meant hiring a cargo plane and paying $8,000 (half of that veterinary fees) to transport the family menagerie west. She quickly commissioned a $100,000 luxury cat residence for her felines in what had been a two-story garage. It included "tile floors, climbing towers, scratching posts, skylights and cozy, low-lying window ledges where the cats could stretch out and watch the world outside their air-conditioned lair."

However, her exclusive new neighbors were not thrilled and stiffly pointed out that local zoning regulations limited each household to three cats. Fifty residents "opposed her . . . arguing that the large number of cats would lower property values and even lure pet-eating coyotes into the neighborhood." After she vowed that none of her cats would ever be allowed outside and that their litter boxes would be changed daily, the neighbors relented. Of course, many people questioned the spending of so much money on mere pets. Replied Katzenbogen in a 1992 *Los Angeles Times* interview, "If I went out and bought a piece of jewelry or an expensive car, nobody would think twice or criticize me. If I want to spend my money and take care of my cats, which are my family, I don't think it's anybody's business."

In her new life, not surprisingly, she became a "mainstay of several animal care agencies both as volunteer and philanthropist." But she also had fun with her $7 million windfall. She bought fancy clothes and entered the local social whirl. However, this was all cut short at the young age of fifty-one. She died, said her aunt, from "a chronic asthma condition aggravated by strong allergic reactions to the very cats that were her overriding passion."

Robert Traub also had one great fascination in his life, but for him it was fleas. During his career at the University of Maryland Medical School (where he was a medical microbiologist), Professor Traub put together the world's second largest flea collection. (The other great flea archive resides at the Natural History Museum in London.) While such an accomplishment seems almost absurd, in the hands of a skilled and inquiring entomologist like Robert Traub it provided fascinating clues to some profound questions. By studying fleas over the decades, reported the *New York Times*, "Dr. Traub developed a theory of how each of the 2,200 species of fleas evolved, each along with its own animal or bird host, over about 125 million years." Based on the evolution of fleas, Dr. Traub posited a theory of continental drift that was later confirmed by geologists. Similarly, he could examine "the hair-grabbing spines" on a flea and make educated assumptions about weather and environment, sometimes millions of years ago.

Born in Manhattan, Traub earned a B.S. in biology from City College of New York in 1938 and an M.S. in medical entomology in 1939. He then entered the Army, where he ended up commanding the Army's research laboratory in Kuala Lumpur in Malaysia. There he worked on figuring out how insects spread disease and what would best cure those diseases. While in the Army, he earned his Ph.D. from the University of Illinois. When Traub retired from the Army, he went to the University of Maryland Medical School. Traub's own son described him as "a genuine eccentric" who also collected such artifacts as blowguns and thought nothing of bringing a gibbon back from a field trip for the Washington Zoo. So impressive were Traub's entomological researches that when he retired from the medical school, he became the Smithsonian's honorary curator of fleas. He had taken what many no doubt saw as an oddball interest and proven its importance. He still had two hundred unidentified specimens awaiting his expert examination when he died.

Kenneth D. Brugger also played a great role in entomology, but in a very different way. Unlike Robert Traub, whose lifetime study of fleas enabled him to describe a whole portion of the insect world over time and place, Brugger was an amateur who, on January 2, 1975, thrilled the world of lepidoptery by discovering the winter resting place of the monarch butterfly.

Brugger's story is telling, for it shows how the path to success can take unexpected twists and turns. Raised in Kenosha, Wisconsin, Brugger showed great mathematical and mechanical ability. But he did not go to college, instead working in his father's garage as an auto mechanic until World War II. The Army was impressed by his intellect and made him a cryptologist. After the war, he returned home, married, and went to work for Jockey International in management. In time he became chief engineer for Jockey's worldwide knitting operations, creating an innovative machine that could manufacture an unshrinkable undershirt. But he also underwent a bitter divorce and decided to start a whole new life in Mexico City as a textile consultant.

In 1973, Brugger noticed an ad in a Mexican newspaper from a University of Toronto scientist who for thirty years had directed efforts to track the annual migration of monarch butterflies. It was well established that the butterflies, which reproduce steadily, somehow dispatched their butterfly grandchildren to some breeding ground in Mexico, but just where was a real mystery. Brugger wrote the Canadian scientist to report that he had once seen huge clouds of the butterflies in mountains west of Mexico City. Letters went back and forth, and Brugger and his second wife, Catalina, agreed to set forth on the quest. They had ascended to ten thousand feet and were driving through groves of towering Oyamel firs when they realized that the trees were alive with millions of resting monarchs, their stained-glass black and red wings slowly undulating in waves of beauty. While North American butterfly enthusiasts were truly thrilled at the solution to this mystery, just as thrilled were the Mexican Indians who lived in the mountains, who had always wondered where the butterflies went each year when they took flight in the spring and disappeared.

Our final unusual life is that of Edward Robb Ellis, "who in 1927 began keeping a diary to fend off the boredom of his small town Midwestern adolescence and emerged nearly 70 years later as the most prolific known diarist in the history of American letters." As a longtime newspaperman who worked in New Orleans, Peoria, and Chicago before coming to the *New York World-Telegram* right after World War II, Ellis had the training to chronicle daily life intelligently. And his diaries deal with matters both large and small, for through his journalism Ellis was in a position to meet many famous people. But he also kept track of what food he ate and what it cost. Writer Pete Hamill said, "I think it is one of those diaries that will be useful to people for a long time. You can always get the memoirs of some general or half-baked politician. But to try to get the diaries of ordinary people is the hardest thing for a certain kind of historian."

The mere fact that Edward Robb Ellis wrote 22 million words took him out of the realm of the ordinary person. Nonetheless, he held no special office but simply aspired to record the passing scene. It all began when he was sixteen and living in Kewanee, Illinois, feeling bored as he was idly shooting basketball hoops with a few friends. He challenged his friends to a contest to see who could keep a diary the longest. He won. At his death, his 22 million words would be half the size of the entire *Encyclopaedia Britannica*. The manuscript filled fifty cartons. In 1995, Knopf published a very pared-down version (1 percent of the total) entitled *A Diary of the Century: Tales From America's Greatest Diarist*.

Fittingly for an American, Ellis was rather obsessed with celebrities. In the course of writing a biography of a high-powered press agent named Steve Hannagan in 1961, Ellis went to Hollywood for some interviews. In his diary, he described the visit he and his daughter made to see Clark Gable's young widow: "Neat and crisp, she wore a blouse, white shorts and handsome leather sandals. Her exquisitely groomed hair was golden, her eyes the color of bluebells, her figure strikingly beautiful." Ellis was also assiduous in recording what he knew were important historical events—for example, the death of Richard Nixon—but also such pop culture happenings as the opening of the Andy Warhol Museum in Pittsburgh in 1994. Ellis always enjoyed a good rant, whether against Nixon or against Warhol.

Ellis gave his diary to the Fales Library, the rare book library at New York University. The director there said of Ellis, "Eddie was a force of nature. He was incredibly intelligent, quick, funny and always on the make. He had an abiding interest in everyone's story, and clearly also in his own." The diary was not all Ellis wrote. He also published, in 1966, an admired history of New York City, *The Epic of New York,* and histories of the Depression and the home front during World War I.

Described by the *New York Times* as a "gregarious eccentric" and "in many ways a classic New York character," Edward Robb Ellis was something of a classic crank, living out his final years in "an increasingly rundown apartment in a 19th-century town house in Chelsea amid mounting towers of manila folders, five sets of encyclopedias and a collection of books whose extent he estimated at various times at 10,000 to 15,000 volumes."

While most of the people in the *New York Times* obituaries have gained renown through traditional careers in business, government, the professions, or arts and entertainment, the free spirits in this chapter—with the exception of the partying anthropologist professor and the expert on fleas—were largely not tethered to institutions. All lived the life they created largely on their own terms. And so our last group are those who pursued unique dreams and talents and made a success of doing so, serving as inspirations to all who dream.

Notes

1. David Kidd, *Peking Story: The Last Days of Old China* (London: Aurum, 1988). This is the English edition of *All the Emperor's Horses,* the American title.

16

Some Final Thoughts on Success and Fame

Alas, we cannot look back on the accomplishments of the many hundreds of successful and famous Americans in our book and unveil the Seven Secrets of Success that served them all so well. Just as the *New York Times* obituaries describe diverse kinds of success, so there are multiple paths that lead people there. But it is worth noting that some ambitions are more realistic than others. If your dream is to become a millionaire, you know that the IRS says that 14,500 Americans have a yearly income of a million or more and five million have assets of a million or more; this is proof that it is possible. You want to be a member of Congress? That's far, far tougher—there are only 535 people in the House and Senate at any given time.

Certain threads do run through many of the obituaries, basic life lessons that resonate long after you've read the stories. One thinks of Gaston the black millionaire businessman who began life in a shack, with almost nothing. His utterly simple life motto: "Start somewhere." Don't wait for things to happen. *Make* them happen. Or the words of a Motorola CEO: "Failure is not falling down. It is failing to get back up—quickly." The beauty of the obits is that one generally learns not just of a person's triumphs but of the rough spots and troughs, too. Again and again you see that sheer perseverance, whether trying new things or just sticking doggedly with the old, *can* get people through. When the young Ella Fitzgerald found her bebop singing career stalled, she re-created herself as a stylish interpreter of classic American tunes. Probably there is no more prominent example of perseverance than the man who occupies the top slot of our Overall Apex of Fame: President Richard F. Nixon. Forced to resign from the nation's highest office, over the next two decades, Nixon slowly but surely repaired his battered reputation by publishing a series of serious books about foreign affairs. By the time of his death, he had remade himself into a Grand Old Statesman.

Character, fortitude, and perseverance are all important qualities. They also imply a certain level of energy and determination. Successful people are often highly energetic. They dedicate more hours, take on more responsibility, churn out more ideas than their colleagues. Burt Lancaster was a successful movie star, but he launched his own production company to expand his professional prospects. Sheer energy enables the ambitious to juggle many roles at once and to foray into new realms. Most people have a natural drive to succeed, but those with unusual energy are more likely to accomplish their goals.

As this book makes abundantly clear, in America success, fame, and money—and the power that come with those—are concentrated in a small number of high-status occupations. While becoming a movie star or best-selling author requires no formal education or training, most high-status work does. Attracted to business, medicine, law, academics, government? Going to a top school will be most helpful but not required. Warren Burger earned degrees from the University of Minnesota and St. Paul College of Law (at night), both decent enough schools. His boyhood friend Harry Blackmun received a scholarship to Harvard, the nation's most prestigious school and then attended the powerhouse Harvard Law School. Blackmun had an elite education, Burger didn't. Both ended up on the U.S. Supreme Court. You can find numerous examples of those with an "ordinary" education achieving tremendous success. But the aggregate pattern shows the incredible advantage of the elite education. While only 1 percent of American undergraduates attend Ivy League schools, 23.1 percent of our database did. A top college or university exposes promising young people to a variety of possible careers, develops their intelligence, and provides mentors and—equally important—a set of friendships and contacts that can last a lifetime. And all trends indicate that more and better education is expected. In the 1999 *Forbes* issue on CEOs at the top eight hundred companies, 91 percent were college grads, while 56 percent held an advanced degree, usually an M.B.A.

What else does one notice about successful people? They generally operate out of important organizations or institutions. Someone high up at IBM or Yale University is almost always more impressive to the outside world than a lone individual. Institutions are proven sources of credibility, money, power, and reinforcement. Indeed, many powerful people have created their own firms, foundations, and schools. An inventor with his own flourishing company, such as Arnold Neustadter and his Rolodex products, will be viewed as a greater success than one who opts to work within a big corporation. Unless, of course, he is like Elmer Wavering, an inventor who spent his career at Motorola, where he developed the first practical car radio and the all-important automotive alternator. Wavering was a successful inventor who also rose to become the CEO of Motorola. Each took a different route, but each ended up with an institutional power base.

Felice Schwartz was another who used her organization to promote her goals. She was a working mother who felt that American companies should acknowledge the reality of families vis-à-vis the workplace. As a lone voice, she could be ignored. By founding an organization, Catalyst, that was dedicated to the issue of women and work, Schwartz became part of an institution whose pioneering studies and activities commanded attention and respect. Set up in 1962, Catalyst remains a force in this field even though its founder is gone.

This might also be the place to mention that success is often linked with a *lifetime* career. This is especially obvious in major corporations, where most top people have been with their company for decades and often their whole working life. But it is equally true in many other fields. Schwartz, for instance, spent decades developing and leading Catalyst. A person who has some success in his field, gets discouraged, and switches to other work is less likely to accumulate the expertise and confidence needed to rise to the top or make an impact. We see that with people in government: the more time served, the more knowledge, power, and contacts are accrued.

Some other observations on success: Location is important. You need to be in the right place to get started: If you want to be a movie star, you better move to Los Angeles, because that's where movies are made. Book publishing remains concentrated in Manhattan. Big-time lawyers tend to be clustered in power cities such as New York, Washington, D.C., and Los Angeles. If you're interested in government, spend time in Washington, D.C., in the belly of the beast. Cutting-edge medicine is conducted mainly at major medical schools. Academics are farther-flung, with first-rate campuses in many parts of the country.

Success is also partly a function of luck and circumstance. The currents of history run through many of our obits and are very much part of their fascination. In our database of people, there were two hugely influential historical events: the Depression but above all World War II. The Depression was generally a constrictor of opportunity, forcing a Gene Kelly into dancing or a Sam Aaron into the wine business when their college degrees yielded no other jobs. But World War II opened the world up as has little else in American history. Young men and women went forth, flung far and wide in extremely demanding circumstances. Millions who left home discovered talents and abilities they had never known they had—the ability to fly, to speak foreign languages, to manage thousands of men and tons of materials, to endure great privations, to inspire their fellow soldiers, to live far from home. In obit after obit, the war was the pivotal transforming event. James Michener wrote his first book, *Tales of the South Pacific*, while a soldier. Numerous inventors saw their creations make huge differences in the course of the war, with Day-Glo paints making possible night landing on aircraft carriers and advances in physics creating radar and the atomic bomb, the ultimate advantages. And then the G.I. Bill of Rights sent millions of veterans to college who otherwise would not have gone. Thomas Watson, Jr., went to war a playboy and returned a serious, seasoned veteran. World War II conferred a confidence and can-do attitude that transformed not just some men and women but a whole country. There are many in our obits for whom World War II turned out to be a catalytic event. Otherwise, they might well have lived out their lives in small towns, never having ventured forth, never having gone to college, and fulfilling a very different destiny. There is without question an element of luck and caprice in success.

Success sometimes translates into fame. But fame comes in many guises—local, national, and, of course, international. In some fields, such as acting and politics, fame is intimately tied to success. All actors and politicians—unlike doctors or scientists—aspire to be on the cover of *People* or *Time*. That means they've arrived and attracted high-profile attention from the media and the popular audience. Far more typical for successful people in non-media-dependent fields is low-level fame among their peers and colleagues. In the world of the Internet, Jonathon Postel was well known as one of the pioneers and the man who for thirty years handled the system for assigning Internet addresses. He was famous among certain techies, by most people unknown.

We showed the Apex of Fame for the university professors to some well-informed neighbors. They knew only one person on the list: astronomer Carl Sagan. Why? Because he had successfully sought national and even international popular fame through two time-tested methods: writing popular books and appearing frequently on TV. Sagan was that rare author whose books won important prizes—the Pulitzer, among others—but were also best-sellers. Books are important valida-tors of status and importance. They say to people that you have ideas or stories important enough to get published. Books make you known to wider circles and promote your agenda, whatever it may be.

But even a top best-selling book barely reaches a million or more people. Today, it's TV that really makes people famous. Contrast the million who read Sagan's books with the 400 million all over the world who watched the handsome astronomer on television in his ten-part PBS *Cosmos* series. Moreover, Sagan was a frequent guest on numer-ous television talk shows. Becoming famous—which these days almost always involves being on TV—means that you and your work have to be of interest to the general media. Columbia University economist William Vickery could interest few in his work on alleviating rush-hour congestion until he won the Nobel Prize. One suspects that the media glare would have subsided quickly, as traffic jams and economics do not enthrall mass audiences. Outer space and aliens—Sagan's pas-sions—do. And so popular fame in this day and age is to a great extent a function of what a mass audience—as the media interpret it—wants to see. Because Bill Gates, CEO of Microsoft Corporation, is now the richest man in America and has developed a product that is used by tens of millions (and reviled by many), he is the object of constant media scrutiny.

Not only do the media have to feel your work merits attention—space and aliens versus traffic jams—you personally have to come across well on the screen. An ugly mumbler has little hope of capturing an audience. Your physical person must be engaging, and you should know how to deliver pithy sound bites. This obviously excludes a great many accomplished people. But it helps explain why Carl Sagan became so famous: He was handsome in a telegenic way and exuded a warm intelligence. He had completely mastered the medium and knew how to communicate. These abilities made him world-famous.

Consequently, our Overall Apex of Fame is heavily weighted toward people seen by tens of millions on their TV or movie screens. Thus we find no businesspeople, no inventors, no engineers, no accountants, no generals, no nurses. What we do see is that the *New York Times* has generally followed its own stated inclinations when it runs an all-out front-page obit: it focuses on the most powerful and creative people. And so there are many actors, entertainers, authors, athletes, and government servants, whether politicians or Supreme Court judges. Three are major cultural figures: Dr. Spock, Allen Ginsburg, and Alger Hiss. There is one journalist, *Times* mandarin James Reston; one artist, Willem de Kooning; and one philanthropist, Paul Mellon. And then there is Jackie Kennedy, third on the list as JFK's widow and all-around icon of elegance and wealth. Most of these people are quite familiar—let us say famous—to regular TV watchers.

One of the mysteries of fame is why some people's fame is so lasting. Which of these folks will still be famous a century from now? Andrew Carnegie and John D. Rockefeller created lasting monuments with their vast wealth. Carnegie left behind numerous foundations, a university, and a famous concert hall in New York City, all of which have kept his name alive. Rockefeller bequeathed the nation a famous university, a foundation, and a celebrated piece of Manhattan real estate, as well as ambitious descendants who have kept the family name in the headlines. Money can create fame (think of all the politicians like Ross Perot and Malcolm Forbes who spent millions of dollars to become public figures, even if they never did manage to get elected to office), and money properly applied can go a long way to ensuring fame in posterity.

Many people have asked as we have gone along whether one can say anything about the success of those in our database as people. Were they better husbands or kinder parents? The *New York Times* is really in the business of summing up life accomplishments, rather than judging who was a good person. Only about a fifth of the time was there even any active comment in the obituaries on people's qualities as human beings. So there is really no way to render collective judgment. Even reading individual obituaries, one is usually left to guess. Multiple marriages may provide clues, but there is little else to go by.

Fame at Last provides a landscape of success and fame in America. Through the daily obits, one meets an amazing group of accomplished people. Through the database, patterns and trends emerge that help explain their success and fame. Where did these outstanding businessmen, lawyers, movie stars, professors, and politicians work? Where did they go to school? What happened in their lives? How did their lives affect ours? The obits cannot give definitive answers, because human lives and society are too complex, but they do provide real stories of real people along with basic information that can inform, guide, and inspire as we too make our way through the journey that is life.

Appendix A-1

Occupational Groups in the U.S. Workforce and the Obituary Database

Occupation	U.S. Workforce		Obituary Database	
	Number	Percent	Number	Percent
I. Management	17,186,000	13.8	2,596	31.4
II. Professions	18,132,000	14.5	5,567	67.3
1. Architects	163,000	0.1	73	0.9
2. Engineers	1,934,000	1.5	108	1.3
3. Mathematicians and computer scientists	1,195,000	1.0	10	0.1
4. Natural scientists	519,000	0.4	108	1.3
5. Physicians and dentists	848,000	0.7	175	2.1
6. Other health care professionals	2,762,000	2.2	23	0.3
7. College professors	846,000	0.7	1,136	13.7
8. Teachers	4,507,000	3.6	59	0.7
9. Counselors	236,000	0.2	9	0.1
10. Librarians	211,000	0.2	107	1.3
11. Social scientists	260,000	0.2	20	0.2
12. Social and religious workers	1,303,000	1.0	174	2.1
13. Lawyers and judges	926,000	0.7	486	5.9
14. Writers, artists, entertainers, and athletes	2,054,000	1.6	3,079	37.2

Occupation	U.S. Workforce		Obituary Database	
	Number	**Percent**	**Number**	**Percent**
III. Technical, sales, and support staff	37,417,000	30.0	22	0.3
IV. Service occupations	16,930,000	13.6	54	0.7
V. Precise production and craft	13,524,000	10.8	0	0
VI. Machine operators and laborers	18,068,000	14.5	14	0.2
VII. Farm, forestry, and fishing	3,642,000	2.9	15	0.2
Total	**124,899,000**	**100.0**	**8,268**	**100.0**

Note: Of the 9,325 men and women in the obituary database, 8,268 were in the U.S. workforce and 1,057 were not. This latter group includes philanthropists, housewives, and military personnel.

Source: Statistical Abstract of the United States, 1996, Table 637.

Appendix A-2

The 176 Millionaires
in the Obituary Database

Name	Age	Obituary Date	Company or Career
George Abbott	107	02/02/1995	Broadway producer, director
John Alessio	87	04/05/1998	Banking; racetrack
Albert Alkek	85	03/06/1995	Alkek Oil Corp.
Charles Allen, Jr.	91	07/17/1994	Allen & Co.
Herbert Allen, Sr.	88	01/23/1997	Allen & Co.
Nathan Ancell	90	06/03/1999	Ethan Allen Co.
Gene Autry	91	10/03/1998	Actor; businessman
William Batten	89	01/27/1999	J.C. Penney/NY Stock Exchange
Joseph Baum	78	10/06/1998	Restaurant Associates
Dave Beck	99	12/28/1993	Teamsters Union
Jeffrey Beck	48	01/31/1995	Drexel Burnham Lambert
Melvin Belli	88	07/11/1996	Lawyer
James Bender	92	11/28/1997	Education; investments
Louis Berger	82	08/19/1996	The Berger Group
Philip Berman	82	12/01/1997	Trucking; Hess's
Zalman Bernstein	72	01/09/1999	Sanford C. Bernstein & Co.
Jack Berry	81	11/30/1997	Citrus baron
John Berry, Sr.	75	05/23/1998	Berry Co.
Erma Bombeck	69	04/23/1996	Columnist/author
Julius Boros	74	05/30/1994	Golfer
George Burns	100	03/10/1996	Actor
Thomas Cabot	98	06/10/1995	Cabot Corp.
William Cafaro	84	04/25/1998	Cafaro Co.
Curtis Carlson	84	02/22/1999	Carlson Co.
Edward Carter	84	04/27/1996	Carter Hawley Hale Stores

Don Clayton	70	04/18/1996	Putt-Putt Golf and Games
Jerry Cohen	70	01/01/1996	Lawyer
Jerry Collins	89	08/06/1997	Racetrack owner
Jack Cooke	84	04/07/1997	Sports team owner
Ann Corio	85	03/09/1999	Actress
Howard Cosell	77	04/24/1995	Sports broadcaster
Hugh Culverhouse	75	08/26/1994	Lawyer; real estate developer
Goerge Dade	85	05/29/1998	Dade Brothers
Shelby Davis	85	06/01/1994	S. C. Davis & Co.
Thomas Davis	81	04/24/1999	Piedmont Airlines
Edward DeBartolo	85	12/20/1994	Edward J. Bartolo Corp.
Hugo de Neufville	90	08/11/1996	Amax
Marion Donovan	81	11/18/1998	Inventor
Seymour Durst	81	05/20/1995	Durst Organization
John Eckman	74	12/20/1993	Rorer Group
Benjamin Eisenstadt	89	04/10/1996	Sweet 'N Low
Alpheus Ellis	89	10/31/1995	Ellis Banking Corp.
Thomas Evans, Sr.	86	07/18/1997	H. K. Porter
Abraham Feinberg	90	12/07/1998	Kayser Roth Corp.
Ben Feldman	81	11/10/1993	New York Life Insurance
Irving Felt	84	09/24/1994	Madison Square Garden Corp.
Avery Fisher	87	02/27/1994	Fisher Radio/Philharmonic
Mel Fisher	76	12/21/1998	Treasure hunter
Zachary Fisher	88	06/05/1999	Fisher Brothers Real Estate
Patrick Frawley, Jr.	75	11/09/1998	Schick
Samuel Fuller	85	11/01/1997	Film director
Betty Furness	78	04/04/1994	Consumer reporter
A. Gaston	103	01/20/1996	Entrepreneur
Harold Geneen	87	11/23/1997	ITT Corp.
Roberto Goizueta	65	10/19/1997	Coca-Cola
John Goldwater	83	03/02/1999	Archie Comic Publications
Linda Goodman	70	10/25/1995	Writer/astrologer
J. Grace	81	04/21/1995	W. R. Grace & Co.
Jerome Greene	93	05/30/1999	New York City law firm

Arnold Habig	91	04/08/1999	Kimball International
John Hadley	64	11/10/1994	Michigan-California Lumber Co.
Vivian Hallinan	88	03/19/1999	Real estate (her own)
John Hanson	88	06/29/1996	Winnebago
Phil Hartman	49	05/29/1998	Comedian/actor
Ira Hechler	80	04/10/1999	Ira J. Hechler & Associates
Harry Helmsley	87	01/06/1997	Helmsley-Spear
Buddy Hirsch	88	10/27/1997	Horse trainer
Jerold Hoffberger	80	04/13/1999	National Brewing Company
Anne Hummert	91	07/21/1996	Soap opera creator
Ted Hustead	96	01/17/1999	Wall Drug Store
Robert Irsay	73	01/15/1997	Indianapolis Colts; heating and AC
David Jackson	96	12/23/1998	Jackson & Segal
Dennis James	79	06/06/1997	Announcer, host
George Jenkins	88	04/10/1996	Publix Supermarkets
Peter Joseph	47	06/26/1998	Rosecliff
Irving Kahn	76	01/25/1994	TelePrompTer Corp.
Fred Kassner	71	10/08/1998	Liberty Travel
Howard Keck	83	12/17/1996	Superior Oil
William Kelly	92	01/08/1998	Kelly Services
Sarah Korein	93	11/04/1998	Real estate investor
M. Lawrence	69	01/11/1996	Entrepreneur, real estate
Jules Lederer	81	01/23/1999	Budget Rent-a-Car
Daniel Lehner	49	06/05/1997	In-flight newspapers and magazines
Henry Leir	98	07/18/1998	Continental Ore Corp.
Jerome Lemelson	74	10/04/1997	Inventor
Alexander Levine	82	09/06/1994	Levco Shopping Centers
William Levitt	86	01/29/1994	Levitt & Sons
Sydney Lewis	79	03/16/1999	Best Products
Albert Lippert	72	03/03/1998	Weight Watchers
Harry Lipsig	93	08/13/1995	Lawyer
Richard Long	46	07/20/1996	GT Bicycles
David Longaberger	64	03/22/1999	Longaberger Co.
Edward Lowe	75	10/06/1995	Kitty Litter

Robert Luby	88	08/15/1998	Luby's Cafeteria
Charles Luckman	89	01/28/1999	Luckman Partnership
John Lusk	91	03/09/1999	Lusk Company
B. Magness	72	11/18/1996	Tele-Communciations Inc.
Paul Manheim	93	01/08/1999	Lehman Brothers
J. Marshall	90	08/08/1995	Koch Industries
Reuben Mattus	81	01/29/1994	Häagen-Dazs
H. McCarty, Jr.	76	06/14/1998	McCarty Farms
Richard McDonald	89	07/16/1998	McDonald's
Arthur Metcalf	88	03/19/1997	Electronics Corp. of America
James Michener	90	10/17/1997	Author
Robert Miner	52	11/17/1994	Oracle Corp.
Morton Mitosky	91	02/06/1999	Lawyer; Broadway investor
Arnold Neustadter	85	04/19/1996	Zephyr American Corp.
Theodore Newhouse	95	11/29/1998	Newhouse Newspapers
Glenn Nielson	95	11/05/1998	Husky Oil Co.
Spencer Olin	96	04/12/1995	Olin Corp.
Donald Othmer	91	11/03/1995	Engineer; inventor
Reece Overcash, Jr.	68	01/18/1995	Associates Corp. of North America
Ara Oztemel	71	02/09/1998	Satra Trading Co.
David Packard	83	03/27/1996	Hewlett-Packard
Michael Palm	47	08/14/1998	Center Re
Frank Pasquirilla	72	04/27/1999	Crown American Realty Trust
Milton Petrie	92	11/08/1994	Petrie Stores Corp.
J. Phifer	82	10/28/1998	Phifer Wire Products
Jesse Philips	80	12/02/1994	Philips Industries
Martha Philips	98	09/10/1996	Fashion retailer
Kenneth Pontikes	54	06/26/1994	Comdisco
Victor Potamkin	83	06/07/1995	Cadillac dealership
Eugene Power	88	12/09/1993	University Microfilm
Lewis Preston	68	05/06/1995	J. P. Morgan
Karl Prindle	95	10/22/1998	DuPont Chemist
Jay Pritzker	76	01/24/1999	Hyatt Hotels
Samuel Rappaport	64	09/10/1994	Real estate speculator

Beze Rebozo	85	05/10/1998	Real estate developer; banker
Jheri Redding	91	03/21/1998	Nexxus; Jhirmack; Redken
Orville Redenbacher	88	09/20/1995	Red Bow Popcorn
Dorothy Rivkin	85	08/08/1998	Dale Carnegie Training Co.
Mary Roebling	89	10/27/1994	National State Bank
Ginger Rogers	83	04/26/1995	Actress/dancer
Ralph Rogers	87	11/06/1997	Texas Industries
Roy Rogers	86	07/07/1998	Actor
Richard Rosenthal	82	06/17/1998	Citizens Utilities
James Rouse	81	04/10/1996	James W. Rouse & Co.
James Ryder	83	03/27/1997	Ryder System
Carl Sagan	62	12/21/1996	Astronomer/TV series host
Lawrence Sanders	78	02/12/1998	Novelist
Alex Schoenbaum	81	12/15/1996	Shoney's Restaurants
George Schultz	77	06/21/1994	Shulton
John Shad	71	07/09/1994	E. F. Hutton & Co.
Sol Shank	83	09/01/1994	Consolidated Stores Corp.
Martin Shugrue	58	03/12/1999	Eastern; Pan Am Airways
Luther Simjian	92	11/02/1997	Reflectone
Frank Sinatra	82	05/16/1998	Singer/actor
Ross Siragusa	89	04/03/1996	Admiral Corp.
Red Skelton	89	09/18/1997	Actor/clown
C. Smith	97	06/11/1996	Westgate-California Corp.
David Smith	67	03/01/1999	Praxis Biologics
Carl Sontheimer	83	03/26/1998	Cuisinart
Benjamin Spock	94	03/17/1998	Author; physician
Dawn Steel	51	12/22/1997	Columbia; Paramount
Ernst Steifel	89	09/07/1997	Lawyer
Wallace Steinberg	61	07/29/1995	Healthcare Investment Group
James Stewart	89	07/03/1997	Actor
Marvin Stone	89	02/22/1999	Stone Container Corp.
S. Taper	92	12/17/1994	First Charter Financial Corp
Arthur Taubman	92	03/22/1994	Advance Stores
Milton Taylor	86	11/09/1994	Caswell-Massey Pharmacy

John Tigrett	85	05/27/1999	Entrepreneur
Elizabeth Tilberis	51	04/22/1999	*Harper's Bazaar*
Rose Totino	79	06/23/1994	Totino's Pizza
Fred Trump	93	06/26/1999	Trump Management Co.
James Walton	73	03/22/1995	Wal-Mart Stores
Louis Ward	76	02/13/1996	Russell Stover Candies
Thomas Watson, Jr.	79	01/01/1994	IBM
Frederick Weisman	82	09/13/1994	Hunt Foods
Frank Wells	62	04/05/1994	Walt Disney Co.
Leighton Wilkie	93	12/16/1993	DoAll Group
Flip Wilson	64	11/27/1998	Comedian; TV host
Charles Wohlstetter	85	05/25/1995	Contel
William Wrigley	66	03/12/1999	William Wrigley Jr. Co.
Tammy Wynette	55	04/08/1998	Singer
Morris Zale	93	03/11/1995	Zale Corp.

Index

Aaron, Sam, 362–363
Abascal, Ralph S., 256
Abbott, George, 36,
    298, 394
Abernathy, Ralph, 79
Abzug, Bella, 58, 244
Adair, Peter, 304
Adams, Elizabeth, 270,
    273–274
Adams, Leon D.,
    363–364
Ahmad, Eqbal, 118
Alessio, John, 394
Al-Jundi, Akil, 271
Alkek, Albert, 394
Allen, Jr., Charles, 394
Allen, Sr., Herbert, 394
Allen, Charles, 195
Altman, Florence
    Skelly, 54
Ameche, Don, 284
Amerine, Maynard,
    358–359
Amory, Cleveland, 150
Ancell, Nathan, 394
Annabella, 290
Anselmo, Rene, 186–187
Ardolino, Emile, 302
Astaire, Fred, 300
Atanasoff, John V.,
    328, 338
Atwood, John, 172
Auerbach, Oscar, 94, 103
Autry, Gene, 36, 284, 394
Ayres, Lew, 286
Bagley, Ben, 300
Bainbridge, Kenneth, 117,
    119–120
Ballantine, Bill, 286

Ballantine, Ian, 141,
    143–144
Barr, Joel, 267, 270
Bartels, John R., 230
Barton, Derek H. R., 119
Baruch, Jr., Bernard, 2
Bass, Saul, 304
Batten, William. M., 191,
    192–193, 394
Baum, Joseph, 36, 347,
    348, 349, 364, 394
Beck, Dave, 268, 270, 394
Beck, Jeffrey P., 394
Beck, Robert A., 190
Belin, David W., 256
Bell, Marion, 290
Belli, Melvin, 38,
    254–256, 258, 394
Bender, James, 394
Beplat, Tristan E., 192
Berger, Louis, 394
Berger, Stuart M., 154
Berman, Pandro, 296, 298,
    300–301, 304–305
Berman, Philip, 394
Bernbaum, Glenn,
    352–353
Bernstein, Zalman C., 22,
    23, 25, 34, 192, 394
Berry, Sr., John William,
    185, 394
Berry, Jack M., 31, 32, 34
Berry, Richard, 77
Bianco, Nicholas, 270
Bing, Rudolf, 302
Bishop, Hazel, 326
Black, Fischer, 192
Blackmun, Harry A., 13,
    230, 238–239, 386

Blackstone, Jr., Harry., 286
Blaine, Vivian, 290
Blevins, James V, 172
Bloch, Irwin, 270,
    272–273
Blumkin, Rose, 63
Blyden, Herbert, 271
Bombeck, Erma, 26–28,
    34, 394
Bonica, John J.,
    97–98, 111
Bono, Sonny, 244
Boros, Julius, 394
Bradley, Owen, 300
Bradley, Tom, 76
Branscomb, Harvie,
    135–136
Brennan, Jr., William, 13,
    227–230, 234–236
Breslin, James E. B., 132
Bridges, Lloyd, 286
Broccoli, Albert, 300
Brodkey, Harold, 162
Brodsky, Joseph, 162
Brown, Bennett A., 192
Brown, Robert, 271
Brown, Ronald, 76
Brownstein, Samuel C.,
    153, 155
Bruckmann, Donald, 192
Brugger, Kenneth D.,
    381–382
Bryant, Betty, 290
Bunting-Smith, Mary, 136
Burger, Warren E., 13,
    230, 235–236, 238, 386
Burke, James, 270,
    274–275
Burnett, Michael, 271

Burnham, Helen Billings, 230, 241–242
Burns, Georg, 36, 284, 377, 394
Burroughs, William S., 162
Buscaglia, Leo, 156–157
Bush-Brown, Albert, 137
Butterfield, L. Joseph, 94
Cabot, Thomas, 394
Cafaro, William, 394
Calderone, Mary S., 59, 94
Calloway, Cab, 77
Camras, Marvin, 328, 333–334
Cantor, B. Gerald, 190
Carlson, Curtis L., 172, 394
Carlson, Violet, 288
Carmichael, Stokely, 76
Carret, Philip, 190
Carson, Johnny, 124
Carter, Betty, 77
Carter, Edward, 394
Castaneda, Carlos, 150
Cater, Douglass, 136
Cates, Joseph, 300
Cave, Vernal G., 94
Chagra, Joseph, 271, 278
Chalmers, Thomas C., 110
Chandler, Dorothy, 204, 212–213
Chandrasekhar, Subrahmanyan, 118
Cheatham, Doc, 76
Chenault, M. W., 271, 277
Clarie, T. Emmet, 232
Clark, Dane, 286
Clark, Patrick, 350–351
Clarke, John Henrik, 119
Clarke, Shirley, 298
Claster, Nancy, 290
Clayton, Don, 189–190, 395

Cleaver, Eldridge, 76
Clifford, Clark M., 14, 254, 256
Coe, Jacques, 192
Cohen, Jerry S., 258, 262–263, 395
Cohen, Morris, 266–267, 270
Colbert, Claudette, 58, 288
Coleman, James, 121–123
Coleman, Thomas, 271
Collazo, Oscar, 270
Colley, Russell, 326
Collins, Jerry, 395
Commager, Henry Steele, 118
Conrad, Clyde L., 270
Cooke, Jack Kent, 38, 395
Cooley III, Robert, 258
Cooper, Irving Ben, 230
Copp, Jim, 300
Corio, Ann, 38, 288, 395
Cornfeld, Bernard, 192
Cosby, Bill   000
Cosell, Howard, 38, 395
Cotten, Joseph, 284
Cray, Seymour, 172, 326, 340–342
Creel, Dana, 222
Crockett, George W, 244
Crowley, Daniel J. 118, 371–372
Culverhouse, Hugh, 395
Cummings, Walter J., 232
Cunanan, Andrew, 271
Cyert, Richard M., 137
Dade, George, 210–211, 395
Dalrymple, Jean, 59, 298
Daly, T. F. Gilroy, 232
Davies, Jack, 360–361
Davies, Ronald N., 232

Davis, Philip, 258
Davis, Shelby, 395
Davis, Thomas H., 32–33, 172, 395
de Kooning, Willem, 13, 390
de Menil, Dominique, 209
de Neufville, Hugo, 395
de Rothschild, Batsheva, 204
DeBartolo, Edward, 395
DeCalvacante, Simone, 270, 275
Delany, Bessie, 77
Delany, Sadie, 58, 76
Deming, W. Edwards, 183–185
Dichter, Misha, 87
Dicke, Robert, 118
Dickerson, Nancy, 60
Dickey, James, 162
Diggs, Jr., Charles C., 244
Dilworth, J. Richardson, 204
DiMaggio, Joe, 13
Disney, Walt, 2
Donovan, Marion, 326, 334–335, 395
Douglas, Marjory, 59, 150
DuBridge, Lee Alvin, 138
Duke, Sr., Lawrence D, 232
Duke, Doris, 58, 202, 204
Durst, Seymour, 38, 395
Dyson, Charles H., 192
East, Catherine, 64
Eccles, Peter W.., 192
Eckert, J. Presper, 326, 339–340
Eckman, John, 395
Edel, Leon, 118
Edey, Winthrop K., 378–379
Edwards, Ben, 302

Ehrlichman, John D., 254, 256

Eisenstadt, Benjamin, 21, 22–23, 25, 35, 328, 395

Eisner, Robert, 119

Elion, Gertrude, 106–107

Elliott, Carl, 246

Ellis, Alpheus, 395

Ellis, Edward Robb, 382–383

Ellison, Ralph, 76, 161–162

Epstein, Diane, 65–66

Epstein, Joseph, 15

Erdos, Paul, 118

Evans, David, 326, 343

Evans, Sr., Thomas Mellon, 190, 197, 395

Fascell, Dante B., 246

Faubus, Orval   000

Faye, Alice, 288

Feder, Abe, 300, 302

Feinberg, Abraham, 395

Felder, Rodney O., 137

Feldman, Ben, 29–30, 395

Felt, Irving, 395

Fenneman, George, 286

Fields, Bernard, 94

Fish, Jr., Hamilton, 246

Fisher, Ada Louise Sipuel, 69–70

Fisher, Avery, 38, 204, 216– 218, 395

Fisher, Mel, 34–35, 395

Fisher, Zachary, 38, 202, 204, 395

Fitzgerald, Ella, 14, 58, 75–78

Fitzgerald, William Burwell, 80–81, 192

Fitzhugh, Gilbert, 192

Fleischman, Lawrence A., 204

Fletcher, James, 192

Flood, Curt, 82–83

Flood, Daniel J., 268–270, 272

Forte, Chet, 304

Fosdick, Dorothy, 250–251

Fowler, Jr., Gene, 304

Foxx, Red, 28

Franey, Pierre, 150, 355–357

Frankfurter, Felix, 2

Franklin, Aretha, 80

Frann, Mary, 290

Frawley, Jr., Patrick, 395

Friedman, Harold, 270

Friendly, Fred, 313–315

Frooks, Dorothy, 258

Fuchsberg, Jacob D., 232

Fulbright, J. William, 14, 244, 249–250

Fuller, Samuel, 38, 302, 304, 306–307, 395

Fulton, John, 374–375

Furness, Betty, 395

Gabrielli, Domenick, 232

Gaddis, William, 162

Gallati, Robert R. J., 326, 344–345

Gallo, Dean, 246

Garcia, Hector Perez, 94

Garfinkel, Stanley, 298

Garon, Jay S., 165

Garson, Greer, 59, 288, 312

Gaston, A.G., 78–79, 395

Gellhorn, Martha, 50, 59

Geneen, Harold S., 38, 172, 181–183, 395

Gill, Brendan, 162

Ginsberg, Allen, 14, 162, 390

Githens, William, 298

Gitlin, Paul, 147–148

Givens, Charles, 270, 273

Goelet, Francis, 204, 218

Goizueta, Roberto C., 36, 172, 178–181, 395

Goldberg, Harold, 192

Goldstein, Leon M., 137

Goldwater, Barry, 13, 244

Goldwater, John, 38, 395

Goodman, Linda, 34, 155–156, 395

Gordon, Archer, 100

Gore, Sr., Albert, 246

Gould, Laurence M., 136

Gould, Milton S., 256

Gould, Samuel B., 137

Grace, J., 395

Granz, Norman, 77

Green, Hannah, 160–161

Green, Joseph, 298

Green, Julian, 162

Greenberg, Florence, 300

Greene, Jerome, 395

Guthrie, Robert , 92–93

Habig, Arnold, 396

Hacker, Andrew, 24, 84, 96, 120, 174

Hadley, John, 396

Hall, John W.., 119, 131–132

Halle, Kay, 48

Hallinan, Vivian, 396

Halperin, Maurice H., 270

Halpern, Seymour, 246

Hamming, Richard, 326

Hampton, Henry, 298

Hanff, Helene, 162

Hanford, William E., 328, 336–337

Hansen Austin, 77

Hanson, John K., 189, 396

Harriman, Pamela, 46–48, 51, 58

Harrington, Sybil, 204

Hartman, Phil, 38, 284, 396

Harvey, A. McGehee, 109

Hatcher, Harlan H, 134, 137
Haydon, Julie, 290
Hazen, Lita Annenberg, 204, 220–221
Head, Murdock, 269–270, 272
Hearne, Paul G., 258
Hechler, Ira J., 192, 396
Helmsley, Harry, 36, 396
Hemphill, Jr., Herbert Waide, 209–210
Hess, Leon, 172
Hewlett, William, 24
Higginbotham, Jr.,A. Leon, 77, 230
Hirsch, Buddy, 396
Hirshon, Dorothy H., 48, 204
Hiss, Alger, 13, 267, 270, 313, 390
Hitchings, George H., 106–107
Hobby, Oveta Culp, 58
Hofberger, Jerold, 396
Hoffman, Walter E., 232
Holmes, Hamilton E., 74–75, 94, 240
Hooker, Janet A., 204
Horne, Marilyn, 86
Horowitz, Wanda Toscanini, 48–49
Horsky, Charles A., 258
Hotson, John 2
Howell, Mary, 9, 54–55
Hubert, Karen 349
Huggins, Charles B., 94, 104–105
Hummert, Anne, 298, 396
Huncke, Herbert, 271
Hunter, Ross, 300
Hunter-Gault, Charlayne, 74, 240
Hustead, Ted, 396

Irsay, Robert 396
Ives, Burl, 284
Jackson, David, 396
Jacobs, Bernard B., 298
Jaffe, Leo, 204
James, Dennis, 309–310, 396
Jeakins, Dorothy, 300, 302
Jenkins, George, 396
Johnson, Harald N., 94
Johnson, Helene, 77, 162
Johnson, Lyndon B., 60, 84–85, 248
Johnson, Reynold, 328, 341–342
Jones, Jr., Bob., 136
Jones, Evan, 357
Jordan, Barbara, 58, 76, 85–86, 244
Joseph, Peter, 396
Joyner, Florence Griffith, 59, 76
Judd, Winnie R., 271, 279–280
Julia, Raul, 286
Junkins, Jerry R., 172
Kahn, Irving, 396
Kallinger, Joseph, 271, 278–279
Kanin, Garson, 302
Kaplan, Helen, 94
Karl, Max H., 192
Kassner, Fred, 396
Katsh, Abraham I., 119
Katzenbogen, Francine, 379–380
Katzman, Leonard, 320
Kazin, Alfred, 162
Keane, Noel, 258
Keck, Howard B., 396
Keller, Helen, 2, 46
Kelly, Gene, 14, 293–294, 388
Kelly, William, 396

Kemp, Jr., Evan J., 258
Kennedy, John F., 43, 58, 60, 84, 252
Kennedy, Rose, 58
Kerley, Ellis R., 119
Kidd, David, 369–371
Kildall, Gary, 326, 342–343
Kiley, Richard, 284
King, Jr., Martin Luther, 2, 79–80, 277–278
Kinsley, Michael, 1–2
Kirk, Grayson, 136
Kirk, Russell, 146–147
Kirstein, Lincoln, 302
Klein, Paul L., 321
Knowles, Legh, 360
Knudsen, Semon, 172
Knutson, Coya, 246
Koenen, Austin, 192
Komarovsky, Mirra, 118
Korein, Sarah, 33, 36, 59, 396
Korshak, Sidney, 256, 270, 276
Koshland, William, 354
Krainik, Ardis, 302
Krim, Arthur, 256
Kroc, Ray, 25–26, 364
Krugman, Saul, 91
Kubrick, Stanley, 300, 302
Kuhn, Thomas, 119
Kunstler, William, 256, 259–260
Kuralt, Charles, 315–316
Lambert, Marie, 56–57, 230
Lamour, Dorothy, 288
Lancaster, Burt 284, 294–295, 310, 386
Langmuir, Alexander, 94, 110–111
Lasker, Mary, 204, 219–220

Lathen, Emma, 158
Latsis, Mary Jane, 159
Lawrence, M., 396
Lawrence, Rosina, 290
Lazard, Wardell R., 77, 190
Learson, T. Vincent, 172, 175–176
Lederer, Jules, 396
Leff, James J., 232
Lehner, Daniel, 396
Leir, Henry, 396
Lemelson, Jerome, 326, 330–331, 396
Leonard, Buck, 77
Leontief, Wassily, 118
LeVeen, Harry H., 99
Levin, Morton L., 102–103
Levine, Alexander, 396
Levitt William, 38, 396
Lewis, Henry, 76, 86–87
Lewis, Janet, 162
Lewis, John 80
Lewis, Ramsey, 80
Lewis, Robert, 302
Lewis, Shari, 288
Lewis, Sydney, 396
Lichtenstein, Roy, 14
Liman, Arthur L., 256
Lindbergh, Charles, 32, 211
Lindley, Audra, 290
Link, Arthur, 119
Lippert, Albert, 365–366, 396
Lippincott, J. Gordon, 172
Lipsig, Harry, 260–261, 396
Loeb, Henry A., 192, 204
Loeb, Sr., John L., 190
Long, Richard, 396
Longaberger, David, 172, 396

Lopata, Sam, 351–352
Lord Annan 5
Lord, Jack, 286
Lortel, Lucille, 58, 204, 298
Louis, Jean, 302
Lowe, Edward, 19–20, 22, 25, 326, 396
Loy, Myrna, 288
Luby, Robert, 397
Luckman, Charles, 38, 397
Lukas, J. Anthony, 152–153, 162
Lumbard, Jr., J. Edward, 232
Lupino, Ida, 290
Lusk, John, 397
Magness, B. J., 318, 397
Malle, Louis 295
Manheim, Paul, 397
Manoogian, Alex, 172
Mantle, Mickey, 13
Marciano, Rocky, 82
Margolis, Ben, 256
Marshall, E. G., 284
Marshall, J., 397
Marshall, Thurgood, 69, 252
Marston, Robert Q., 137
Martin, David B. H., 252–253
Martin, Dean, 284
Martin, Louis E., 251–252
Martini, Louis P, 361–362
Mattus, Reuben, 397
Mauchly, John W., 339
Maxim, Joey, 81, 82
Maxwell, Vera, 52, 53
McCarthy, Michael W., 194–195
McCarty, Jr., H., 397
McDonald, Maurice, 25
McDonald, Richard, 25–26, 40, 364, 397

McDowall, Roddy, 286
McElroy, William, 137
McGill, William, 136
McGivern, Owen, 230
McHenry Dean E. 137
McKean, Hugh F., 136
McLamore, J. W., 364
McLaughlin, Leo, 137
McMahon, Thomas 115
McMurry, Lillian, 298
McQueen, Butterfly, 288
Meadows, Audrey, 288, 310–311
Mehta, Zubin, 86
Mellon, Paul, 14, 201–204, 206–207, 209, 390
Menuhin, Yehudi, 14
Meredith, Burgess, 284
Metcalf, Arthur, 397
Metzger, Juan, 172
Metzger, Michael, 271
Meyers, Stephen, 263–264
Michener, James A., 36, 149–150, 152, 388, 397
Mills, Victor, 326, 335
Milne, Christopher Robin, 5
Miner, Robert, 397
Mitchum, Robert, 284
Mitford, Jessica, 150
Mitosky, Morton, 397
Monk, Julius, 298
Moody, Helen Wills, 59
Moore, Archie 76, 81, 82
Moreno, Wenceslao, 286
Morris, Robert J., 256
Moses, Gilbert, 304
Moss, Calrton, 300
Moss, Jeffrey, 150
Moss, John E., 244
Motley, Marion, 77
Murphy, Joseph, 137
Murphy, Thomas, 230

Murray, Jerome, 326, 331–332
Muskie, Edmund S., 244
Nabrit, Jr., James M., 77, 136
Natcher, William, 246
Natwick, Mildred, 290
Nelson, Ralph L., 213
Neu, Harold C., 94
Neustadter, Arnold, 323–324, 328, 397
Newhouse, Theodore, 397
Nielson, Glenn, 397
Nixon, Richard M., 12–13, 85, 235–237, 385
Nizer, Louis 256
Noyce, Elizabeth Bottomley, 204, 222–224
O'Brien, Mark, 90
O'Dwyer, Paul, 256
O'Neill, Jr, Thomas P., 243–244, 246–249
O'Sullivan, Maureen, 288
Obletz, Peter E., 304
Olin, Spencer, 397
Oliphant, Jack, 271
Olney, Richard, 355
Onassis, Jacqueline Kennedy, 13, 43, 46–47, 52, 58, 254, 261, 353–354, 390
Ong, Benny, 270, 274
Orr, Alice Greenough, 375–376
Osrow, Harold, 326, 329–330, 334
Othmer, Donald, 397
Overcash, Jr., Reece, 397
Oztemel, Ara, 397
Packard, David, 23–24, 38, 172, 397
Packard, Vance, 150
Pakula, Alan J., 302

Palm, Michael, 397
Paredes, Americo, 119
Parrish, Robert, 304
Paschal, Robert H., 80
Pasquerilla, Frank, 397
Patterson, Floyd 000
Patton, Arch, 198, 199
Pauling, Linus, 118
Pearl, Minnie, 290
Penick, Harvey 000
Perkins, James A., 136
Perlman, Itzhak, 87
Perry, Frank, 304
Peterson, Roger Tory, 150
Petrie, Milton, 204, 397
Phifer, J. Reese, 35, 397
Philips, Jesse, 397
Phillips, Martha, 397
Plunkett, Roy J., 328, 336–337
Pollack, Michael L., 94, 101–102
Polykoff, Shirley, 188
Pontikes, Kenneth N., 397
Postel, Jonathan B., 326, 345
Potamkin, Victor, 397
Powell, Jr., Lewis, 13, 230, 236–238
Power, Eugene, 397
Powers, J. F., 162
Pregel, Alexander, 172
Preston, Lewis T., 190, 195, 196, 397
Price, Eugenia, 157–158
Prindle, Karl E., 326, 397
Pritzker, Jay, 172, 397
Proctor, Haydn, 232
Provost, Daniel E., 172
Quintero, Jose, 302
Rabb, Ellis, 286
Ragano, Frank, 270
Railey, Suzanne, 372–373
Randolph, Jennings, 246

Rappaport, Samuel, 397
Ray, James Earl, 271, 277–278
Raye, Martha, 288
Rebozo, Bebe, 38, 398
Redding, Jheri, 172, 398
Redding, Louis L., 258
Redenbacher, Orville, 398
Regnery, Henry, 146
Rene, Norman, 304
Reston, James, 13, 390
Rewald, John, 119
Rey, Margaret E., 164
Ribicoff, Abraham A., 244
Rich, Giles S., 230
Richey, Charles R., 232
Riding, Laura, 5
Ridley, Walter, 70–72, 136
Riese, Murray, 364–365
Rifkind, Simon, 256, 261–262
Ringel, William, 232
Rivkin, Dorothy, 398
Robbins, Harold, 147, 150
Robbins, Jerome, 13
Robinson III, Spottswood W., 77, 256
Rockefeller, Mary C., 59
Rodriguez, Irwin Flores 270
Roebling, Mary, 50–51, 192, 398
Rogers, Buddy, 286
Rogers, Ginger, 36, 49, 58, 282–283, 288, 300, 398
Rogers, Ralph, 316–317, 398
Rogers, Roy, 36, 398
Romero, Cesar, 286
Roosevelt, Franklin Delano, 83
Rose, Margo, 302
Rosenthal, A. M., 2, 4
Rosenthal, Richard, 398

Rosenwald, William, 204
Rosten, Leo, 150
Roth, Arthur T., 192
Roth, Henry, 162
Rothenberg, Marvin, 304
Rothkrug, Leonard F, 258
Rothwax, Harold J.,
    230, 241
Rouse, James, 38, 398
Rudolph, Wilma, 77
Ruopp, Richard, 136
Rusk, Dean, 14
Russell, Donald S., 246
Ryan, Sheila, 40
Ryder, James, 398
Sagan, Carl, 36, 118,
    123–125, 389, 390, 398
Salk, Jonas, 89–90, 94
Saltzman, Charles E., 192
Sanders, Lawrence
    159–160, 398
Sanford, Terry, 136
Santi, Gino P.., 326
Sarnoff, Robert W., 172
Sarton, May, 59, 162
Saudek, Robert, 298
Savino, Peter, 270, 275–276
Savio, Mario, 119
Scarry, Richard, 161, 164
Schapiro, Meyer, 118
Schele, Linda, 126–127
Schermerhorn,
    Richard E., 270
Schinitsky, Charles, 258
Schoenbaum, Alex, 398
Schultz, George, 398
Schwartz, Felice,
    64–65, 387
Segal, Bernard G., 258
Semon, Waldo, 326
Sepkoski, Jr., J. John, 118
Serber, Robert, 118
Shabazz, Betty, 58, 76
Shad, John, 398

Shannon, Jr., Edgar F., 137
Sheehan, George, 94
Shepard, Richard, 3
Shinn, Richard, 192
Shirer, William L., 150
Shore, Dinah, 290
Shouse, Catherine Filene,
    204, 214–215
Shugrue, Jr., Martin, 398
Simjian, Luther G.,
    325–326, 328, 398
Simmons, Adelma
    Grenier, 357
Simon, Julian, 129–130
Simpson, Alan, 136
Simpson, Don, 298,
    307–308
Simpson, Nicole, 58
Sinatra, Frank, 12–13, 398
Siragusa, Ross, 398
Sister Parish, 51–52, 59
Sitka, Emil, 286
Skelton, Red, 36, 284, 398
Sleet, Jr., Moneta, 77
Slepack, Steven, 373–374
Smith, C. Arnholt,
    269–270, 398
Smith, David H., 36, 398
Smith, Louise
    Rheinhardt, 204
Smith, Margaret Chase,
    59, 244
Smith, Oliver, 302
Snell, George Davis, 106
Sobek, Joseph, 326
Sobel, Nathan R., 232
Sobel, Robert, 119
Sontheimer, Carl, 398
Spann, William, 271
Spencer, Frank, 119
Sperry, Roger, 105–106
Spitzer, Jr., Lyman,
    118, 125
Spivak, Lawrence E., 313

Spock, Benjamin, 13, 36,
    91, 94, 153, 390, 398
Stanley, Harry, 377–378
Steel, Dawn, 34, 38,
    59–62, 298, 398
Steinberg, Saul, 13
Steinberg, Wallace, 398
Steiner, Pau, 144–146
Stennis, John C., 244
Stewart, Jr., Charles, 232
Stewart, James, 13, 36,
    282, 284, 293, 398
Stickney, Dorothy, 288
Stiefel, Ernst C., 258
Stoddard, Thomas, 256
Stokes, Carl B., 84–85
Stokes, Lewis, 84
Stone, Jon, 298
Stone, Marvin, 398
Stout, Juanita K., 77, 230
Strasberg, Susan, 288
Stratton, Julius, 137
Strax, Philip, 94, 98–99
Struger, Oto J., 344
Sturgis, Frank A., 271
Sunn, Rell, 62–63
Suomi, Verner E., 128–129
Switzer, Robert, 326,
    332–333
Synar, Mike, 246
Taft, William　84
Talley, Madelon, 57, 192
Tandy, Jessica, 14, 58,
    288, 292–293
Taper, S., 398
Tartikoff, Brandon,
    319–320
Taubman, Arthur, 398
Tavoulareas,
    William P., 172
Taylor, Milton, 398
Tchelistcheff, Andre,
    359–360
Temin, Howard M., 94

Terrell, St. John, 286
Thomas, Jr.,
Robert McG., 3
Thornberry, Homer, 232
Tigrett, John, 399
Tilberis, Elizabeth, 399
Totino, Rose, 399
Traub, Robert 380, 381
Trell, Bluma L., 133
Trilling, Diana, 58, 162
Trump, Fred, 36, 399
Tsongas, Paul, 244
Tucker, Albert W., 127–128
Tully, Alice, 59, 204,
215–216
Turner, Lana, 283, 288,
290–293, 309
Tuttle, Elbert P., 230,
239–240
Tversky, Amos, 130–131
Udall, Morris K., 235
Ulasewicz, Anthony, 271
van Urk, Jack, 367–368
Vickery, William, 115,
118, 125, 389
von Clemm, Michael, 192
Walker III, John, 207–208
Wallace, George, 13

Wallis, W. Allen, 137
Walsh, Michael, 172
Walsh, William. B., 94,
111–112
Walton, James, 399
Wanderone, Rudolph, 376
Ward, Louis, 399
Warpick, Matthew, 94
Watson, Jr., Thomas, 38,
167–169, 171–172,
175–177, 181, 388, 399
Wavering, Elmer, 326,
337–338, 387
Weaver, Robert C., 83–84
Weidman, Jerome, 150
Weiler, Jack D., 204
Weinstein, Edwin A., 94
Weintz, William H., 187
Weiser, Mark, 172
Weisman, Frederick, 399
Weisz, William. J., 183
Wells, Frank, 399
West, Dorothy, 76, 150
West, Louis J., 94
Whitman, Alden, 3
Whitney, Betsey
Cushing, 204
Whyte, William H., 150

Wiesner, Jerome, 136
Wigner, Eugene, 118
Wikberg, Ron, 267, 271
Wilentz, Robert, 230
Wilkie, Leighton, 399
Williams, Joe, 76
Wilson, Flip, 28, 38, 76,
284, 399
Winfrey, Oprah 75
Wisdom, John Minor, 230
Wohlstetter, Charles, 399
Wolpe, Joseph, 94
Wright, Stephen J., 73–74
Wrigley, William, 399
Wylie, Chalmers, 246
Wynette, Tammy, 34, 36,
38, 59, 399
Yarborough, Ralph,
248–249, 252
Yeargin, James, 232
Yoder, John H., 119
Young, Coleman, 76
Young, Robert, 284,
311–312
Youngman, Henny, 284
Zale, Morris, 399
Zambelli, Irene, 59
Zoll, Paul M., 94, 99–100